Race and the Law in South Carolina

From Slavery to Jim Crow

JOHN WILLIAM WERTHEIMER

Amherst College Press
Amherst, Massachusetts

The complete manuscript of this work was subjected to a partly closed ("single-blind") review process. For more information, visit https://acpress.amherst.edu/peerreview/.

Published in the United States of America by
Amherst College Press
Manufactured in the United States of America

DOI: https://doi.org/10.3998/mpub.12531540

ISBN 978-1-943208-32-6 (paper)
ISBN 978-1-943208-33-3 (OA)

CONTENTS

Acknowledgments

Each of this book's six chapters began as a class-wide collaborative project in HIS 455: Law and Society in American History, an undergraduate research seminar that I teach in the History Department at Davidson College. In all, eighty students cowrote these pages. My greatest debt is to them.

Chapter 1, "*State v. Posey*," originated in HIS 455 in the fall of 2015. Jean Atkinson, Tait Jensen, Wells King, Wade Leach, John S. Marsh, Daniel Martin, J. G. Walker Mogen, Caroline Turner, Molly B. Walker, E. B. Whitener, Robby Woodward, and Hugh Xu brought the troubling story of Martin Posey and Appling to life. Molly Walker proposed the topic in the second week of class. Late in the semester, Mark Jones and Cristy Russell visited campus and helpfully discussed a rough draft with us. The class also presented its work to the Davidson College History Forum, prompting useful feedback from Dan Aldridge, Robin Barnes, Vivien Dietz, Amy Kohout, Sally McMillen, Anelise Shrout, Trish Tilburg, and Alice Wiemers. Students Daniel Martin and Walker Mogen worked on the project over the summer of 2016, funded by the Davidson Research Initiative. That fall, Daniel Martin, Molly Walker, and I presented a short version of our paper to the American Society for Legal History (ASLH) at its annual meeting in Toronto, and Walker and I presented a longer version to the Triangle Legal History Seminar, which the University of North Carolina Law School hosted that day. These presentations prompted valuable feedback from Al Brophy, Ed Balleisen, Elizabeth Dale, Andrew Fede, Sally Hadden, and others. Back in Davidson, Paul Finkelman and Dan Rodgers provided suggestions during serendipitously timed campus visits.

Chapter 2, "*Willis v. Jolliffe*," began in HIS 455 in the fall of 2008. Chad Barnes, Kevin Birney, Caitlyn Culbertson, Patrick de Visscher, Owen Fitzpatrick, Daphne Fruchtman, Andrew Gorang, and Andrew Kengeter collaborated on the initial draft. At the beginning of the semester, Daphne

Fruchtman proposed this topic. At the end, Carol Higham visited class and provided helpful feedback. Daphne Fruchtman subsequently did additional research and then presented the project at the Philadelphia meeting of the ASLH, on a panel organized by Lyndsay Campbell and Tony Freyer. Campbell and Freyer then skillfully coedited a book in which a version of this chapter appeared. I wrote a song called "Swing Low," about this chapter's dramatic story. An informal recording of "Swing Low," sung by Daphne Fruchtman, is available upon request. To commemorate our collaborative work on this project, Patrick de Visscher gave me a beautiful historical print called *Scenes on the Ohio, Above and Below Cincinnati*. It hangs in my office in the Chambers Building.

Chapter 3, "*Burgess v. Carpenter*," emerged from the Law and Society seminar in the fall of 2011. Heidi Rickes proposed the topic and then helped to research it, along with classmates Akoua Enyo Abalo, Aaron Jordan, Alexander Kaplan, Ellis Martin, Claire McDonald, James Mietus, James P. Mooney IV, Bryan Wesley Reynolds II, and Anna Van Hollen. Late in the semester, Al Brophy drove over from UNC Law School and commented on a preliminary draft. The Davidson Research Initiative subsequently enabled William H. Mogen to advance the project. He presented his research at the 2013 ASLH meeting, in Miami, where Robert Steinfeld provided commentary. After doing some additional work, I presented different versions of this project to the Princeton History Department and the Duke Law School, respectively. Various professors and students there—among them Walter Johnson, Sarah Igo, Dan Rodgers, James McPherson, and Guy-Uriel E. Charles and his smart Duke Law students—provided challenging feedback.

Chapter 4, "*Tucker v. Blease*," was one of two chapters whose seeds were planted in HIS 455 in the fall of 2007. Harper Addison proposed that we study this case. Joining her in working on the paper in class were Jessica Bradshaw, E. Dudley Colhoun, Samuel Diamant, Andrew Gilbert, Jeffrey Higgs, and Nicholas Skipper. Shep McKinley of the University of North Carolina at Charlotte commented on an early draft. The Davidson Research Initiative funded Jess Bradshaw and Allyson Cobb's summer work with me in 2008. Dillon County genealogist Helen Belden Moody provided valuable research suggestions. The following fall, Jess and I presented the paper at the ASLH meeting in Ottawa, Canada, where Ariela Gross provided wonderful commentary. We then published a version of that paper in the *Law and History Review*, enabling us to benefit from the thoughtful suggestions of editor David Tanenhaus and two anonymous reviewers, as well as the published remarks of Ariela Gross and Peter C. Caldwell.

Chapter 5, "*State v. Sanders*," has the book's most complicated origin story. It resulted from the hard work of two different groups of seminar students. In the fall of 2009, Peter Bruton, Andrew Jones, Emily May, Kayla McCann, Alexander Merritt, Lee Mimms, Rex Salisbury, Alex Sineath, and David Warren tackled the daunting topic of Jim Crow juries through the case *State v. Middleton* (South Carolina, 1946), which Andy Jones originally proposed. Jim Goodman of Rutgers-Newark visited class that fall and commented on our paper. At the Davidson College History Forum, my History Department colleagues Dan Aldridge, Vivien Dietz, Ralph Levering, Sally McMillen, and wonderful visitor Michael Meng commented on our collaborative research presentation. Davidson College's then president Tom Ross also contributed his thoughts. Right at the end of that semester, class member David Warren discovered some "jury books" in a South Carolina archive. These handwritten tomes were compiled by jury commissioners in South Carolina counties as part of the jury-selection process. Although we did not have time to dig deeply into these books that semester, I took note of David's discovery. In the spring of 2014, a different group of HIS 455 students—Gerardo Alvarez Sottil, Katy Boyle, Katie Burwick, Bridget Flynn Kastner, Daniel Guenther, Katherine Herold, William Mahler, Everett Muzzy, Robin Malloch, Cameron Parker, CT Talevi, and Lawrence Wall—chose to study the history of Jim Crow juries in South Carolina through a different case, this one proposed by Bridgett Flynn Kastner: *State v. Sanders* (South Carolina, 1915). Thanks to the efforts of the 2009 group, I knew to direct the 2014 group directly to the jury books. Steven Weinberg commented on an early draft that spring. The following fall, Bridget Flynn Kastner, Katherine Herold, Cam Parker, Everett Muzzy, Daniel Guenther, Will Mahler, and CT Talevi joined me for a road trip to Durham, to copresent a revised version of our paper to the Duke University History Department. Duke historians Ed Balleisen, Nancy MacLean, John Jeffries Martin, and others received us with good questions and lunch.

Chapter 6, "*Tessie Earle v. Greenville County*," originated in HIS 455 in the fall of 2007. Charles Horwitz proposed the case and subsequently worked on it along with classmates Jess Bradshaw, Kathryn Finnigan, Joe Harvey, Randall McLeod, Sam Morris, and Madeline Stough. Shep McKinley commented on a rough draft. Will Gravely and Christopher Waldrep helped us with our research. With funding from the Davidson Research Initiative, Joe Harvey and Gabrielle Jones conducted additional research over the following summer. Joe and I then copresented our research at the Organization of American Historians' 2009 meeting in Seattle, Washington, where we received helpful feedback from Bobby Donaldson, Kari Frederickson, Will Gravely, and Bryant Simon. Years later, in the spring of 2018, I returned to this chapter's topic in a course called Filming Southern History, in which my students and I collaboratively produced a documentary film, in partnership with filmmakers Thomas Espy and Colin Sylvester, who, at the time, were graduate students in the Documentary Film Program at nearby Wake Forest University. Davidson undergraduates EJ Canny, Francis Scalia Carroll, Hannah Cohen, Olivia Coral Daniels, Cassandra M. Harding, Stephanie Jefferis, William Stuart Kaskay II, Emilee Lord, Nate MacKenzie, Bryce Simmons, Ellen M. G. Spearing, and Seth W. Stancil took that course. The research that they did while making that film contributed to this chapter. Dan Aldridge, E. M. Beck, Myisha Eatmon, Kari Frederickson, Will Gravely, Kenneth Janken, Mark Jones, Kuba Kabala, Steve Kantrowitz, Fuji Lozada, Bryant Simon, Melissa Milewski, and Molly Walker all provided research consultation during that exciting semester. The ultimate result of that filmmaking exercise was *Remembering Willie Earle* (2020), a powerful documentary short directed by Frank Carroll, Cassie Harding, Stevie Jefferis, and Thomas Espy. *Remembering Willie Earle* won Best Documentary Film in the "History Plus" category at the 2021 Longleaf Film Festival of Raleigh, North Carolina, and was an official selection at six other film festivals, mostly in the Carolinas. Throughout this long research-and-filmmaking process, we benefited greatly from the generous collaboration of Dr. Will Gravely, the world's leading expert on the history of the Willie Earle lynching. And without the extraordinary help of the late Acquillious "AQ" Jackson, we never could have made *Remembering Willie Earle*. AQ's memories anchor that film and inform the narrative that we provide in chapter 6.

I began experimenting with collaborative-research pedagogy in 1997. The Davidson College History Department's support was immediate and enduring. I thank its members, past and present.

I also thank the many funders whose generosity made these projects possible: the Davidson Research Initiative, the George L. Abernethy Research Fund, the Bacca Foundation Visiting Scholar and Artist Program, the Andrew W. Mellon Foundation, the Malcolm Lester fund, the William R. Kenan Jr. Charitable Trust, and the Mark Jones Mentorship Fund.

Four of this book's six chapters debuted as presentations at annual meetings of the American Society for Legal History. Although few undergraduates attend ASLH conferences, and fewer still present research there, the legal history community has consistently received my undergraduate copresenters with respect and warmth. In their interactions with my students, legal historians such as Constance Backhouse, Ed Balleisen, Laurie Benton, Al Brophy, Lyndsay Campbell, Elizabeth Dale, Dan Ernst, Andrew Fede, Tony Freyer, Sally Gordon, Michael Grossberg, Sally Hadden, Dirk Hartog, Michelle McKinley, Patti Minter, Matthew Mirow, Dylan Penningroth, Gautham Rao, Reuel Schiller, Chris Schmidt, Rebecca Scott, David Tanenhaus, Chris Tomlins, Barbara Welke, and others embodied the legal history community's reputation for taking mentorship seriously. I thank them all.

With good humor and an editor's eye, Reuel Schiller helped me to think through the challenges that I would face while weaving six independently written chapters into a coherent book. Thanks, Reuel. Once I started weav-ing, Beth Bouloukos and her editorial team at Amherst College Press— Trevor Perri, Hannah Brooks-Motl, and two anonymous reviewers—provided valuable assistance. I appreciate their patience with me, their commitment to liberal arts education, and their determination to get it right. At the end of the process, my sharp-eyed departmental colleague Ralph Levering provided valuable proofreading.

Mark Jones, an exemplary Davidson College undergraduate, took my collaborative research seminar in the spring of 2000 and taught me by example how exciting it can be when student-faculty collaboration works. As an alumnus, Mark has continued to support my collaborative teaching by volunteering his considerable expertise whenever asked and by encouraging me to continue this sort of mentorship.

Year after year, my father, Richard Wertheimer— affectionally known to generations of Davidson College students as "The Esquire"— v i sited my classes and showed my students (and me) how to read and write about the law. We thank him.

At home in Davidson, Glenda, Sharad, and Marco Wertheimer provided love and support, as did my parents down the street, Richard and Loretta Wertheimer. To them all I say, *gracias.*

Acknowledgments

Preface

This book has unusual origins. Each chapter originated as a collaborative research project in my legal history seminar at Davidson College. Whenever I teach this course, a dozen or so advanced undergraduates and I collaboratively explore a single topic. I designed this seminar to teach students, in a hands-on way, how to research, analyze, and write about the legal past. When designing the course, I expected students to learn a ton—and they do. I expected them to enjoy working together to create something important—and they do. What I did not expect was that the resulting scholarship would be worth sharing—but it is. The first batch of collaboratively produced essays to emerge from this seminar concerned North Carolina's legal history. In 2009, the University Press of Kentucky published these essays as a book.[1] You are reading the South Carolina follow-up.

These books develop slowly. They begin in class. Students start by rummaging through old state supreme court reports, itself an eye-opening experience for them. I instruct them to look for cases that touch on important historical issues, raise interesting legal questions, and concern intriguing people. Each student identifies such a case and presents it to the group. After extensive discussion, the group selects a winner. Year after year, between 2007 and 2015, students gravitated to race-related cases, reflecting both the bounty of such cases contained in South Carolina court records and the values that my students brought with them to class.

Topic in hand, we research. Like physicians in training, students cycle through secondary, primary, and archival research rotations. Some start with secondary sources. They read scholarly books and journal articles and start to sketch the historical background against which our case will be set.

1. *Law and Society in the South: A History of North Carolina Court Cases* (Lexington: University Press of Kentucky, 2009).

Others start with primary sources. They might seek old press accounts of our case or comb legal records, in search of similar cases. Still others head to the state archives in Columbia, South Carolina, to pan for gold. After several rotations, we know enough about our story to build a working outline. By design, the number of sections in our outline equals the number of students in the course. Students draw lots to determine the order in which they select writing assignments. They then spend the rest of the semester researching and writing their assigned segments—an individual task serving a collective end. Communication is constant, particularly among writers of adjacent sections. Research finds get passed around. Unexpected discoveries here demand revisions there. Two-thirds of the way through the term, an outside reader visits class to critique an inevitably ragged draft. Smart feedback results. Near the end of the term, we present our work on campus, prompting additional smart feedback.[2]

The semester ends; work continues. Thanks to Davidson College's generous support for undergraduate research, one or two students usually continue to work on the paper, often over a summer. Summer students deepen our excavations, especially in the archives. Sometimes, their digging undermines classroom assumptions, compelling us to rethink our arguments.

The students then leave the paper with me. I do additional research. I take the paper apart and reassemble it. I discard much and add new material. Some papers shrink to half their original length. Others double in size. On my good days, I sharpen the analysis. On my best days, I make it sing.

I then prepare a condensed version to test-drive before an academic audience and invite student coauthors to copresent. All of the chapters in this book debuted either as invited lectures on university campuses or as parts of research panels at academic conferences. Although undergraduates rarely present in such contexts, my students regularly do. They always perform marvelously. Sometimes, conference presentations serendipitously lead to publications.[3]

---

2. For a more detailed discussion of this course's mechanics, see John Wertheimer, "The Collaborative Research Seminar," *Journal of American History* 88 (March 2002): 1476–81.

3. "*Willis v. Jolliffe*: Love and Slavery on the South Carolina-Ohio Borderlands," in *Freedom's Conditions in the U.S.-Canada Borderlands in the Age of Emancipation*, ed. Tony Freyer and Lyndsay Campbell (Durham, NC: Carolina Academic Press, 2011), 257–84; and "'The Law Recognizes Racial Instinct': *Tucker v. Blease* and the Black-White Paradigm in the Jim Crow South," *Law and History Review* 29, no. 2 (2011): 471–95.

The final stage in the evolution from seminar project to scholarly book is the fusing of the separate papers. I assemble the chapters in chronological order. Because all of the chapters touch on the same general theme, the relationship between racial distinctions and the law in South Carolina history, patterns quickly emerge. Stories interweave. Locations recur. Characters with leading roles here reappear in cameos there. This synergy binds the book. I revise each chapter in light of all others, write section-to-section transitions, and prepare an introduction and a conclusion. Feedback from wise readers polishes my glasses along the way. Some former students stay in touch and offer helpful advice. Despite all of this help, flaws remain. Those are mine alone.

John Wertheimer
Davidson, North Carolina

INTRODUCTION

Continuity and Change in the Palmetto State

Although the scale of federal litigation in the United States has grown immeasurably since the nation's birth, state litigation remains far more common. For every case filed in a federal court, a hundred are filed in state courts.[1] That federal-to-state imbalance surely was even greater during the century or so covered in this book, from the 1840s to the 1940s, a stretch of South Carolina's history that began during slavery and ended during Jim Crow.

Despite the submerged bulk of state law, federal law remains the iceberg's looming tip in popular memory. Utter the phrase "the legal history of slavery" to an American and you are likely to evoke such infamies as the three-fifths clause (a federal constitutional provision), the Fugitive Slave Act (a federal statute), and *Dred Scott* (a federal court case). Yet state law, which built on colonial law, was vastly more important to the history of US slavery than was federal law. Likewise, for all of the retrospective attention paid to the US Supreme Court's infamous "separate but equal" reasoning in *Plessy v. Ferguson* (1896), the Jim Crow system was, first and foremost, a state-level creation. *Plessy* segregated nothing. It merely permitted states to continue segregating. When asked why he robbed banks, the celebrated thief Willie Sutton allegedly replied, "Because that's where the money is." The present exploration of race and the law, from slavery through Jim Crow, focuses on state law for a similar reason: that's where the legal history is.

1. Fitz Tepper, "Legalist Is Making It Easier for Lawyers to Find State Court Records," Tech Crunch, July 19, 2016, https://techcrunch.com/2016/07/19/legalist-is-making-it-easier-for-lawyers-to-find-state-court-records/; Dana H. Shultz, "What Percentage of Court Cases in the United States Are Heard by Federal Courts?" Quora, Aug. 5, 2016, https://www.quora.com/What-percentage-of-court-cases-in-the-United-States-are-heard-by-federal-courts.

This book examines various ways in which perceived racial distinctions interacted with the law in South Carolina, from the 1840s through the 1940s. For much of the twentieth century's second half, scholars snapped together these historical eras—slavery, Reconstruction, Jim Crow—in a configuration that zigged and zagged but ultimately bent toward justice. Slavery, standard accounts held, poisoned the new nation. Thankfully, the Civil War did away with it, allowing freedom fleetingly to sprout during the post–Civil War Reconstruction period, when a newly powerful federal government enforced equality and civil rights. Before long, however, a reactionary "Redemption" movement, led by southern Democrats, violently plowed under these tender shoots, allowing the noxious weeds of Jim Crow to spread across the South and beyond. The plowed-under sprouts of Reconstruction, America's "unfinished revolution," however, would not die. By the mid-twentieth century, they had resurfaced, and a "Second Reconstruction" bloomed.[2]

Around 2000, in response to the sputtering out of Civil Rights–era progress, a different and less hopeful interpretation emerged. Frustrated by what one scholar dubbed the "permanence of racism,"[3] writers asked themselves, "Why has formal legal equality been achieved in most spheres while social and structural inequalities persist?"[4] Race scholars, Black and white, including historians of whiteness, concluded that American white suprem-

2. The phrase "unfinished revolution" comes from the subtitle of Eric Foner's *Reconstruction: America's Unfinished Revolution, 1863–1877* (New York: Harper & Row, 1988). The phrase "Second Reconstruction" comes from C. Vann Woodward, "The Political Legacy of Reconstruction," *Journal of Negro Education* 26, no. 3 (Summer, 1957): 231–40. For a discussion of the conventional scholarly wisdom surrounding Reconstruction, see Susan J. Pearson, "Review Essay: A New Birth of Regulation: The State of the State after the Civil War," *Journal of the Civil War Era* 5, no. 3 (September 2015): 422. For a discussion of the conventional scholarly wisdom about the relationship between Reconstruction and the mid-twentieth-century civil rights movement, see Kenneth W. Mack, *Representing the Race: The Creation of the Civil Rights Lawyer* (Cambridge, MA: Harvard University Press, 2012), 3.

3. Derrick Bell, *Faces at the Bottom of the Well: The Permanence of Racism* (New York: Basic Books, 1995).

4. Cornelia H. Dayton and Lisa Levenstein formulated this rhetorical question, capturing the perspective of progressive scholars who were frustrated by the lack of social justice progress in many fields. Dayton and Levenstein, "The Big Tent of U.S. Women's and Gender History: A State of the Field," *Journal of American History* 99, no. 3 (Dec. 2012): 793–817, at 802.

acy is an "intractable problem"[5] that morphs and mutates but never dies.[6] White supremacy simply "reproduce[s]" itself in a "new form in every era,"[7] allowing the color line to remain "an organizing principle of U.S.-American life."[8] Scholars drove this point home rhetorically by connecting historical dots. "Slavery became 'separate but equal,'" Jennifer Harvey wrote early in the twenty-first century, "which now has become color-blindness."[9] David Roediger drew a similarly continuous line from "slave patrols to lynchings to contemporary mass incarceration."[10] US racial history was a story of continuity. The "preferential treatment of white people" survived emancipation and remained a force "so fundamental to America that it is difficult to imagine the country without it," wrote Ta-Nehisi Coates.[11] Racialized "privilege and subordination" were among the nation's most "fundamental continuities," added Barbara Welke.[12] Ibram X. Kendi surveyed American history and found that patterns of racial discrimination were "stamped from the beginning" and persisted.[13]

The scholarly emphasis on continuity has had a huge impact, both within and beyond the academy. Its unwavering spotlight has illuminated some important truths: racial inequality in the United States survived emancipation. It survived the Equal Protection Clause of the Fourteenth Amendment. It survived the demise of Jim Crow and the passage of civil rights laws in the 1960s. At no point—no point—in American history have Black people, by any meaningful metric, experienced equality with white

5. Jennifer Harvey, "Race and Reparations: The Material Logics of White Supremacy," in *Disrupting White Supremacy from Within: White People on What We Need to Do*, ed. Jennifer Harvey, Karin A. Case, and Robin Hawley Gorsline (Cleveland: Pilgrim Press, 2004), 92.

6. Jacqueline Jones, "Back to the Future with *The Bell Curve:* Jim Crow, Slavery, and G," in *Critical White Studies: Looking behind the Mirror*, ed. Richard Delgado and Jean Stefancic (Philadelphia: Temple University Press, 1997), 179.

7. George Lipsitz, *The Possessive Investment in Whiteness: How White People Profit from Identity Politics* (Philadelphia: Temple University Press, 1998), 3.

8. Harvey, "Race and Reparations," 111.

9. Ibid.

10. David Roediger, *Colored White: Transcending the Racial Past* (Berkeley: University of California Press, 2002), 23.

11. Ta-Nehesi Coates, "The Case for Reparations," *The Atlantic*, June 2014, https://www.theatlantic.com/magazine/archive/2014/06/the-case-for-reparations/361631/.

12. Barbara Young Welke, *Law and the Borders of Belonging in the Long Nineteenth Century United States* (New York and Cambridge: Cambridge University Press, 2010), 2, 13.

13. Ibram X. Kendi, *Stamped from the Beginning: The Definitive History of Racist Ideas in America* (New York: Nation Books, 2016).

people.[14] This powerful message has done important political work. By its very nature, however, continuity scholarship deemphasizes historical distinctions among different systems of racial hierarchy. It also deemphasizes the processes by which the coil of history turns.

Take education. Antebellum South Carolina had some of the nation's strictest laws limiting the education of Black people.[15] The state made it illegal for anyone to teach an enslaved person to read or write.[16] It also restricted educational opportunities for so-called free Negroes.[17] Emancipation brought dramatic change. Black delegates to the state's Constitutional Convention of 1868 pushed hard for a system of "free public schools throughout the state."[18] The resulting system of public education persisted even after Reconstruction fell. South Carolina's Jim Crow constitution of 1895 mandated that "separate schools" be provided "for children of the white and colored races."[19] Without question, the spirit of white supremacy infused South Carolina's system of education under both slavery and Jim Crow. Thanks largely to the efforts of Black leaders, however, education went from being illegal to being constitutionally mandated—segregated, yes, and always insultingly unequal, but nominally free and compulsory "for all children."[20] And these constitutional promises were not entirely empty. Although Black literacy trailed white literacy throughout, it advanced dramatically during the century under study.[21] That change seems

14. See Nicholas Kristof's multipart series, "When Whites Just Don't Get It," *New York Times*, 2014 and 2016, https://impactamerica.com/the-new-york-times-when-whites-just-dont-get-it-parts-1-7/

15. Walter Edgar, *South Carolina: A History* (Columbia: University of South Carolina Press, 1998), 299. Note that some white South Carolinians defied the laws and taught enslaved people to read, particularly for purposes of religious instruction. An estimated 5 percent of the state's Black population had some level of literacy as of 1860.

16. John Belton O'Neall, *The Negro Law of South Carolina* (Columbia, SC: J. G. Bowman, 1848), 23.

17. Edgar, *South Carolina*, 176, 299.

18. A. A. Taylor, "The Convention of 1868," *Journal of Negro History* 9, no. 4 (Oct. 1924): 390–94. For the quoted words, see S. Carolina Const. , art. X, § 3 (1868); S. Carolina Const. , art. X, "Education" (1868).

19. S. Carolina Const. art. XI, § 7 (1895).

20. "Constitution of the State of South Carolina, Ratified in Convention, Dec. 4, 1895," art. XI, § 5 (Abbeville, SC: Hugh Wilson, 1900), 43.

21. See chapter 4 in this monograph.

worth noting. The role of Black South Carolinians in bringing it about also seems worth noting.

In part, this book supplements continuity scholarship's top-down focus on white supremacy and its persistence by highlighting the historically variable experiences of nonwhite actors, including attorneys, plaintiffs, defendants, jurors, and even a state supreme court justice. When viewed from their perspectives, the needle measuring racial oppression during the century under study jumps around dramatically. The degree of Black access to the public sphere goes a long way toward explaining the timing of these jumps. Under slavery, Black South Carolinians had essentially no claims-making ability. The public sphere briefly opened wide to them during Reconstruction. Then it reclosed, though only partially. Continued Black legal agency, combined with at least partial buy-in to the "rule-of-law" ideal on the part of some white leaders, moderated some of the worst abuses of Jim Crow. This moderation arguably strengthened Jim Crow in the short run but weakened it in the long run, paving the way for the civil rights and post–civil rights eras that followed.

Slavery

This book's first two chapters explore slavery in antebellum South Carolina. They show that the Old South's reputation for racist oppression is richly deserved. According to black-letter law, enslaved people in South Carolina were their masters' personal property. They could be bought, sold, inherited, rented out, and "stolen."[22] Enslaved people could not marry,[23] make contracts,[24] or, as previously mentioned, be "taught to read or write."[25] Worse still, enslavement, under South Carolina law, was entirely racialized.[26] Legal experts had good reason for labeling it "*negro* slavery [empha-

22. John Belton O'Neall, *The Negro Law of South Carolina* (Columbia, SC: J. G. Bowman, 1848), 17–18, 43.

23. Ibid., 23.

24. Ibid., 22.

25. Ibid., 23.

26. "An Act for the Better Ordering and Governing Negroes and Other Slaves in this Province," in *The Statutes at Large of South Carolina*, vol. 7, *Containing the Acts Relating to Charleston, Courts, Slaves, and Rivers*, ed. David J. McCord (Columbia, SC: A. S. Johnston, 1840), 397.

sis added]."[27] Skin color, as one legal expert noted, was "prima facie evidence," that the "party bearing the color of a negro, mulatto or mestizo [was] a slave."[28] White people could not legally be enslaved.[29] The "burden of proof of freedom" rested heavily on the shoulders of Black people "claiming to be free."[30] Slavery's racialization may have been its most enduringly vile feature.

The legal abuse of so-called free Negroes in antebellum South Carolina compounded the system's racial vileness. Free Negroes were a negligible portion of the state's population, consistently below 2 percent of the total.[31] They faced stark legal disabilities that did not apply to whites. They could not legally migrate into the state.[32] If they left South Carolina, they were "forever prohibited from returning."[33] They could not "lawfully strike any white person," even if the white person struck first.[34] They could not hold certain jobs[35] or own certain things.[36] In short, the so-called free Negro, though not formally enslaved, was, as one South Carolina jurist matter-of-factly noted in 1848, "subject to all the disabilities of the degraded class . . . into which his color thrusts him."[37] None of this was veiled or coded. State leaders unapologetically chiseled racism into the white marble of law. And South Carolina was hardly alone. Whereas slavery divided the states, unequal legal treatment of "free Negroes" existed nationwide, though to different degrees.[38]

South Carolina's roller-coaster movement up and down the axes of

27. O'Neall, *The Negro Law of South Carolina*, 12.

28. Ibid., 5.

29. The existence of some cases in which arguably white people were enslaved, perhaps due to racial ambiguity, does not change the legal presumption that whites were ineligible for enslavement. For some instances in which arguably white people were enslaved, see Carol Wilson and Calvin D. Wilson, "White Slavery: An American Paradox," *Slavery and Abolition* 19, no. 1 (1998): 1–23.

30. O'Neall, *The Negro Law of South Carolina*, 8.

31. Donald J. Senese, "The Free Negro and the South Carolina Courts, 1790–1860," *South Carolina Historical Magazine*, vol. 68, no. 3, July 1967, 140.

32. O'Neall, *Negro* Law, 15, quoting an 1835 state law.

33. Ibid., 16.

34. Ibid., 28.

35. Ibid., 23.

36. Ibid., 32.

37. Ibid., 17.

38. Timothy Walker, *Introduction to American Law, Designed as a First book for Students* (Philadelphia: P. H. Nicklin & T. Johnson, 1837), 166.

racial oppression closely tracks the varying ability of nonwhite people, at different points in time, to participate in state governance. During the era of slavery, South Carolina's political and legal systems were effectively closed to Black voices. By constitutional fiat, all voters and all legislators were white.[39] The state contained no Black lawyers or judges.[40] Black men were not allowed to serve on juries.[41] They could not testify in court, except "against other blacks."[42] These political and legal disabilities constituted an unhappy variation on Lincoln: it was government of one people, by another people, for that other people.

The law of slavery placed substantial constraints on everyday life. Chapter 1 describes how such constraints drove an enslaved South Carolinian named Appling to propose a desperate bargain to his enslaver, Martin Posey. Appling knew that Martin was unhappily married and that South Carolina did not permit divorce. Lacking any other bargaining chips, Appling offered to kill his enslaver's wife, in exchange for a promise of freedom. Appling's subsequent crime presented South Carolina's courts with legal questions that scholars have neglected: When enslaved people committed crimes on behalf of their enslavers, should the law treat "masters" as jointly responsible "principals"? Or should the law credit enslaved people with sufficient humanity to be found guilty as principals, while treating enslavers as mere "accessories"? More generally, did the common law, which usually did not apply to enslaved people, apply when they committed common-law crimes? In addition to analyzing these legal questions, chapter 1 carefully sketches the case's social context. It emphasizes the agency that enslaved people exercised. Appling was not ordered to kill. He volunteered to kill. And he struck his deadly bargain only after a rival (and less competent) enslaved worker had unsuccessfully attempted contract murder. In other words, Appling's criminal negotiations were not unique. They reflected a broader tradition in which at least some enslaved people sought advantage through a willingness to commit crimes on behalf of their enslavers. This would not be the last time in American history that an unjust system inclined oppressed people to criminal behavior, with unfortunate consequences.

39. S. Carolina Const., art. I, §4, 6, and 8 (1790).

40. William Lewis Burke, *All for Civil Rights: African American Lawyers in South Carolina, 1868–1968* (Athens: University of Georgia Press, 2017).

41. O'Neall, *Negro Law*, 13.

42. Ibid. 13, 23.

Slave law constrained all South Carolinians—including enslavers. One measure of its restrictiveness is the length to which dissenting enslavers went to avoid legal constraints. In the late 1840s, chapter 2 recounts, Elijah Willis, an unmarried and childless South Carolina planter, wrote a will leaving his estate to his siblings. Around the same time, he started a family with Amy, one of his enslaved laborers. Amy and Elijah effectively lived as husband and wife and produced several children. Like Appling, the enslaved man considered in chapter 1, Amy sought to escape the straightjacket of slavery through her dealings with the white man who claimed ownership in her. South Carolina law, however, barred Elijah and Amy from marrying. It also prohibited Elijah from writing a new will that would free Amy and leave his property to her, as he wished to do. Elijah, therefore, traveled to Ohio, where a Cincinnati lawyer prepared a new will, ordering that Elijah's estate descend to Amy and the children following Elijah's death. Elijah then returned south, gathered Amy and the children, and the whole family headed north, toward freedom. On the wharf in Cincinnati, Elijah collapsed and died, setting off a dramatic confrontation in the South Carolina courts about the validity of the northern will. South Carolina ultimately upheld the Ohio will, allowing Amy, now in Ohio, to inherit Elijah's property. The South Carolina court's seemingly emancipatory reasoning, however, actually reinforced the logic of slavery. Amy could inherit only because it was her late enslaver's demonstrated wish that she do so. South Carolina law did not act out of respect for Amy's rights. It acted out of regard for her late enslaver's right to control his property.[43]

Reconstruction

South Carolina's position on the axis of racial oppression flipped dramatically during the Reconstruction era. Between 1865 and 1877, slavery ended, never formally to reappear, and Black South Carolinians, supported by federal forces, fleetingly gained something close to formal political and legal equality. Although neither social integration nor true equality were ever achieved, or even approximated,[44] Reconstruction,

43. Willis v. Jolliffe, 32 S.C. Eq. (11 Rich. Eq.) 447 (S.C. 1860).

44. Albert Sanders, "Jim Crow Comes to South Carolina," *Proceedings of the South Carolina Historical Association* (1966): 28–29.

while it lasted, was revolutionary, starting with equal manhood suffrage. At the time, Black South Carolinians constituted almost 60 percent of the state's population, so political equality meant that Black voters were in the majority. Between 1867 and 1876, Black officeholders were in the majority too.[45] South Carolina had more Black legislative representation than any other state.[46] Its assembly arguably did more than any other state legislature to serve the needs of its Black residents.[47] South Carolina established a system of public education, mandated that it be operated "without regard to race or color,"[48] and prohibited racial discrimination in public accommodations and conveyances.[49]

In addition to these political and civil rights, Black South Carolinians during Reconstruction also achieved genuine advances in the legal system. Prior to 1865, the state had no Black lawyers. By 1877, almost fifty Black lawyers had been admitted to the South Carolina bar.[50] New laws guaranteed equal access to the courts.[51] Black and white jurors served in rough proportion to their share of the local population.[52] And Black people could testify freely in court. These stark changes produced starkly different legal outcomes.

Chapter 3 focuses on arguably the single most conspicuous example of the state's legal opening during Reconstruction. Jonathan Jasper Wright, a Black lawyer, joined the South Carolina Supreme Court in 1870, becoming the first Black member of any appellate bench in US history.[53] Most scholarly treatments of egalitarian legal change during Reconstruction understandably focus on federal constitutional amendments and civil rights laws.

45. This includes state and federal officeholders elected in South Carolina. Thomas Holt, *Black over White: Negro Political Leadership in South Carolina during Reconstruction* (Urbana: University of Illinois Press, 1977), 1.

46. Foner, *Reconstruction*, 354

47. Hyman S. Rubin III, "Reconstruction," in *The South Carolina Encyclopedia*, ed. Walter Edgar (Columbia: University of South Carolina Press, 2006), 780.

48. S. Carolina Const., art. X, § 10 (1868); Sanders, "Jim Crow," 28.

49. South Carolina General Assembly, Acts and Joint Resolutions of the General Assembly of the State of South Carolina . . . Designed to Form a Part of the Fourteenth Volume of the Statutes at Large, Columbia, SC, 1872, 179, 386–88; Sanders, "Jim Crow," 28.

50. Burke, *All for Civil Rights*, 5, 8, 19.

51. South Carolina General Assembly, Acts and Joint Resolutions, 337; Sanders, "Jim Crow," 28.

52. See chapter five of this book.

53. Burke, *All for Civil Rights*, 25.

This chapter shows that Justice Wright pursued equally egalitarian ends using common-law judging at the state level. In particular, the chapter explores Wright's ruling in *Burgess v. Carpenter* (1870), an employment dispute. Burgess, a white landowner, sued Carpenter, also white, for injuring one of Burgess's Black agricultural workers.[54] Burgess sued under a common-law rule that allowed "masters" to recover damages from third parties who inhibited their "servants'" labor. In resolving this dispute, Justice Wright looked backward, to egalitarian free-contract ideology from the Jacksonian era. Although Wright's free-contract-based efforts failed, never really to be resurrected among civil rights advocates, they represent an intriguing path not taken. When civil rights activism revived during the Second Reconstruction following World War II, the Jacksonian-style free-contract ideology that infused Justice Wright's jurisprudence during the First Reconstruction was nowhere to be found. The quivers of post–World War II civil rights activists now contained other arrows, such as equal protection litigation and civil rights statutes.

Jim Crow

Although Black people initially hoped that Reconstruction had ushered in a "new era"[55] that would raise them "to the full stature of . . . citizens,"[56] it was not to be. Southern Democrats violently retook power in the 1870s. At first, much of the public equality achieved during Reconstruction persisted.[57] By the turn of the twentieth century, however, a populistic and virulently racist wing of the Democratic Party had taken command. These Democrats largely strangled Black political rights and obsessively banned racial mixing in an ever-growing number of venues: trains, steamboats, ferries, reformatories, penitentiaries, public parks, poolrooms, textile mills, traveling tent shows, and on and on.[58]

54. Burgess v. Carpenter, 2 S.C. 7 (1870).

55. "Letter from Richmond," *National Anti-Slavery Standard* (New York), Aug. 1, 1868, 2.

56. "Celebration at Elko, Nev.: Introductory Remarks of W. A. Scott, President of the Day," *The Elevator* (San Francisco), May 6, 1870, 1.

57. Sanders, "Jim Crow," 31–33.

58. Burke, *All for Civil Rights*, 131–32; Sanders, "Jim Crow," 37–39; and Patrick Huber, *Linthead Stomp: The Creation of County Music in the Piedmont South* (Chapel Hill: University of North Carolina Press, 2008), 13.

Jim Crow laws of this sort gave segregation not just the state's tangible "police-power" backing but also its intangible seal of approval. As discussed in chapter 4, the South Carolina Supreme Court buttressed Jim Crow by articulating a supposed "racial instinct" that inclined "those with and those without negro blood" to seek separation from each other.[59] Judicial pronouncements of this sort influenced how South Carolinians thought about race and made segregation seem natural.

Even after the political system's door had slammed in the faces of Black South Carolinians, however, the legal system's door remained ajar. Black people retained the right to litigate, to testify in court, and to practice law.[60] It was not a large opening, but it mattered. Black litigants fared surprisingly well. When they litigated against whites in Jim Crow–era appellate courts, they usually won.[61] Trial courts, too, remained open venues within which racism could be openly challenged.[62] Black legal activism, together with elite white commitment to the rule-of-law ideal, limited Jim Crow's worst abuses and banked the embers of civil rights, to be rekindled in the mid-twentieth century.

Civil rights activists were fully aware of the law's norm-setting functions. Black lawyers worked hard to counter the legal system's white-supremacist leanings. They forcefully argued that racism was incompatible with the rule of law. Occasionally, as in chapters 5 and 6, they won. The experiences of these Black lawyers highlights both continuity and change in South Carolina legal history. The need to battle white supremacist outrages, again and again, highlights white supremacy's tenacity. But their ability to fight in court and the legal victories that they achieved—victories that were not terribly unusual in the New South[63]—showed how much had changed since the days of slavery.

Law is not an autonomous realm. Society deeply influenced it during the Jim Crow years. Chapter 5 shows how racist local officials implemented neutral laws in discriminatory ways. Private citizens also unofficially

59. Tucker v. Blease, 97 S.C. 326 (1914).

60. In 1900, the South Carolina bar had proportionally more Black lawyers—twenty-nine—than did the bar of any other southern state. Burke, *All for Civil Rights*, 4.

61. Melissa Milewski, *Litigating across the Color Line: Civil Cases between Black and White Southerners from the End of Slavery to Civil Rights* (New York: Oxford University Press, 2017).

62. See chapter 5 in this book.

63. Milewski, *Litigating across the Color Line.*

policed racial lines, allowing grassroots understandings of race to influence the law from below, as shown in chapters 4 and 6.

Vigilantes acted as if lynching were a quasi-official wing of the criminal justice system. In addition to killing thousands, lynching indirectly affected the workings of the legal system. Judicial officials knew that in any racially charged criminal case with a Black defendant, the slightest procedural delay or pro-defendant ruling could stir a murderous mob to life. Courts responded by accelerating their procedures and curtailing due process protections, hoping to preempt lynchings, which they regarded as a regional embarrassment.

Each of the three chapters in this section focuses on a different facet of Jim Crow. Chapter 4 concerns segregated schooling. In 1913, an all-white public school dismissed three siblings on racial grounds. The South Carolina Supreme Court upheld their expulsion. Superficially, this case illustrates the important role that law played in sorting Americans into two piles: "those with and those without negro blood," to quote the ruling. There was, however, a twist. Contrary to the consistent assumptions of subsequent scholars, the expelled students in this case were *not* alleged to have any "negro" ancestry at all. Instead, they were alleged to be part Croatan Indian; their neighbors sought to send them to Indian schools, not Black schools. This case demonstrates how the South Carolina courts used their statewide power to reinforce community-based racism. It also shows how courts imposed the "one-drop rule" to divide those with from those without "negro blood" and how they effectively filtered out multicultural local complexity in favor of a statewide Black-white dualism, showcasing the local community's bottom-up ability to patrol racial lines as well as the statewide legal system's top-down ability to influence popular understandings of race.

Chapter 5 explores the 1915 trial of James Sanders, a Black man accused of murdering a white man. One prospective trial juror, R. L. Bailey, who was white, admitted to being severely biased against Black lawyers, including the ones representing Sanders. Although Sanders's attorneys argued that Bailey's admitted racial bias rendered him unfit for jury service, the trial judge deemed Bailey fit to serve, despite his open admission that his prejudice might sway his vote. *Sanders* serves as a point of departure for a deep exploration of Jim Crow juries generally. Scholars typically focus on quantitative measures of jury composition and generally conclude, without looking too closely, that Blacks "disappeared" from southern juries from the late nineteenth century through World War II. This chapter agrees that the exclusion of Black jurors was pervasive, though perhaps a bit less so than most scholars assume. The chapter also investigates something that historians generally overlook: how courts dealt with the racism, and not just the race, of prospective jurors. Especially in racially charged cases, it finds, courts often had to decide whether or not to impanel jurors who admitted to holding racist views. Black attorneys challenged these views as incompatible with jury service. In a series of cases that included *Sanders*, Black lawyers systematically grilled white would-be jurors about their racial opinions and challenged those who admitted prejudice. They often succeeded in getting jurors struck for cause, thanks to the nominal commitment of trial judges to the rule-of-law ideal. When defense lawyers failed at the trial level, they appealed, sometimes successfully. One such appeal saved James Sanders's life.

Chapter 6 uses a well-documented lynching to explore a little-known feature of South Carolina's legal history. In Greenville County, South Carolina, in 1947, a white mob lynched Willie Earle, a Black man. South Carolina prosecuted dozens of the lynchers, but an all-white jury acquitted them all. The story's legal history, however, does not end there. Willie Earle's mother, Tessie Earle, subsequently sued Greenville County under an 1895 South Carolina law that enabled family members of lynching victims to recover monetary damages from the counties in which their relatives perished. Seemingly incongruously, this antilynching law originated during the same 1895 Constitutional Convention that signaled Jim Crow's statewide triumph. Black delegates to the 1895 convention, though virtually powerless, initially proposed what became the antilynching measure. The measure passed thanks to dogged support from an unexpected source: "Pitchfork" Ben Tillman, a racist demagogue who was the state's dominant political figure. Tillman had come to believe that the disorder and bad press associated with lynching were ultimately bad for white supremacy. By penalizing lynching in the 1895 Constitution, Tillman hoped to eradicate it—and thereby strengthen Jim Crow. Tillman's white supremacist opposition to lynching arguably buttressed Jim Crow in the short run, by making it appear more compatible with the rule of law, but weakened it in the long run by calling attention to lynching's illegitimacy and by empowering Black litigants to challenge it openly in state court. The surviving family members of over 10 percent of subsequent lynching victims would eventually sue under this measure, and they usually won.

Each of the book's six chapters is a case study of a particular legal dispute. The case-study approach to the writing of legal history has cons as well as pros. Like painted portraits, case studies, however revealing of inner life, lack the breadth of landscape. That said, case studies offer legal historians many compensating virtues. Humans are storytelling animals.[64] Thanks to the legal system's genius for preserving quotidian details, for channeling private conflicts through public institutions, for creating naturally swelling dramas of tension and resolution, and for capturing flesh-and-blood legal actors acting both courageously and venally, legal history lends itself to narrative portraiture. The results remind us, again and again, of the human causes—and human consequences—of legal history.

64. Jonathan Gottschall, *The Storytelling Animal: How Stories Make Us Human* (New York: Houghton Mifflin Harcourt, 2012).

CHAPTER ONE

State v. Posey: Slavery's Criminal Bargains[1]

In 1849, amid the pine trees and sweetgums of the Edgefield district in western South Carolina, two men, Appling and Martin, hashed out a bargain. It was the nineteenth century, the golden age of contract, and such negotiations were in vogue.[2] Even in the backwoods of western South Carolina, the restless ambitions of a young nation led Americans, rich and poor, to seek advantage through exchange.[3]

Appling and Martin's 1849 contract, however, was neither typical nor enforceable. For one thing, it called for Appling to murder Martin's wife, an illegal act for which no lawful contract could be made. For another, Appling technically could enter no contract at all. He was enslaved, and South Carolina law was clear: "A slave cannot contract [or] be contracted with."[4] Technicalities aside, the bargain was sealed. Appling agreed to murder the wife of his enslaver, Martin, in exchange for a promise of freedom. At least figuratively, the two men shook on it.[5]

---

1. Daniel Martin, J. G. Walker Mogen, Jean Atkinson, Tait Jensen, Wells King, Wade Leach, John S. Marsh, Caroline Turner, Molly B. Walker, John Wertheimer, E. B. Whitener, Robby Woodward, and Hugh Xu coauthored this chapter.

2. Lawrence M. Friedman, *A History of American Law* (New York: Simon & Schuster/ Touchstone Books, 1985), 275.

3. James Willard Hurst, *Law and the Conditions of Freedom in the Nineteenth-Century United States* (Madison: University of Wisconsin Press, 1956), 18.

4. John Belton O'Neall, *The Negro Law of South Carolina* (Columbia: John G. Bowman, 1848), 22.

5. A Junior Member of the Edgefield Bar, *Report of the Trial of Martin Posey, for the Murder of His Wife, Matilda H. Posey before the Court of Common Pleas and General Sessions of South Carolina, held at Edgefield on October 3, 1849, with an appendix containing all of the new testimony developed at the subsequent trial of Martin Posey, Elbert Posey, and Francis Posey, for the murder of a negro slave, Appling* (Advertiser Print, 1850), 35 From the testimony of Wilson Kirkland, the overseer on the Posey plantation. This document hereafter referred

The murderous bargain that Martin and Appling struck in 1849 suggests just how tightly law constrained everyday life in antebellum South Carolina. Although Martin desperately wanted to flee his marriage, the law permitted no escape short of death. Appling, for his part, wanted to be free. Yet the law bound him at every turn. Indeed, even if Martin Posey had wanted to manumit Appling, state law would not have permitted it.[6]

Lacking legal options, the two men came to an illegal agreement. This was just one of multiple Black-white handshakes in the Old South whereby enslaved people, playing one of the few bargaining chips available to them, offered to commit crimes on behalf of white enslavers in exchange for benefits. These deals, widely overlooked in previous scholarship, are troubling examples of what historians call "slave agency"—that is, instances in which enslaved people, demonstrating independent volition, exerted control over their own lives.[7]

Prior to the 1960s, scholars paid scant attention to the agency of enslaved people.[8] The most influential historians of the early twentieth century depicted slavery as a benign institution marked by, as U. B. Phillips put it in 1929, "gentleness, kind-hearted friendship and mutual loyalty."[9] In Phillips's words, enslaved people, being "more or less contentedly slaves,"[10] lacked ambition[11] and generally accepted their condition with "passive acquiescence."[12] Following World War II, scholars rejected this rosy portrait of slavery and the racist assumptions that underlay it.[13] But the picture that

---

to as *Report of the Trial of Martin Posey*. Also, "Report of the Trial of Martin Posey" (unpublished manuscript, 1850), South Caroliniana Library, University of South Carolina.

6. O'Neall, *Negro* Law, 11.

7. Walter Johnson, "On Agency," *Journal of Social History* 37, no. 1 (Autumn, 2003): 113–24.

8. Peter J. Parish, *Slavery: History and Historians* (New York: Harper & Row, 1989); Paul Finkelman, ed., *Slavery and Historiography* (New York: Garland Publishing, 1989); and David Brion Davis, "Slavery and the Post-World War II Historians," *Daedalus* 103 (Spring 1974): 2.

9. Ulrich Bonnell Phillips, *American Negro Slavery: A Survey of the Supply, Employment and Control of Negro Labor as Determined by the Plantation Régime* (New York: D. Appleton, 1929), 514.

10. Ulrich Bonnell Phillips, "Southern Negro Slavery: A Benign View," in *American Negro Slavery: A Modern Reader*, ed. Allen Weinstein and Frank Otto Gatell (New York: Oxford University Press, 1968), 38, from U. B. Phillips, *Life and Labor in the Old South* (Boston: Little, Brown, 1927).

11. Phillips, "Southern Negro Slavery," 38.

12. Ibid., 37.

13. Kenneth M. Stampp, "The Historian and Southern Negro Slavery," *American Historical Review* 57 (1952): 620.

they hung in its place was equally inattentive to the agency of enslaved people. Postwar racial liberals reinterpreted slavery as an unremitting "reign of tyranny"[14] that "infantilized" enslaved people and rendered them docile victims, much as had occurred, these historians explicitly noted, to concentration camp victims during World War II.[15] The entrepreneurial Appling of Edgefield was neither passively acquiescent nor docile.

Starting in the 1960s and '70s, and continuing for decades,[16] scholars rejected both the early-century "contented acquiescence" approach and the post–World War II "infantilized-victimhood" approach to the history of slavery.[17] Instead, they found example after example of what they called "slave agency." Enslaved people, they argued, maintained substantial cultural autonomy beyond white control through such things as "slave religion,"[18] "the black family,"[19] "slave folklore,"[20] "black culture,"[21] and "the slave community."[22] "Agency" scholars depicted enslaved people working to

14. John Hope Franklin, "Slavery and the Martial South," *Journal of Negro History* 37 (1952): 38.

15. Stanley M. Elkins, *Slavery: A Problem in American Institutional and Intellectual Life* (Chicago: University of Chicago Press, 1959). Elkins was influenced by psychological studies of Nazi concentration camps. See also Kenneth M. Stampp, *The Peculiar Institution: Slavery in the Ante-Bellum South* (New York: Alfred A. Knopf, 1956), 141–91.

16. In 1999, one historian observed that scholarship of this sort may have passed its apex. Gary B. Nash, review of Philip D. Morgan's *Slave Counterpoint* in *William and Mary Quarterly* 56, no. 3 (July 1999): 614.

17. Peter Kolchin, "American Historians and Antebellum Southern Slavery, 1954–1984," in *A Master's Due: Essays in Honor of David Herbert Donald*, ed. William J. Cooper Jr., Michael F. Holt, and John McCardle (Baton Rouge: Louisiana State University Press, 1985), 93.

18. Albert J. Raboteau, *Slave Religion: The "Invisible Institution" in the Antebellum South* (New York: Oxford University Press, 1978). See also Mechal Sobel, *Trabelin' On: The Slave Journey to an Afro-Baptist Faith* (Westport, CT: Greenwood Publishing Group, 1979); and Milton C. Sernett, *Black Religion and American Evangelicalism: White Protestants, Plantation Missions, and the Flowering of Negro Christianity, 1787–1865* (Metuchen, NJ: Scarecrow Press, 1975).

19. Herbert Gutman, *The Black Family in Slavery and Freedom, 1750–1925* (New York: Pantheon Books, 1976); and Cheryl Ann Cody, "Naming, Kinship, and Estate Dispersal: Notes on Slave Family Life on a South Carolina Plantation, 1786 to 1822," *William and Mary Quarterly* 39, no. 1 (Jan. 1982): 192–211.

20. Sterling Stuckey, "Through the Prism of Folklore: The Black Ethos in Slavery," *Massachusetts Review* 9, no. 3 (Summer 1968): 417–37.

21. Lawrence Levine, *Black Culture and Black Consciousness: Afro-American Folk Thought from Slavery to Freedom* (New York: Oxford University Press, 1977).

22. John W. Blassingame, *The Slave Community: Plantation Life in the Antebellum South* (New York: Oxford University Press, 1972).

improve their circumstances through economic exchange,[23] or even by influencing their own sales at slave markets.[24] Scholars also showed that enslaved people actively resisted and sometimes revolted against enslavement.[25]

Appling's story adds a new sort of agency to this list: criminal bargains that enslaved people struck with white people. Unlike some other forms of "agency" that scholars have explored, Appling's bargain does not give the misleading impression that human bondage was not particularly onerous—that, as one critic of "slave agency" scholarship sarcastically put it, enslaved people were "able to flourish independently, little scathed by slavery."[26] Although Appling exercised plenty of agency, he acted very much within (and, indeed, in direct response to) slavery's oppressive constraints. His story highlights the tragic limits of the agency of enslaved people. Far from being emancipatory, the criminal bargain that Appling struck proved to be, in the most literal sense, a dead end. The bargain's dreadful outcomes highlight anew the horrors of slavery and the injustice of the racialized legal system that undergirded it.[27]

---

23. Robert W. Fogel and Stanley L. Engerman, *Time on the Cross*, vol. 1: *The Economics of American Negro Slavery*, and vol 2: *Evidence and Methods* (Boston: Little, Brown, 1974); Alfred H. Conrad and John R. Meyer, "The Economics of Slavery in the Antebellum South," *Journal of Political Economy* 66 (1958): 95–130; Loren Schweninger, "Slave Independence and Enterprise in South Carolina, 1780–1865," *South Carolina Historical Magazine* 93 (April 1992): 101–25; and Kathleen Hilliard, *Master, Slaves, and Exchange* (New York: Cambridge University Press, 2014), 186.

24. Walter Johnson, *Soul by Soul: Life Inside the Antebellum Slave Market* (Cambridge, MA: Harvard University Press, 1999), 175–80.

25. T. Stephen Whitman, *Challenging Slavery in the Chesapeake: Black and White Resistance to Human Bondage, 1775–1865* (Baltimore: Maryland Historical Society, 2007); "'Sisters in Arms': Slave Women's Resistance to Slavery in the United States," *Past Imperfect* 5 (1996): 141–74; Daniel E. Walker, *No More, No More: Slavery and Cultural Resistance in Havana and New Orleans* (Minneapolis: University of Minnesota Press, 2004); James Oakes, "The Political Significance of Slave Resistance," *History Workshop* 22 (Oct. 1986): 89–107; Robert L. Paquette, "Social History Update: Slave Resistance and Social History," *Journal of Social History* 24, no. 3 (Spring 1991): 681–85.

26. Kolchin, "American Historians," 93.

27. For more on this story, see Elizabeth Dale, "A Different Sort of Justice: The Informal Courts of Public Opinion in Antebellum South Carolina," *South Carolina Law Review* 54 (2003): 627–47; and Dale, "Getting Away with Murder," *American Historical Review* 111, no. 1 (2006): 95–103. Dale discusses such things as extralegal punishment and why South Carolina's legal system seemingly tolerated homicides in some antebellum cases but not others but does not explore Appling and Posey's bargain at any length.

Scholars have yet to explore the complex legal questions raised by informal criminal contracts between white enslavers and enslaved Black people. In these cases, enslaved people did not commit crimes under compulsion. They were not merely following orders.[28] They agreed to commit crimes in exchange for some consideration. In some cases, including Appling's, they initially proposed the bargain themselves. When adjudicating the crimes that resulted from these bargains, southern courts had to decide how to apportion legal responsibility. One option was to consider the white people who paid for the crimes to be morally responsible "principals" and the enslaved people who carried out the crimes to be mere "agents" who, in legal presumption, were not fully responsible for their actions. Another option was to credit enslaved people with sufficient humanity to be found guilty as principals, while treating white criminal contractors as mere "accessories" before the fact. Court rulings in these cases reveal judicial assumptions about the nature of slavery and how morally responsible—that is, how human—enslaved people were. In Martin and Appling's case, the court decided that, for purposes of criminal punishment, at least, enslaved people were fully human and therefore bore the lion's share of criminal responsibility for their actions, even when they acted on behalf of their enslavers.

The South Carolina Supreme Court also had to decide whether or not the common law, whose protections usually did not extend to the enslaved, could be used to find enslaved people guilty of common-law crimes. It held in the affirmative.[29] Never did the law treat the enslaved more fully as people, not things, than when punishing them for criminal behavior.[30] Abolitionists of the day noted the inhumanity of this logic. As one indignantly observed, "The slave . . . is allowed to be human, so far as to be punishable. . . . He is entitled to the penalty, though not the benefit of law."[31]

28. For a discussion of crimes that enslaved people committed at the command of their enslavers, a related though distinct phenomenon, see Craig Buettinger, "Did Slaves Have Free Will? *Luke, a Slave, v. Florida* and Crime at the Command of the Master," *Florida Historical Quarterly* 83, no. 3 (Winter 2005): 241–57.

29. Scholars have payed scant attention to these questions. Thomas D. Morris, *Southern Slavery and the Law, 1619–1860* (Chapel Hill: University of North Carolina Press, 1996), 362; Thomas D. Morris, "Slaves and the Rules of Evidence in Criminal Trials," *Chicago-Kent Law Review* 68, no. 3 (1992): 1209–40.

30. Alfred L. Brophy, *University, Court, and Slave: Pro-Slavery thought in Southern Colleges and Courts and the Coming of Civil War* (New York: Oxford University Press, 2016), 262.

31. *National Anti-Slavery Standard* (New York), Dec. 17, 1840, p. 2.

Finally, Martin and Appling's bloody tale reminds us that legal inequality in antebellum South Carolina was not just a matter of free people versus enslaved people. It also was very much a matter of white people versus Black people. White criminal defendants, such as Martin Posey, were tried in General Sessions courts, which offered all of the due-process protections that the day's law afforded. By contrast, Black criminal defendants, free and enslaved, were tried in "Magistrates and Freeholders courts," slapdash tribunals where legal protections were scant. Critics seeking historical examples of racial injustice will find a rich harvest in the legal system of antebellum South Carolina.

Martin Posey of Edgefield District

In the nineteenth century, South Carolina's Edgefield District, on the state's western edge, just across from Georgia, had a reputation for mayhem. One visitor memorably described life there as "pandemonium itself."[32] It was the homicide capital of the state.[33] The South's murder rate was seven times the North's;[34] Edgefield's was four times the South's.[35] Combative politicians flourished in the district's frontier soil. Native sons included cane-wielding Preston Brooks, a proslavery congressman who pummeled Senator Charles Sumner, a Massachusetts abolitionist, on the floor of the United States Senate in 1856; "Pitchfork" Ben Tillman, a fire-breathing, populist champion of Black disfranchisement during the Jim Crow era; and Strom Thurmond, a filibustering "Dixiecrat" who opposed federal civil rights protections in the mid-twentieth century. Revealingly, the state's Democrats dubbed their

---

32. Mason Locke Weems, *The Devil in Petticoats, or God's Revenge against Husband Killing* (Edgefield, SC: Edgefield Advertiser Press, 1878), 1.

33. Orville Vernon Burton, *In My Father's House Are Many Mansions: Family and Community in Edgefield, South Carolina* (Chapel Hill: University of North Carolina Press, 1985), 6.

34. Dickenson D. Bruce Jr., *Violence and Culture in the Antebellum South* (Austin: University of Texas Press, 1979), 242, note 4.

35. Edgefield's coroners recorded sixty-five murders between 1844 and 1859. Burton, *In My Father's House*, 145. Edgefield's population, according to the 1850 census, was 39,505. See *The Seventh Census of the United States: 1850* (Washington, DC: US Census Bureau, 1850), 338. This works out to an annual murder rate in Edgefield District of 10.28 per 100,000.

1876 scheme to suppress Black votes and wrest control from Republicans at the end of Reconstruction the "Edgefield Plan."[36]

It was here, in untamed Edgefield, that Martin Posey was born in 1815 to a large, nonelite white family.[37] Census records from 1830, when Martin was a teen, report that his family included his parents (Francis and Mary Posey), several siblings, and no enslaved people.[38] At the time, almost half of Edgefield's households contained enslaved people.[39] The enslavement of people was a sign of wealth, for enslaved workers were the most valuable form of "property" in the South.[40] The Poseys' lack of enslaved people marked them as nonelite.

Possessed of boundless ambition but little else, young Martin Posey went a-courtin'. In part, his interest in marriage was social. He aspired to elite-planter status, and elite planters were expected to marry, produce children, and enslave humans.[41] More enticing than the distant appeal of paterfamilias status, however, may have been the immediate jingle of gold coins.

---

36. Lacy K. Ford Jr., "Origins of the Edgefield Tradition: The Late Antebellum Experience and the Roots of Political Insurgency," *South Carolina Historical Magazine*, vol. 98, no. 4, Oct. 1997, 328–48.

37. For biographical information on Martin Posey, see "Edgefield County Marriages 1769–1880 Implied in Edgefield County South Carolina Probate Courts," South Carolina Department of Archives and History, 86, 205. Hereafter cited as SCDAH; Edgefield District (SC), 1850 Census and 1820 US Census, Edgefield, South Carolina, roll M33 . . . 118, img. 302, SCDAH, p. 113A; *Edgefield County Marriages*, 86, 205.

38. Record for "Frances Posey, Edgefield, South Carolina," 1830 Census, Edgefield, South Carolina, Family History Library Film 0022506, series M19, roll 172, p. 202.

39. Burton, *In My Father's House*, 44.

40. Steven Deyle, *Carry Me Back: The Domestic Slave Trade in American Life* (New York: Oxford University Press, 2005), 41

41. Burton, *In My Father's House*, 366–67; Bertram Wyatt-Brown, *Southern Honor: Ethics and Behavior in the Old South* (New York: Oxford University Press, 1982), 373; Stephanie McCurry, *Masters of Small Worlds: Yeoman Households, Gender Relations, and the Political Culture of the Antebellum South Carolina Low Country* (New York: Oxford University Press, 1995), viii, 56, 72; Hendrik Hartog, *Man and Wife in America: A History* (Cambridge, MA: Harvard University Press, 2002), 147, 247; Harry Hammond to James Henry Hammond, June 29 and 30, 1859, Hammond Bryan, Cummings Papers, South Caroliniana Library, University of South Carolina; J. William Harris' *The Making of the American South: A Short History, 1500–1877* (Malden: Blackwell Press, 2006), 126; Loren Schweninger, *Family in Crisis in the South: Divorce, Slavery, and the Law* (Chapel Hill: University of North Carolina Press, 2012), 1–49.

Most Old South enterprises started with family capital, something that Martin lacked.[42] Like many other young strivers, Martin found his seed money at the altar, just in time for the pivotal years of early adulthood.[43] He said "I do" to Matilda Holmes of Edgefield District on February 23, 1838,[44] putting himself in a position to pick himself up by his father-in-law's bootstraps. The same 1830 census that listed Martin's father as enslaving no people reported that Matilda's father, Lewis Holmes, enslaved eighteen.[45] By 1840, two years after the Posey-Holmes wedding, Lewis Holmes enslaved thirty-three.[46]

Newly flush, Martin sought investment opportunities. All around, he saw trees. Edgefield was a veritable arboretum, its lumber the finest in the state.[47] Perhaps inspired by ads in the local press,[48] Martin invested in log-milling equipment, and the sawdust flew. By the 1840s, Martin Posey claimed to produce "the very best plank or lumber, of any kind."[49] His mill was a local landmark.[50]

In Edgefield, however, the big money was in small plants. Cotton was king, but the Edgefield's fertile soil also produced plenty of princes: corn, wheat, oats, rice, and tobacco, as well as cattle and hogs.[51] By 1850, Edgefield topped the state in crop and livestock production.[52] Those who acquired land there did well. Those who also acquired people did better.

---

42. Wyatt-Brown, *Southern Honor*, 213.

43. Ibid.

44. Carlee T. McClendon, *Edgefield Marriage Records: Edgefield, South Carolina, from the Late 18th Century up through 1870* (Columbia, SC: R. L. Bryan, 1970), 126.

45. "Lewis Holmes," 1830 Census, Edgefield, South Carolina, Family History Library Film 0022506, series M19, roll 172, p. 20.

46. "Lewis Holmes," 1840 Census, Edgefield, South Carolina, Family History Library Film 0022509, roll 511; p. 107, img. 224.

47. Tom Downey, *Planting a Capitalist South: Masters, Merchants, and Manufacturers in the Southern Interior, 1790–1860* (Baton Rouge: Louisiana State University Press, 2009), 56; Burton, *In My Father's House*, 55–57; Tom Downey, *Planting a Capitalist South*, 54; John Abney Chapman, *History of Edgefield County: From the Earliest Settlements to 1897* (Newberry, SC: E. H. Aull, 1897), 24.

48. See "Saw Mills," *Edgefield (SC) Advertiser*, May 21, 1845; and "From the New York Star, Something New," *Edgefield Advertiser*, February 4, 1841.

49. "Lumber for Sale," *Edgefield Advertiser*, March 21, 1849.

50. *Report of the Trial of Martin Posey*, 13, 14, 17, 27, and 37.

51. Burton, *In My Father's House*, 35–36; Walter Edgar, ed., *The South Carolina Encyclopedia* (Columbia: University of South Carolina Press, 2006), 284.

52. Ibid.

And those who acquired more people did better still.[53] Edgefield enslavers tended to be "middle-class masters" whose social positions, though locally elevated, were several rungs below the titans of the tidewater back east, whose massive plantations and huge bound workforces generated enormous wealth and prestige.[54] Edgefield's frontier openness made it a good place for white strivers such as Martin Posey.

Rung by rung, Posey climbed. He fathered children, acquired land, bought farm equipment, and enslaved human beings. By 1840, just two years into marriage, Martin's household included his wife Matilda, a newborn daughter, and four enslaved laborers.[55] Martin was a regular at "Sherriff Sales," at which distressed Edgefield debtors auctioned off possessions, often at deeply discounted prices. Frequently in the early 1840s, Posey submitted winning bids for land, livestock, and farm equipment.[56] His itchy auction finger occasionally got him into trouble, as in 1843, when he bid beyond his means, forcing him to file for bankruptcy.[57] The setback did not last long. By their tenth anniversary, in 1848, the Poseys possessed four children, a thousand acres, and about twenty enslaved people.[58] Martin had entered Edgefield's top wealth quintile,[59] on the lower edge of the planter elite.[60]

---

53. Ibid., 44.

54. James Oakes, *The Ruling Race: A History of American Slaveholders* (New York: Alfred A. Knopf, 1982), 153.

55. United States Census, 1840, Edgefield, South Carolina, Family History Library Film 0022509, roll 511, p. 116, img. 242.

56. *Edgefield Advertiser*, December 31, 1840, and February 18, March 18, and September 16, 1841.

57. "United State District Court," *Southern Patriot* (Charleston, SC), January 19, 1843; "United State District Court," *Southern Patriot*, July 28, 1843.

58. State v. Posey, 35 S.C.L. 103, 6 (1849), Testimony of Cullen Rhodes, Westlaw version; Dale, "Getting Away with Murder," 98.

59. *Slave Records of Edgefield County South Carolina*, SCDAH, 313–14, reports that Martin Posey owned twenty enslaved people. Several enslaved people understood to have belonged to Posey, including Appling, however, do not appear in this list, indicating that Posey enslaved more than twenty people. Assertions about Martin Posey's total holdings and their position within Edgefield come from Dale, "Getting Away with Murder," 98.

60. Mark W. Geiger, *Financial Fraud and Guerrilla Violence in Missouri's Civil War, 1861–1865* (New Haven, CT: Yale University Press, 2010), 122–23; Peter Kolchin, *American Slavery 1619–1877* (New York: Hill and Wang, 1993), xiii; John M. Vlach, "The Plantation Landscape," in *American Architectural History: A Contemporary Reader*, ed. Keith L. Eggener (New York: Routledge, 2004), 101; Burton, *In My Father's House*, 183.

From the outside, the Poseys' story was a happy one. People knew Matilda as "exemplary in all relations of life."[61] Martin was rougher around the edges but had established himself as a financial success, a devoted family man, and a respectable community member.[62] In 1847, for instance, Martin Posey and a neighbor, Cullen Rhodes, jointly posted a job listing for a teacher for the local schoolhouse. The two fathers would pay the salary themselves.[63]

But behind Martin Posey's proper exterior, inner demons lurked. At the end of the 1840s, they took control and rampaged. As in countless nineteenth-century morality tales, three deadly sins drove Martin into the abyss.

Lust

Martin's lust for his wife's younger sister Eliza went a long way toward explaining his precipitous fall. Eliza was just six years old in 1838, when Martin became her brother-in-law.[64] But she grew. Martin already had a thing for her in 1847, the year in which her father, Lewis Holmes, passed away. By then, Eliza was fifteen. Martin, thirty-two, attended the estate sale and purchased as much of his deceased father-in-law's property as his young sister-in-law wanted.[65] Shortly thereafter, Eliza married another man, but the marriage did not last. As luck would have it—or was it something other than luck?—Eliza's husband died in August of 1848, less than a year after their wedding, leaving Eliza a sixteen-year-old widow.[66] Not to worry. Brother-in-law Martin was there to provide comfort. Martin and Eliza could not stay away from each other.[67]

Matilda suspected something but had no proof. Early in 1849, she

---

61. *Report of the Trial of Martin Posey*, 11.

62. The State v. the Dead Body of Matilda H. Posey (S.C. 1849), James Rainsford acting as coroner.

63. "Wanted, a Female Teacher," *Edgefield Advertiser*, February 17, 1847.

64. Edgefield District (SC), 1850 Census, SCDAH, details that Eliza Holmes was born in 1832 and was a daughter of Lewis Holmes.

65. This story was told by Gabriel Holmes, the brother of Matilda and Eliza and the brother-in-law of Martin Posey. See *Report of the Trial of Martin Posey*, 12.

66. Ibid., 12.

67. For a discussion of southern gentlemen and sex, including their attraction to younger women, see Wyatt-Brown, *Southern Honor*, 202, 293–94.

aired her suspicions. "Well, old fellow," Matilda told Martin at breakfast one morning, "I have caught you at last."[68] Matilda had spied him and Eliza together in the garden the previous evening. Martin pleaded innocent. When Matilda pressed her case, Martin reasoned that, if she were right, his footprints should be in the garden. He suggested that they set the record straight once and for all by "measur[ing] tracks."[69] Martin led her to the back of the garden, where he triumphantly showed that the footprints there were not his. If the tracks don't fit, you must acquit, he implied.

The footprint test was rigged. According to the overseer who related this story subsequently at trial, Martin, anticipating trouble, had taken preemptive measures. Before breakfast, he had "made Franklin," an enslaved worker, "go and substitute his tracks" for Posey's. Martin's crude cover-up did not convince Matilda. With her own eyes, after all, she had seen her husband and her little sister together in the garden the previous evening.[70] But Martin's clumsy footprint cover is telling. Besides showing his general propensity for deceit, it illustrates his willingness to use enslaved people to do his dirty work for him. Franklin likely derived some benefit in exchange for his willingness to play along. At the very least, he attained leverage over Posey in the form of compromising knowledge.

The magnet-strong attraction between Martin and Eliza strained the Posey marriage. One day, Martin admitted to a neighbor that "his wife had fallen out with him" because she was "jealous of him and Eliza." Martin asked for a drink to calm his nerves, because his wife "had fretted him." The drink soothed his nerves. It also loosened his lips, causing him to admit that he indeed "had something to do with Eliza." Indeed, "some day or other," Martin "intended to make a wife of her."[71]

Martin's inappropriate attraction to Eliza also tore at other family relations. Gabriel Holmes, Matilda and Eliza's brother, grew increasingly angry with Martin. The two had previously engaged in routine trade relations, but once Martin's philandering ways became known, Gabriel's demeanor changed. He unfraternally took Martin to court over a minor property dispute and won, forcing Posey to sell some belongings at a sheriff's sale to pay

68. State v. Martin Posey, testimony of John Shaw35 S.C.L. 103 (1849).

69. *Report of the Trial of Martin Posey*, 34.

70. Ibid., 34. For a different version of this same story, see ibid., 13.

71. State v. Martin Posey, 8–9, Testimony of Wilson Kirkland, Westlaw version.

him back.[72] Martin Posey cursed Gabriel and blamed him for bad things that happened around his plantation.[73]

Eliza's role in the affair likewise strained her relationship with her sister. In early February 1849, the tension reached a breaking point. The two sisters "had a fray," after which Matilda "rose on Eliza" and "r[a]n her off." Eliza's flight caused Martin Posey to panic. He mumbled that he "was confused and would as soon die" as live without his young sister-in-law. He desperately wanted to chase after her, but she had taken his horse. Martin grabbed a saddle, found another mount, and uttered an ominous threat: Within "one week there would be hell to" pay.[74]

Greed

Eliza's physical maturation, the precipitous death of her husband, and the mutual attraction between her and Martin help to explain why Martin and Matilda's marriage disintegrated when it did. Around the same time, Matilda and Eliza's father, the wealthy Lewis Holmes, passed away. The patriarch's death triggered a different deadly sin in Martin Posey: greed. Greed, his lifelong companion, helped him prosper and impelled him to crow about his prosperity. Neighbors complained that he "often boasted of his wealth," which was especially irritating given that he was not all that wealthy.[75]

When his rich father-in-law died, Martin's relentless striving, one of his greatest strengths, became a deadly weakness. As long as Lewis Holmes lived, Martin had a financial incentive to stay on his good side, so that he and Matilda would remain in the will. When Lewis Holmes passed away on November 3, 1847, just shy of Martin and Matilda's tenth anniversary, he left a substantial inheritance to his six children.[76] The estate sale following

72. "Edgefield County Book of Sheriff's Writs, 1846–1851," Microfilm, County Collections, SCDAH.

73. *Report of the Trial of Martin Posey*, 15, 28.

74. State v. Martin Posey, 5, testimony of Allen Smith; *Report of the Trial of Martin Posey*, 16.

75. *Report of the Trial of Martin Posey*, 21, 23.

76. Ibid., 12.

his death brought in about $29,000.[77] Matilda and Martin inherited $2,834.[78] With that disbursement, Martin's profit motive for remaining married to Matilda evaporated. In strictly economic terms, a different temptation may have beckoned seductively: Eliza Holmes inherited $6,264, far more than her older sister did.[79] Martin may have calculated what Matilda's death would mean to him in strictly material terms. He would get to keep Matilda's inheritance of $2,834. Thereafter, were he to marry Eliza, he would acquire an additional $6,264, more than tripling his share of the Holmes estate. Martin might have had a difficult time suppressing these diabolical thoughts. That, at least, is what the solicitor in Martin Posey's subsequent murder trial suggested when accusing Martin of "murdering his own wife—his life companion and bosom friend, for the sake of a guilty paramour, and her petty fortune."[80]

Gluttony

Martin's troubles drove him to the bottle, and the bottle made everything worse. His slide from respectable family man to, as one neighbor put it, "habitual sot" began in the summer of 1848.[81] There was nothing secretive about Martin's tendency to "drink in excess."[82] Everyone noticed. Matilda fumed. One of Martin's drinking companions pointedly avoided her, "as Mrs. Posey might fall out with me for fetching him some liquor."[83] Cullen Rhodes, Martin's neighbor and friend, "took the liberty" of "beseeching [Martin,] in the most eloquent terms that I could, to quit drink."[84] It was no use. By February of 1849, neighbors reported that Martin "had been drinking to excess for several months"[85] and was "almost always drunk."[86] He "*did* drink a *great* deal

77. Ibid.

78. "Estate of Lewis Holmes Deed," box no. 57, pkg. no. 2377, Edgefield County Archives, Edgefield, South Carolina.

79. Ibid.

80. *Report of the Trial of Martin Posey*, 12.

81. Ibid., 20, 12.

82. Ibid., 14, 20.

83. State v. Posey, 9, testimony of Wilson Kirkland.

84. *Report of the Trial of Martin Posey*, 20.

85. Ibid.

86. State v. Posey, 9, testimony of Wilson Kirkland.

between June 1848 and Feb. 1849," Rhodes acknowledged. "In truth, every time I had any intelligence of him he was intoxicated."[87]

Matilda bore the brunt of Martin's intemperance. When sober, Martin was "at least kind, if not affectionate."[88] But when drunk, he was horrible—"unpleasant to strangers" and "forbidding to his household."[89] At least one old friend "cut his acquaintance" when Martin slid into the bottle.[90] If only Matilda had done the same. Even before Martin's drinking escalated, he had "whipped his wife" at least once.[91] When he was under the influence, the mistreatment multiplied.[92] Although Martin's drinking caused pious tongues to wag, his spousal abuse generated little criticism. Some chivalrous South Carolinians boasted that "the whipping of [white] women is the only crime for which a [white] man should be whipped,"[93] but such threats were largely empty. For the most part, spousal abuse was quietly tolerated. Patriarchal norms held that husbands, as heads of household, were responsible for disciplining their wives and therefore needed to be able to correct them as they would a misbehaving child, animal, or slave.[94]

Spousal murder, however, was a different matter altogether.

The Marriage Yoke

By February of 1849, Martin Posey—an abusive, alcoholic, adulterer—was desperate to leave his wife and wed his wife's little sister. One option would have been simply to abandon Matilda and run away with Eliza. At one point, indeed, Martin fantasized about fleeing with Eliza to California.[95] It was, after all, the era of the Gold Rush. Martin Posey, a lifelong treasure-seeker, would have fit right in. But he and Eliza stayed put. Legally speaking, abandoning Matilda, even across state lines, would not necessarily dissolve their marriage. Any subsequent marriage could theoretically trigger a crim-

---

87. *Report of the Trial of Martin Posey*, 21.
88. Ibid., 22; State v. Posey, 6.
89. *Report of the Trial of Martin Posey*, 22.
90. Ibid.
91. State v. Posey, 6, testimony of Cullen Rhodes6.
92. *Report of the Trial of Martin Posey*, 22.
93. Ibid, 7.
94. Hartog, *Man and Wife*, 116.
95. *Report of the Trial of Martin Posey*, 66.

inal prosecution for bigamy.[96] Furtive flight to California also would presumably have meant abandoning much of the property that Posey had worked so hard to amass in South Carolina: the sawmill, the land, the human beings.

Divorce must also have crossed Martin's mind. In most states, divorce was possible under at least some circumstances. Divorce petitions in other states commonly mentioned infidelity and alcoholism—two boxes that Martin certainly checked.[97] South Carolina, however, prohibited divorce.[98] Local traditionalists staunchly defended this policy, viewing the state's divorce ban as evidence of moral superiority. They argued that the absence of divorce in their state protected married women against abandonment and destitution.[99] Religious leaders preached that divorce was incompatible with the sacredness of the marital union.[100] The *Edgefield Advertiser* in 1839 criticized the increasing popularity of divorce in the Northeast. "The marriage yoke," the paper sniffed, "is evidently galling to a number of [Connecticut's] people."[101] Unhappily married South Carolinians occasionally filed desperate divorce petitions, despite their futility. Eliza Ransom of Barnwell County, South Carolina, for instance, petitioned for divorce in 1841. She had a pretty good case, meaning a pretty horrible marriage. Her husband drank to excess, gambled compulsively, ran up crippling debts, and "repeatedly" beat her. Her petition was denied.[102]

Martin Posey's case seemed equally futile. He was unhappily married in a state that allowed no divorce. The only escape from "the marriage yoke" that he could see was the one suggested by his vow to Matilda eleven years previously: "'Til death do us part."[103]

---

96. Hartog, *Man and Wife*, 147.

97. Hartog, *Man and Wife*, 64, 74; Schweninger, *Family in Crisis*, 18–19.

98. Kellen Funk, "'Let No Man Put Asunder': South Carolina's Law of Divorce, 1895–1950," *South Carolina Historical Magazine*, vol. 110, no. 3/4, July–October, 2009, 134; Janet Hudson, "From Constitution to Constitution, 1868–1895: South Carolina's Unique Stance of Divorce," *South Carolina Historical Magazine*, 1997, 79.

99. Burton, *In My Father's House*, 137, 141.

100. Woodson Hortense's *Giant in the Land: A Biography of William Bulletin Johnson, First President of the Southern Baptist Convention* (Nashville, TN: Broadmaess, 1950), 66–72; Burton, *In My Father's House*, 137, 140–41.

101. "Working of the Divorce Bill," *Edgefield Advertiser*, July 4, 1839.

102. *Petition of Eliza Taylor Ransom to the Equity Court of Barnwell District, South Carolina, October 8, 1841*, Equity Court Records, microfilm reel BW83, frames 116–24, SCDAH.

103. McCurry, *Masters of Small Worlds*, 87.

Appling

We know much less about Appling, the enslaved laborer who was the other party to the criminal bargain that culminated in the death of Matilda Posey in early 1849. Appling, who went by App, was around thirty years old at the time of the bargain, making him about four years younger than Martin and three years younger than Matilda.[104] A subsequent advertisement for Appling's capture described him as being about "5 feet 8 or 10 inches high," "straight," and of "ordinary size."[105]

As of early 1849, Appling had been on the Posey plantation for less than a year and a half. He previously had been enslaved by Lewis Holmes, Matilda and Eliza's father, though for how long we do not know. If it was a long time, as seems possible, he and Matilda might have grown up together.[106] As mentioned above, Martin Posey bid aggressively at the estate sale following his father-in-law's death in November of 1847. Martin bought his fifteen-year-old sister-in-law Eliza whatever she wanted.[107] For himself, his purchases included "a negro man App, or more properly Appling."[108] The price that Martin paid for Appling, $300, was strikingly low. At the same sale, Martin paid over twice that amount—$700 each—for "1 Negro Boy Henry" and "1 Negro Girl Emily."[109] Compared to these two children, who presumably had many productive years ahead of them, Appling was almost thirty, well advanced toward his life expectancy.[110] Yet age alone fails to explain the discount. After all, Posey paid $655, over twice what he paid for App, for Tom, an adult man, at the same sale.[111] In all likelihood, the price that Martin paid for Appling reflected a couple of perceived defects. Posey subsequently described App as speaking with a stammer. More significantly, given the context, App had a bum leg. A trial witness later testified,

104. "$100 Reward!," *Edgefield Advertiser*, March 21, 1849, 1; "Proclamation," *Edgefield Advertiser*, March 21, 1849, 1.

105. Ibid.

106. Ibid.; Edgefield District (SC), 1850 Census, SCDAH; *Edgefield County Marriages*, 86, 205.

107. *Report of the Trial of Martin Posey*, 12

108. Ibid.

109. "Estate of Lewis Holmes Deed," Edgefield County Archives.

110. "$100 Reward!," 1; "Proclamation," 1.

111. "Estate of Lewis Holmes Deed," Edgefield County Archives.

"I knew he [App] had a sore leg . . . saw his leg sore the day he was sold."[112] Others described App's leg as "much swollen." The problem was serious enough that "one leg bone was affected." App's "knot on the bone" inhibited his mobility during his life and would facilitate the identification of his body after his death.[113]

At one point, Posey posted a "Wanted" ad for App that contained two racialized descriptions. App was, in Posey's words, "a little copper-colored," and he sported a "long beard on his chin."[114] "Copper-colored" implied mixed racial ancestry.[115] Similarly, a "long beard," to Americans of that day, signified at least some white blood. One mid-nineteenth-century American writer, an advocate of white supremacy and racial pseudoscience, wrote that the "full, flowing, and majestic beard of the Caucasian, in contrast with the negro or other subordinate races, is as striking and imposing as the mane of the lion when compared with the meaner beasts of the animal world. . . . The Caucasian is the only bearded race," this writer continued, "and the negro is furthest removed of all, for the . . . negro, except a little tuft on the chin and sometimes on the upper lip, has nothing that can be confounded with a beard." Any bearded Black man, this writer asserted, must have had a "large infusion," or perhaps even a "vastly predominating infusion," of "Caucasian blood."[116]

App's "copper" color and long beard likely caused people to categorize him as a mixed-race "mulatto." In the day's racial ideology, mulattoes occupied an intermediary position "between European and African."[117] Racists deemed them "decidedly superior to negroes" in "cleanliness, capacity, activity, and courage."[118] Enslaved mulattoes benefited from these stereotypes. Mixed-race enslaved people—many of whom were blood relatives of their owners—often occupied desirable positions, such as domestic work-

112. *Report of the Trial of Martin Posey*, testimony of Luke Lott, 53.

113. State v. Posey, 8, testimony of Cullen Rhodes; "$100 Reward!," 1; "Proclamation," 1; *Report of the Trial of Martin Posey*, testimony of Luke Lott, 53.

114. "$100 Reward!," 1; "Proclamation," 1.

115. Ariela J. Gross, "Litigating Whiteness: Trials of Racial Determination in the Nineteenth-Century South," *Yale Law Journal* 108, no. 1 (Oct. 1998): 109–88; Claire Kahane, "The Artificial Niggers," *Massachusetts Review* 19, no. 1 (Spring, 1978): 196.

116. John H. Van Evrie, *Negroes and Negro "Slavery": The First an Inferior Race: The Latter Its Normal Condition* (New York: Van Evrie, Horton, 1861), 102–3.

117. Ibid., 92.

118. Ibid.

ers and artisans.[119] Appling appears to have enjoyed such privileges during his year-and-a-half stay on the Posey plantation. He drove a wagon, a less grueling task than working in the fields or toiling in a sawmill.[120] App also had unusual access to the Posey family's domestic space. A worker who visited the plantation to build a chimney for Martin Posey recalled seeing App, but "no other negro," "in the house playing with the children."[121] The chimney-builder likewise reported seeing App spend "a day or two about the house"—meaning the Poseys' "big house"—while recovering from an illness.[122]

Appling may have enjoyed playing with the Posey children, but he was no angel. His reputation, like his owner's, was not good. "App's character was bad," declared one witness in early 1849.[123] In particular, he drank. By law and custom, South Carolina tightly controlled enslaved people's access to liquor,[124] but witnesses were "quite certain" that App "drank at the jug."[125] Given the norms of the Old South, the local white community would have held App's moral shortcomings against Martin Posey, under the paternalistic assumption that an honorable enslaver, like an honorable parent, was responsible for the behavior of those under his authority.[126]

App may have enjoyed an unusual degree of leeway, but no amount of pleasure "at the jug," and no number of plantation privileges, could alter his legal status. He was a slave, meaning he had precious little control over his life and endless cause for complaint.

Some of App's grievances were specific. He complained, for instance, that "his mistress," Matilda Posey, "would not give him enough to eat."[127] Other grievances were systemic, for the slave status bound him, and the rest of South Carolina's enslaved majority, at every joint. The same racialized

---

119. Joel Williamson, *New People: Miscegenation and Mulattoes in the United States* (New York: Free Press, 1980), 20.

120. *Report of the Trial of Martin Posey*, 33.

121. Ibid., 15.

122. Ibid.

123. State v. Posey, 12, testimony of James Ransford.

124. Slave Codes of South Carolina, sec.23, 1740. Transcription from David J. McCord, ed., *The Statutes at Large of South Carolina*, vol. 7: *Containing the Acts Relating to Charleston, Courts, Slaves, and Rivers* (Columbia, SC: A.S. Johnson, 1840).

125. *Report of the Trial of Martin Posey*, 15.

126. Ariela Gross, *Double Character: Slavery and Mastery in the Antebellum Southern Courtroom* (Princeton, NJ: Princeton University Press, 2000), 98–99.

127. Ibid., 58; State v. Posey.

frontier culture that freed Martin Posey to rise prevented App from doing so. Martin was born poor but white, and thus free. The debasing law of "negro slavery"[128] would not—could not—apply to him. By contrast, App was owned the moment he was born. Under South Carolina law, the "offspring of a slave mother must also be a slave." Whoever enslaved App's mother instantly enslaved App.[129]

As an adult, Martin Posey could live wherever he wished. Appling could not. Enslaved people were not allowed to own land.[130] South Carolina also prevented them from "renting or hiring any house" or room.[131] The enslaved lived where their enslavers commanded them to live. App resided on the Posey plantation not through any volition but because Martin Posey purchased him following the death of Lewis Holmes, his previous enslaver.

Martin Posey jump-started his rise by marrying the wealthy Matilda Holmes and further fueled it by inheriting his wife's share of her father's estate. Appling, by contrast, remained single, not because that was his preference—his marital preference is unknown—but rather because South Carolina did not permit enslaved people to marry.[132] (App's inner marital preference might have been known had he kept a diary, but South Carolina also made it illegal to teach him to read or write.)[133] And even if App had had a free and wealthy relative—even if his own father had been wealthy and free—App, by law, was not allowed to inherit a thing.[134]

Hoping to get ahead, Martin Posey ambitiously made business contracts, purchased land, and acquired supplies. Appling also appears to have been ambitious, but his legal status as a slave prevented him from doing any of the things that Martin did to get ahead. He could not "contract" or "be contracted with."[135] With Martin's consent, App theoretically had the right to "acquire and hold *personal* property" (though not land—a hugely important caveat, given the agricultural basis of Edgefield's economy). At the end of the day, however, the law stipulated that anything that App managed to

---

128. O'Neall, *Negro Law*, 12.

129. Ibid., 17.

130. Roy W. Copeland, "In the Beginning: Origins of African American Real Property Ownership in the United States," *Journal of Black Studies* 44, no.6 (Sept. 2013): 649.

131. O'Neall, *Negro Law*, 25.

132. Ibid., 23.

133. Ibid., 23.

134. Ibid., 23.

135. Ibid., 22.

acquire would ultimately belong to Martin.[136] Under South Carolina law, "whatever is given to the slave belongs to the master."[137]

Manumission fantasies were hardly worth entertaining. For one thing, Martin Posey appears to have been a hard-hearted scoundrel with no interest in freeing anyone. For another, even if Martin had wanted to emancipate Appling, South Carolina law would not have permitted it. By the late 1840s, only an act of the state legislature could emancipate a South Carolina slave.[138] Posey could not even have established a bequest, trust, or conveyance whereby App would be moved out of state and freed following Posey's death. Any such instrument would have been void under South Carolina law. App would have remained a slave, and his ownership would likely have passed to Posey's next of kin.[139]

Finally, even if Appling, bum leg and all, had managed to escape, his in-state prospects were dim. South Carolina law considered the color of App's skin to be "prima facie evidence that the party bearing the color of a negro, mulatto or mestizo, is a slave."[140] Because he was a "Negro," App would have borne the heavy burden of proving his freedom.[141] And even if he managed to slip through the cracks and live as a free person, his legal status would have persisted. South Carolina insisted that "if a negro be at large, and enjoy freedom," even for decades, "he or she is still a slave."[142]

Appling, thus, had many reasons to complain about his legal status and ample incentive to want to improve it. But his negotiating position was weak. He may have thought that, being enslaved, he had no bargaining leverage at all. But then an enslaved conjurer appeared on the Posey plantation and showed him otherwise. His name was Jeff.

Jeff

Martin Posey's desperation to escape marriage in a divorceless state created bargaining opportunities for the people around him. The first person to

136. Ibid., 21.
137. Ibid., 11.
138. Ibid., 11.
139. Ibid., 11–12.
140. Ibid., 5.
141. Ibid., 8.
142. Ibid., 39.

take advantage of Posey's predicament was an unlikely one. He was Jeff, an enslaved "conjuror" on a distant plantation.

The roots of slave conjuration stretch back to Africa, where conjurors often served as community leaders, healers, and priests.[143] Like their African predecessors, enslaved conjurers in the Americas called upon spirits or used potions or talismans to produce desired effects. One conjurer sought to use talismans to make himself and other enslaved people impervious to physical harm.[144] Another gave a special powder to a companion to prevent his enslaver from punishing him.[145] A third was said to be able to call down lightning and thunder in order to prevent enslaved people from being convicted in criminal trials.[146] Conjurors sometimes failed to achieve their objectives, but failure did not necessarily destroy others' faith in their powers.[147]

Some enslavers sought to suppress conjuration because of its non-Christian nature and because it posed a threatening form of resistance to white authority.[148] Others doubted but tolerated conjuration, believing that its controlled use could improve slave morale and productivity. Martin Posey seems to have belonged to a third group: enslavers who genuinely believed in conjuration's powers. This belief led him to Jeff. Jeff the conjurer "belong[ed] to Boatwright, of Lexington," a wealthy planter whose estate was a considerable distance away.[149] At the time, during the autumn of 1848, some of the enslaved laborers on Posey's plantation had health concerns. Martin Posey negotiated a temporary rental agreement with Boat-

143. Douglas R. Egerton, *He Shall Go Out Free: The Lives of Denmark Vesey* (Madison, WI: Madison House, 1999), 118.

144. Edward A. Pearson, ed., *Designs against Charleston* (Chapel Hill: University of North Carolina Press, 1999), 126.

145. Henry Bibb, "Conjuration and Witchcraft," in *African American Religious History: A Documentary Witness*, ed. Milton C. Sernett (Durham, NC: Duke University Press, 1999), 78.

146. Jeffrey E. Anderson, *Conjure in African American Society* (Baton Rouge: Louisiana State University Press, 2005), 85.

147. Maude Barragan, interview with Julia Henderson, *American Slavery: A Composite Autobiography*, accessed nov. 11, 2015, http://gem.greenwood.com/pdf-files/AS/gwsn_03s_hen_j.pdf

148. Theophus H. Smith, *Conjuring Culture: Biblical Formations of Black America* (New York: Oxford University Press, 1994), 4; Pearson, *Designs against Charleston*, 122–24; Anderson, *Conjure in African American Society*, 57.

149. "From the South Carolinian—Boatwright's Plantation Mills," *Edgefield Advertiser*, March 24, 1847.

wright to bring Jeff to Edgefield to "doctor some of [Posey's] negroes."[150] Posey's eagerness to bring Jeff from afar suggests his faith in Jeff's effectiveness. Jeff arrived and began "doctor[ing] some of [Posey's] negroes." Jeff quickly concluded two things. First, life in Edgefield was preferable to life in Lexington. We do not know what made the Boatwright estate so bad, but Jeff's preference for the Posey plantation was clear. In order to remain, however, Jeff would have to convince Martin Posey to extend his stay. He would need bargaining leverage.

The second thing that Jeff discovered provided that bargaining leverage. Through the plantation grapevine, Jeff quickly learned that Martin Posey was desperate to be rid of his wife. This information led Jeff to propose a mutually advantageous (albeit criminal) bargain: Jeff would use his conjuring arts to do away with Matilda Posey; in exchange, Martin would purchase Jeff. Importantly, this was not a direct command from enslaver to enslaved. It was a contractual bargain, one that Jeff proposed. As later related by a courtroom witness: "The negro himself [Jeff] had told [Posey that] he could do something which would secretly cause his wife's death." In exchange, "the negro wanted him [Posey] to buy him." Posey agreed, but added a contractual condition of his own: Posey would not make the purchase "till Jeff had first conjured his wife away."[151] Metaphorically, at least, the two men shook on it.

Even though Jeff initiated the bargain, he found Martin Posey to be an eager negotiating partner. Martin seems to have been quite fond of dealing with people—white or Black, free or enslaved—who were willing to do nasty things for him in exchange for a reward. Several courtroom witnesses later testified to that effect. One reported that "Martin Posey told me he would give me $1000 if I would get Polly Rowe to ride [Martin's brother-in-law] Gabriel Holmes to death." Polly Rowe, the witness explained, "is supposed to be a witch."[152]

Jeff's negotiation with Posey was a bargain between unequals. Posey had lots of bargaining chips. Jeff had few. The most powerful thing that Jeff could offer was a willingness to commit a crime on behalf of his enslaver. That was enough. By playing that chip, Jeff put himself in a position to convince a much more powerful person to do his bidding. Criminality

150. *Report of the Trial of Martin Posey*, 32

151. Ibid.

152. Ibid., 70.

enhanced Jeff's control over his circumstances. All that remained was to follow through on the contract and do away with Matilda Posey. Jeff's magic, however, fizzled. He tried "several times" to kill Matilda "but kept failing." Finally, at the end of January 1849, Posey ran out of patience and returned Jeff to Boatwright of Lexington.[153]

Appling's Criminal Bargain

Jeff's sudden arrival seems to have threatened Appling's privileged position on the Posey plantation. Copper-colored and full-bearded, Appling enjoyed high standing. He drove the wagon. He strolled the big house and played with the Posey children. Then Jeff, the fancy conjurer, moved into App's sunlight and threatened App's honor. Male honor played an important role within enslaved communities.[154] Honor-based conflicts sometimes produced fisticuffs among the enslaved. Appling, perhaps because he had a bum leg,[155] took a different route to solve his problem. He realized that Jeff served at Martin Posey's pleasure. In order to get rid of Jeff, Appling needed to persuade Martin Posey not to purchase him. That meant offering something that his enslaver wanted. App's extensive plantation knowledge made that easy. He knew, as everyone knew, that Martin wanted Matilda dead. App concluded that his strongest bargaining leverage was his willingness to commit murder.

Like Jeff before him, Appling initiated the negotiations. Martin Posey did not order either enslaved man to act criminally. They both volunteered. In exchange for Matilda's death, Appling appears to have asked Martin for two things. First, Appling wanted Jeff gone. "App said [that] if Jeff were gone, he could put Mrs. Posey out of the way" a witness later reported.[156] According to this same witness, Martin Posey, presumably as an act of good faith, then "sent Jeff home because he found he would not, or could not, put his wife out of the way, and he had no longer use for him, and as App said

153. Ibid., 32; State v. Posey, 9, testimony of Wilson Kirkland.

154. Wyatt-Brown, "The Mask of Obedience: Male Slave Psychology in the Old South," *American Historical Review* 93, no. 5 (Dec. 1988): 1228–52; Jeff Forret, *Slave against Slave: Plantation Violence in the Old South* (Baton Rouge: Louisiana State University Press, 2015), 288.

155. *The Report of the Trial of Martin Posey*, 60.

156. State v. Posey, 9, testimony of Wilson Kirkland; *Report of the Trial of Martin Posey*, 32.

he could [kill Matilda] if Jeff were gone, he [Martin] wanted Jeff out of the way that App might [proceed with the killing of Matilda]."[157]

Appling's second condition was a promise of freedom, an enticement so alluring that South Carolina jurist John Belton O'Neall described it as "the only reward" that a master could give "which . . . his slave appreciates."[158] App described the deal to Wilson Kirkland, the plantation's overseer, who later testified as follows: "At the mill, App came to me . . . and he stated his master had promised to send him away if he would put his wife out of the way."[159]

Appling was not naïve. He realized that his enslaver was not a completely reliable negotiating partner. He had reason to suspect that Martin might not follow through on his end of the bargain, even if App fulfilled his promise to kill Matilda.[160] App shared his worries with Kirkland, the overseer, one day at Posey's mill. If App "put his mistress [Matilda] out of the way," Kirkland explained, "his master [Martin] was to carry him away," but App "feared he would not." Kirkland did not believe that App would kill Matilda, but he told App that if he did, and if Martin still failed to "carry him away to freedom," Kirkland would do so himself.[161] Hearing this from Kirkland, and observing that Martin had satisfied the bargain's first condition by sending Jeff away, App apparently figured that it was worth a try. He would follow through on his end of the bargain. What could he lose?

Murder

When the sun rose on Saturday, February 17, 1849, Matilda Posey was nowhere to be found. About two and a half weeks had elapsed since Jeff's departure. Time passed; still, no Matilda. Neighbors and family members eventually formed a search party and went looking for her, day after day.[162] Five people privately knew what had happened: Appling, Martin Posey, Posey's overseer Wilson Kirkland, and Luisa and Franklin, both enslaved. When Matilda's body was discovered, a week and a half after her disappear-

157. State v. Posey, 9, testimony of Wilson Kirkland.

158. O'Neall, *Negro Law*, 12.

159. *Report of the Trial of Martin Posey*, 58.

160. Ibid.

161. State v. Posey, 11, testimony of Wilson Kirkland.

162. *Report of the Trial of Martin Posey*, 13, 60.

ance, all but Appling, who had vanished, testified at a coroner's inquest.[163] Later still, during the criminal trial of Martin Posey for the death of his wife, neither Louisa nor Franklin testified, because Black people—free or enslaved—were not allowed to testify against white people.[164] Kirkland, however, testified extensively, making his words—carefully preserved by the official court reporter, and also by a commercial publication that covered the trial—the ones upon which historians must principally rely. Here is the story that emerges from these accounts.

On Friday evening, February 16, 1849, Appling performed his end of the bargain. He set a trap in the woods, by the springhouse, a small structure designed to keep fallen leaves and animals out of the plantation's water supply. A couple of Black children wandered down in search of kindling. App sent them to tell Matilda Posey that the springhouse door was broken. When Matilda arrived, App tried to lure her into the woods by preying on the suspicions that he knew she harbored about her husband's infidelities. "You have often accused master Martin," App reportedly said, "and if you will go with me I will show you the fact." At that very moment, App said, Martin was "with another woman."[165] Matilda was tempted. She started following Appling. But then she stopped short. "App, I know what you are after," she said: "You want to kill me."[166]

Matilda's perception that App "want[ed]" to kill her is revealing. She clearly sensed that her husband wanted her dead. She also knew that Martin was capable of using enslaved people to do his dirty work for him. The wording of her statement to App—"You *want* to kill me [emphasis added]," rather than "You have been ordered to kill me"—could indicate her belief that App exercised volition in the matter. Her reaction reveals a plantation culture in which criminal bargains between enslavers and enslaved people were easy to imagine.

Back near the springhouse, Matilda, realizing her peril, started back toward the big house. Appling caught hold of her and said, "I want to do it."

Matilda responded with her last reported words: "App, I'll have you hung."

163. The State vs. the dead body of Matilda Posey (Murder), James Rainsfort, Magistrate, acting as coroner, South Carolina, Edgefield District, Examination of Witness[es], February 26, 1849, SCDAH.

164. Morris, "Slaves and the Rules of Evidence in Criminal Trials," 1209.

165. *Report of the Trial of Martin Posey*, 58; State v. Posey, 10, testimony of Wilson Kirkland.

166. Ibid.

"You might have me hung, and you might not," App replied.[167]

At this point, the record clouds. The official trial report proceeds right from this exchange to App drowning Matilda in the mill pond. An unpublished coroner's inquest, however, contains additional testimony from Franklin, an enslaved man, suggesting that Appling raped Matilda before killing her. Franklin explained that, about a week after Matilda's disappearance, App had told him what he had done to "Miss Tilda." "When she went to the spring," Franklin said, paraphrasing App's confession, "he took hold of her and had to do with her."[168] Only then did App kill her. If true, this part of the story opens the possibility that, among App's motivations were some not yet mentioned: power, domination, violence, and pleasure.

Whether or not Appling raped Matilda, the available evidence suggests that he killed her by beating her with a hoe and then drowning her in the millpond. Later that night, he retrieved the corpse and buried it, with the help of Louisa and Franklin.[169] App and his coconspirator Martin Posey sought to cover up the affair, but Franklin's knowledge of the crime ultimately led the cover-up to unravel. Franklin approached Kirkland the overseer and told him that "he had found out that App had killed his mistress."[170] Franklin, aware of the culture of criminal bargaining that prevailed on the Posey plantation, may have believed that he, too, had some bargaining leverage by virtue of his knowledge. He may have hoped for some reward in exchange for his silence. It did not work out that way. Kirkland immediately alerted Posey, who threatened to kill Franklin if he revealed the truth.

Many of the events described above are known to history only because Franklin or other enslaved people reported them. Yet, in theory, enslaved people were not supposed to be able to testify in court. Indeed, even so-called free negroes, under South Carolina law, could not serve as witnesses in trials, "with the single exception" of criminal trials of Black criminal defendants[171]—not an issue in the Martin Posey case. Nevertheless, Black voices are audible in the legal record. Some informal legal proceedings,

167. *Report of the Trial of Martin Posey*, 58; State v. Posey, 10, testimony of Wilson Kirkland.

168. Testimony of "Franklin a negro fellow," the State v. the Dead Body of Matilda H. Posey, James Rainsford acting as coroner, South Carolina, Edgefield District, February 26, 1849, SCDAH.

169. State v. Posey, 10.

170. *Report of the Trial of Martin Posey*, 37.

171. O'Neall, *Negro Law*, 13.

such as coroner's inquests, did record and preserve the testimonies of enslaved people. And even in more formal legal settings, such as criminal trials in superior courts, white witnesses regularly recounted things told to them by Black people. In these ways, Black perspectives made more of an imprint on the legal record than the state's formal law might lead one to expect.[172]

Martin Posey then told an enslaved plantation hand named Jake to take App into hiding and tell him to lie low, for it would not be long before Martin Posey sent someone to "carry [App] away, as he was to have his freedom for killing his mistress." The scheming Posey, however, had other ideas. Concocting yet another criminal bargain with an enslaved person, Posey reportedly "sent Jake down to Ergle's bridge," with orders to "kill him [App]," "if he could get a chance." No record remains of what, if anything, Posey offered Jake in exchange for killing App. Jake, however, showed good judgment and left App under Ergle's bridge, very much alive. (Jake's account, relayed indirectly through a white witness, ultimately made it into the legal record.)[173]

One morning, after over a week of fruitless hunting, the community search party chanced upon Martin Posey. Cullen Rhodes asked Posey if he had any news about his wife's whereabouts. "Yes," Posey replied: "App confessed to Franklin last night that he had to do with my wife, and then drowned her and buried her . . . above the spring branch!" Rhodes asked if App was in custody. "No!" Posey said: "Kirkland and I looked for him but he's gone!"[174]

Franklin's information quickly led the search party to Matilda's rotting body. (Recall that Franklin had long known what happened, and indeed had helped bury the body.) A postmortem examination occurred on February 26, ten days after Matilda's disappearance.[175] Dr. Addison, the examiner, noted that "wounds extended from near the top of the right side of the head to the lowest rib on the right side, and on and under the right arm." He believed that "the beating had produced her death" rather than the drowning.[176]

Meanwhile, the search turned from Matilda to Appling. Notices urging

172. For more on this phenomenon, see Gross, *Double Character.*

173. Ibid., 35; State v. Posey, 10.

174. *Report of the Trial of Martin Posey*, 19.

175. Ibid., 55.

176. State v. Posey, 5.

his apprehension circulated throughout the state. Both Martin Posey and the Office of the South Carolina Governor advertised substantial rewards for Appling's capture. Posey offered $100 for the "apprehension and delivery of my negro man." The governor offered $250.[177]

The searchers eventually found Appling's remains on an island in a swamp near the county line. "Putrifaction" had begun; "little flesh yet remained." The head "was dislocated from the body and had neither hair nor flesh upon it."[178]

All along, of course, Martin Posey knew where Appling had gone to hide because he had told Jake where to take him. In an attempt to hide his guilt forever, Martin had urged Jake to kill App. Jake, however, left App alive.[179] Posey then gave the omnipresent Franklin "weapons to kill" and urged him to take Appling's life,[180] but Franklin, too, left App alive. Wilson Kirkland was next, but the overseer, like the enslaved people before him, refused to carry out Posey's wishes.[181] Finally, the scheming patriarch took matters into his own hands. On March 1, 1849, Martin Posey lured Appling from his hiding spot, tied him up, and shot him through the chest and the neck with two horse pistols.[182]

The ultimate discovery of Appling's murdered body turned suspicions toward Martin Posey and his overseer, Wilson Kirkland. From the outset, Martin had acted strangely. Search-party members had noticed Martin's seeming disinterest in finding either Matilda or, later, App.[183] Confronted with his wife's death, Posey showed no grief and conspicuously little sadness. He "never once complained of his wife being dead,"[184] one suspicious searcher remarked. Posey worried only about the woman he called "poor Eliza."[185] He "was afraid to leave home, for Eliza . . . was afraid to stay by herself."[186]

177. "$100 Reward!," 1; "Proclamation," 1; "Proclamation," *Camden Journal* (Camden, SC), April 4, 1849, 1; and "Proclamation," *Sumter Banner* (Sumter, SC), March 28, 1849, 3.

178. *Report of the Trial of Martin Posey*, 26.

179. Ibid., 35; State v. Posey, 10.

180. State v. Martin Posey, in James A. Strobhart, *Report of Cases Argued and Determined in the Court of Appeals and Court of Errors of South Carolina, on Appeal from the Courts of Law* (Charleston, SC: A. S. Johnston, 1847–51), 147.

181. Strobhart, *Report of Cases*, 147.

182. State v. Posey, 8.

183. *Report of the Trial of Martin Posey*, 19; State v. Martin Posey, 7.

184. *Report of the Trial of Martin Posey, 25.*

185. Ibid.

186. Ibid., 19.

The interrogations of Franklin, Louisa, and other enslaved persons confirmed the worst suspicions about Martin Posey. These witnesses told "a straight and familiar tale" that incriminated Posey and his overseer, Kirkland.[187] Based on these tales, the authorities arrested Kirkland and searched for Posey. The following evening, a group of outraged citizen law enforcers tracked him to his father's house, where they arrested him for the murders of Matilda and Appling, two people entrusted to his supposedly paternalistic care. After a brief standoff, Martin Posey came down from the second floor with Eliza by his side. "You have not got the right man," he insisted. "Gabriel Holmes [Matilda's brother] was the last man seen with my wife."[188] But they had the right man. And they would soon put him on trial.

Martin Posey on Trial

On October 3, 1849, Martin Posey entered the Court of General Pleas and Common Sessions in Edgefield County, South Carolina, to stand trial for the murder of his wife, Matilda Posey. One week later, he would be tried again, this time for the murder of Appling. The same team of lawyers represented him both times. Martin's life depended on the outcomes of the two trials. His prospects were bleak.

People flocked from around the state and beyond to witness the Matilda Posey murder trial. In the words of one reporter, the Edgefield courtroom was "crowded almost to smothering,"[189] and additional people waited outside, hoping to get in. Edgefield had never seen such crowds.[190] Then again, no man had ever so spectacularly flouted both state law and the norms of his social class. Wealthy planters imagined themselves to be God-fearing paternalists who protected and provided for those entrusted to their care. If the charges in the indictment were true, however, Martin Posey, "not having the fear of God before his eyes, but being moved and seduced by . . . the Devil," had conspired to murder both his wife and a slave, two people entrusted to his paternalistic care.[191]

The courtroom scene was spellbinding. "Who that was present," one

187. Ibid., 21.
188. Ibid., 27.
189. Ibid.
190. *Report of the Trial of Martin Posey*, 4.
191. The State of South Carolina v. Martin Posey, 35 S.C.L. 103, 2 (1849).

observer wrote, "can ever forget the deep feeling, the awful solemnity, the death-like stillness that pervaded?"[192] Neck-craning spectators rooted for a conviction, overwhelmingly convinced of Posey's guilt. Presiding judge Thomas Jefferson Withers, a respected magistrate in his third year on the bench, sought to uphold the rule of law in the face of an indignant public. At one point, when Judge Withers called for a recess, he made sure to separate the jury from the agitated throng. "If the jury were to go forth [and mingle with the public during the recess]," he reasoned, "they would not try the prisoner according to the law and the evidence . . . but by the . . . arguments of blind passion and by the charge of revenge."[193]

Solicitor Bonham stoked the crowd's outrage with dramatic opening remarks. The cold-blooded murder of Matilda Posey, a "poor, helpless woman," by Martin Posey, a "monster" and "heartless wretch," he thundered, was "perhaps without a parallel in the annals of crime."[194]

Many of the state's eighteen witnesses attacked Martin Posey's character, starting with his drinking. A reputation for drinking hurt, especially given the strength of South Carolina's temperance movement at the time.[195] Temperance meetings, lectures, books, and "Temperance Stories" in the local press equated drinking with a loss of control and respectability—the very antithesis of the patriarchal code that was supposed to prevail among men of Martin Posey's class.[196] Shortly after the Posey trials, Edgefield would elect a prohibition ticket and impose a tavern ban.[197] Witnesses in Posey's trial echoed larger temperance themes. Martin's drinking had turned him from an attentive father into an abusive monster.[198] It had wrecked his marriage,[199] destroyed friendships,[200] and broken the heart of his poor

192. *Report of the Trial of Martin Posey*, 5.

193. Ibid., 24.

194. Ibid., 12.

195. Douglas W. Carlson, "'Drinks He to His Own Undoing': Temperance Ideology in the Deep South," *Journal of the Early Republic* 18, no. 4 (Winter 1998): 666; Joseph R. Gusfield, *Symbolic Crusade: Status Politics and the American Temperance Movement* (Urbana: University of Illinois Press, 1963), 30; "Thoughts on Temperance," *Christian Observer*, July 31, 1846.

196. "Temperance Story, Now Ready," *Edgefield Advertiser*, June 27, 1849; *Report of the Trial of Martin Posey*, 3.

197. J. William Harris, *Plain Folk and Gentry in a Slave Society: White Liberty and Black Slavery in Augusta's Hinterlands* (Middleton, CT: Wesleyan University Press, 1985), 67.

198. *Report of the Trial of Martin Posey*, 22.

199. Ibid., 32.

200. Ibid., 20.

father.[201] It had led to a dangerous breakdown of discipline on his plantation.[202] And it had sent him sliding into debt.[203]

Solicitor Bonham then systematically demonstrated Martin Posey's clear role in the "foul and diabolical murder" of his wife, a crime that had no mitigating elements whatsoever: "It was not done in self-defense—nor in sudden heat and passion—it was not even done against a man, but against a poor helpless woman, and one who, so far as I am informed, was *exemplary* in all the relations of life."[204] Witnesses described the entire story: Martin's affair with Eliza, his oft-expressed desire to be rid of Matilda, his criminal bargains with Jeff the conjurer and App. The state rested, having forged what it called "a connected chain between the prisoner and the deed."[205]

The Defense

Posey's attorneys seem to have realized that their case was unwinnable. The law was against them. The facts were against them. The public was against them. Given how flagrantly Posey had violated patriarchal norms, the well-heeled jury was surely against them too. Defense lawyers basically threw in the towel. They half-heartedly cross-examined some of the state's witnesses, trying to plant a few grains of doubt amid the bushels of evidence against their client. For example, after the doctor who performed the postmortem on Matilda Posey testified that multiple blows to her head "were enough to kill her, or anyone else," the defense's cross-examination forced the doctor to admit that he had not actually seen "any *fracture* of the skull," nor had he "carefully dissect[ed] for one, as I only took off sufficient hair to locate the wounds, and omitted to strip the skin."[206] Defense lawyers also did some procedural maneuvering. They persuaded the trial judge to keep jurors away from the public overnight.[207] This small victory was more than overwhelmed by a large defeat: the defense failed to persuade Judge Withers to

201. Ibid., 55.
202. Ibid., 15.
203. Ibid., 20–21.
204. Ibid., 11. Emphasis is in the original.
205. Ibid.
206. Ibid., 16.
207. Ibid., 22–23.

exclude the testimony of Wilson Kirkland, overseer and star witness for the prosecution, on grounds that he was an accomplice trying to save his own skin by testifying for the state.[208] Their failure on this point sealed their client's doom. Other than these small arguments, however, the defense had nothing. When the state rested, the defense lawyers, their quivers empty, rested too. They called no witnesses, presented no evidence.[209]

Interestingly, the very same defense lawyers put up much more of a fight a week later in a separate (and much less closely watched) trial of Martin Posey for the murder of Appling. The defense team seems to have concluded that, although aggressively defending a wife-killer was unseemly, aggressively defending a slave-killer was good lawyering.

In the second murder trial, for the killing of Appling, Posey's lawyers argued that their client's admittedly compromised character had left him vulnerable to the insidious scheming of his underling.[210] They exhorted jurors to focus not on the irresponsibility of their propertied client but rather on the threat to social order posed by an ambitious and unprincipled poor white man: the prosecution's star witness, Posey's overseer, Wilson Kirkland.

Playing on the popular elite stereotype of the scoundrel overseer,[211] the defense argued that Kirkland, landless and unctuous, had deviously taken advantage of Posey, whose personal turmoil had left him "we[a]k minded" and "besotted with drink."[212] Kirkland was "poor" but "sighed for a fortune." Longing to "feast upon Posey's bounty," Kirkland cunningly "[fed Posey's] appetite for liquor" and exerted an "unbounded influence" over Posey's enslaved laborers. He bewitched Posey with the dark powers of conjuration (Posey was convinced that Kirkland, like Jeff, had mastered the dark arts), and "stir[red] the darkest and meanest passions of his soul."[213] With cold-blooded cunning, this "smooth faced villain and whining hypocrite" managed to invert the power dynamic between owner and overseer,

---

208. Ibid., 28–32.

209. Ibid., 40.

210. Ibid., 62.

211. Ibid., 61; William E. Wiethoff, *Crafting the Overseer's Image* (Columbia: University of South Carolina Press, 2006), 32, 36, 75–104; William Kauffman Scarborough, *The Overseer: Plantation Management in the Old South* (Baton Rouge: Louisiana State University Press, 1966), 44, 106, 123–32; Wyatt-Brown, *Southern Honor*, 377.

212. *Report of the Trial of Martin Posey*, 61.

213. Ibid., 61–62.

reducing Posey, his "hands tied," to Kirkland's "dupe." And all Kirkland needed to finish his "designing game" was to put an end to the nosy Matilda and leave a trail of hearsay that would lead investigating authorities wrongly to blame his boss.[214]

In contrast to the robust defense that Posey's lawyers presented in the trial for Appling's murder, their defense in the earlier trial was anemic. By killing Matilda—his own wife, a white woman—Posey had apparently violated his class's code of proper conduct so egregiously that his lawyers did not even attempt to mobilize anti-overseer sentiment in his favor. The defense team's divergent approaches to the two trials provide a crude measure of the different values assigned to the lives of white women and enslaved Black men in the Old South.

The Verdict

The twelve jurors who decided Martin Posey's fate in the Matilda Posey murder trial were all, like the accused, affluent white men. Their real estate holdings averaged a robust $4,000 and their occupations included farmer, physician, merchant, and planter.[215] Their first task was to decide whether to find Posey guilty or not guilty. If they found him guilty, as everyone expected, they would then face a trickier question: how to divvy up criminal responsibility between the disgraced enslaver, Martin, and the deceased slave, Appling, who actually put Matilda to death.

The grand jury indictment had charged Posey with multiple counts related to the murder of Matilda Posey. Trial jurors would have to choose among several possibilities. The first charged Martin as "principal in the first degree" in the murder of Matilda, meaning that "he himself" had killed her. A second set of counts charged Martin as "principal in the *second* degree," meaning that he had been present and provided assistance but that Appling had done the actual killing.[216]

Both the first and the second set of counts assumed that Martin was physically present at the killing of Matilda. All evidence in the case, however, suggested that Martin was far away when Appling murdered Matilda.

214. Ibid., 61–63.

215. Dale, "Getting Away with Murder," 98–99.

216. *Report of the Trial of Martin Posey*, 9.

Why, then, did the grand jury include these easily refuted "principal" charges? The answer has to do with the day's prevailing assumptions about master-slave relations and slave autonomy. Although Martin was not physically present at the time of Matilda's murder, the trial jury could presumably have found him guilty as a "principal" if they believed that he, a master, was akin to a sniper and Appling, a slave, was akin to a bullet. Although bullets might technically cause death, moral accountability for shootings must fall to trigger-pullers, however distant. A hierarchical view of master-slave relations and an assumption that enslaved people were incapable of independent moral thought could have inclined jurors to find Martin guilty as a "principal" in the murder of his wife, even though he was not physically present for the killing. The grand jury had these thoughts in mind when composing the indictment. The solicitor also had these thoughts in mind during opening arguments when he told the jury that he would prove that Martin Posey, "either by his own hand, or by his procuration"—that is, by using App as a weapon—"is the monster . . . who . . . planned *and executed* the crime . . . of murdering his own wife [emphasis added]."[217]

There was, however, a third set of criminal charges. These deemed Posey to be criminally responsible, but less so. They charged him as an "accessary [*sic*] before the fact," meaning that he was not physically present at the killing but "did incite, move, procure, counsel, command, [and] hire" Appling to murder Matilda.[218] This third group of charges was the most consistent with the facts, but it assumed that Appling, though enslaved (and, of course, though now deceased), was sufficiently accountable morally to be treated as the "principal" in the case, even though he was doing his enslaver's bidding. It assumed that Appling understood right from wrong and was capable of exercising independent moral judgement. These charges assumed, in other words, that App was an ethically responsible human being, not merely an extension of his enslaver's will.

The jury returned to the courtroom, and Judge Withers called for order. Silence spread. The most silent of all was Martin Posey, who looked on with a cold stare. The jury foreman delivered the verdict: "guilty" on the third set of charges: accessory to murder before the fact. This was a telling verdict. In

217. Ibid., 12.

218. State v. Martin Posey, 35 S.C.L. 103, 1849 WL 2709, 14 (S.C.App.L.). A seventh count stated that Posey was an accessory before the fact to App and diverse other persons. The jury found that App alone had committed the murder.

convicting Martin as an accessory before the fact, rather than as a principal, in the murder of Matilda Posey, the jury implicitly found Appling, the deceased slave, guilty as principal. In the minds of jurors, therefore, Appling was not merely the property, the tool, the volitionless weapon of his master. He was a moral agent who consciously, deliberately, and with malice aforethought chose to murder Matilda Posey.

App, however, could be punished no more. Martin could. Barring a successful appeal, he would hang in the courthouse square.

The Appeal

At the time of the Posey trial, the South Carolina Court of Appeals, the state's highest court, was not a separate, freestanding institution. It was a panel made up of sitting trial judges. The tribunal that heard appeals in South Carolina, in other words, included the very judges whose actions at trial were under review. Worse still, in particular appeals, the judge who presided at trial, being the most familiar with that case, often wound up writing the appellate opinion, and therefore ruling on the legitimacy of his own actions. Needless to say, this was a very appellant-unfriendly system. South Carolina eventually created a freestanding appellate court, but not until 1859.[219] Thanks to this convoluted system, the justice who ruled on Martin Posey's appeal was the very same man who had presided at his trial: Thomas Jefferson Withers. This boded ill for Martin Posey.

Withers was born poor but quickly rose. He excelled at legal study, married up, and embraced the southern paternalistic ideal with both arms.[220] He was the patriarch of a large, extended household that included several children of his own, two children of a deceased friend, and many enslaved people. He also provided financial support to his own younger siblings. A self-serving local legend maintained that Withers treated the people he

219. Donald J. Senese, "Building the Pyramid: The Growth and Development of the State Court System in Antebellum South Carolina, 1800–1860," *South Carolina Law Review* 24, no. 3 (1972): 357–79; "The Judiciary System of South Carolina," *Southern Quarterly Review* 2, no. 4 (November 1850): 467.

220. Ezra J. Warner and W. Buck. Yearns, *Biographical Register of the Confederate Congress* (Baton Rouge: Louisiana State University Press, 1975); B. F. Perry and Elizabeth Frances Perry, *Reminiscences of Public Men, with Speeches and Addresses* (Greenville, SC: Shannon,1889), 222–23, 229.

enslaved so humanely that neighbors complained that he was demoralizing the people whom they enslaved.[221] Withers believed that the health of southern society depended on the willingness of privileged patriarchs to protect those entrusted to their care.[222] This, too, boded ill for Martin Posey.

Judge Withers used the law as a tool to reinforce his paternalistic values.[223] In an 1850 case, white members of a slave patrol were accused of unjustifiably whipping several enslaved people who had gathered in a public place for a quilting. Normally, such slave gatherings were not allowed, but these enslaved people had their masters' permission to assemble. The whip-wielding slave patrollers were convicted and appealed. Withers upheld their convictions in a ruling that referenced his own experiences as a benevolent plantation paternalist:

> How many of us have permitted to our slaves the enjoyment of a wedding party and ceremony, in imitation of the custom of the higher class, and even contributed liberally, to the good cheer of the occasion? . . . It would be painful to find that the law forbids masters to permit or to encourage the slave in honoring the humble virtues that may be consistent with his condition. . . . The true spirit of our law does not aim at such an end.[224]

Withers's paternalism also extended to wives. During a trial concerning a land dispute between a widow and her deceased husband's family, Withers showed extreme sympathy to the former. He nudged the jury in the direction of his personal belief that a wife should be protected against the moral and economic failings of her husband. The recently deceased husband in this case was, like Posey, known to have been a lush and a wife-beater. An indignant Withers was willing to invoke the law to punish the misdeeds of dishonorable planters.[225] This, too, boded ill for Martin Posey.

Posey appealed to the Court of Appeals of South Carolina in December of 1849. The last three of his six grounds for appeal were, to quote the court,

---

221. Ibid.

222. Martin Bauml Duberman, "Writhing Bedfellows" *Journal of Homosexuality* 6, no.1–2 (1981): 85–101.

223. Perry and Perry, *Reminiscences of Public Men*, 224.

224. State v. Boozer, 36 S.C.L. 21, 23–24 (1850).

225. Wyatt-Brown, *Southern Honor*, 260–61.

"manifestly . . . unsubstantial."[226] The first three, however, were serious. All three focused on the law's treatment of Appling. Posey's first ground was that the grand jury's indictment of Martin for being an "accessory before the fact" to a crime committed by Appling was fatally flawed because it did not specify which criminal statute Appling had supposedly violated. "The indictment," Posey's lawyers argued, did "not charge the murder by the principal [Appling] to be against the Act of General Assembly in such case."[227] Absent any reference to a South Carolina statute, Posey's indictment necessarily assumed that Appling had committed the *common-law* crime of murder—that is, the crime of murder as defined by traditional, English, judge-made law.[228] There was reason to suspect, however, that the common law might not apply to enslaved people. In *State v. Maner* (1834), a South Carolina appeal brought by a white man who had been convicted of committing a common-law crime against an enslaved person, South Carolina's highest court had held that enslaved people were outside the protections of the common law. "The criminal offence of assault and battery cannot at common law be committed on the person of a slave," Justice O'Neall stated: "The peace of the state is not thereby broken; for a slave is not generally regarded as legally capable of being within the peace of the State."[229] Posey's lawyers hoped that the high court would extend the logic of *Maner* and conclude that the common law, as a general proposition, simply did not apply to enslaved people. If the court went that way, it could possibly conclude that Appling was not guilty of the common-law crime of murder and therefore that Martin could not be convicted as accessory to a noncrime.

Justice Withers rejected this argument. He noted that the prosecution here was against Martin, not Appling. The indictment, therefore, had to be precise in its description of Martin's crime, but did not have to be comparably precise in its description of Appling's infraction: "The prosecution here was against the prisoner [Martin] . . . and not against the principal [Appling], whose felony need be set forth only with such form and certainty as may comport with the rules of criminal pleading, which rules

226. State v. Posey, 35 S.C.L. 103, 1849 WL 2709 (S.C. App. L.) 29–30. This phrase actually applied to the fourth and fifth grounds. The sixth ground was equally weak. Ibid.

227. State v. Posey, 35 S.C.L. 103, 1849 WL 2709 (S.C. App. L.), 13.

228. Ibid.

229. State v. Maner, 20 S.C.L. (2 Hill) at 453 (1834); Thomas D. Morris, "Slaves and the Rules of Evidence in Criminal Trials"; Morris, *Southern Slavery and the Law*, 229.

require that the legal characteristics of the crime be averred for the proper information of the party called to answer." As long as the indictment clearly explained every relevant aspect of the crime of which Martin had been charged, it was valid.[230]

Justice Withers, however, recognized that the case raised a "graver question": Could the common law's sword of criminal prosecution strike enslaved people, even though its shield of rights-protection would not safeguard them? Withers answered in the affirmative. "We are of the opinion that murder by a slave is a felony . . . at the common law," he stated. Even if this had been a prosecution of Appling for murder, not a prosecution of Martin for being an accessory before the fact, the common-law accusation would have been sufficient to convict. No criminal statute was required to find an enslaved person guilty of murder.[231]

Withers realized the implication of his ruling: that common-law punishments applied to enslaved South Carolinians, even though common-law protections did not. He neither hid nor sugarcoated this harsh outcome. "However unfit the slave has been, and is, to receive the boon of common law rights and privileges," he rhetorically asked, "does not [the common law's] definition of murder well fit him [the slave] as an agent to perpetrate it; and death, the sanction of its sentence, suit him as a convict?"[232] Enslaved people, in other words, could commit common-law crimes. Consequently, Martin could be found guilty as accessory before the fact, even absent any allegation that Appling's actions violated any South Carolina statute.[233] Martin Posey's first ground for appeal failed.

Posey's second ground for appeal was that he could not be convicted as an accessory to a crime that nobody had previously been convicted of committing. The basis for this claim was an English common-law rule that held that principals must be convicted before accessories could be tried. The "crime of the accessory," the logic ran, "is derivative, not substantive—no principal no accessory." And the existence of a principal had to be "ascertained judicially." Rumors and hearsay would not suffice. Only a trial conviction would suffice. The purpose of this rule was to "avoid the abhorrent consequence of the accessary being hanged, and the principal acquitted."[234]

230. State v. Posey, 35 S.C.L. 103, 13 (1849), Westlaw version.

231. Ibid., 14.

232. Ibid., 15.

233. Ibid., 16.

234. Ibid., 18.

Previous white South Carolinians who had been convicted as accessories to crimes committed by enslaved people had argued that the conviction of an enslaved principal could never serve as the basis for the conviction of a free accessory. Enslaved people were not tried in the whites-only, regular courts, they noted. They were tried in the Blacks-only Court of Magistrates and Freeholders, which lacked the due process protections that prevailed in the white courts. "The evidence sufficient to convict a negro," the argument ran, "would not be sufficient to convict a white man."[235] To make the conviction of an enslaved person a component of the circumstances that could convict a free white person would be fatally to compromise white legal protections.[236] These arguments highlighted the obvious: the legal system was separate and unequal for Black South Carolinians, free and enslaved alike.

Posey's case was slightly different than these precedents, however, in that Appling had died before he could stand trial, much less be convicted. Posey's lawyers therefore argued that Appling's pretrial death, which Martin himself had caused, meant that Martin could not be convicted "as accessary before the fact to the murder of Matilda Posey" because the principal, Appling, had never been convicted of committing the murder.[237] No principal conviction, no accessory conviction.

Justice Withers gave this argument the dismissive swat that it deserved. He first noted that South Carolina courts had never affirmed the English common-law provision upon which Posey relied, the one that required the conviction of a principal before an accessory could be tried. Indeed, South Carolina courts had repudiated this rule in three known cases.[238] Withers then closed the law books and lectured. Posey had made criminal conviction of Appling impossible by murdering him before he could stand trial. "Shall one take advantage of his own wrong?" Withers fumed. Shall the brazen Martin Posey "derive his exemption from conviction for one shocking murder by the perpetration of another?" Withers indignantly concluded that "it was not necessary that there should have been any . . . conviction of

235. State v. Cynthia Simmons, and Laurence Kitchen, 1 Brev. 6 (Cont. C. App. S.C. 1794) at 7.

236. State v. David G. Sims, 2 Bail. 29 (C. App. L. and E. S.C. 1831); State v. Cynthia Simmons; and State v. Thomas Crank, 2 Bail. 66 (C. App. L. and E. S.C. 1831).

237. State v. Posey, 16.

238. State v. David G. Sims, 18 S.C.L. 29, 2 (C. App. L. and E.S.C. 1831); State v. Cynthia Simmons, 2–3; State v. Thomas Crank, 5.

the slave" as principal before Posey could be convicted as accessory.[239] Second argument: overruled.[240]

The final serious ground for appeal was more promising. It claimed that Posey "could not, by the law of the land, be an accessary before the fact to a murder committed by his *own* slave, by his command and coercion [emphasis in original]."[241] Some common-law doctrines appeared to support this argument. One held that "where an offence is committed through the medium of an innocent agent, the employer, though absent when the act is done, is answerable as a principal."[242] Another held that "if a child under years of discretion, or any other person of defective mind, is incited to commit a murder or other crime, the inciter is the principal . . . though he were absent when the thing was done."[243]

Posey's application of these doctrines to the master-slave relationship played on the cultural presumption that the master was the ultimate plantation authority. To deny this ground for appeal would be to deny several commonly held assumptions: that enslaved people were their masters' tools; that in terms of moral accountability, the enslaved were akin to children; and that enslaved people were essentially "person[s] of defective mind." To find Martin Posey guilty as accessory before the fact would be to reject these assumptions and to acknowledge instead that Appling had been a free moral agent, possessed of the power to bargain with his enslaver as an independent equal. It would be to recognize that enslaved people could rationally evaluate their enslavers' wishes and, if they disagreed, refuse to obey them. The bottom-line premise of this argument was that the enslaved person, even when breaking the law, remained the enslaver's tool. The inherently hierarchical master-slave relationship made the term "master accessory" an oxymoron, Posey's legal team argued. The master must either be a principal or not guilty.

---

239. State v. Posey, 16.

240. Ibid., 28–29.

241. Ibid., 13.

242. Quoted in Ibid., 29. See R. v. Giles, 1 Moo. C.C. 166; Reg. v. Michael, 2 Moo. C.C. 120; Reg. v. Michael, 9 C. & P. 356; John Davison Lawson, *Defences to Crime: Disabilities of Parties* (San Francisco: Sumner Whitney, 1885), 282. For a discussion of this doctrine's relationship to slavery, see Andrew Fede, *People without Rights: An Interpretation of the Fundamentals of the Law of Slavery in the U.S. South* (New York: Garland, 1992).

243. State v. Posey, 29; Sir William Oldnall Russell, *A Treatise on Crimes and Misdemeanors*, vol. I (Philadelphia: T. & J. W. Johnson, 1877), 53.

Justice Withers, a patriarchal master par excellence, was sympathetic to the appellant's argument that Posey "could not, by the law of the land, be an accessary before the fact to murder committed by his . . . slave, by his command and coercion." "This proposition," Withers acknowledged, "may be true."[244] But it did not fit the facts of Posey's case. In particular, Withers found no evidence that Appling had acted under Martin's "command and coercion." "The most diligent examination" of the "voluminous testimony," Withers argued, "will be vain to discover any single fact that imports command or coercion, directed by the prisoner to App." True, trial testimony suggested that Martin had despicably enticed Appling to murder his wife through "the arts of persuasion," the "temptation of high bribery," and the "wicked debauchery of the slave's lingering sentiment of duty." The shameless Martin had "smother[ed] that still small voice of a feeble though better conscience than his master's" and had prepared App's heart for "the perpetration of the bloodiest and the darkest deed." These acts, committed by Posey, were criminally evil, but they were "an accessary's [*sic*] crime," not a principal's. Appling was not Martin's marionette. He was a free moral agent, accountable for his crimes. Withers therefore concluded that "the master may be accessary to his own slave in murder." Posey's third ground of appeal "must, therefore, be resolved against the prisoner."[245] Case closed.

If Appling Had Lived

Some scholars have been impressed by what they call the "essentially decent" treatment that Black litigants, including the enslaved, received in the state supreme courts of the Old South, high courts in which elite jurists dressed up the law in its Sunday best.[246] But in lower-level, community-based tribunals, the story was different. Had Appling lived, that's where his case would have begun. Justice Withers considered this scenario. He justified Martin Posey's conviction as an accessory by noting that Appling, had he survived, "could have been punished" as principal.[247] It is a scenario

244. State v. Posey, 29.

245. Ibid., 29.

246. A. E. Keir Nash, "The Texas Supreme Court and the Trial Rights of Blacks, 1845–1860," *Journal of American History* 58, no. 3 (Dec. 1971): 622.

247. State v. Posey.

worth considering. What legal processes would have awaited Appling, had Martin not killed him?

To state the obvious, much of slavery occurred beyond the law's reach. Enslavers enjoyed virtually unchecked authority to act as judges, juries, and punishers. In some circumstances, however, enslavers were required to submit enslaved people to the state for trial. Appling's murder of Matilda, a capital crime, would have been one such circumstance. But Appling would not have joined Martin Posey in the Court of General Sessions. This court was for white people only. Instead, App would have appeared in the Magistrates and Freeholders Court, which was for Black people only. Far from representing blind justice, the rule-of-law ideal, or "essentially decent treatment," these racially specific criminal courts institutionalized white supremacy. They were separate and unequal. Black defendants, whether nominally "free" or enslaved, were sent there. One's race, not one's freedom status, determined one's access to justice in the criminal courts of antebellum South Carolina.[248]

In the Blacks-only Court of Magistrates and Freeholders, Appling would have found few of the legal protections that prevailed in the whites-only Court of General Sessions. The Black court's legal procedures were extremely informal. Magistrates and Freeholders trials did not even have to be held in courthouses. Trials sometimes occurred on farms or at alleged crime scenes.[249] Evidentiary standards scarcely existed. Jury selection was haphazard, with magistrates sometimes favoring speed and convenience over fairness by selecting jurors from a single family or neighborhood. Unlike Martin Posey, who was tried by a jury of his racial peers, App would have been tried by a panel of white men, most of whom would likely have been enslavers.[250] Jury decisions in the Magistrates and Freeholders Court did not have to be unani-

---

248. Daniel J. Flanigan, "Criminal Procedure in Slave Trials in the Antebellum South," *Journal of Southern History* 40, no. 4 (Nov. 1974): 540; Michael Hindus, *Prison and Plantation: Crime, Justice, and Authority in Massachusetts and South Carolina, 1767–1878* (Chapel Hill: University of North Carolina Press, 1980), 132–37, 577–78; Court of Magistrates and Freeholders Records, SCDAH,; Terry W. Lipscomb and Theresa Jacobs, "The Magistrates and Freeholders Court," *South Carolina Historical Magazine*, vol. 77, no. 1, Jan. 1976, 62–63; and Philip N. Racine, "The Spartanburg District Magistrates and Freeholders Court," *South Carolina Historical Magazine*, vol. 87, no. 4, Oct. 1986, 198.

249. Hindus, *Prison and Plantation*, 155; Racine, "Spartanburg District,"198.

250. Lipscomb and Jacobs, "Magistrates and Freeholders," 62.

mous for a conviction to stand.[251] The timing differed too. The Court of General Sessions, where white suspects were tried, met just twice annually, giving defendants such as Martin Posey ample time to secure lawyers and prepare defenses. By contrast, the Magistrates and Freeholders Court, where Black people were tried, was supposed to convene within six days of the commission of an offense, leaving precious little time for passions to cool or lawyers to prepare.[252] The prosecution held virtually all the procedural advantages; Black defendants held next to none. In one egregious Spartanburg case, testimony clearly revealed that Reuben, a slave, never touched a female complainant. Nevertheless, Reuben was found guilty of rape.[253]

In 1833, South Carolina established an appeals procedure for Black people convicted in the Magistrates and Freeholders Court.[254] If App had been convicted, as certainly would have happened, he (via his enslaver, Martin Posey) could have appealed. Cost considerations, however, discouraged most enslavers from appealing.[255]Not surprisingly, unequal courts and unequal procedures produced unequal outcomes. Our quantitative analysis of criminal court records from five South Carolina counties during the period under study reveals that the conviction rate for Black defendants was about twice high as the conviction rate for white defendants.[256] Whereas

251. Flanigan, "Criminal Procedure," 540.

252. Ibid., 541.

253. Hindus, *Prison and Plantation*, 151–52.

254. Racine, "Spartanburg District," 198.

255. Ibid.

256. Magistrates and freeholders records from Edgefield County no longer exist, so we analyzed records at SCDAH from five demographically similar South Carolina counties: Anderson/Pendleton District Court of Magistrates and Freeholders, Trial Papers (1819–1865); Fairfield District Court of Magistrates and Freeholders, Trial Papers Index (1839–1865); Kershaw District Court of Magistrates and Freeholders, Trial Papers (1802–1861); Laurens District Court of Magistrates and Freeholders, Trial Papers (1808–1865); and Spartanburg District Court of Magistrates and Freeholders, Trial Papers (1824–1865). Using Court of General Sessions indexes from the Fairfield, Laurens, and Spartanburg Districts, also held at SCDAH, we estimated conviction rates for white criminal defendants. These indexes were massive, with hundreds of entries, so we chose to sample the first twenty cases from the beginning of each decade from 1800 until 1860. In the end, our numbers came out within 1 percent of the number that Hindus provides. Hindus, *Prison and Plantation*, 144. Like Hindus, we grouped the "Nol Pros"/"No Bill" references along with the "Not Guilty" cases. See Fairfield District Court of General Sessions, Session Rolls (1800–1839), SCDAH; Fairfield County Court of General Sessions, General Sessions Indexes (1840–1882), microfilm reel FA42, SCDAH; Laurens County Court of General Sessions, Index to Sessions Rolls

about 34 percent of white criminal defendants were found guilty, 67 percent of enslaved and free Black people in sampled districts—Laurens, Fairfield, Kershaw, Spartanburg, and Pendleton/Anderson—were found guilty. (Of course, this sky-high conviction rate for Black criminal defendants does not take into account the private punishments that enslaved people endured on plantations, where conviction rates were whatever masters wanted them to be.[257])Once convicted, Black people received much harsher punishments than did white people. The disparity was particularly pronounced when it came to whippings. In our sample, only 6 percent of white people convicted in the court of General Sessions between 1800 and 1860 received lashes.[258] By contrast, almost all—96 percent—of the enslaved and free Black people convicted in sampled Magistrates and Freeholders courts in those same years felt the sting of the lash.

Moreover, the number of lashes administered to convicts varied dramatically by race. The few white convicts who did receive lashes rarely received more than the traditional scriptural limit of thirty-nine.[259] By contrast, more than 45 percent—almost half—of the enslaved and free Black people convicted in our sample received more than thirty-nine lashes as punishment for their crimes. Roughly 7 percent received over one hundred lashes. In one extreme case, a slave was sentenced to five hundred lashes and was then "put out of the district."[260]

(1801–1912), microfilm reel LR14, SCDAH; Spartanburg County Court of General Sessions, Index to General Sessions Indictments (1800–1908), microfilm reel SP43, SCDAH.

257. We analyzed the three crimes that appeared in the two courts with greatest frequency: larceny, stealing, and various forms of assault.

258. Unfortunately, the indexes for the Court of General Sessions often did not specify or elaborate on the sentences when individuals were convicted. To get a general idea of sentencing for white people, we perused court journals that sometimes, but not always, included sentences for Spartanburg, Fairfield, and Laurens. Some of these source books were in horrible condition and nearly impossible to read, so we sampled to derive an estimate of the number of white individuals who received lashes as their punishment. Because of this, the punishment sample from the Court of General Sessions and the Court of Magistrates and Freeholders are vastly different. See Fairfield County, Office, Clerk of Court (General Sessions), Journal (1825–1829, 1840–1863, 1866–1868), microfilm reel C372, SCDAH; Laurens County, Office, Clerk of Court (General Sessions), General Sessions Journal (1800–1810, 1810–1824, 1825–1840, 1840–1868), microfilm reels C37, C37, SCDAH.

259. Racine, "Spartanburg District," 203; Hindus, *Prison and Plantation*, 145; Fogel and Engerman, *Time on the Cross: Evidence and Methods, a Supplement* (Boston: Little, Brown, 1974), 116.

260. Court of Magistrates and Freeholders Records, SCDAH.

Given the severity of Appling's crime, lashes would not have been an issue. His was a capital crime. Capital punishment was rare for enslaved people, because slavers did not wish to lose their investments. Just 2 percent of the enslaved and free Black convicts in our sample faced capital punishment. Had Appling lived to stand trial in the Magistrates and Freeholders Court, he surely would have been convicted, making this capital punishment figure just a little bit higher.[261]

In 1848, amid the events described here, South Carolina's John C. Calhoun proudly told the US Senate that, in the South, "the two great divisions of society are not the rich and poor, but white and black; and all the former, the poor as well as the rich, belong to the upper class."[262] He was right. All Black criminal defendants in South Carolina, free or enslaved, but zero white criminal defendants, were tried in the draconian Magistrates and Freeholders courts.[263] Although things have improved mightily since then, traces of this racialized and unjust inheritance arguably remain visible to this day.

Conclusion

Both Appling and Martin hoped that the criminal bargain that they hashed out amid the pine trees and sweetgums of Edgefield in 1849 would free them from binding legal restrictions. They were not alone. Indeed, App was not even the first enslaved person on his plantation to offer to murder Matilda Posey in exchange for benefits. Jeff the conjurer beat him to it, though, lucky for him, he failed to perform his end of the bargain. The published records of antebellum southern courts contain several other instances in which free white people were convicted as accessories to felonies committed by enslaved Black people, as happened in the case of Martin and Appling. Although the published reports of these other cases do not specify

---

261. Racine, "Spartanburg District," 208.

262. US Senator John C. Calhoun, "Speech on the Oregon Bill, delivered in the Senate, June 27th, 1848," in *The Works of John C. Calhoun*, vol. 4 (New York: D. Appleton, 1883), 505.

263. Note that southern states varied in their handling of criminal prosecutions of Blacks, free and enslaved. South Carolina was as unjust as any, though was not alone on that end of the spectrum. See Flanigan, "Criminal Procedure"; and William W. Fisher III, "Ideology and Imagery in the Law of Slavery," *Chicago-Kent Law Review* 68 (1993): 1052–53.

the natures of the criminal bargains between enslaved principals and enslaving accessories, negotiations of some sort are implied. As Justice Withers reasoned in *Posey*, the convictions of white people as accessories, not principals, meant that the enslaved principals were impelled not by "command or coercion" but rather by what Withers called the "temptation of high bribery,"[264] meaning some sort of contractual inducement. This implies negotiation, which in turn suggests a degree of slave agency. Antebellum cases from North Carolina,[265] Tennessee,[266] and several from South Carolina[267] all involved free white conspirators who were found guilty as accessories to crimes committed by enslaved people. [268]

Other white people were tried as principals, not accessories, for crimes that enslaved people committed following a bargain of some sort. Elizabeth Green, a white South Carolinian who "lived unhappily" with her hard-drinking husband Henry, openly offered to "give any man $100 to kill" her spouse. According to Elizabeth, an enslaved man named Edom voluntarily accepted her offer. Two days after Christmas, in 1835, as Henry Green walked home through the woods following a religious gathering, with Elizabeth and some others trailing thirty or forty yards behind, Edom stole upon Henry Green and shot him dead. Elizabeth instantly cried out, "Henry is killed—the negroes have risen—we shall all be killed" and turned her party around, allowing her husband's killer to escape. Notably, Elizabeth was not Edom's enslaver. Another white man, Tommy Ray, claimed ownership in Edom. The murderous bargain that Edom and Elizabeth struck, therefore, took place outside the context of a direct master-slave relationship. Edom was charged with murder but was acquitted due to lack of evidence. Elizabeth Green was not so lucky. Having spoken so openly, and so frequently, of her willingness to purchase her husband's death, she was convicted as principal in his murder, a murder committed, in the eyes of the law, "by the agency of an unknown person."[269] Historians have long over-

264. State v. Posey, 29.

265. State v. Chittem, 13 N.C. 48 (1828).

266. State v. McCarn, 30 Tenn. 494 (1851).

267. State v. Cynthia Simmons; State v. David G. Sims; State v. Thomas Crank.

268. Note that enslaved people, as well as free people, could be convicted as accessories to crimes committed by enslaved people. See Byrd v. State, 2 Miss. 247 (1835); Thornton (a slave) v. State of Georgia, 23 Ga. 301 (1858).

269. State v. Elizabeth Green (1836), reported in full in a footnote within State v. Martin Posey, 129–40.

looked this troubling form of slave agency, whereby enslaved people, their life options severely limited by slave law, agreed to commit crimes in exchange for negotiated benefits.

After Justice Withers struck his gavel, closing the curtains on *State v. Martin Posey*, the cast scattered. Eliza, Matilda's little sister, had married Martin sometime after his arrest.[270] Martin's death on the gallows left her a two-time, teenaged widow. Eliza was never indicted for her role in the conspiracy that led to her sister's death. One contemporary observer remarked that her avoidance of criminal liability owed "more to her sex than to her innocence."[271] Perhaps legal chivalry would have prevented male jurors from convicting Eliza of a capital crime, this observer continued, "for we never hang a woman in this State, no matter what she does."[272] But if Eliza "had been tried by a jury of women, her fate would doubtless have been similar to [Martin] Posey's"—that is, death.[273] Eliza escaped legal punishment but faced harsh social repudiation. She lost her inheritance. She lost her adult status and became her cousin's ward. She lost custody of her stepchildren (Martin and Matilda's children). Ostracized from South Carolina society, Eliza moved out of the state and remarried.[274]

Franklin, the footprint-altering enslaved worker who unsuccessfully tried to benefit from his knowledge of Appling and Posey's criminal bargain, may have achieved what Appling sought. Following the discovery of Matilda's corpse, officials arrested Franklin and several other enslaved people for questioning. According to a trial reporter, Franklin and the others said nothing "to criminate themselves" but told "such a straight and familiar tale against Kirkland and Posey" that authorities released them and arrested the overseer and master, leading, ultimately, to Posey's conviction.[275] During all of this commotion on the Posey plantation, Franklin seems to have slipped away. "It is generally known," a published account of the *Posey* trial noted in a footnote, "that this negro [Franklin] has been *run*; he was taken off soon after his release from prison."[276] We would like to imagine that Franklin found freedom, though we really do not know.

---

270. Dale, "A Different Sort of Justice," 635.
271. *Report of the Trial of Martin Posey*, 6.
272. Ibid.
273. Ibid.
274. Dale, "A Different Sort of Justice," 634–36.
275. *Report of the Trial of Martin Posey*, 20.
276. Ibid., 34.

Justice T. J. "Jeff" Withers remained prominent in South Carolina for years to come. He continued judging, supported secession, signed the Confederate Constitution, and served in the Confederate Congress.[277] This upright plantation patriarch's greatest renown, however, may have come posthumously, when historians discovered some randy letters that he wrote to a college friend, future South Carolina governor James Henry Hammond. In one such letter, Withers playfully asked Hammond "whether you yet sleep in your shirt-tail, and whether you yet have the extravagant delight of poking and punching a writhing Bedfellow with your long fleshen pole—the exquisite touches of which I have often had the honor of feeling!" Sincerely, the "old stud, Jeff."[278] Although scholars believe that these letters reveal a nineteenth-century culture of jocular masculinity more than a modern-style homosexual identity, the letters nonetheless became a bit of a sensation. Surely more people have read them than have read any of Withers's judicial opinions. The letters earned "old stud, Jeff" Withers a prominent place on such websites as Gay History & Literature[279] and Gay and Southern: A Website Dedicated to All Things Queer in Dixie.[280]

Martin Posey was put to death on the Edgefield courthouse square on February 1, 1850. An estimated four to five thousand people gathered to watch the scoundrel swing.[281] The crowd included "men, women, children, and negroes"[282]—as if the first three categories did not include the fourth. Posey reportedly "made no confessions under the gallows, but met his doom with a calm, determined silence."[283] Although Posey's hanging punished him for both of the crimes of which he was convicted—the murder of

277. Perry, *Reminiscences of Public Men*, 223; Thomas Jefferson Withers, "Letters from Hon. T. J. Withers," Southern Rights and Co-Operation Documents, South Caroliniana Library, University of South Carolina.

278. Quoted in Drew Gilpin Faust, *James Henry Hammond and the Old South: A Design for Mastery* (Baton Rouge: Louisiana State University Press, 1982), 18–19, note 18.

279. Rictor Norton, "The Gay Love Letters of Thomas J. Withers and James H. Hammond," Gay History & Literature, 1997, http://rictornorton.co.uk/withers.htm.

280. "James Henry Hammond's Long Fleshen Pole," Gay and Southern, Dec. 7, 2005, http://gayandsouthern.blogspot.com/2005/12/james-henry-hammonds-long-fleshen-pole.html

281. *Report of the Trial of Martin Posey*, 52–53.

282. Ibid.

283. Ibid.

Matilda[284] and the murder of Appling[285]—commentators focused their moralizing on the former crime. "Woe! Woe!! to the man that harms a woman here, or anywhere else [in] the South," a reporter wrote following the Posey hanging: "Let him kill his wife here, and the gold of California cannot buy eloquence enough to save him."[286]

As for Appling, he had proved himself a man of his word. He upheld his end of the bargain by murdering Matilda Posey. He then fled to an agreed-upon hiding place to wait several agonizing days for Martin to follow through on his promise of freedom. Martin's payment instead took the form of two pistol shots: one in the side below App's left nipple, the other on the left side of his neck, a little below his head.[287]

Appling surely knew that such an outcome was possible. His willingness to strike a criminal bargain with Martin, even in the face of such an easily foreseeable outcome, suggests how desperate App was, how few his options were, and how enticing the prospect of freedom must have been. One of App's few bargaining chips to play in pursuit of freedom was his willingness to kill. Playing this chip enabled him to believe that he was exerting some control over his circumstances. But criminal bargaining failed to deliver its seemingly emancipatory promise. Even had App lived, the legal system offered Black people, free or enslaved, only racist injustice. Revealingly, the state's top legal treatise on slavery was not called *The Slave Law of South Carolina*. It was called *The Negro Law of South Carolina* (1848). It provided lawyers with "a digest of Law in relation to Negroes (slave or free)."[288] In the long run, the race-based discriminations of Old South law may have left a more insidious legacy than slavery itself.[289] Appling would not be the last American to respond to unjust circumstances by being willing to commit crimes, only to pay a tragically high price for doing so.

---

284. "Trial of Martin Posey," *Edgefield Advertiser* Oct. 10, 1849, 2.

285. "State Trials," *Edgefield Advertiser* Oct. 17, 1849, 2.

286. *Report of the Trial of Martin Posey*, 5.

287. From the indictment of Martin Posey for the murder of Appling, *Report of the Trial of Martin Posey*, 53.

288. O'Neall, *Negro Law.*

289. Alejandro de la Fuente and Ariela J. Gross, *Becoming Free, Becoming Black: Race, Freedom, and Law in Cuba, Virginia, and Louisiana* (Cambridge: Cambridge University Press, 2020).

CHAPTER TWO

Willis v. Jolliffe: Slavery's Inheritance[1]

On a spring day in 1855, Amy and Elijah Willis led their children off the steamboat *Jacob Strader* and onto a Cincinnati wharf. They had traveled hundreds of miles from South Carolina, where Elijah had enslaved Amy and their children. The couple looked forward to a future of freedom in Ohio. But on the wharf, his daughters' hands in his, Elijah collapsed and died. His death thrust Amy into a prolonged inheritance battle with Elijah's white relatives. Perhaps surprisingly, Amy won.

This inheritance dispute, *Willis v. Jolliffe*,[2] highlights the constraints that slave law placed on everyday life. Enslaved people, under the law of testamentary succession, could be forcibly transferred from one enslaver to another, like so much livestock or furniture. Slave law also restricted enslavers, albeit in incomparably milder ways. South Carolina law, for example, prohibited Elijah Willis from freeing his children and their mother in his will and leaving his property to them.[3] The only way to accomplish these objectives was to travel to a jurisdiction with different laws. If one measure of a law's significance is the distance that forum-seekers will travel to escape

1. Chad Barnes, Kevin Birney, Caitlyn Culbertson, Patrick de Visscher, Owen Fitzpatrick, Daphne Fruchtman, Andrew Gorang, Andrew Kengeter, and John Wertheimer coauthored this chapter. A version originally appeared as "*Willis v. Jolliffe*: Love and Slavery on the South Carolina-Ohio Borderlands," in *Freedom's Conditions in the U.S.-Canada Borderlands in the Age of Emancipation*, ed. Tony Freyer and Lyndsay Campbell (Durham: Carolina Academic Press, 2011), 257–84.

2. Willis v. Jolliffe, 11 Rich. Eq. 447, 32 S.C. Eq. 447 (S.C.), 1860 WL 3897 (S.C.). All citations to this case use Westlaw's page numbering. For more on this case, see Bernie D. Jones, *Fathers of Conscience: Mixed-Race Inheritance in the Antebellum South* (Athens: University of Georgia Press, 2009); and Adrienne D. Davis, "The Private Law of Race and Sex: An Antebellum Perspective," Stanford Law Review 51 (January 1999): 221–88.

3. Thomas D. Morris, *Southern Slavery and the Law, 1619-1860* (Chapel Hill: University of North Carolina Press, 1996), 371–80.

its reach, slave law was significant indeed. At a time when travel beyond even county lines required considerable effort, Elijah Willis ventured north repeatedly, in search of different laws.

Amy and Elijah

Elijah Willis grew up on a sprawling Barnwell County plantation containing thousands of acres and over forty enslaved people.[4] Knowing that he would have to share his parents' wealth with his ten siblings,[5] Elijah set off on his own—and prospered. By 1840, Elijah, then in his mid-forties, had acquired a nearby plantation and eighteen enslaved laborers.[6] By 1850, the value of his landholdings had swelled to $10,000 and his enslaved workforce had grown to twenty-seven.[7]

Although Elijah never officially married, he quasi-wed a woman named Amy in the mid-1840s. Elijah was around fifty at the time.[8] Amy was substantially younger. She already had three children and would go on to have several more with Elijah.[9]

Witnesses described Amy as a racially mixed "mulatto" with a "black negro" mother, Celia.[10] Although no references to Amy's father have been found, her brother Gilbert was described as "nearly white," suggesting that he, and probably Amy, had a white father—perhaps Celia's enslaver.[11] At the

4. 1820 Federal Census, Barnwell County, South Carolina, roll 119, p. 52; Will of Robert Willis of Barnwell District, 1844, microcopy no. 9, will book D, p. 49, South Carolina Department of Archives and History. Hereafter cited as SCDAH; Will of Elijah Willis of Barnwell District, 1846, microcopy no. 9, will book D, p. 268, SCDAH.

5. Will of Robert Willis of Barnwell District, 49; Will of Elijah Willis of Barnwell District, 268.

6. 1840 Census Population Schedules Barnwell County, South Carolina, roll 501, book 1, p. 239, SCDAH.

7. 1850 Federal Census, Slave, South Carolina, roll 861, pp. 439–40, SCDAH; 1850 Federal Census, Barnwell County, South Carolina, roll 849, p. 380, SCDAH.

8. 1850 Federal Census, 439–40; 1850 Federal Census, 380; "Manumission of Slaves—The Sudden Death of their Master," *Exeter News-Letter and Rockingham Advertiser* (New Hampshire), June 4, 1855, 3.

9. "The Jolliffe Will Sustained," *National Anti-slavery Standard*, July 14, 1860, 2, 24; 1860 Federal Census, Clermont County, Ohio, roll 944, p. 225; Jolliffe v. Fanning & Phillips, 10 Rich. 186 (S.C. App. Law 1856), WL 3237, 2.

10. Willis v. Jolliffe, 11 Rich. Eq. 447, 32 S.C. Eq. 447 (S.C.), 1860 W.L. 3897 (S.C.), 25.

11. Ibid., 24.

time, South Carolina conceptualized race somewhat differently than it would decades later. State law included more racial categories for Black people—"negro," "mulatto," "mestizo"—than it later would, and the borders separating these categories were fuzzier. By "negro," South Carolina law meant what it revealingly called "slave African[s] . . . and their descendants."[12] "Mulatto" meant "the issue [offspring] of the white and the negro."[13] A "mestizo," in South Carolina parlance, blended "negro" and "Indian."[14]

The division between mulatto and white was blurry. "No specific rule, as to the quantity of negro blood . . . has ever been adopted," a South Carolina judge admitted in 1848. The boundary between the two categories appears to have fallen somewhere between one-eight and one-quarter Black.[15] Though fuzzy, the distinction between white and mulatto was hugely consequential. Whites enjoyed many legal rights denied to those with legally actionable African ancestry.

The line separating mulatto from negro was even blurrier but lacked consequence. All of the legal disabilities that faced negroes also faced mulattoes—and, for that matter, mestizos. None of these groups could be witnesses in superior court.[16] None could serve on juries.[17] In other words, South Carolina operated not just a slave system but a racialized caste system. Even if you were "free," your "color"—that is, your degree of what jurists called "African taint"[18]—determined your "caste," a word from which legal writers of the day did not shy.[19]

Amy, the daughter of a "black negro" mother,[20] faced all the disabilities of legal blackness.[21] What, exactly, was she, in racial terms? Opinion differed. Some witnesses considered her "negro,"[22] others "mulatto,"[23] others

12. John Belton O'Neall, *The Negro Law of South Carolina* (Columbia, SC: John G. Bowman, 1848), 5.

13. Ibid.

14. Ibid., 8.

15. Ibid., 6.

16. Ibid., 13.

17. Ibid.

18. Ibid.

19. Ibid., 6.

20. Willis v. Jolliffe, 25.

21. Ibid., 17.

22. Ibid., 22, 24.

23. Ibid., 25.

"colored."[24] One witness described her as a "dark yellow woman."[25] Legally speaking, however, it made no difference. She bore the "African taint."[26]

No such ambiguity surrounded Amy's freedom status. Her mother was enslaved, and the law was clear: "The offspring of a slave mother must also be a slave," regardless of the father's status.[27] Amy's birthright enslavement affected her every experience, including how she and Elijah met. Elijah purchased her. State law structured the deal. It defined enslaved people as "chattels personal,"[28] meaning nonreal-estate property. Elijah bought Amy, her three "black" sons, and her "black negro"[29] mother from a Barnwell County planter in 1842.[30]

Amy and Elijah soon developed a sexual relationship.[31] Had Amy been free, she and Elijah technically could have married. Under South Carolina law, free people of color could marry one another and could also marry whites.[32] Amy, however, was enslaved and therefore could marry no one. Nor could Elijah have freed Amy in order to marry her. Since 1820, South Carolina had barred private manumissions. Only the legislature could free enslaved people, and it was not inclined to exercise this power.[33]

Sex between enslaving males and enslaved females was common, particularly when the men were unmarried.[34] This, too, reflected the legal context, at least in part. Southern states would later use "fornication and adultery" prosecutions aggressively to suppress extramarital sex, particularly when it crossed racial lines.[35] South Carolina, however, did not (yet)

24. Ibid., 26.

25. Ibid., 28.

26. Ibid., 6.

27. O'Neall, *Negro Law*, 17.

28. First section of the Act of 1740, quoted in ibid., 17.

29. Willis v. Jolliffe, 25.

30. The planter's name was William Kirkland. See Willis v. Jolliffe, 23, 24; "Selected Matter," *Frederick Douglass' Paper* (Rochester, NY), June 8, 1855.

31. Willis v. Jolliffe, 24.

32. O'Neall, *Negro Law*, 13.

33. "An Act to Restrain the Emancipation of Slaves, and to Prevent Free Persons of Color from Entering into this State; and for Other Purposes," no. 2236 (1820), in David J. McCord, *Statutes at Large of South Carolina* (Columbia, SC: A.S. Johnston, 1840), 459; O'Neall, *Negro Law*, 11.

34. John W. Blassingame, *The Slave Community: Plantation Life in the Antebellum South*, rev. ed. (New York: Oxford University Press, 1972, 1979), 154.

35. Charles Frank Robinson II, *Dangerous Liaisons: Sex and Love in the Segregated South* (Fayetteville: University of Arkansas Press, 2003), 19.

consider fornication an indictable offence.[36] More importantly, southern law did nothing whatsoever to obstruct white male sexual access to enslaved Black women.[37] The law of rape simply did not apply. No white man, whatever the circumstances, could be prosecuted for raping an enslaved woman.[38]

Although sexual relationships between enslaving men and enslaved women was common, Amy and Elijah's relationship was not. For one thing, it was entirely unconcealed.[39] Perhaps the most important explanation for its openness was Elijah's lifelong bachelorhood, itself an unusual circumstance for someone of his social class. Elijah was one of eleven children. He alone remained unmarried.[40] There being no wife from whom to hide their relationship, Elijah and Amy were completely open about it. The local court of public opinion deemed Elijah and Amy's intimacy to be, at most, a misdemeanor. Some locals disapproved,[41] but not enough to make him mask, much less end, his relationship with Amy.

Even more atypically, Elijah and Amy's relationship was, as far as the evidence reveals, marriage-like in duration, depth, and, perhaps even emotional character. Witnesses reported that Elijah and Amy "acted pretty much as man and wife."[42] The quasi-marital nature of their relationship was "generally reported and believed in the neighborhood."[43] Newspapers reported the same thing: Elijah treated Amy "as his wife."[44] Amy and Elijah

36. State v. Brunson, 2 Bail. 149, 18 S.C.L. 149 (S.C. App. 1831). Early-nineteenth-century Barnwell County prosecuted card playing, public drunkenness, and other moral offenses but apparently did not indict anyone for fornication. Criminal Journals, Barnwell County Court of General Sessions, 1800–1822, SCDAH.

37. James Oakes, *Slavery and Freedom: An Interpretation of the Old South* (New York: Vintage Books, 1990), 7.

38. Morris, *Southern Slavery*, 305; Merril D. Smith, ed., *Encyclopedia of Rape* (Westport, CT: Greenwood Press, 2004), 235.

39. The openness of Elijah and Amy's quasimarriage was unusual but not unique. See Philip D. Morgan, *Slave Counterpoint: Black Culture in the Eighteenth-Century Chesapeake and Lowcountry* (Chapel Hill: University of North Carolina Press, 1998), 403.

40. Will of Elijah Willis of Barnwell District, 258–69; Joan E. Cashin, "The Structure of Antebellum Planter Families: 'The Ties that Bound us was Strong,'" *Journal of Southern History* 56 (Feb. 1990): 57.

41. Willis v. Jolliffe, 26; Willis v. Jolliffe, Deposition of Willison B. Beazley, 26.

42. Ibid., 24.

43. Ibid., 22.

44. "The Jolliffe Will Sustained," *National Anti-slavery Standard*, July 14, 1860, 2, quoting *Cincinnati Gazette*.

would remain together until death parted them. As he approached his end, Elijah did what he could to provide for Amy after he was gone. Theirs was by no means the nation's only enslaver-enslaved relationship of this sort.[45] But it was certainly not the norm.

Elijah's First Will

In 1846, Elijah Willis, middle-aged and mindful of mortality, prepared a will that would have left all of his property to his white relatives.[46] Amy would receive nothing. Indeed, she was among the "property" to be distributed. Even if Elijah had wanted to leave property to Amy, state law would have presented a formidable barrier. South Carolina would neither permit him to free her nor name her, while still enslaved, as a beneficiary.[47]

That had not always been the case. Up through the early nineteenth century, South Carolina law had permitted enslavers to manumit the people they enslaved and then leave property to them in their wills. Manumissions contributed to the growth of a small community of free Blacks in the state; inheritances of human property by the mixed-race children of wealthy enslavers fed a tiny but growing group of wealthy, mixed-race enslavers.[48]

All of this changed between the 1820s and 1840s, when South Carolina and other states clamped down on free Black populations. [49] Reducing the number of free Black people, legislators reasoned, would tighten the correlation between freedom status and race, strengthening social control. The goal was a society in which all white people were free and all Black people enslaved. Between 1820 and 1841, South Carolina outlawed private emancipations,[50] barred free Black people from migrating into the state,[51]

45. Steven Weisenburger, *Modern Medea: A Family Story of Slavery and Child-Murder from the Old South* (New York: Hill and Wang, 1998), 90; O'Neall v. Farr, 1 Rich. 80 (S.C. 1844).

46. Willis v. Jolliffe; Will of Elijah Willis of Barnwell District, 268.

47. Alfred L. Brophy, *University, Court, and Slave: Pro-slavery Thought in Southern Colleges and Courts and the Coming of Civil War* (New York: Oxford University Press, 2016), 200.

48. Larry Kroger, *Black Slaveowners: Free Black Slave Masters in South Carolina, 1790–1860* (Columbia: University of South Carolina Press, 1995).

49. Morris, *Southern Slavery*, 371–80.

50. O'Neall, *Negro Law*, 11.

51. Ibid., 15.

barred free Black people who left from ever returning,[52] and prohibited testamentary emancipations.[53] Calls for all Black South Carolinians to be enslaved or deported continued to circulate throughout the antebellum years.[54]

By the time Elijah got together with Amy, his testamentary options were limited. State law barred him from freeing Amy during his life; from freeing her in his will, even if she were sent elsewhere; and from leaving any property to her as long as she remained enslaved.[55] Elijah's 1846 will thus divided his estate among his white relatives.

But Elijah's relationship with Amy soon deepened. Most importantly, they had children together, four of whom survived.[56] The first surviving child was Elizabeth, born in 1847, five years after Elijah bought Amy and one year after Elijah prepared his first will.[57] They became a family. Evidence of their domestic life is scant but telling. After Elijah's death, newspapers referred to Amy as his "wife" and reported that the two had been "married . . . about thirteen years."[58] Articles stated that Elijah had "always manifested towards [Amy] and the children a warm affection."[59] One witness reported seeing Elijah dine with his "children in his lap," "giving them the best victuals from the table," and in other ways "treat[ing] them as his own children"—which, of course, they were.[60]

---

52. Ibid., 16.

53. Ibid., 11–12. For a discussion of what these measures did and did not accomplish, see Larry Kroger, "Black Masters: The Misunderstood Slaveowners," *Southern Quarterly* (Jan. 2006): 60, 62, 66.

54. Michael P. Johnson and James L. Roark, eds., *No Chariot Let Down: Charleston's Free People of Color on the Eve of the Civil War* (Chapel Hill: University of North Carolina Press, 1985).

55. "Act to Prevent the Emancipation of Slaves, and for Other Purposes," no. 2836 (1841), in *Statutes at Large of South Carolina*, vol. 11 (Columbia: Republican Printing Company, 1873), 168–69.

56. Note that sources diverge regarding the number of surviving children that Amy and Elijah had together. Some say three; others say four. We believe that four is more likely to be the correct number. 1860 Federal Census, Clermont County, Ohio, Roll 944, p. 225; Jolliffe v. Fanning & Phillips, 10 Rich. 186 (S.C. App. Law, 1856), WL 3237, 2, Westlaw version; Willis v. Jolliffe, 2, 24, 25. Note that Amy already had three children at the time Elijah bought her. Elijah was not the father of these children.

57. 1860 Federal Census, Clermont County, Ohio, roll 944, p. 225.

58. "The Sudden Death at Cincinnati," *Baltimore Sun*, May 26, 1855, 1.

59. Ibid.

60. Willis v. Jolliffe, 22.

Amy, though enslaved, appears to have enjoyed extraordinary freedom, thanks to her intimate connection to Elijah. Newspapers and courtroom witnesses alike reported that Elijah "permitted [Amy] to act as the mistress of his house."[61] Amy "watchfully superintended [Elijah's] domestic affairs," "attended to the wants of the slaves," and "advised as to the [lumber] business."[62] She routinely took Willis's carriage into nearby Williston (named after his ancestors) to buy provisions.[63] In town, Amy "traded considerably," and did so "as freely as a white woman." One Williston merchant was James Willis, Elijah's nephew. When Amy visited his store, he welcomed her patronage. He "would make much of" her, even calling her "Aunt Amy."[64] Hearing such testimony, a judge came to an extraordinary conclusion: Elijah had "allowed [Amy], though his slave, to occupy a level with himself."[65]

Elijah's feelings for Amy and the children altered his estate planning. His health was poor, and he worried about what would befall Amy and the children after his death. He wanted to provide for them, but South Carolina law would not let him free them or leave them any property. The only way to secure their future was to cross legal borders. As early as 1851, he explored the possibility of selling his property and leaving his home state.[66] According to a neighbor, Elijah intended to take Amy and the children beyond South Carolina's borders, "to some country where they would be free."[67]

Elijah, however, was unsure where to go. After briefly considering free Black communities in Tennessee and Virginia,[68] he turned to Baltimore, Maryland, which one historian dubbed the "nineteenth-century black capital."[69] Baltimore was home to one of the nation's largest free Black communities.[70] And Maryland, unlike South Carolina, allowed private manumission.[71] In 1853, Willis took Amy and the children to Baltimore, then returned

---

61. Jolliffe v. Fanning & Phillips, 2.

62. "Sudden Death—An Interesting Case," *(Madison) Wisconsin Patriot*, June 9, 1855, 2.

63. Willis v. Jolliffe, 25.

64. Ibid., 22–24.

65. Ibid., 6.

66. Ibid., 23.

67. Ibid., 24.

68. Ibid., 26.

69. Leroy Graham, *Baltimore: The Nineteenth Century Black Capital* (Washington, DC: University Press of America, 1982).

70. Christopher Phillips, *Freedom's Port: The African American Community of Baltimore, 1790–1860* (Champaign: University of Illinois Press, 1997), 235.

71. "An Act Relating to Negroes, and to Repeal the Acts of Assembly Therein Mentioned,"

home himself to attend to some business. But he quickly had second thoughts. Perhaps Maryland's status as a slave state troubled him. Perhaps he missed his family. Two months later, he brought Amy and the children back to South Carolina where, once again, they were enslaved and unable to inherit.[72]

Willis intensified his search for a jurisdiction where private emancipation was legal and slavery was not. He acted urgently, for he suffered from heart palpitations and did not want to die before securing his family's future. His search led him to Ohio, a common destination for enslavers wishing to manumit. Just as, in future years, Nevada's easy marriage laws would draw flocks of impulsive lovebirds, Ohio's antislavery laws and lawyers attracted antebellum southerners who wished to free their human property.[73] In 1854, Elijah Willis crossed the Ohio River.

Cincinnati

Willis went to Cincinnati in search of William Henry Brisbane, a Baptist minister from South Carolina.[74] Like Elijah, Rev. Brisbane grew up in a wealthy family and enslaved many people.[75] But then he found religion, and everything changed. He took to preaching against slavery, quickly becoming a hated man—among whites, at least—in his corner of low-country South Carolina.[76] In 1837, Brisbane moved to Cincinnati,[77] where he freed his previously enslaved workers.[78]

---

in *Proceedings and Acts of the General Assembly, 1796*, vol. 105 (Annapolis: Maryland State Archives, 2000), 255.

72. Willis v. Jolliffe, 21.

73. For example, see Hooper v. Hooper, 32 Ala. 669 (1858); Barclay v. Sewell, 12 La. Ann. 262 (1857); Mary v. Brown, 5 La. Ann. 269 (1850); Mitchell v. Wells, 37 Miss. 235 (1859); Hinds v. Brazealle, 3 Miss. 837 (1838); Thompson v. Newlin, 8 Ired. Eq. 32 (N.C. 1851); and Thomas v. Palmer, 54 N.C. 249 (1854).

74. "Selected Matter."

75. William Alcorn, "Dissenting Baptists: The Glory of a Hated People," *Baptist History and Heritage* 38, no. 3 (Summer–Fall 2003): 49–56.

76. Lawrence S. Rowland, Alexander Moore, and George C. Rogers Jr., *The History of Beaufort County, South Carolina*, vol. 1: *1514–1861* (Columbia: University of South Carolina Press, 1996), 417.

77. Alcorn, "Dissenting Baptists," 2.

78. "Slaveholding Examined in the Light of the Holy Bible," *National Era* (Washington, DC), October 14, 1847.

From his Ohio pulpit, Rev. Brisbane sought to redeem the Palmetto State. His long-distance abolitionist preaching linked the two states in a communications network based on differences in state law. Brisbane urged South Carolina enslavers to see the light and emancipate in Ohio, as he had done. His abolitionist writings, including "A Letter . . . to the Baptist Denomination in South Carolina," filtered south.[79] Most white South Carolinians probably agreed with the *Spartanburg Spartan*'s characterization of Brisbane as an "arch-traitor" engaged in a "vile attempt to disturb the peace and harmony of the State."[80] A few, however, found inspiration.[81] Among this latter group was Elijah Willis of Barnwell County, a Baptist[82] who enslaved his own children and their mother. Heart palpitating troublingly, Elijah Willis looked north.

Cincinnati was a good location for Willis's manumission efforts. It was a major city—the nation's sixth largest in 1850.[83] It sat on the northern banks of the Ohio River, making it the only major northern city located right on the slave-free border.[84] An antislavery paradise it was not. Extensive social and economic ties between Cincinnati and points south prompted some white Cincinnatians to oppose abolitionism vigorously. Occasionally—in 1829, in 1836, in 1841—antiabolitionism, economic competition, and flat-out racism flared into ugly, anti-Black Cincinnati riots.[85]

But when viewed from the southern banks of the Ohio, and through

79. Alcorn, "Dissenting Baptists," 4.

80. "Rev. Wm. Henry Brisbane, the Traitor," *Spartanburg (SC) Spartan*, reprinted in *The Liberator* (Boston), Oct. 19, 1849, 165.

81. Alcorn, "Dissenting Baptists," 4; Alcorn, "William Henry Brisbane."

82. "History—Churches," Town of Williston, South Carolina, accessed August 21, 2022, http://www.williston-sc.com/history/churches.

83. "Population of 100 Largest Urban Places: 1850," United States Bureau of the Census, table 8, https://www2.census.gov/library/working-papers/1998/demographics/pop-twps0027/tab08.txt.

84. Keith P. Griffler, *Front Line of Freedom: African Americans and the Forging of the Underground Railroad in the Ohio Valley* (Lexington: University Press of Kentucky, 2004), 1.

85. Nikki M. Taylor, *Frontiers of Freedom: Cincinnati's Black Community, 1802–1868* (Athens: Ohio University Press, 2005); Julie A. Mujic, "A Border Community's Unfulfilled Appeals: The Rise and Fall of the 1840s Anti-Abolitionist Movement in Cincinnati," *Ohio Valley History* 7, no. 2 (March 2007): 53–69; Patrick Allen Folk, "'The Queen City of Mobs': Riots and Community Reactions in Cincinnati, 1788–1848" (PhD diss., University of Toledo, 1978); and Charles R. Wilson, "Cincinnati a Southern Outpost in 1860–1861?" *Mississippi Valley Historical Review* 24 (Mar. 1938), 473–82.

Black people's eyes, Cincinnati shimmered as freedom's gateway.[86] Enslaved people escaping across the river often found refuge there, thanks largely to the city's Black community. Black Cincinnatians numbered more than three thousand in 1850; although this represented just 2.7 percent of the city's booming population, Cincinnati's Black community was the largest in the old Northwest Territory and the fifth most concentrated Black community in the nation.[87] Despite hardship, this community found the strength to shield Black refugees and to help Black transplants restart their lives.[88] Some white Cincinnatians lent a hand. Antebellum Cincinnati was a major stop on the Underground Railroad and a hotbed of abolitionism. A group of white Cincinnati women met weekly to sew clothing for escapees from slavery. Cincinnati was home, at least for a time, to such antislavery luminaries as *Uncle Tom's Cabin* author Harriet Beecher Stowe (who opened her Cincinnati home to Underground Railroad passengers), abolitionist writer and politician James G. Birney (himself a transplanted southerner and a former enslaver), Levi Coffin ("national president" of the Underground Railroad), and Salmon P. Chase (later governor of Ohio, a US senator, a member of President Abraham Lincoln's cabinet, and chief justice of the United States).[89]

Demographic patterns suggest that Cincinnati's Hamilton County was a magnet that attracted Black migrants northward. Southern migrants dominated the local Black community. Only 19 percent of Black heads of household in Hamilton County were native to Ohio; less than 10 percent came from other northern states. Most Black household heads—72 percent of the total—had migrated to Cincinnati from slave states. Although two-thirds of these northward Black migrants had come from neighboring Kentucky or Virginia, the remaining third had crossed multiple state lines within the South before reaching free soil.[90] Cincinnati lay at the heart of a churning borderland.

---

86. Henry L. Taylor, "Spatial Organization and the Residential Experience: Black Cincinnati in 1850," *Social Science History* 10 (Spring 1986): 45.

87. Ibid., 49.

88. Stephen Middleton, "The Fugitive Slave Crisis in Cincinnati, 1850–1860: Resistance, Enforcement, and Black Refugees," *Journal of Negro History* 72 (1987): 23; Charles Cist, *Sketches and Statistics of Cincinnati in 1859* (Cincinnati: n.p., 1859), 164–65.

89. Taylor, "Spatial Organization and the Residential Experience," 60–61; and Larry Gara, *Liberty Line: The Legend of the Underground Railroad* (Lexington: University Press of Kentucky, 1996), 1, 77–78, 91, 94, 96, 117, 160.

90. 1860 Federal Census, Hamilton County, Ohio; 1860 Federal Census, Jefferson County, Kentucky.

The substantial Black migration northward across the Ohio River is even more impressive when contrasted with two other migratory trends. The first is the comparatively puny northward migration of whites across the same river. While 72 percent of Black household heads in Hamilton County as of 1860 had migrated from slave states, only 5 percent of the county's white household heads had done so.[91]

A second way to confirm the substantial Black migration northward across the Ohio River is to contrast it to Black migration southward. That migration scarcely existed. Although Covington, Kentucky, lay right across the river from Cincinnati, the 1860 census records not a single Ohio native in its small community of free Black people.[92] The free Black population of Louisville, Kentucky, a border city about a hundred miles southwest of Cincinnati, was much larger than Covington's. As of 1860, 993 Black households resided in Jefferson County, home to Louisville. None of these Black heads of household—not one—was originally from Ohio.[93] Legal differences explain the one-way Black migration.

John Jolliffe

Among the former southerners whom Elijah Willis met in Cincinnati was a white attorney named John Jolliffe. Jolliffe was born to a Quaker family in Virginia. Although not all Quakers opposed slavery,[94] John's parents did. In 1799, prior to John's birth, and apparently as a condition of marriage to a devout Quaker named Rebecca Neill, John's father William Jolliffe freed all of the people he had enslaved.[95] John followed his parents' antislavery path. He explained his abolitionism largely in terms of his strong religious faith. Slavery, he believed, violated such core biblical maxims as "Thou shalt love

91. Ibid.

92. 1860 Federal Census, Kent County, Kentucky.

93. 1860 Federal Census, Hamilton County, Ohio; 1860 Federal Census, Jefferson County, Kentucky.

94. Ryan P. Jordan, *Slavery and the Meetinghouse: The Quakers and the Abolitionist Dilemma, 1820–1861* (Bloomington: Indiana University Press, 2007).

95. William Jolliffe, *Historical, Genealogical, and Biographical Account of the Jolliffe Family of Virginia, 1652 to 1893. Also Sketches of the Neill's, Janney's, Hollingsworth's, and Other Cognate Families* (Philadelphia: J. B. Lippincott, 1893), 109–10; Weisenburger, *Modern Medea*, 91.

thy neighbor as thyself" and "Inasmuch as ye have done unto one of the least of these my brethren, ye have done it unto me." In future years he would incorporate these biblical commands into his political and legal advocacy.[96]

John Jolliffe studied law under Henry St. George Tucker, one of Virginia's legal luminaries.[97] Having trained with so prominent a lawyer, Jolliffe surely could have found comfortable in-state employment. But his antislavery views put him on a different path. In 1827, having completed his legal studies, he migrated northward.[98] He soon established himself in Cincinnati as a prominent abolitionist lawyer, a leading member of the Cincinnati Anti-Slavery Convention, and an (unsuccessful) candidate for public office on the Abolition Party ticket.[99]

In addition to his legal and political advocacy, Jolliffe sought to spread his antislavery views by writing novels. He wrote *Belle Scott* (1856), a sentimental indictment of slavery, while working on the Willis case. The novel depicts one proslavery southerner after another experiencing a change of heart and accepting the antislavery gospel. *Belle Scott* implicitly urged good-hearted enslavers to repent and travel across as many state lines as necessary to find a jurisdiction where they could manumit the people they enslaved. In the novel that jurisdiction was Ohio.[100]

Steamboat rides between South and North figure prominently in *Belle Scott*. Belle, an enslaved person in New Orleans, is taken on a steamboat trip north. When the boat makes an unscheduled stop on the northern banks of the Ohio River, Belle flees, having heard that slavery is not allowed in Ohio. She is caught and sent to jail, causing Mrs. Johnston, a kindly Buckeye, to lament that unjust national laws were turning Ohio jails into slave pens. A southern attorney, having been persuaded of slavery's injus-

96. Weisenburger, 101.

97. E. Lee Shephard, "Breaking into the Profession: Establishing a Law Practice in Antebellum Virginia," *Journal of Southern History* 48, no. 3 (Aug. 1982): 398.

98. Ibid., 92.

99. Jolliffe, *Historical*, 115; Bernie D. Jones, "Southern Free Women of Color in the Antebellum North: Race, Class, and a 'New Women's Legal History," *Akron Law Review* 41 (2008): 788–89; Weisenburger, *Modern Medea*, 94; Everts, *History of Clermont County*, 114, 126; "Cincinnati Convention," *Pennsylvania Freeman*, May 1, 1851; and "The States," *Emancipator* (New York], Nov. 18, 1841, 115; "The Free Democrats of Hamilton County," *National Era* (Washington, DC) Sept. 30, 1852, 159.

100. John Jolliffe, *Belle Scott; or Liberty Overthrown: A Tale for the Crisis* (Cincinnati: D. Anderson, 1856).

tice by an abolitionist's critique, defends Belle in court. Alas, Belle loses. Her enslaver is determined to take his prize south as quickly as possible, but Mrs. Johnston locks the would-be getaway craft to the wharf.[101] In the nick of time, another steamboat arrives from New Orleans, carrying crucial evidence that leads to Belle's emancipation. Jolliffe's novel vividly illustrates the salience of interstate legal differences in the age of slavery.[102]

John Jolliffe was not the only antislavery novelist whose characters deliberately crossed legal borders. Harriet Beecher Stowe, a more accomplished novelist than Jolliffe, incorporated a border-crossing subplot into *Dred: A Tale of the Great Dismal Swamp* (1856), her follow-up to *Uncle Tom's Cabin* (1852). Among the many characters in *Dred* is Cora Gordon, a "beautiful and good" mixed-race woman who was "born the slave" of her own father, in the South.[103] Cora nurses her Mississippi enslaver back to health after a bout of smallpox. He is a "man of honor," and the two soon fall in love. They move to Ohio, secure Cora's emancipation, marry, and have two children.[104]

"Why didn't he live with her on his [Mississippi] plantation?" one character asks.

"He couldn't have freed her there; it's against the laws," was the reply. But then her husband dies, leaving his valuable Mississippi estate to Cora and the children, according to the terms of his Ohio will. An evil lawyer, representing a greedy, white southern relative of Cora's deceased husband, files suit and overturns the act of emancipation that freed Cora.[105] Cora and the children are returned to slavery, "as incapable of holding property as the mule before the plough."[106] Resisting reenslavement, Cora whisks her children back north, to Cincinnati, but because they are now fugitive (escaped) enslaved persons, rather than voluntarily transported ones, the border fails them. They are recaptured, returned south, and re-reenslaved. The night before she is to be forcibly separated from her offspring, a des-

101. Jolliffe, *Belle Scott*, 356.

102. Stephen Lucasi, "William Wells Brown's Narrative and Traveling Subjectivity," *African American Review* 3 (2007): 521–39.

103. Harriet Beecher Stowe, *Dred: A Tale of the Great Dismal Swamp* (Boston: Houghton, Mifflin, 1856), 462.

104. Ibid., 61–62.

105. Ibid., 459.

106. Ibid., 457.

perate Cora kills her own children in an act of anguished mercy, losing her soul to save theirs.[107]

In real life, John Jolliffe handled few cases as dramatic as Belle Scott's or Cora's, but he was "extensively known," according to the press, as "a friend and advocate of the slave in court cases."[108] Cincinnati's abolitionist and free Black communities knew that "lawyer Jolliffe" was always available to help.[109] He handled most of the antislavery legal work in southwestern Ohio, often working for free.[110] By the 1850s, many of his cases involved escapees from southern slavery who sought refuge in the North. These cases were virtually impossible to win, thanks to the slavery-friendly Fugitive Slave Law of 1850. Jolliffe lost case after case but kept litigating, in part to raise public awareness of slavery's horrors.[111] He was precisely the sort of lawyer that Elijah Willis needed when he reached Cincinnati in 1854.

Elijah's Second Will

Willis had crossed the Ohio River in search of Rev. Brisbane, the antislavery Baptist from South Carolina. Although Brisbane had recently moved to Wisconsin, Elijah's search for the minister in early 1854 soon led him to the offices of John Jolliffe, the transplanted abolitionist lawyer.[112] Willis explained that his "object in coming to Ohio was to make his will, and provide for certain persons whom he held as slaves in South Carolina."[113] The "certain persons" included Amy and her immediate family, but no one else. Willis did not intend to emancipate the many other people he enslaved. Family love drove him, not abolitionism.

Reporting that he was in good health and sound of mind, Elijah dictated his revised estate plan. His new will voided his old will and directed that, following his death, his property be left to Amy and all seven of her chil-

107. Ibid., 462

108. "John Jolliffe; Cincinnati," *Alban Evening Journal*, June 4, 1857, 2.

109. Ibid., 90.

110. Ibid., 91.

111. Weisenburger, *Modern Medea*, 100–3; Middleton, "Fugitive Slave," 26.

112. "Anti-Slavery Convention in Cincinnati," *National Era* (Washington, DC), January 22, 1852.

113. Willis v. Jolliffe, 27–28.

dren, the four youngest of which were Elijah's.[114] It called for his executors "to bring . . . said persons and their increase . . . to the State of Ohio, and to . . . set them free."[115] The will also gave the executors "full power to sell all or any of [Willis's] personality," except Amy and the children.[116] The proceeds from these sales, and the sale of Willis's South Carolina land, were to be used to pay all outstanding obligations and then to purchase new land in a free state, which Amy and the children would receive, along with all remaining money.[117]

Fearing that he might die at any moment, Willis requested duplicate copies of his new will. He kept one on his body and left the other with lawyer Jolliffe. One of his brothers had died very suddenly, he explained. He himself suffered from "palpitation of the heart" and was "liable to be also summoned to another world at moment's notice."[118]

Back in South Carolina, he inventoried his possessions, recorded all debts due to him and owed to others, "made preparations for disposing of his entire estate," and prepared his family to travel.[119]

The *Jacob Strader*

In May of 1855, Elijah Willis took his final journey. Accompanied by Amy, her children, and Amy's mother, he traveled from Barnwell County, South Carolina, to Louisville, Kentucky. The party then boarded the steamboat *Jacob Strader* and headed northeast on the Ohio River, to Cincinnati.[120]

Ohio was a good choice for the Willis family. It permitted interracial

---

114. As mentioned above, there is some uncertainty about how many surviving children—three or four—Elijah and Amy had together, in addition to the three that Amy brought with her to the relationship. One witness reported that Elijah and Amy had four surviving children. Willis v. Jolliffe, 25. Others said that the couple had three. Ibid., 23. Another unhelpfully estimated that the couple had "three or four mulatto children" together. Ibid., 22. Based on reports in the US Census, we believe that the more likely number is four. 1860 Federal Census, Clermont County, Ohio, Roll 944, p. 225.

115. Ibid., 2.

116. Ibid.

117. Willis v. Jolliffe, 2.

118. "Sudden Death," 2.

119. Ibid.

120. "Sudden Death of a Slaveholder," *National Era* (Washington, DC), June 7, 1855.

marriage.[121] Moreover, had Elijah and Amy merely cohabited there, their conduct, to quote a nineteenth-century legal ruling about another enslaver who freed an enslaved woman and then lived with her in Cincinnati for several years, "may have been such as to raise a legal presumption of a marriage."[122] A presumption of marriage certainly characterized some of the news reporting following Elijah Willis's death. Cincinnati papers referred to Amy as Elijah's "wife"[123] and described the couple as "married."[124]

The *Jacob Strader* reached Cincinnati on the morning of May 21, 1855. Elijah alit, hailed a carriage, and gathered two of his young daughters by the hand. "Just as he went to reach one of the small children into [the carriage]," the press reported, he stopped and "breathed heavily."[125] Concerned, Amy asked if he had been struck by another "attack of palpitation of the heart." Elijah nodded and expelled some "heavy breathings." Then he crumpled.[126]

Among the items found thereafter on Willis's lifeless body was his last will and testament. A local lawyer read the document and announced that Elijah had willed his entire South Carolina estate to Amy and her children. "If the property is attained," the newspapers reported, "each of these colored children will have a fortune of twenty-five or thirty thousand dollars."[127] But Amy and her children would inherit this fortune only if the South Carolina courts, confronted with two wills, upheld the validity of the more recent one, which had been made out of state. That was no sure bet.

In the South Carolina Courts: Round One

Cincinnati lawyer John Jolliffe was the executor of Willis's second will. On May 23, 1855, two days after Willis's death, a Cincinnati probate court vali-

121. David H. Fowler, "Northern Attitudes Towards Interracial Marriage: A Study of Legislation and Public Opinion in the Middle Atlantic States and the States of the Old Northwest" (PhD diss., Yale University, 1963); and Peter Wallenstein, *Tell the Court I Love My Wife: Race, Marriage, and Law—An American History* (New York: Palgrave MacMillan, 2004), 254.

122. Bonds v. Foster, 36 Tex. 68, 69 (1872).

123. "Sudden Death of a Slaveholder," *Cincinnati Gazette*, May 22 1885.

124. "The Sudden Death at Cincinnati," 1.

125. "Sudden Death," 2; "Manumission of Slaves-Sudden Death of Their Master," *Daily Ohio Statesman* (Columbus, SC), May 23, 1855.

126. Ibid.

127. "Sudden Death," 2.

dated ("proved") this 1854 will.[128] This was a victory for Jolliffe, but an inconsequential one. Willis's estate lay in South Carolina, not Ohio. In order to carry out Willis's testamentary wishes, Jolliffe would have to prevail in the South Carolina courts. Although he raced south with a copy of the new will, news of Willis's death beat him there. By the time Jolliffe arrived, a Barnwell County probate court had already validated Willis's first will—the 1846 document leaving everything to his siblings.[129] The executors of that first will, Patrick Fanning and Hughey Phillips, had acted rapidly. Both were brothers-in-law of the deceased. If Willis's first will prevailed, Fanning and Phillips would receive healthy chunks of his huge estate, the estimated value of which reached as high as $150,000.[130] If the second will prevailed, the two would receive nothing.

Jolliffe immediately met a jarring obstacle. The probate court in Barnwell County refused to admit the Ohio will. Jolliffe challenged that refusal, prompting a jury trial in the local Court of Common Pleas. Fanning and Phillips contended that the Ohio will was void for several reasons. They argued that Willis was insane when he prepared it, that Amy had manipulated him unduly, that lawyer Jolliffe had committed fraud in its preparation, and that its central terms violated South Carolina's antimanumission laws.[131] They presented witness testimony purporting to show Elijah's troubled state of mind in his last years. One witness claimed that Willis was frequently "under gloomy depression of spirits," often "avoiding society on account of his connection with Amy."[132] Others attacked Amy's character and challenged the legitimacy of the couple's relationship.[133]

Other testimony, however, suggested just how closely Amy and Elijah's relationship adhered to nineteenth-century domestic ideals. According to witnesses, Elijah "permitted [Amy] to act as the mistress of his house." She "exercised great influence over [Elijah] in reference to his domestic affairs." She took enslaved people from their plantation labors "to make wheels for little wagons for his mulatto children." Even Willis's supposed late-life gloom indicated familial devotion. After taking Amy and the children to

128. Jolliffe v. Fanning & Phillips.

129. Ibid.

130. Will of Elijah Willis of Barnwell District, 268; "Married to His Own Slave," *Selma State Sentinel* (Alabama), June 21, 1855.

131. Jolliffe v. Fanning & Phillips.

132. Ibid., 2.

133. Ibid.

Baltimore, Elijah returned south, alone, "abstracted and reserved." His loneliness apparently impelled him to retrieve them from Baltimore. Three local doctors testified that Willis indeed was "anxious" late in life but explained why: "It appeared, he was always anxious to secure the freedom of, and make provision for, Amy, and her children by him."[134]

The trial judge, John Belton O'Neall (who will reappear later, in round three), concluded that the Ohio will was valid and told the all-white jury as much. The jury disregarded O'Neall's views and found against the will.[135] Jolliffe appealed to the Law Court of Appeals, where Judge Thomas Jefferson Withers, whom we met in the Martin Posey case in chapter 1, presided. Like Judge O'Neall before him, Withers saw no legal basis for rejecting the Ohio will. He acknowledged that the Ohio will's first provision, ordering the emancipation of Amy and her family, violated South Carolina's Act of 1841, which banned testamentary emancipations. The point was moot, however, since emancipation had occurred out of state and prior to Willis's death. Elijah himself had carried "said slaves" to freedom in Ohio. By the time Willis died, Amy and her children were neither in South Carolina nor enslaved. They were in Ohio, free, and eligible to inherit property.[136]

Judge Withers found no other defects in the Ohio will. As to Amy's allegedly "undue influence" over Willis, Withers pointed out that Willis had made his second will in Cincinnati, hundreds of miles away from Amy—clearly, a "free and voluntary act." As to fraud, Withers noted that the will was executed in duplicate and "one copy was read while [Willis] had before his eyes the other." There was no reason to doubt the will's validity.[137] The insanity claim was equally baseless, Judge Withers thought. Willis's brothers-in-law had argued that any enslaver who hired an abolitionist attorney must be insane. Withers disagreed. "Not in the least does it argue insanity that Willis should resort to such a man as Jolliffe," the South Carolina judge wrote. "To what other description of people should he apply to aid in the object he had in view?"[138]

---

134. Ibid., 2.

135. Ibid.

136. Ibid., 4.

137. Ibid., 6.

138. Ibid., 7. For more on how American jurists grappled with claims of insanity in the context of civil litigation, see Susanna L. Blumenthal, Law and the Modern Mind: Consciousness and Responsibility in American Legal Culture (Cambridge, MA: Harvard University Press, 2016).

Judge Withers grounded his opinion on a straightforward understanding of legal borders. South of the Ohio River lay the law and culture of slavery, where Willis's emancipationist goals would have been "met by the opposition of the law, and no doubt that of individual and general sentiment." North of the river, by contrast, neither the law nor the culture of slavery prevailed. Elijah Willis reasonably concluded that only northern laws could help him achieve his emancipationist goals. So he traveled north. The instant Willis crossed the Ohio River, Judge Withers reasoned, everything changed. He had reached a land "beyond the limits where slavery prevails."[139]

Judge Withers rejected all of Fanning and Phillips's claims and ordered a new trial. That trial resulted in a "verdict for the [1854 Cincinnati] will."[140] Round one went decisively to John Jolliffe.

Round Two

Willis's white relatives appealed to the Barnwell County Court of Equity. This time they conceded that Elijah's Cincinnati will was valid and could be probated in South Carolina's courts, just as Judge Withers had ordered. They argued, however, that Amy and her children could not inherit anything under that will because, under South Carolina law, they remained enslaved at the time of Elijah's death.[141]

Fortunately for Willis's white relatives, the chancellor who presided over the Barnwell County case was Francis Hugh Wardlaw, a passionate proslavery ideologue. Just two years after his 1858 ruling in *Willis v. Jolliffe*, Wardlaw would sign—and was rumored to have been a principal drafter of—South Carolina's Ordinance of Secession.[142] Chancellor Wardlaw's proslavery ideology influenced his approach to *Willis*. Although *Willis* was a "wills and testaments" case that did not directly challenge the legitimacy

139. Ibid.

140. Willis v. Jolliffe.

141. Ibid.

142. Francis Hugh Wardlaw file, SCDAH; U. R. Brooks, *South Carolina Bench and Bar*, vol. 1 (Columbia, SC: State Company, 1908), 96; John Amasa May and Joan Reynolds Faunt, *South Carolina Secedes* (Columbia: University of South Carolina Press, 1960), 224; Yates Snowden and Harry Gardner Cutler, *History of South Carolina*, vol. 3 (Chicago: Lewis Publishing, 1920), 190–91.

of slavery, Wardlaw peppered his opinion with rhetorical defenses of the institution. Slavery, Wardlaw wrote in *Willis*, was consistent with divine law.[143] Its lawfulness in the here-below, where it had existed since "the earliest periods of . . . history,"[144] was beyond question. Moreover, Wardlaw cited the recently decided *Dred Scott* case and stated that slavery was a "cornerstone" of the US Constitution.[145]

Chancellor Wardlaw had a proslavery understanding of the slave-free border. Unlike Judge Withers, who understood the Ohio River to be a sharp divide between slavery and freedom, Chancellor Wardlaw conceptualized that border as stretchy and blurry. Wardlaw rejected the proposition that Amy and the children "became free simply by breathing the atmosphere of Ohio."[146] Geographical location alone did not determine status. As far as South Carolina law was concerned, Wardlaw declared, Amy and her children were still enslaved at the moment of Elijah's death, "wherever in space their bodies might be."[147]

Wardlaw defended his interpretation by invoking legislative history. South Carolina had sought to affect developments both within and beyond state lines when it banned testamentary emancipations in 1841, he noted. The "object of the legislature" was to "check . . . the growth of free persons of color" both "in our midst" and in "our vicinage." He found that the "policy of the State" was "against emancipation of slaves" and against the settlement of "free negroes" both "among us" and beyond state lines.[148]

"Amy and her brood" were considered free persons under Ohio law, Wardlaw conceded. But Ohio law had no bearing on the case. Only South Carolina law mattered, for Elijah Willis was a South Carolinian and his estate lay in South Carolina. The central question, thus, was whether, at the instant of Elijah's death, Amy and her children were free under South Carolina law. If so, they could inherit everything; if not, they could inherit nothing.[149]

Had Amy and her children "become free by mere landing on the

143. Willis v. Jolliffe.

144. Ibid., 8, reports Wardlaw's 1858 ruling.

145. Ibid., 8–9, 12, 16. Dred Scott v. Sandford, 60 U.S. 393, 19 How. 393 (U.S. 1857).

146. Reported in Willis v. Jolliffe, 4.

147. Ibid., 3.

148. Ibid., 5.

149. Ibid., 3.

northern shore of the Ohio [R]iver," as John Jolliffe claimed?[150] Wardlaw thought not, for three reasons. First, Elijah Willis never resided in Ohio and thus never established legal "domicil" there. Had he done so, Wardlaw asserted, Amy and the children would have been free the moment they hit Ohio's shores. But Elijah remained legally domiciled in South Carolina. South Carolina law accompanied him—and his enslaved workers—across the river.

Second, Wardlaw asserted, Elijah never formally emancipated anyone in Ohio. Amy and the children were enslaved in South Carolina, remained so throughout their journey ("it being through a slave region"), and were "not manumitted in Ohio by any formal act." Amy's enslaver "did not express in any form, *after she reached Ohio*, his purpose . . . to make her free [emphasis added]." (Of course, Willis's death immediately upon reaching Ohio prevented him from expressing this or any other thought, but that did not trouble Wardlaw.) Wardlaw also noted that lawyer Jolliffe eventually executed "formal deeds of emancipation" for Amy and the others in Ohio, but not until after Willis's death. To Chancellor Wardlaw, that made all the difference. At the instant of Willis's passing, Amy and the others remained unfree.[151]

Third, Wardlaw considered the evidence that, long before the group reached Ohio, Elijah had frequently announced his intent to emancipate. Wardlaw admitted that Elijah had "repeatedly expressed" this "general intent." But "every intention or purpose is revocable." Nothing in the case record proved that Willis's previously expressed "general intent" to emancipate in Ohio persisted "after his arrival there." Wardlaw noted that Elijah had previously taken Amy and the children to Baltimore, only to reconsider and return them to South Carolina. In the Baltimore instance, Willis did not carry out his previously stated intent. The same might have happened in Cincinnati.[152]

For all these reasons, Chancellor Wardlaw held that, under South Carolina law, Amy and the children remained unfree at the time of Elijah's death, and therefore could inherit no property. The mere crossing of legal borders had not altered their status.[153]

150. Ibid., 16.

151. Ibid., 7.

152. Ibid., 20.

153. Ibid.

Round Three

John Jolliffe appealed to the Court of Appeals of Equity, the highest equity court in South Carolina. That tribunal's three members presented him with bad and good news. The bad news was that Chancellor Wardlaw had recently been promoted and would hear the appeal of his own 1858 ruling.[154] The good news was that the court's other two members during that May 1860 term, John Belton O'Neall and Job Johnstone, opposed Wardlaw's states' rights stridency. Indeed, while Wardlaw pushed secession late in 1860, O'Neall and Johnstone actively advocated unionism.[155] The same two-to-one split prevailed in *Willis v. Jolliffe* (1860).[156]

Chief Justice O'Neall wrote the majority opinion. Like Wardlaw, he had participated in an earlier hearing in the case. He had presided over the original round one trial, during which he demonstrated sympathy for Jolliffe's arguments. O'Neall's long public record (he had been a judge since 1828)[157] suggested that he might side with Jolliffe once again. As mentioned, he was a unionist. He had opposed Nullification in the 1830s and would go on to oppose secession at the dawn of the 1860s.[158] His wariness of states' rights radicalism may have led him to regard Ohio law more respectfully than Chancellor Wardlaw did.

Furthermore, O'Neall, who enslaved many people, strongly believed that enslavers should be able to do as they wished—even emancipate. South Carolina originally had permitted enslavers to manumit. In 1820, however, the state legislature banned private manumissions, and in 1841 it outlawed testamentary manumissions. O'Neall opposed both statutes. "My experience as a man and a Judge," he wrote in 1848, "leads me to condemn the Acts of 1820 and 1841. They ought to be repealed." "All laws unnecessarily restraining the rights of owners are unwise."[159]

An additional factor that may have inclined O'Neall in Jolliffe's direc-

154. Ibid., 33.

155. Lillian Kibler, "Unionist Sentiment in South Carolina in 1860," *Journal of Southern History* 4 (1938): 361–62.

156. Willis v. Jolliffe.

157. John Belton O'Neall and John A. Chapman, *The Annals of Newberry: In Two Parts* (Newberry, SC: Aull & Houseal, 1892), 367–70; John Belton O'Neall, *Biographical Sketches of the Bench and Bar of South Carolina* (Charleston, SC: S.G. Courtenay, 1859), xii–xiv.

158. O'Neall, and Chapman, *Annals of Newberry*, 100; Kibler, "Unionist Sentiment."

159. All quotations in this paragraph come from O'Neall, *Negro Law*, 10–12.

tion was the role that he played in *O'Neall v. Farr* (1844), a relevant South Carolina precedent. Like Elijah Willis, William Farr lived quasi-maritally with a woman he enslaved, Fan. Farr wrote a will designed to emancipate and provide for Fan and her offspring upon his death. Chief Justice O'Neall was to Farr as Jolliffe was to Willis: he drafted Farr's will and agreed to serve as executor. When Farr died, O'Neall went to court to defend the will against resentful white relatives who claimed that Fan had exerted "undue influence" over the testator. O'Neall prevailed. His Jolliffe-like participation in *Farr*, on behalf of an enslaver who wanted to free and endow his enslaved "paramour" and her son, likely informed O'Neall's ruling in *Willis*, sixteen years later.[160]

In *Willis*, Chief Justice O'Neall analyzed the slave-free border in a new way. He did not share Judge Withers's round one view that slave status automatically disappeared the instant a nonfugitive enslaved person entered free territory.[161] Nor did he share Chancellor Wardlaw's round two understanding of the slave-free border, whereby the voluntary transit of an enslaved person into free territory had no effect on that person's status, absent another legal act such as the swearing out of a deed of freedom. Rather, O'Neall concluded that the slave-free border could mean everything or nothing, depending on the will of the enslaver. If an enslaver brought an enslaved person into Ohio with no emancipatory intent, border-crossing would have no emancipatory effect. If, however, an enslaver brought an enslaved person into Ohio with emancipatory intent, border-crossing alone would do the trick. An enslaver's volition, in other words, determined what effect, if any, border-crossing would have on the status of a nonfugitive enslaved person.

O'Neall acknowledged that Elijah Willis never officially changed his domicile; he remained a South Carolinian until death. Nonetheless, Willis transported Amy and the others across the Ohio River for the demonstrated purpose of freeing them. Witness after witness had testified that Willis planned to "carry [Amy and the children] to Ohio . . . and free them, so they could have the benefit of his property."[162] His plan originated before the journey and remained consistent throughout the journey. Even in the trip's last leg, as the *Jacob Strader* steamed toward Cincinnati, Elijah told a fellow

160. O'Neall v. Farr.

161. Willis v. Jolliffe,.

162. Ibid., 32.

passenger that he was "going to Ohio, to set them . . . free, and school the children.'" Citing such testimony, O'Neall concluded, "There can be no doubt what was his purpose."[163] O'Neall concluded that Amy and the children "were free from the moment when, by the consent of their master, they were placed upon the soil of Ohio to be free." This was so not because "soil of Ohio *per se* confers freedom," but rather because "the act of the master . . . has that effect."[164]

O'Neall realized that his ruling might be unpopular in South Carolina. But he stood his ground. "I should feel myself degraded," he wrote, "if, like some in Ohio and other abolition States, I trampled on law and constitution, in obedience to popular will. There is no law in South Carolina which, notwithstanding the freedom of Amy and her children, declares that the trusts in their favor are void. As soon as they are acknowledged to be free one moment before the death of Elijah Willis, they are capable to [inherit property] . . . under his will."[165] South Carolina's highest equity court thus ruled that Amy and the children were entitled to Elijah Willis's estate.

Conclusion

South Carolina law regulated Elijah and Amy's lives at every turn. It declared Amy an enslaved negro, like her mother, even though her father was free and white. It therefore authorized Elijah to purchase Amy. It meant that Amy's previous quasi-marriage to a "slave husband"[166] was no impediment to her eventual relationship with Elijah, even in divorceless South Carolina. It gave Elijah unfettered sexual access to Amy, since the law of rape did not apply.[167] It meant that Elijah and Amy's children were unfree, unwhite, and incapable of inheriting their father's estate. It prevented Elijah from manumiting his family in-state. It meant that, barring legislative action, which was vanishingly unlikely, or escape, which was perilously risky, the only way for Amy to secure freedom for herself and her children was to convince her enslaver to relocate them to a free jurisdiction.

Legal differences create legal borderlands. The more consequential the

163. Ibid.

164. Ibid., 31.

165. Ibid.

166. Jolliffe v. Fanning & Phillips, 2.

167. Morris, *Southern Slavery*, 305; Smith, *Encyclopedia of Rape*, 235.

differences, the further those borderlands reach. In antebellum America, legal differences between free and slave states were so stark that they motivated people to migrate great distances, seeking legal advantage. Black people drifted northward across the Ohio River, attracted by the magnet pull of freedom, if not equality. (Plenty of anti-Black discrimination existed in antebellum Ohio, it should be noted.[168]) Rev. Brisbane, lawyer Jolliffe, and other white southern abolitionists migrated to Ohio, where they agitated against slavery, wrote abolitionist novels featuring interregional steamboat travel, and sent messages south, hoping to inspire followers. Elijah Willis and other southern enslavers who wished to emancipate their "chattels personal" traveled north, seeking favorable legal climes in a borderland legal culture that reached from the Deep South to the northern shores of the Ohio River and beyond, into Canada.[169]

Chief Justice O'Neall's final ruling in *Willis v. Jolliffe* emphasized Elijah Willis's legally driven migrations. Willis, O'Neall wrote, had "travelled hundreds of miles to consummate [his emancipationist] intention, and had reached a point" where he could do so. South Carolina, O'Neall believed, was powerless to reverse this enslaver's voluntary act. "Can we reach a hand to Ohio and draw back those people to servitude?" O'Neall rhetorically asked. The answer was no. Elijah had won. Amy and her children were "in the enjoyment of freedom and we [South Carolina officials] cannot and ought not to interfere."[170]

Elijah Willis was buried in Cincinnati, in a "negro-graveyard."[171]

Late in 1860, seven months after filing his *Willis* dissent, Chancellor Wardlaw signed—and may have helped draft—South Carolina's declaration of secession. This document justified secession as a response to the "increasing hostility . . . to the institution of slavery" demonstrated by northern states.[172]

Chief Justice O'Neall passed away in 1863. Wartime South Carolina

168. Paul Finkelman, "The Strange Career of Race Discrimination in Antebellum Ohio," *Case Western Reserve Law Review* 55, no. 2 (2004): 373–408.

169. Tony Freyer and Lyndsay Campbell, eds., *Freedom's Conditions in the U.S.-Canadian Borderlands in the Age of Emancipation* (Durham, NC: Carolina Academic Press, 2011).

170. Willis v. Jolliffe, 32.

171. Ibid., testimony of Jonathan Pender, 22.

172. South Carolina, Convention (1860–1862), *Declaration of the Immediate Causes Which Induce and Justify the Secession of South Carolina from the Federal Union; and the Ordinance of Secession* (Charleston, SC: Evans & Cogswell, 1860).

eulogists spun his softness on secession and slavery—including, one imagines, rulings such as *Willis*—into left-handed compliments: "If Judge O'Neall had faults, they were all on virtue's side; if he committed errors, they were errors on the side of humanity and benevolence."[173]

Amy remained free, in Ohio.[174] During the Civil War, two of her sons defended Cincinnati as part of that city's "Black Brigade."[175] Amy apparently later married a mulatto man who had migrated from North Carolina.[176] She and most of her children remained in Ohio, working as housekeepers, coal miners, and wage laborers.[177] They worked humble jobs in part because they had difficulty securing their South Carolina inheritance. The Civil War, which began less than a year after round three ended, was largely to blame. The Confederate States of America seized the Willis estate, on the grounds that its inheritors were not loyal southerners.[178] The war also severely diminished the value of the estate, largely due to the emancipation of Elijah's enslaved workers, the most valuable part of his property. Amy, however, continued to seek her due in court. Early in the 1870s, representatives in South Carolina, acting on Amy's behalf, sold several remaining parcels of Elijah Willis's land. If all went as planned, the three or four thousand dollars yielded by those sales made their way northward across the Ohio River, to Amy and her family.[179]

173. "Tribute to Chief Justice John Belton O'Neall," *Charleston Mercury*, Feb. 17, 1864, 2.

174. 1860 Federal Census, Clermont County, 225.

175. Sharon Wick, transcriber, "The Black Brigade: Muster Roll of the Black Brigade, Cincinnati" (1864), Ohio Genealogy Express, 2008, http://www.ohiogenealogyexpress.com/military/black_brigade_roster.htm; Edgar A. Toppin, "Humbly They Served: The Black Brigade in the Defense of Cincinnati," *Journal of Negro History* 48, no. 2 (April 1963): 75–97.

176. Jones, *Fathers of Conscience*, 148.

177. 1870 Federal Census, Athens County, Ohio, roll 1171, p. 45; 1880 Federal Census, Athens County, Ohio, roll 993, p. 172 and 292, SCDAH; 1900 Federal Census, Pike County, Ohio, roll 1314, p. 13; 1880 Federal Census, Clermont County, Ohio, roll 1000, p. 194; 1900 Federal Census, Clermont County, Ohio, roll 1247, p. 172; and 1910 Federal Census, Clermont County, Ohio, roll 1160, p. 164.

178. Jones, *Fathers of Conscience*, 148.

179. Ibid., 163; "Petition of Amy Ash and Clarissa Sloan," Barnwell County Probate Records, July 4, 1870, bundle 184, pkg. 12, book M 311, SCDAH; ibid., book AAA 529, SCDAH.

CHAPTER THREE

Burgess v. Carpenter: The Reconstruction of South Carolina Labor Law[1]

The first important case decided by South Carolina's first Black Supreme Court Justice involved agricultural labor. *Burgess v. Carpenter* began when one white landowner, W. R. Burgess, sued another, W. R. Carpenter, for shooting and injuring Henry Burgess, a Black worker on W. R. Burgess's land. W. R. Burgess sought monetary damages to compensate him for the economic losses that he suffered due to Henry Burgess's injuries. The justice, Jonathan Jasper Wright, would have to decide whether W. R. Burgess could recover money from the man who shot an agricultural laborer who worked his land.[2]

Had these events occurred during the era of slavery, and had W. R. Burgess enslaved Henry Burgess, the plaintiff, W. R. Burgess, would have had a slam-dunk case. South Carolina law endowed "masters" with powerful tools with which to defend the bodies and labor of the workers they enslaved. As South Carolina jurist John B. O'Neall explained in 1848, "The right of protection, which would belong to a slave, as a human being, is by the law of slavery, transferred to the master."[3] The South Carolina enslaver could protect his enslaved workers preemptively by "repelling force with force."[4] Subsequently, he could sue in court to recover monetary damages

1. Akoua Enyo Abalo, Aaron Jordan, Alexander Kaplan, Ellis Martin, Claire McDonald, James Mietus, William H. Mogen, James P. Mooney IV, Bryan Wesley Reynolds II, Heidi Rickes, Anna Van Hollen, and John Wertheimer coauthored this chapter.

2. Burgess v. Carpenter, 2 S.C. 7 (1870).

3. John Belton O'Neall, *The Negro Law of South Carolina* (Columbia, SC: J. G. Bowman, 1848), 18.

4. Ibid, 18.

for "any injury done to the person of his slave."[5] South Carolina also defended enslavers' property interests by making it a felony, punishable by death, for anyone to "steal" an enslaved person or "aid any slave in . . . departing from his master's . . . service."[6] South Carolina sternly enforced this ban on so-called "negro stealing"[7] because, in O'Neall's words, it was "a most valuable safeguard to property."[8] By some accounts, indeed, South Carolina punished the "stealing" of an enslaved person more vigilantly than it did any other crime, including the killing of such a person.[9]

By the time W. R. Carpenter shot Henry Burgess, on June 7, 1866, however, none of these legal concepts mattered. They had been wiped off the books, along with slavery itself, by the Thirteenth Amendment, which was ratified on December 6, 1865, six months before Carpenter shot Henry Burgess. What once would have been an open-and-shut case was suddenly difficult to handicap. Justice Wright's ruling would set precedent for postslavery South Carolina.

By the time *Burgess v. Carpenter* reached the state Supreme Court in the spring of 1870, Reconstruction was under full sail. The federal government, in a historic burst of constitutional amendments and civil rights statutes, had abolished slavery, established birthright citizenship, and promised basic civil rights and equal protection of the law to all persons. Most recently, just three months before the South Carolina Supreme Court's *Burgess* ruling, the Fifteenth Amendment was ratified, declaring that no state could deny citizens the right to vote on account of race, color, or previous condition of servitude. In the later words of US Supreme Court justice John Marshall Harlan, these momentous reforms had "removed the race line from our governmental systems."[10]

South Carolina law changed just as much as federal law did during Reconstruction. Early in 1868, elected delegates convened in Charleston to produce a new, postslavery Constitution for South Carolina. The majority of

---

5. Ibid., 19.

6. Ibid., 17.

7. "Negro Stealing," *Charleston Courier*, June 3, 1858, 2

8. O'Neall, 17.

9. Robert Olwell, *Masters, Slaves, and Subjects: The Culture of Power in the South Carolina Low Country, 1740–1790* (Ithaca, NY: Cornell University Press, 1998), 70–71; "A Sad Picture," *Charleston Courier*, Sept. 10, 1858, 2; "Negro Stealing," 2; "Commutation of Sentence," *Charleston Courier*, Jan. 24, 1857, 4; O'Neall, 19.

10. Plessy v. Ferguson, 163 U.S. 537, 555 (1896).

the delegates who attended this convention, like the majority of the state's population at the time, were Black people. The Charleston convention produced a strikingly democratic state constitution. Gone were the racial designations that had stained South Carolina's previous constitutions. In their place were glittering egalitarian principles: "All men are born free and equal"; all men are "endowed by their Creator with certain inalienable rights";[11] "Slavery shall never exist in this State."[12] With surgical precision, the new document excised every racially discriminatory feature of preemancipation South Carolina law. Voting and office-holding had always been, by law, a whites-only prerogative in the state. Now, the right of suffrage spread to all male citizens twenty-one years and up "without distinction of race, color, or former condition" of servitude.[13] Racial designations were similarly removed as qualifications for public office-holding. (Voting and office-holding eligibility were also purged of property qualifications—with important implications, given how poor most Black—and many white—South Carolinians were.[14]) Previously, Black people had not been allowed to testify against whites in court. The new constitution countered: "No person shall be disqualified as witness."[15] Previously, the state's enslaved majority had not been allowed to own property, make contracts, or receive lessons in reading or writing. Now, no person could be "prevented from acquiring, holding, and transmitting property, or be hindered in acquiring education."[16]

The Reconstruction Constitution of 1868 did not transform South Carolina into an egalitarian paradise. For one thing, white people retained overwhelming economic supremacy, even after emancipation had released the more than four hundred thousand Black South Carolinians whom enslavers had considered their personal chattel and who collectively had constituted the state's most valuable form of property.[17] The facts of *Burgess v. Carpenter* illustrated economic disparities. The two white litigants were affluent landowners, while the injured Black man was a landless agricultural laborer.

---

11. S.C. Const. of 1868, art. I, § 1.
12. Ibid., art. I, § 2.
13. Ibid., art. VIII, § 2.
14. Ibid., art. I, § 31–32; art. II, § 10; art. III, § 3; art. IV, § 10.
15. Ibid., art. I, § 12.
16. Ibid.
17. Walter Edgar, *South Carolina: A History* (Columbia: University of South Carolina Press, 1998), 285.

The 1868 Constitution also faced formidable political obstacles. Most white South Carolinians thoroughly rejected it and eventually embraced an almost religious crusade to restore white supremacy.[18] That crusade was led by a Democratic party that had played no role in the constitution's creation. (All 124 delegates to the Constitutional Convention of 1868 were Republicans.[19]) South Carolina Democrats complained of Republican corruption, bewailed what they called their state's "Africanization," and fought ruthlessly to retake power. The Ku Klux Klan and like groups contributed violence and intimidation. These white terror groups threatened, beat, and murdered Republicans, white and Black. Among their murder victims were three sitting members of the state legislature. Political violence of this sort prompted South Carolina's Republican governor to decry, in the fall of 1868, the "systematic effort, by abuse and intimidation, to deter colored persons from the exercise of the elective franchise."[20]

And yet, the new constitution was no dead letter. For a time, at least, it ushered in real change. Black people then constituted around 60 percent of South Carolina's population. As one might expect in a democracy, slightly over half of the 487 elected officials in South Carolina between 1867 and 1876 were Black men. In other words, Black representation was roughly proportional. And public officials in South Carolina were attentive to the needs of their constituents. The State Assembly adopted antidiscrimination measures that sought to equalize access to restaurants, theaters, and other public accommodations.[21] It also obeyed the new Constitution's command to "provide for a . . . uniform system of free public schools" for "all the children and youths of the State, without regard to race or color."[22] Although, in practice, most schools were racially segregated,[23] public education for all

18. Thomas Holt, *Black over White: Negro Political Leadership in South Carolina during Reconstruction* (Urbana: University of Illinois Press, 1977), 4.

19. Hyman S. Rubin III, "Reconstruction," in *The South Carolina Encyclopedia*, ed. Walter Edgar (Columbia: University of South Carolina Press, 2006), 780.

20. "Proclamations by His Excellency Robert K. Scott, Governor of South Carolina," *Tri-Weekly Mercury* (Charleston, SC), Oct. 24, 1868, 4.

21. Holt, *Black over White*, 1; Joel Williamson, *After Slavery: The Negro in South Carolina during Reconstruction, 1861-1877* (Chapel Hill: University of North Carolina Press, 1965); Edgar, *South Carolina*, 389–93.

22. S.C. Const. of 1868, art. X, § 3, 10.

23. In one Charleston school, Black and white children occupied separate floors but shared a playground. This limited experiment in semiintegration ended when the local white

children, whatever their race, was nonetheless one of South Carolina's major Reconstruction-era successes.[24]

In addition to revolutionizing South Carolina's political system, Reconstruction revolutionized its legal system. For the first time ever, Black South Carolinians had equal access to all of the state's courts as litigants, witnesses, and jurors. And because jurors were fished from the pool of registered voters, the new Constitution's democratization of voting also democratized jury service. Throughout Reconstruction, Black South Carolinians served proportionally on juries.[25]

Reconstruction likewise transformed the state bar. No Black lawyers are known to have served in South Carolina prior to 1866.[26] From that year until 1877, the state bar admitted forty-nine Black lawyers, almost one-quarter of all new admittees during those years.[27] The first Black lawyers to practice in South Carolina were northerners who came south with the Union Army, the Freemen's Bureau, or groups such as the abolitionist American Missionary Association. By the end of Reconstruction, however, native-born South Carolinians had overtaken outsiders in the state's Black bar.[28] South Carolina's new Black lawyers made a difference. They helped write the egalitarian Constitution of 1868. They held public office. They educated the Black community about their new rights. And, of course, they represented clients in court. Overwhelmingly, they did criminal defense work, since most of their clients were too poor for civil litigation. They won more than they lost in court. It surely helped that Reconstruction-era South

---

community erupted in protest. Racial segregation resulted there and in almost all parts of the state. Edgar, *South Carolina*, 390.

24. Ibid.

25. "An Act to Regulate the Manner of Drawing Juries," in *The Constitution of South Carolina, adopted April 16, 1868, and the Acts and Joint Resolutions of the General Assembly Passed at the Special Session of 1868, Together with the Military Orders Therein Re-Enacted* (Columbia: John W. Denny, 1868), 119. For more on jury composition during and after Reconstruction, see chapter 5.

26. William Lewis Burke, *All for Civil Rights: African American Lawyers in South Carolina, 1868–1968* (Athens: University of Georgia Press, 2017), 8.

27. Burke, *All for Civil Rights*, 220.

28. John Oldfield, "The African American Bar in South Carolina, 1877–1915," in *At Freedom's Door: African American Founding Fathers and Lawyers in Reconstruction South Carolina*, ed. James Lowell Underwood and W. Lewis Burke Jr. (Columbia: University of South Carolina Press, 2000), 116–17.

Carolina was a majority-Black state and its juries—for a time—were racially representative. This pioneering cohort of Black lawyers asserted the rights of the recently rightsless and defended the freedoms of the recently unfree. They were the state's first civil rights lawyers.[29]

Black South Carolinians had less of an impact on the state's bench than on its bar, but Black judges did serve. Some worked in minor courts, such as probate courts.[30] Some served on more influential tribunals, such as a high-profile criminal court in Charleston County.[31] The state's most prominent Black jurist was Jonathan Jasper Wright, who joined the South Carolina Supreme Court in 1870 and served until 1877. He was the first Black member of any state supreme court in US history.[32]

One of Justice Wright's first tasks on the state's high court was to write the opinion in *Burgess v. Carpenter* (1870), the case of the injured farm worker. Wright would have to decide whether agricultural employers in South Carolina could sue for tortious interference with their employees' labor. Now that slavery had ended, how would South Carolina law define the relationship between landowning employers, most of whom were white people, and landless agricultural workers, most of whom were Black people? One easy option would have been to replace the discarded categories "master and slave" with the common-law categories "master and servant." Justice Wright did not want to do this.

Master and Servant

The legal term "master" originated in the English common law of "master and servant." Americans were aware of this long history. A northern treatise published in the 1870s noted that English courts originally restricted the categories "master and servant" to domestic employment contexts. Like the similarly domestic categories of "husband and wife" and "parent and child," "master and servant" originally suggested household relationships. Unlike

29. Burke, *All for Civil Rights*.

30. Ibid., 34–35.

31. Ibid., 33–34.

32. J. Clay Smith Jr., "The Reconstruction of Justice Jonathan Jasper Wright," in *At Freedom's Door*, 72; Frederic D. Schwarz, "The Reluctant Judge," *American Legacy* 10, no. 3 (fall 2004): 16; Susan Coleman, "Wright, Jonathan Jasper, 1840–1885," in *The Great American Judges: An Encyclopedia*, ed. John R. Vile (Santa Barbara, CA: ABC-CLIO, 2003), 828.

other sorts of employees, "servants" typically lived with "masters'" families, were employed for long terms, and performed household tasks. The servant's central objective was "to serve about the master's house and to attend upon him personally." The English common law referred to other sorts of workers—"clerks, farm hands, etc."—by other terms, such as "laborers or workmen." Nondomestic workers of this sort were "subjected to different rules" than servants.[33]

The "master and servant" category expanded over time. As English industrialization advanced, home-based employment declined, wage labor increased, and the old legal terms stretched. By the late eighteenth century, "master and servant" had become a catch-all term for employer and employee, generally. William Blackstone's famous *Commentaries on the Laws of England* (1765–1769) referred to all employees, not just domestic workers, as servants, and all employers as masters.[34]

American law, like the American economy, lagged. During the colonial era, a wide range of status existed among American workers, including (in roughly descending order) free artisans, journeymen, apprentices, domestic servants, indentured servants, and enslaved laborers. The "master-servant" legal category remained largely confined to household-based, domestic work relations.[35] In 1795, in what was arguably the young republic's first legal treatise, Connecticut's Zephaniah Swift affirmed America's comparatively narrow understanding of servanthood. "Labourers, or persons hired by the day . . . or any longer time," Swift wrote, "are not by our law . . . considered as servants."[36]

Between the Founding Era and the Civil War, however, the market

33. H. G. Wood, *A Treatise on the Law of Master and Servant: Covering the Relation, Duties, and Liabilities of Employers and Employees* (Albany, NY: John D. Parsons Jr., 1877), 2–3; Douglas Hay and Paul Craven, eds., *Masters, Servants, and Magistrates in Britain & the Empire, 1562–1955* (Chapel Hill: University of North Carolina Press, 2004).

34. William Blackstone, "Of Master and Servant," *Commentaries on the Laws of England* (Oxford: Clarendon Press, 1765–1769); Robert J. Steinfeld, *The Invention of Free Labor: The Employment Relation in English & American Law and Culture, 1350–1870* (Chapel Hill: University of North Carolina Press, 2002), 20–22; Christopher L. Tomlins, *Law, Labor, and Ideology in the Early American Republic* (New York: Cambridge University Press, 1993), 236–38.

35. Christopher L. Tomlins, "The Ties that Bind: Master and Servant in Massachusetts, 1800–1850," *Labor History* 30, no. 2 (Spring 1989): 199–208; Tomlins, *Law, Labor, and Ideology*, 239–41, 255–58.

36. Zephaniah Swift, *A System of the Laws of the State of Connecticut* (Windham, CT: John Byrne, 1795), 1:218, quoted in Tomlins, *Law, Labor, and Ideology*, 255.

economy and industrialization vigorously expanded in the United States. English courts previously had responded to similar economic developments by expanding "master and servant" to cover new employment circumstances.[37] American jurists followed suit, often citing English precedents.[38] Legal scholars noticed. In an 1816 treatise, Connecticut's Tapping Reeve defined masters and servants in terms of interpersonal power dynamics. "A master is one who, by law, has a right to a personal authority over another," Reeve explained, "and such person, over whom such authority may be rightfully exercised, is a servant."[39] Reeve reasoned that, because all workers—be they free factory workers, apprentices, "day-labourers," "menial" domestic workers, debtors forced to work to pay off debts, or enslaved laborers—were subject, to one degree or another, to the "personal authority" of their "masters," they all qualified as "servants."[40] Timothy Walker of Ohio agreed. In his *Introduction to American Law: Designed as a First Book for Students* (1837), Walker acknowledged that the legal phrase "master and servant" did "not sound very harmoniously to republican ears." Nevertheless, he argued, "the legal relation of master and servant must exist . . . wherever civilization furnishes work to be done." Walker specified that, by "the relation of master and servant," he meant "nothing more or less, than that of the *employer* and the *employed*."[41]

Three caveats are due. First, a handful of northern judges resisted the spread of the terms "master" and "servant" on egalitarian grounds. The term "servant," these dissenting judges believed, was demeaning to nondomestic workers, because it implied an un-American degree of social hierarchy. This view was most pronounced in Pennsylvania, which arguably had the nation's

37. Tomlins, *Law, Labor, and Ideology*, 259–92; and William E. Nelson, *The Americanization of the Common Law: The Impact of Legal Change on Massachusetts Society, 1760–1830* (Cambridge, MA: Harvard University Press, 1975).

38. Christopher L. Tomlins, *Freedom Bound: Law, Labor, and Civic Identity in Colonizing English America, 1580–1865* (New York: Cambridge University Press, 2010), 306, 350, 354, 357; John Nockleby, "Tortious Interference with Contractual Relations in the Nineteenth Century: The Transformation of Property, Contract, and Tort," *Harvard Law Review* 93, no. 7 (1980): 1521.

39. Tapping Reeve, *The Law of Baron and Femme, of Parent and Child, of Guardian and Ward, of Master and Servant, and of the Powers of Courts of Chancery* (New Haven, CT: Oliver Steele, 1816), 339.

40. Ibid., 339–78.

41. Timothy Walker, *Introduction to American Law, Designed as a First Book for Students* (Philadelphia: P. H. Nicklin & T. Johnson, 1837), 243.

most egalitarian political culture at the time.[42] The two most important cases of this sort emerged from the Pennsylvania Supreme Court in the 1810s. *Ex parte Meason* (1812) concerned a 1794 state law that was designed to help "servants" recover back wages from the estates of deceased "masters." Pennsylvania's high court had to decide whether, as far as this statute was concerned, ironworkers counted as "servants." The court acknowledged that some people considered the term "*servants*, in its largest extent," broad enough to include "all those employed by another to do any kind of work." But the Court rejected this broad definition, in line with what it called "the common understanding of the country." Popular usage, the Court found, confined servanthood to domestic workers: "That class of persons who make part of a man's family, whose employment is about the house or its appurtenances . . . or who, residing in the house, are at the command of the master."[43] Ironworkers were not "at the command of the master" in this way, and thus were not "servants." Being "unconnected with the domestic scene," ironworkers "may be properly called workmen," but not "servants."[44]

Five years later, that same Pennsylvania court backtracked slightly by ruling, in *Boniface v. Scott* (1817), that barkeepers in taverns legally qualified as servants. The court admitted that a person's job need not be wholly domestic in order for that person to be considered a servant: "If he be partially employed for that purpose, it will be sufficient." But reiterating its awareness of the popular aversion to demeaning labels of servitude, the court stood by its previous ruling that only domestic workers were servants. "In Pennsylvania none are called servants whose persons are not subjected to the coercion of the master," the court explained. "No person to whom wages could be due for his services would endure the name, as it would be considered offensive and a term of reproach." The *Boniface* court considered "all who are employed for hire in the domestic concerns of the family" to be "servants."[45] Tavern barkeepers were sufficiently domestic to qualify for servanthood. Many other sorts of jobs, however, were not.

42. See Andrew Shankman, *Crucible of American Democracy: The Struggle to Fuse Egalitarianism and Capitalism in Jeffersonian Pennsylvania* (Lawrence: University Press of Kansas, 2004); Kim T. Phillips, "Democrats of the Old School in the Era of Good Feelings," *Pennsylvania Magazine of History and Biography* 95, no. 3 (July 1971): 363–82; Eric Foner, *Tom Paine and Revolutionary America* (New York: Oxford University Press, 1976).

43. *Ex parte Meason*, 5 Binn. 167, 175 (P.A. 1812).

44. Ibid., 176.

45. Boniface v. Scott, 3 Serg. & Rawle 351, 352 (PA, 1817).

These two early-nineteenth-century Pennsylvania cases, however, were outliers. As the century progressed, northern legal authorities increasingly applied "master and servant" to the full range of work relations. New York jurist James Kent confidently expressed what had become conventional wisdom by mid-century: "I know of no legal distinction between . . . domestic and other hired servants."[46] All workers—domestics, apprentices, wage laborers, the enslaved—were "servants," according to Kent.[47] Nevertheless, *Meason* and *Boniface*, the two outlying Pennsylvania rulings, remained on the books and would supply future egalitarians with precedents to cite.

A second limitation on the general spread of the "master and servant" category was the growing divide that emerged in the first half of the nineteenth century between legal language and popular language. Within the legal system, as we have seen, "master and servant" expanded, becoming a catch-all term for employment relations generally. But beyond the legal system, many workers, steeped in free-labor ideology,[48] indignantly refused the "servant" label. Inspired by a blend of egalitarianism and racism, white laborers in the North rejected the term "servant," which they associated with Old World hierarchy and New World slavery. They insisted, as one Philadelphia paper put it in 1837, that, outside of the slave states, employment in America "was considered a relation of contract," which "placed both laborer and employer on terms of equality."[49] Charges of "submission" and "oppression," commonly made by English labor radicals, "were not heard among us," this paper claimed, for in egalitarian America, such charges "had no meaning." [50] European visitors were repeatedly struck by the prickly aversion of northern workers—even domestics—to being called "servants." "There is no such relation as *master and servant* in the United States," one English visitor remarked in 1818. "Indeed, the name [servant]

46. James Kent, *Commentaries on American Law*, 6th ed., vol. 2 (New York: William Kent, 1848), 260.

47. Kent, *Commentaries on American Law*, vol. 2, 9th ed. (Boston: Little, Brown, 1858), 274.

48. Eric Foner, *Free Soil, Free Labor, Free Men: The Ideology of the Republican Party before the Civil War* (New York: Oxford University Press, 1970); Jonathan A. Glickstein, *Concepts of Free Labor in Antebellum America* (New Haven, CT: Yale University Press, 1991).

49. "The Laboring Classes," *[Philadelphia] Public Ledger*, Oct. 14, 1837, 2.

50. Ibid.

is not permitted."[51] Another British visitor to the North observed something similar: "If you call at the door of any man, and ask the servant if his master is at home, he will say, 'Master! I have no master: do you want Mr. Such-a-one?'"[52] The white working class's objections to the language of social hierarchy had consequences. It underlay some important early-nineteenth-century reforms, including the effective end of slavery in the North, resistance to slavery's westward spread, the decline of adult indentured servitude, the democratizing (and racist) reforms associated with the Democratic Party in the Age of Jackson,[53] and the "free labor" impulses of the Republican Party during the 1850s, complete with its rejection of the language of servitude and its self-congratulatory distinction between English and American labor relations.[54]

A third caveat regarding the spread of "master and servant" law is that it was regional. It was a northern phenomenon, even though northern jurists presented it as a national one. Our comparative analysis of pre-1865 labor-relations appeals from the New York and South Carolina courts, respectively, reveals clear regional differences.[55] We included in this study pre-

---

51. John Bristed, *America and Her Resources* (London: Henry Colburn, 1818), 459–60; Tomlins, "The Ties that Bind," 193.

52. Richard Parkinson, *A Tour in America 1798, 1799, and 1800* (London: n.p., 1805), 19. For more of the same, see ibid., 30–31; Francis Grund, *The Americans, in their Moral, Social and Political Relations* (Boston: Longman, Rees, Orme, Brown, Green, and Longman, 1837), 2:66; Thomas Colley Grattan, *Civilized America*, vol. 2 (London: Bradbury and Evans, 1859), 155–56, 256–59; and Albert Matthews, *The Terms Hired Man and Help* (Cambridge, 1900), 28–31.

53. Steinfeld, *Intervention of Free Labor*, 8, 11; Sean Wilentz, *The Rise of American Democracy: Jefferson to Lincoln* (New York: W. W. Norton, 2005).

54. Eric Foner, *Free Soil*, 11–12, 15–16; *The Debates of the Constitutional Convention of the State of Iowa*, 2 vols. (Davenport: n.p., 1857), 1, 193, http://www.statelibraryofiowa.org/services/collections/law-library/iaconst; Abraham Lincoln, "Address before the Wisconsin State Agricultural Society, Milwaukee, Wisconsin, September 30th 1859," in *The Collected Works of Abraham Lincoln*, vol. 3: *1858–1860*, ed. Roy P. Basler (New Brunswick, NJ: Rutgers University Press, 1953), 478–79.

55. Similar to the study of New York cases mentioned above, we explored forty-eight South Carolina state court cases from 1801–1865. The same problems apply to the South Carolina data as with New York, but at least rough conclusions have been reached. South Carolina had fewer overall employment-related cases, which is not surprising given New York's overall population advantage. Between 1800 and 1860, as New York's population exploded, South Carolina's population shrank from about 60 percent to about 20 percent of New York's.

1865 cases that post-1865 legal indexers would eventually file under the heading "Master and Servant." The cases concern such issues as employers' liability for injuries to third parties caused by employee negligence, employers' liability for employees' workplace injuries, and workers' suits to recover unpaid wages. Collectively, these cases show that, when it came to embracing the "master and servant" category prior to the Civil War, the North led and the South lagged.

The New York cases track the story described above.[56] Early in the nineteenth century, New York courts largely reserved the term "master and servant" for domestic-based economic relationships, such as apprenticeships.[57] Then, around the 1830s, as railroads chugged and industrialization accelerated, New York courts, often relying on English precedents, applied master-and-servant logic to an ever-widening array of cases. Railroads became "masters"; railroad workers became "servants."[58] Similar things happened

56. William Mogen conducted this research while an undergraduate at Davidson College, funded by a Davidson Research Initiative grant. He used the Westlaw database to explore 147 labor-relations cases from New York State appellate courts from 1801 until 1865. New York was neither the most industrialized of the northern states (that would be Massachusetts) nor was it the least, so it serves as a useful example. Similar trends occurred in other northern states around the same time. See Grinnell v. Phillips, 1 Mass. 529 (1805); Stone v. Codman, 32 Mass. 297, 299 (1834); Inhabitants of Lowell v. Boston & Lowell Railroad Corporation, 40 Mass. 24 (1839); Elder v. Bemis, 43 Mass. 599 (1841); Sproul v. Hemmingway, 31 Mass. 1 (1833). These Massachusetts cases and more are discussed at length in Christopher Tomlins, "Ties that Bind." For further examples spread across the northern states, see Hill v. Morey, 26 Vt. 178 (1854); Cleveland, C. & C. R. Co. v. Keary, 3 Ohio St. 201 (1854); McGuire v. Grant, 25 N.J.L. 356 (1856); Flinn v. Philadelphia, W. & B. R. Co., 1 Houst. 469 (Del., 1857); Byron v. New York State Printing Tel. Co., 26 Barb. 39 (N.Y. 1857); and Chicago & R.I. R. Co. v. Whipple, 22 Ill. 105 (1859).

57. Out of 114 cases actually using master and servant law/language in New York from 1801 to 1865 (the other thirty-three were either only categorized as such or were inapplicable), 20.2 percent referred to it in the domestic context and 15.8 percent with reference to apprenticeship. But most of those cases came before 1840. In the next twenty-five years, either the absolute number of cases was dropped (for apprenticeship) or the rate of increase relative to other categories slowed (for domestic).

58. In the New York case study, after zero railroad-related master-servant cases before 1840, there were seventeen in the next twenty-five years, which overall came to 13.7 percent of the cases actively using master-servant language. For some examples, see McMillan v. Saratoga & W.R. Co., 20 Barb. 449 (N.Y. 1855); Keegan v. Western R. Corp., 4 Seld. 175 (N.Y. 1853); Langlois v. Buffalo & R.R. Co., 19 Barb. 364 (N.Y. 1855); Green v. Hudson River R. Co., 16 How. Pr. 230 (N.Y. 1858). Often, it must be noted, these cases applied the

in manufacturing[59] and municipal employment.[60] Sometimes, as when liability for worker negligence passed to "masters," workers benefited. At other times, as when nondomestic "masters" were allowed to limit the right of their "servants" to contract elsewhere, workers suffered. Either way, the point remains: northern courts enlarged the categories of master and servant during the antebellum years.

South Carolina courts lagged. About 40 percent of the preemancipation South Carolina cases that legal indexers would later file under the heading "Master and Servant" failed to include the actual terms "master and servant." (In New York, the corresponding figure was just 16 percent.) Many of these antebellum South Carolina employment disputes pitted enslavers against white overseers of enslaved workers. Usually, overseers sued for back wages after being fired. Northern courts at the time likely would have invoked master-and-servant doctrine to resolve these run-of-the-mill employment disputes. South Carolina courts, however, resisted invoking the terms "master and servant" in such cases, perhaps due to the day's racial politics, according to which only enslaved people had "masters."[61]

When the South Carolina courts did invoke master-and-servant language, the employment relations at issue spanned a narrower range than was true in New York. Over two-thirds of the South Carolina cases that did include "master and servant" language concerned apprenticeships (40 percent of the total) and slavery (28 percent of the total). The New York sample, by contrast, contained far fewer apprenticeship and slavery cases (under one-fifth of the total, combined), and correspondingly more cases involving

---

fellow servant rule: Coon v. Syracuse & U.R. Co., 6 Barb. 231 (N.Y. 1849); Sherman v. Rochester & S.R. Co., 15 Barb. 574 (N.Y. 1853); Boldt v. New York Cent. R. Co., 4 E.P. Smith 432 (N.Y. 1858); and Wright v. New York Cent. R. Co., 11 E.P. Smith 562 (N.Y. 1862). But those cases still considered a master's liability first, and so are relevant to this study of the master-servant relationship.

59. Ryan v. Fowler, 10 E.P. Smith 410 (N.Y. 1862).

60. Conrad v. Village of Ithaca, 16 N.Y. 158 (1857); and Carmen v. City of New York, 14 Abb. Pr. 301 (N.Y. 1862).

61. For examples of overseer cases that did not invoke "master and servant" language, see McClure v. Pyatt, 4 McCord 26 (S.C. 1826); Byrd v. Boyd, 4 McCord 246 (S.C. 1827); Rogers v. Collier, 2 Bail. 581 (S.C. 1832); State v. Gay, 1 Hill 364 (S.C. 1833); Holcombe v. Townsend, 1 Hill 399 (S.C. 1833); Craig v. Pride, 2 Speers 121 (S.C. 1843); Suber v. Vanlew, 2 Speers 126 (S.C. 1843); Hunter v. Gibson, 3 Rich. 161 (S.C. 1846); Boone v. Lyde, 3 Strob. 77 (S.C. 1848); and Atkinson v. Fraser, 5 Rich. 519 (S.C. 1852).

not only domestic workers but also railroad workers, free agricultural workers, maritime workers, municipal workers, and manufacturing workers.[62]

The South's industrial lag also underlay a change over time. Up through the 1830s, cases indexed under "master and servant" constituted a higher percentage of the total in South Carolina than in New York. As New York industrialized, it overtook South Carolina. For the rest of the century, employment disputes indexed under "master and servant" constituted a higher percentage of total appellate cases in New York than in South Carolina.

The absence of a robust industrial economy in South Carolina explains many of these differences. But the presence of slavery also mattered. Like the Pennsylvania judges considered above, at least some South Carolina judges explicitly argued that England's law of master and servant was ill-suited to South Carolina. But whereas the Pennsylvania judges resisted the master-and-servant category because it was too demeaning to Pennsylvania's workers, South Carolina judges rejected "master and servant" because it was not demeaning enough.

In *Snee v. Trice* (1802), Trice's enslaved workers caused a fire that destroyed three hundred bushels of Snee's corn. Snee sued, under the common-law provision that held masters accountable for their servants' negligence. In charging the jury, the trial judge observed "that there appeared to be a wide difference between white servants in England" and enslaved "negroes" in South Carolina. In England, masters could, in turn, sue negligent servants to recover money after third parties had recovered money from them. The workers' awareness of this possibility "made them extremely careful" at work. By contrast, the trial judge pointed out, enslaved laborers in South Carolina had no money with which to pay monetary damages, and in any event neither enslavers nor anyone else could sue them "for any civil injury." Therefore, the English law of master and servant ill-suited slavery. South Carolina must devise different rules, ones "adapted to the regulation of slaves," a class of workers "unknown in Great Britain." Furthermore, the trial judge argued, the English doctrine holding "masters" liable for the negligence of their "servants" would unfairly leave all enslavers

62. Note that South Carolina courts did invoke "master and servant" analysis in some cases involving labor relations other than those involving apprenticeship, slavery, or overseers. These included a sheriff and his deputy (Barksdale v. Posey, 2 Hill 657 [S.C. 1835]); city employees (Charleston Gaslight Co. v. City Council of Charleston, 9 Rich. 342 [S.C. 1856]); and railroad employees (Murray v. South Carolina R. Co., 1 McMul. 385 [S.C. 1841]).

at the "mercy of their numerous slaves, who might commit what trespasses, or be guilty of what neglects and omissions they thought proper, to the ruin of their masters."[63]

The *Snee* jury disregarded the trial judge's logic and ordered the enslaving defendant to compensate the plaintiff for the whole value of the destroyed corn. An appellate court reversed this plaintiff-friendly verdict. On the very grounds suggested by the trial judge's charge to the jury, the appellate court held that English employment law was ill-suited to South Carolina society due to the distinctiveness of enslaved workers and enslavement. English master-and-servant law was "by no means applicable to the local . . . circumstances of Carolina, where almost the whole of our servants are slaves," the court held. Enslaved workers could not be sued, and therefore lacked that disincentive to negligence. The court also invoked race. Black people, who constituted "almost the whole" of South Carolina's workforce, were "in general a headstrong, stubborn race of people." They "had a volition of their own, and the physical power of doing great injuries to neighbours and others, without the possibility of their masters having any control over them; especially when they happened to be at a distance from them," the court argued. Furthermore, experience had taught the court "how little [enslaved workers] adhered to advice and direction when left alone." The English common law was devised for whites. It would be "a most dangerous thing" to apply it to Blacks by making enslavers "liable in damages for the unauthorized acts of their slaves."[64]

Other South Carolina judges also found master-servant law a bad fit for slavery-based South Carolina, but for different reasons. In an 1824 case, an enslaver sued someone who had injured his enslaved worker. The injuring party invoked master-servant law in an attempt to escape liability. The court rejected this attempt, distinguishing southern slavery, which was based on ownership, from English employment, which was based on the free-labor contract. "An argument . . . has been drawn from a supposed analogy in the relation of master and servant in England . . . and that of master and slave in this country; but it will not hold," the court wrote:

> In England the master has no immediate and direct interest in the person of the servant, and consequently can only be mediately or consequentially

63. Snee v. Trice, 2 S.C.L. 345, 347–48 (S.C. Const. App. 1802).

64. Ibid., at 349–50.

> affected, by an injury done to him; but in this country [South Carolina], the master's property in the slave, is as absolute as in any other article of property. Force committed on a slave, is, therefore an immediate injury to the master.[65]

As time went on, these objections softened, and South Carolina courts grew increasingly willing to apply master-and-servant logic to cases involving slavery.[66] The embrace was never complete, however. Exceptions persisted, based on slavery's distinctive racialization and its chattel-property nature.[67]

The Black Codes

The end of slavery following the Civil War intensified debates about employment law in the US South. Powerful white southerners, once leery of the term "master and servant" out of a preference for "master and slave," now reached for "master and servant" with both arms, dreading the social and economic consequences of an unshackled Black population. Former enslavers had "little faith," as one wrote in a private letter, "in the reliability of the negro as a voluntary laborer."[68] Seeking to recreate the control that they had exercised under slavery, southern whites enacted "Black Codes." These legal codes, which applied exclusively to Black people, replaced the old racial hierarchy of slavery with a new racial hierarchy of "master and servant." South Carolina enacted its Black Code on December 19, 1865, one day after the Thirteenth Amendment formally ended slavery. The code was racially specific, applying only to "persons of color." Among other things, it created a separate district court system for Blacks, perpetuating the antebellum tradition of separate and unequal justice.[69]

South Carolina's Black Code also racialized the term "servant": "All persons of color who make contracts for service or labor, shall be known as servants, and those with whom they contract, shall be known as masters."[70]

65. Carsten v. Murray, Harp. 113, 114–15 (SC, 1824).

66. O'Connell v. Strong, 23 S.C.L. 265, 268 (S.C. App. L. 1838).

67. Bell v. Lakin, 26 S.C.L. 364, 366 (S.C. App. L. 1841).

68. [______] to My Dear Mr. Grimball, Feb. 16, 1866, box 3, John Berkley Grimball Papers, David M. Rubenstein Rare Book & Manuscript Library, Duke University.

69. Williamson, *After Slavery*, 74–79; Edgar, *South Carolina*, 383–84.

70. "An Act to Establish and Regulate the Domestic Relations of Persons of Color and to

The code also sketched out the basic obligations that masters and their Black servants owed each other. The latter were to rise at dawn, "feed, water and care for the animals on the farm," "do the usual and needful work about the premises," and prepare the day's meals. They were to complete all of these tasks by "sun-rise," at which time they would turn to the real work of the day: farm labor.[71] Other provisions of the South Carolina Black Code extended beyond workplace control. For example, servants could not be absent from the premises—or invite guests to the premises—without their masters' permission.[72]

Like the Old South slave codes, the postemancipation Black Codes assumed that "masters" had a quasi-ownership interest in their "colored" "servants'" labor. Criminal and civil penalties awaited "any person who shall deprive a master of the service of his servant." Convicted violators risked fines ranging from twenty dollars to $200, as well as imprisonment or hard labor of up to sixty days. Violators also faced the possibility that masters would file civil suits, seeking to "recover damages for loss of services."[73] One of South Carolina's goals was to discourage labor-starved landowners from poaching each other's workers, thereby driving up labor costs. This was a widespread concern. Other southern states included similar antienticement provisions in their post–Civil War Black Codes. North Carolina empowered masters to sue labor enticers for double the value of the damages.[74] Alabama threatened fines of up to $500.[75] Among the possible punishments that labor enticers faced in Florida were fines of up to $1,000 and up to thirty-nine whip stripes across the bare back.[76]

Amend the Law in Relation to Paupers and Vagrancy, Act No. 4733," *The Statutes at Large of South Carolina*, vol. 12: *Containing the Acts from December 1861 to December 1866* (Columbia, SC: Republican Printing, 1875), 274, South Carolina Department of Archives and History, Columbia, South Carolina.

71. Ibid., 275.

72. Ibid., 275.

73. Ibid., 276.

74. N.C. Public Laws, *Public Laws of the State of North Carolina, Passed by the General Assembly, 1865–1866* (Raleigh: Robert W. Best, 1866), 126; James B. Browning, "The North Carolina Black Code," *Journal of Negro History* 15, no. 4 (Oct. 1930): 468.

75. Alabama Black Codes, February 16, 1866, in Edward McPherson, *The Political History of the United States of America during the Period of Reconstruction* (Washington: Solomons & Chapman, 1875), 33–34; David Martin, "The Birth of Jim Crow in Alabama, 1865–1896," *National Black Law Journal* 13, no. 1 (1993): 187.

76. McPherson, *Political History*, 39–40.

Southern Black Codes provoked northern outrage. Republicans saw them as proof that the South was unrepentant and sought to reestablish slavery in everything but name. Pointing to the South Carolina Code, including its antienticement provisions, the *Chicago Tribune* found "no words adequate to express our sense of the baseness of such efforts to smuggle slavery back into existence."[77] The *Tribune*, however, rejoiced that at least the all-white South Carolina legislature and its oppressive Black Codes had "hatched out [of] the serpent's egg of [lenient, Presidential] 'Reconstruction'" in time for northerners "to see its offspring wriggle."[78]

Northerners vowed to stamp out this neo-Confederate wriggling. Union military commanders, still occupying the South, took political control. In South Carolina, Major General Daniel E. Sickles, local commander of the Union's occupation forces, declared the state's Black Codes null and void in January of 1866, shortly after their passage.[79] White South Carolinians were indignant. In the far west of the state, the *Keowee Courier* grumbled, referring to Sickles's order voiding the Black Codes: "We do not relish the idea clearly put forth in this order, namely: That, for all legal purposes, equality exists between the races."[80] But local supporters of the voided Black Codes could do little. As the northern press reported, South Carolina was "thoroughly subject to the will and control of the national authority."[81]

The Freedmen's Bureau

One of the national government's most pressing concerns was the replacement of slavery with an orderly system of free labor. The body initially charged with this undertaking was the Freedmen's Bureau, which Congress

---

77. "Black Codes," *Chicago Tribune*, reprinted in *New Orleans Tribune*, Dec. 24, 1865, 3.

78. Ibid.

79. "South Carolina Freedmen: Improved Condition of Labor and Laborers," *New York Herald*, Jan. 29, 1866, 8; "From the South," *Jackson Citizen Patriot* (Michigan), Jan. 29, 1866, 4; "The Real Enemies of Speedy Restoration," *New York Herald-Tribune*, Jan. 29, 1866, 4; Edgar, *South Carolina*, 384; "Official: Headq'rs, Department of South Carolina, Charleston, Jan. 1, 1866," *Keowee Courier* (Walhalla, SC), Feb. 3, 1866, 1.

80. "Official: Headq'rs," 2.

81. "Reconstruction," *Commercial Advertiser* (New York), Jan. 27, 1886, 2.

established within the Department of War in March of 1865.[82] The Bureau's tasks were mammoth: to oversee the South's conversion from slavery; to manage abandoned and confiscated lands in the former Confederacy; and to handle "all subjects"—food, shelter, legal services, education, health care, and more—"relating to refugees and freedmen from rebel states."[83] Considering the enormity of these goals, the Bureau's tools were puny. It relied on the War Department for funding and staff and never had enough of either.[84] Although it was charged with serving millions of formerly enslaved people across the South, the Bureau never had more than nine hundred agents in the field at any one time. In addition to being overstretched and underfunded, the Bureau was short-lived. It ceased most of its functions by 1869, just four years after its founding. Congress pulled the plug on it entirely in 1872.[85] But the Bureau's short existence came at a crucial time, enabling it to make an important mark on the postemancipation South.

The voluntary labor contract was the cornerstone of the Freedmen's Bureau's approach to labor relations. Signing labor contracts, however, did not come naturally to some postemancipation South Carolinians. In a private letter written in January 1866, one South Carolina landowner described an informal labor arrangement with Josey, a recently emancipated laborer who had chosen to remain: "I have made no written agreement with Josey. . . . People up here do not make [written] agreements."[86] The Freedmen's Bureau feared that the lack of labor contracts gave the advantage to

82. Donald G. Nieman, *To Set the Law in Motion: The Freedmen's Bureau and the Legal Rights of Blacks, 1865–1869* (Millwood NY: KTO Press, 1979), 72–73.

83. "Chap. XC—An Act to Establish a Bureau for the Relief of Freedmen and Refugees," approved March 3, 1865, *U.S. Statutes at Large, Treaties, and Proclamations of the United States of America*, vol. 13 (Boston: n.p., 1866), 507–9.

84. Eric Foner, *Reconstruction: America's Unfinished Revolution 1863–1877* (New York: Harper & Row, 1988), 69.

85. James L. Roark, "From Lords to Landlords," *Wilson Quarterly* 2 (Spring 1978): 127; David S. Leventhal, "'Freedom to Work, Nothing More or Less:' The Freedmen's Bureau, White Planters, and Black Contract Labor in Postwar Tennessee, 1865–1868," *Journal of East Tennessee History* 78 (2006): 23–49; James D. Schmidt, "'A Full-Fledged Government of Men': Freedmen's Bureau Labor Policy in South Carolina, 1865–1868," in *The Freedmen's Bureau and Reconstruction: Reconsiderations*, ed. Paul C. Cimbala and Randall M. Miller (New York: Fordham University Press, 1999), 247.

86. Meta Grimball to John Berkley Grimball, Jan. 5, 1866, box 3, John Berkley Grimball Papers, David M. Rubenstein Rare Book & Manuscript Library, Duke University.

powerful landowners over landless workers. Hoping to empower freedmen, Bureau officials distributed template contracts, pressured landowners and workers to sign, and adjudicated contractual disputes.[87]

The labor rules that the Freedmen's Bureau established differed from the short-lived post–Civil War Black Codes in two crucial ways. Perhaps most obviously, they were not racially specific. South Carolina's Black Code applied only to "persons of color." By contrast, the military order that voided South Carolina's Black Code, and which foreshadowed the Freedmen's Bureau policy to come,[88] declared that, henceforth, "all laws shall be applicable alike" to all inhabitants, regardless of race.[89]

Second, the Freedman's Bureau meticulously avoided using the terms "master" and "servant." The South Carolina Black Code had relied heavily on those terms. A template labor contract included in the Black Code had begun: "I (*name of servant*) do hereby agree with (*name of master*) to be his (here insert the words '*household servant*' [domestic worker] or '*servant in husbandry* [field hand],' as the case may be)."[90] Freedman's Bureau officials carefully dodged these terms. The Bureau's template labor contracts, and its recommended "Plantation Rules and Regulations," studiously avoided these words. Rather than referring to "masters," they referred to landowners as "employers," "farmers," "planters," or "landowners." For "servants," they wrote "employees," "laborers," "hands," or sometimes "freedmen and women."[91] Occasionally, Bureau officials slipped, as when one used the term

87. "Monthly Report of Contracts Approved by Lt. M. J. De Forest A.A.A. General Sub District of Darlington, and Sub. Dist. Commr. Dist. Darlington for the month of January 1867," reel 1478, South Carolina State Archives, Columbia; regarding the Bureau's adjudicative role in South Carolina, see Martin Linton Abbott, *The Freedmen's Bureau in South Carolina, 1865–1872* (Chapel Hill: University of North Carolina Press, 1967), 103–4; Foner, *Reconstruction*, 143.

88. Schmidt, "A Full-Fledged Government of Men,'" 228.

89. "Official: Headq'rs," 1; Foner, *Reconstruction*, 209; Edgar, *South Carolina*, 384; James D. Schmidt, "'A Full-Fledged Government of Men,'" 227–28; Holt, *Black over White*, 23.

90. "An Act to Establish," 279; D. L. Wardlaw and Armistead Burt, "Report of the Committee on the Code," South Carolina General Assembly (1865), 11, University of South Carolina Library, Caroliniana Room.

91. "The State of South Carolina, Chesterfield District, Articles of Agreement Entered into by and between the freedmen and women whose names are hereunto signed on the one part and Allan MacFarlan," Jan. 27, 1866, Allan A. MacFarlan Papers, David M. Rubenstein Rare Book & Manuscript Library, Duke University; "Freedmen's Contracts," *Keowee Courier* (Walhalla, SC), Mar. 3, 1866, 1; "Military Orders," *Keowee Courier* (Walhalla, SC), Mar. 31, 1866, 1; "Our Sumter Correspondence," *Charleston Courier*, Sept. 30, 1868, 1.

"servant" to distinguish domestic workers (servants) from field workers (laborers).[92] On the whole, however, the move from the Black Code to the Freedmen's Bureau was a move away from the logic of master and servant.

The Bureau's days, however, were numbered. The enfranchisement of Black men and the rise of Republican governments in the South seemed to reduce the need for the institution. The embarrassing failure of the Freedmen's Bank, a financial institution that the Bureau established to help freedmen save money, further eroded northern support. By 1872, the Bureau ceased operations.[93] Southern labor disputes reverted to the control of state governments.

Master and Servant in an Age of Emancipation

Despite the centrality of the terms "master and "servant" to northern labor law, many abolitionists objected to them, due to the words' association with slavery. "Master 'is synonymous with owner' in the slavery parlance," a New England newspaper complained in the summer of 1865, as the Thirteenth Amendment was working its way toward ratification.[94] The *Philadelphia Inquirer* came to a similar conclusion later that year, when criticizing the South Carolina Black Code for attempting to reestablish a new version of slavery following emancipation. Under the Palmetto State's Black Code, the *Inquirer* warned, the "legal relation of 'master' and 'servant' supplants that of 'master and slave.'"[95]

During the intoxicating early days of Reconstruction, northern apostles of free labor traveled south, bringing their egalitarian critique of "master and servant" with them. They urged freedpeople to reject the terms, too. Freedpeople were "now responsible no longer to the master, but to the law," South Carolina's Massachusetts-born attorney general Daniel Chamberlain declared in 1870.[96] White southerners protested and cursed the "carpetbag-

92. "Important Circular," *Baltimore Sun*, Mar. 30, 1866.

93. William S. McFeely, *Yankee Stepfather: General O.O. Howard and the Freedmen* (New Haven, CT: Yale University Press, 1968), 327.

94. "A Sad State of Affairs," *Providence Evening Press*, July 12, 1865, 2.

95. "The Black Law of South Carolina," *Philadelphia Inquirer*, Nov. 25, 1865, 4.

96. "The Facts and Figures: The Practical and Truthful Record of the Republican Party of South Carolina; Speech of Hon. D. H. Chamberlain," *Daily Republican* (Charleston, SC), Oct. 15, 1870, 3. For a discussion of Chamberlain's later turn to white supremacy, see Wilton B.

gers" who, in the words of one southern newspaper, taught the Black "servant . . . to regard himself as good as his master [*sic*]."[97]

Free-labor egalitarianism exerted a profound legal impact during Reconstruction. On the national level, it underlay the Reconstruction Amendments and Civil Rights laws. It also prompted some legal thinkers to question the wisdom of using the inherently hierarchical terms "master and servant" to describe labor relations generally. For decades, legal thinkers on both sides of the Atlantic had treated "master-servant" as synonymous with "employer-employee." Now, some reconsidered. Massachusetts scholar James Schouler's *Treatise on the Law of the Domestic Relations* (1870) provides a case in point. Schouler followed Tapping Reeve's early-nineteenth-century example by defining the master in an employment relationship as the "one who has legal authority over another" and the servant as "the person over whom such authority may be rightfully exercised."[98] Yet whereas Reeve (1816) had found nothing problematic in this definition, Schouler, writing at the height of Reconstruction, struggled with it. "The relation of master and servant presupposes two parties who stand on an unequal footing in their mutual dealings," Schouler wrote, "yet not naturally so, as in other domestic relations," such as parent and child. "This relation [of master and servant] is, in theory, hostile to the genius of free institutions. It bears the marks of social caste." Schouler sought to soften these troubling features by asserting, without evidence, that master-servant hierarchies were on their way out, being "of more general importance in ancient than in modern times." Equally free of evidence was his insistence that such hierarchies were "better applicable at this day to English than American society."[99] Were he "untrammeled by authority," Schouler claimed, he would restrict the terms "master and servant" to domestic workers only—a category, he thought, of diminishing importance. But in order to meet "the practical wants of the lawyer," Schouler swallowed his objections and discussed the

Fowler, "A Carpetbagger's Conversion to White Supremacy," *North Carolina Historical Review* 43, no. 3 (July 1966): 286–304.

97. "The Freedmen's Bureau and Northern Interference with the Negro—What Is to Be the Result," *Macon Daily Telegraph* (Georgia), Mar. 30, 1866, 2.

98. James Schouler, *A Treatise on the Law of the Domestic Relations: Embracing Husband and Wife, Parent and Child, Guardian and Ward, Infancy, and Master and Servant* (Boston: Little, Brown, 1870), 599.

99. Ibid.

law of "master and servant" broadly, however "offensive," and "anomal[ous]" it might be.[100]

In 1870, the same year in which Schouler's treatise appeared, *Burgess v. Carpenter* reached the South Carolina Supreme Court, inviting that tribunal to consider what place, if any, master-and-servant law deserved in the postemancipation South.

Burgess v. Carpenter

After emancipation, some formerly enslaved workers did something that, though completely mundane, was intoxicatingly new: they voluntarily moved. Others, however, stayed put. Predicting who would stay and who would go was difficult. "It does seem strange," one former enslaver wrote in 1866 of a formerly enslaved worker who had stuck around, "that this man so bad tempered . . . should be the one to remain with us."[101]

One Black worker who seems to have stayed put was Henry Burgess, a "ploughman" in Clarendon County, South Carolina, roughly midway between Charleston and Columbia.[102] His employer was W. R. Burgess. The shared surname suggests that W. R. or his ancestors may have claimed ownership in Henry or his ancestors.[103] At the beginning of 1866, W. R. Burgess hired Henry Burgess for the year. Their contract described a typical sharecropping arrangement. W. R. would provide Henry and other workers with the use of farmland, provisions, and stock, including a plow horse for Henry, in exchange for two-thirds of the resulting crop. Henry and the other workers would provide their labor and split a one-third share.[104]

A bullet shattered this arrangement. That June, a white man named W. R. Carpenter shot and injured Henry Burgess, idling his horse and stilling his plow.[105] According to witness testimony, W. R. Burgess, the landowner,

100. Ibid., 599–601.

101. Meta Grimball to John Berkley Grimball.

102. Burgess v. Carpenter.

103. John C. Inscoe, "Carolina Slave Names: An Index to Acculturation," *Journal of Southern History* 49, no. 4 (Nov. 1983): 548–49.

104. Burgess v. Carpenter.

105. The circumstances of the shooting remain unknown. On white-on-Black violence generally during these years, see Stephen Kantrowitz, *Ben Tillman and the Reconstruction of*

"took [Henry] to his house and nursed him for several weeks . . . while he was unable to work." All summer, W. R. fed Henry, at an estimated cost of two or three dollars per month. He also fed the horse. Hiring a replacement was apparently not an option. Most local agricultural workers had entered annual labor contracts the previous winter, rendering them unavailable in June. The stoppage of Henry's plow "seriously damaged" Burgess's yield. By the time Henry was back on his feet—"some time in August"—the crop's value had dropped "at least $400."[106]

W. R. Burgess sued W. R. Carpenter, the shooter, seeking to recover damages sustained due to "loss of service of a hired servant." The trial in Clarendon County had scarcely begun when the trial judge called it off. The trial judge found that the sharecropping agreement made the two Burgesses contracting copartners, not "master and servant." Because Henry Burgess was not W. R. Burgess's servant, W. R. could not recover damages from Carpenter for "loss of service of a hired servant," as his suit sought to do. Judge Green ordered an immediate nonsuit.[107]

W. R. Burgess appealed to the South Carolina Supreme Court. The case raised several essential questions: What would replace slavery? What claims did landowners have to the labor of their workers? Would the banned legal categories "master and slave" give way to the different but still hierarchical categories "master and servant"? Or would postemancipation southern law reconceptualize plantation employment relations in terms of voluntary labor agreements between juridical equals? Early in Reconstruction, these questions were entirely up for grabs.

Jonathan Jasper Wright

Responsibility for writing the *Burgess v. Carpenter* decision fell to a brand-new member of the South Carolina Supreme Court: Associate Justice Jona-

White Supremacy (Chapel Hill: University of North Carolina Press, 2000); LeeAnn Whites, *Gender Matters: The Civil War, Reconstruction, and the Making of the New South* (New York: Palgrave MacMillan, 2005); Bertram Wyatt-Brown, *Southern Honor: Ethics and Behavior in the Old South* (New York: Oxford University Press, 1982); Michael Stephen Hindus, *Prison and Plantation: Crime, Justice, and Authority in Massachusetts and South Carolina, 1767–1878* (Chapel Hill: University of North Carolina Press, 1980); and Elizabeth Fox-Genovese, *Within the Plantation Household* (Chapel Hill: University of North Carolina Press, 1988).

106. Burgess v. Carpenter.

107. Ibid.

than Jasper Wright. Wright had extensive experience helping freedmen adjust to life after slavery but scant experience as a judge. When he and two others were admitted to the state bar in September of 1868, they became the first three Black lawyers in South Carolina history.[108] Just a year and a half later, in February of 1870, he joined the state's highest court. The *Burgess* ruling, three months later, was his second judicial opinion of any sort, making the case something of a milestone, for Justice Wright was the first Black member of a state supreme court in United States history.[109]

Much about *Burgess v. Carpenter* (1870) must have resonated with Justice Wright, given his past. Although the case's two named parties were both white farmers, Wright's ruling emphasized a third party: Henry Burgess, the Black farmworker whose injury was the case's central fact. Wright's background helps explain his emphasis. He, too, had been a Black farm worker. The 1860 census, compiled ten short years before he joined South Carolina's top court, lists Wright as a twenty-one-year-old Black, "farm laborer" (not "servant") in Pennsylvania.[110]

Wright was born in Pennsylvania in 1840, making him a young thirty or so at the time of *Burgess*. "My father [Samuel Wright]," Jonathan Wright later told an interviewer, "was a runaway slave from Baltimore, but my mother was always free."[111] Samuel Wright rose from Maryland slavery to become a land-owning Pennsylvania farmer.[112] He taught his son about slavery, social mobility, and the dignity of land ownership.

Jonathan Wright became a lifelong advocate of education, perhaps because he struggled so hard to attain one. "My early educational advantages were not good," he later explained, "for my parents were very poor. I went to [local, segregated] school some winters and worked summers [on neighboring farms] to pay my way."[113] At age fifteen, Jonathan was fortunate enough to be taken on by a private tutor, a staunch opponent of slavery and

108. Burke, *All for Civil Rights*, 224, app. A.

109. Greg Goelzhauser, "Diversifying State Supreme Courts," *Law and Society Review* 45, no. 3 (2011): 762.

110. United States Census (1860), Pennsylvania, Susquehanna County, series M653, roll 1186, 859.

111. "The Black Judge," *Cincinnati Commercial* (Ohio), May 12, 1871, 2.

112. Susan Coleman, "Wright, Jonathan Jasper," in *Great American Judges: An Encyclopedia*, John R. Vile (Santa Barbara, CA: ABC-CLIO, 2003), 828.

113. "The Black Judge," 2; "Hon. J. J. Wright," *Harpers Weekly*, Mar. 5, 1870, 149, http://blackhistory.harpweek.com/7Illustrations/Reconstruction/JJWright.htm.

a member of a formerly all-white Presbyterian church that Wright had joined. Wright studied privately for three years, absorbing antislavery values along with school lessons. He then studied for two additional years at an academy in upstate New York.[114]

Wright graduated in 1860 and spent the next four years teaching in Pennsylvania's segregated schools. Concurrently, he read law, first in a lawyer's office and then in a judge's chambers.[115] The free-labor-based Pennsylvania law that he learned would influence his later jurisprudence. *Meason*[116] and *Boniface*,[117] the distinctively egalitarian employment rulings from Pennsylvania during the Early Republic, described above, may well have been part of his studies; Wright would later cite these Pennsylvania precedents on the South Carolina bench. In 1864, Wright sought admission to the Pennsylvania bar but was turned down on account of his race.[118] He gained admission two years later, following passage of federal civil rights laws, becoming Pennsylvania's first Black lawyer.[119]

The Civil War stirred Wright to activism. In 1864, he attended Frederick Douglass's National Convention of Colored Men in Syracuse, New York, a gathering that urged abolition, legal equality, and universal manhood suffrage. The following year, at the State Equal Rights Convention of the Colored People of Pennsylvania, Wright decried the Keystone State's disfranchisement of Black men and demanded political equality. "We have come [to this convention]," Wright declared, "to ask that our white fellow-citizens . . . act as though they believe in their own Declaration of Independence, and especially in its assertion, that all men are equal."[120] Wright also

114. Richard Gergel and Belinda Gergel, "'To Vindicate the Cause of the Downtrodden': Associate Justice Jonathan Jasper Wright and Reconstruction in South Carolina," in *At Freedom's Door*, 36–37; Ronald G. Coleman, "Wright, Jonathan J.," BlackPast, Jan. 29, 2007, http://www.blackpast.org/?q=aah/wright-jonathan-j-1840-1885; Frederic D. Schwarz, "The Reluctant Judge," *American Legacy* 10, no. 3 (Fall 2004).

115. Susan Coleman, "Wright, Jonathan Jasper," in *Great American Judges*, 828.

116. *Ex parte Meason*, 175.

117. Boniface v. Scott, 352.

118. Arnold H. Taylor, "Wright, Jonathan Jasper," *Dictionary of American Negro Biography*, Rayford W. Logan and Michael R. Winston, eds. (New York: W. W. Norton, 1982), 669–70; Schwarz, "The Reluctant Judge," 16.

119. Coleman, "Wright, Jonathan Jasper," 828; Schwarz, 16.

120. *Proceedings of the State Equal Rights' Convention of the Colored People of Pennsylvania, Held in the City of Harrisburg, February 8th, 9th, and 10th, 1865* (Philadelphia: C. Crummill, 1865), 4. On the disfranchisement of nonwhite Pennsylvanians, see Edward Price, "The

thanked God for "bringing upon the country this bloody rebellion [the Civil War] as an exterminator of the barbarous system of American slavery."[121] Wright urged Black Americans to "lose no time" in demanding their overdue rights and predicted that they would prevail. The convention erupted in "deafening applause."[122]

Inspired, Wright, under the auspices of the American Missionary Association, headed south in April of 1865, to help build a postslavery world. In South Carolina, he experienced a Horatio Alger-like ascent and had a powerful impact. He organized and taught in freedmen's schools, dispensed legal advice, lectured on public issues, and established himself as a powerful moderate in the state's Republican politics.[123]

The Freedmen's Bureau hired Wright as a lawyer in 1867. His charge was "assisting free people in legal affairs."[124] Much of his work concerned agricultural labor. He urged Black workers to seek the fairest possible terms in their negotiations with white landowners and endorsed the Radical Republican ideal of Black landownership—achieved, if necessary, by "the breaking up of land monopolies."[125] His father's example surely informed Wright's support for Black land ownership. If Black people could not acquire land, Wright thought, they should at least strive to become renters (tenant farmers), rather than wage laborers.[126] Renters were comparatively less subservient to landowners, he reasoned.

In 1868, Wright left the Freedmen's Bureau to participate in South Carolina's state constitutional convention. He played a leading role, serving as one of the convention's five vice presidents, three of whom were white

---

Black Voting Rights Issue in Pennsylvania, 1780–1900," *Pennsylvania Magazine of History and Biography* 100, no. 3 (July, 1976): 356–73.

121. Ibid., 26.

122. Ibid., 37.

123. Gergel and Gergel, "To Vindicate," 39; Julie Saville, *The Work of Reconstruction: From Slave to Wage Laborer in South Carolina, 1860-1870* (New York: Cambridge University Press, 1994), 161; "South Carolina Colored Convention," *The Liberator* (Boston, Mass.), Dec. 8, 1865, 195; "Reconstruction. South Carolina. Another Meeting of Colored Men in Columbia," *San Antonio (Texas) Express*, May 15, 1867, 1.

124. Quoted in Gergel and Gergel, "To Vindicate," 40.

125. From a resolution proposed by the Republican Association of Beaufort District, of which Wright was a leading member, quoted in "Reconstruction. South Carolina. Another Meeting of Colored men in Columbia," *San Antonio Express* (Texas), May 15, 1867, 1.

126. Saville, "The Work of Reconstruction," 190.

men.[127] All told, he addressed the convention some eighty times, mostly on the need to improve public education, to eradicate "all elements of the institution of slavery,"[128] and to avoid the inadvisable excesses pressed by more radical delegates.[129] The *Charleston Daily News*, no cheerleader for Republicans or Black people, reported that Wright "could out talk any man on the floor of the convention." He was "clear headed, quick as a flash, [and] by no means a bitter Radical."[130] Wright's prominence at the convention launched him into a state senate race in April 1868. He and nine other Black candidates won, becoming the first Black state senators in South Carolina history.[131] A New York newspaper deemed Wright "the most notable negro in the Legislature."[132]

Early in 1870, a vacancy opened on the South Carolina Supreme Court. The state legislature selected Wright to fill it. The *New York Times* recognized this as "an event of no ordinary significance." At the time, the paper reckoned, state supreme court justice was "the highest position ever yet attained by a negro" not just in the United States, but in the history of the world. Or "at least," the *Times* qualified, "in any civilized country."[133]

Burgess v. Carpenter on Appeal

Scholars have characterized Justice Wright as a timid judicial formalist whose "strict adherence to the law"—along with a "proclivity not to offend the white establishment"—led him to sublimate his "personal attitudes and ideology about the subject matter of the litigation."[134] This assessment may characterize some of Wright's later opinions, but it misconstrues *Burgess v.*

127. R. H. Woody, "Jonathan Jasper Wright, Associate Justice of the Supreme Court of South Carolina, 1870–77," *Journal of Negro History* 18 (Apr. 1933): 116.

128. Quoted in Taylor, "Wright, Jonathan Jasper," 669.

129. Woody, "Jonathan Jasper Wright," 116.

130. Quoted in Gergel and Gergel, "To Vindicate," 43; and Woody, "Jonathan Jasper Wright," 117.

131. Gergel and Gergel, "To Vindicate," 43.

132. "South Carolina: The Legislature," *New York Daily Tribune*, Feb. 2, 1870, 2.

133. "Election of Senator Wright (Colored) to the Supreme Bench of South Carolina," *New York Times*, Feb. 7, 1870, 5.

134. Coleman, "Wright," 831; Clay J. Smith Jr., "The Reconstruction of Justice Jonathan Wright," in *At Freedom's Door*, 77.

Carpenter (1870), his first important decision.[135] In *Burgess*, Wright's enslaved ancestry, rural and working-class upbringing, anti-slavery schooling, Pennsylvania legal training, Freedmen's Bureau legal advocacy, and Reconstruction-era political activism combined to produce a bold ruling.

As described above, the case began when W. R. Burgess (white) sued W. R. Carpenter (white) for wounding Henry Burgess ("colored"), whom the plaintiff had "employed as a ploughman." W. R. Burgess sued under a common-law rule that allowed "masters" to recover damages caused by the "loss of service of a hired servant." The trial court had ruled that the plaintiff had no case because the injured worker was not a "hired servant." W. R. Burgess appealed.[136]

Justice Wright's ruling for the South Carolina Supreme Court upheld the trial court's nonsuit but was much more expansive in its reasoning. The trial judge had found that sharecroppers such as Henry Burgess were not servants but left open the possibility that other agricultural workers might be. Justice Wright, by contrast, refused to apply the hierarchical, demeaning label "servant" to any agricultural worker, whatever the nature of the employment relationship.[137]

Wright began with an egalitarian flourish. Echoing the free-labor ideology to which he had been exposed in the antislavery movement, in the Republican Party, and in the Freedmen's Bureau, Wright declared that, "the relation of master and servant, as it existed in England, was wholly different from the relation of employer and employed as it exists in this county."[138] This was untrue.[139] But the notion that America's democratic air was too pure for "masters" or "servants" to breathe provided a powerful, patriotic, egalitarian preface.

Next, Wright conceded that the common law indeed empowered masters to sue third parties who interfered with their servants' labor. But, he argued, this rule applied only to "menial servants"—that is, domestic servants, to whom masters stood in loco parentis. "No such relation existed between W. R. and Henry Burgess," Wright stated. The nature of the

---

135. Wright's previous two majority opinions for the South Carolina Supreme Court were *Byrd v. Small*, 2 S.C. 388 (1870); and *Reilly v. Whipple*, 2 S.C. 277 (1870).

136. Burgess v. Carpenter.

137. Ibid.

138. Ibid., at 9.

139. Steinfeld, *The Invention of Free Labor*, 20–22; Tomlins, *Law, Labor, and Ideology*, 259–92; Tomlins, *Freedom Bound*, 330–31.

contract—sharecropping, tenant farming, wage labor—made no difference. All that mattered was that Henry was not a domestic worker. "Henry Burgess being exclusively concerned in the cultivation of the soil," Wright explained, "and there being no domestic cast within the nature of his service, he does not fall within the class to which the term 'servant' can, in any sense, be applied."[140]

On behalf of this proposition, Wright quoted the only two precedents that he would cite in the entire ruling: *Meason*[141] and *Boniface*,[142] the two previously mentioned labor-law cases from Pennsylvania in the 1810s. Wright's exclusive reliance on these Pennsylvania precedents was unusual. Given Wright's legal education in Pennsylvania and his overall lack of legal experience at the time of *Burgess*, these two rulings may have been among the only labor-relations cases he knew. But this seems unlikely. During the course of his legal training, his legal practice, or his *Burgess* research, Wright probably ran across other, more recent master-servant cases. Most would have contradicted the half-century-old *Meason* and *Boniface* rulings by treating "master" and "servant" as mere synonyms for employer and employee.[143] Perhaps Justice Wright preferred to overlook these other rulings. He wrote in an age of emancipation, when he and other egalitarians feared that master-servant hierarchies would simply replace master-slave hierarchies.[144] Wright and others hoped to do away with legal hierarchies altogether, to the extent possible. Consequently, Wright reached back to the egalitarianism of Early National Pennsylvania to find useful precedents. "No person to whom wages could be due for his services would endure the name [servant], as it would be considered offensive, and a term of reproach," the Pennsylvania Supreme Court had asserted in *Boniface* (1817). Justice Wright agreed.[145]

Wright would not necessarily shield Carpenter, the shooter, from all liability. His ruling noted that Henry Burgess, the victim, was a free and independent man who could, in his own name, sue the gunman "for any

140. Burgess v. Carpenter, 10

141. *Ex parte Meason*, 175.

142. Boniface v. Scott, 352.

143. James Kent, *Commentaries on American Law*, vol. 2, 9th ed. (Boston: Little, Brown, 1858), 274; Stone v. Codman, 32 Mass. 297, 299 (1834); Sproul v. Hemmingway, 31 Mass. 1 (1833); and Haywood v. Miller, 3 Hill 90 (N.Y. 1842).

144. See Schouler, *A Treatise on the Law of the Domestic Relations*, 599.

145. Boniface v. Scott, 352, quoted in Burgess v. Carpenter, 9.

private injury . . . sustained at his hands."[146] Moreover, "as each of the parties to the contract"—W. R. Burgess, Henry Burgess, and the other workers with whom Henry would divide a share—"contributed his special portion of the means necessary to the production of the crop, and each was to receive his special portion after an equitable division," Wright reasoned, "if there was a loss it was a common loss." If Carpenter, the shooter, "committed an unlawful act which was the cause of such loss, then the parties to the contract, severally, have the legal right of action against the defendant for damages."[147] And presumably criminal prosecution of the shooter remained an option. The record does not reveal whether the trigger-happy Carpenter was sued by the injured Henry Burgess, by W. R. Burgess along with all of his sharecroppers, by the state, by all of the above, or by none. But Justice Wright was clear: W. R. Burgess could not sue Carpenter separately for loss of Henry Burgess's labor. Unlike Old South enslavers, New South employers owned neither their workers' bodies nor their workers' labor. They could not unilaterally sue third parties who deprived them of either.

Wright seems to have been playing a long game. He hoped that, over time, his ruling would help Black people generally, even if it hurt particular Black workers. After all, when Henry Burgess was shot, W. R. "took him to his house and nursed him for several weeks . . . while he was unable to work."[148] W. R.'s assumption that he could recover damages from the shooter may have enhanced his willingness to care for Henry. Arguably, Wright's ruling in *Burgess*, by making it harder for employers to sue third parties who injured their employees, might have decreased the likelihood that future landowners would care for workers unlucky enough to be injured by third parties. Wright was willing to take that chance. His aim was more foundational. He seems to have been trying to bake into the private law of South Carolina the antislavery, free-labor ideals of the Thirteenth Amendment and the egalitarian ideals of the Fourteenth Amendment. This was most visible toward the end of the ruling, when Wright considered the nature of the legal relationship between the two Burgesses. W. R. Burgess was not a master, Wright insisted. And Henry Burgess was no servant. The two men were free and equal parties to a contract. In Wright's words, W. R. Burgess "sustained the same relation to Henry Bur-

146. Burgess v. Carpenter, 10.

147. Ibid.

148. Burgess v. Carpenter, 7.

gess that Henry Burgess did to him. Each was *sui juris*"—possessing full rights, able to manage his own affairs, under the power of no one. Neither was "the servant of the other." After all, Wright reminded readers, Henry Burgess was "a free man."[149]

At the time of *Burgess v. Carpenter* (1870), the South Carolina Supreme Court contained three members, all appointed recently by the Republican-dominated state legislature.[150] Wright was brand new. The two other members—Chief Justice Franklin J. Moses Sr., a Charlestonian, and Amiel J. Willard, a New Yorker—had served since 1868. Together, the court formed something of a microcosm of the state's Republican party: a white southerner, a white northerner, and a Black man (or, in the day's discourteous lexicon, a "scalawag," a "carpet-bagger," and a "Negro."[151])

Chief Justice Moses joined Wright's *Burgess* ruling. Justice Willard, however, wrote a separate concurrence, meaning he agreed with the majority outcome, but not its reasoning. At first glance, this split between Wright and Willard surprises, for the two had much in common. Both were northern Republicans who had moved south during the Civil War to work with the formerly enslaved. After the war, both remained in South Carolina and worked for the Freedmen's Bureau.[152] Wright, however, occupied the Bureau's activist wing. He saw his charge as, in his words, "assisting free people in their legal affairs."[153] He sympathized with formerly enslaved workers, not former enslavers.[154] Willard was less of an activist. Believing the restoration of plantation discipline to be an economic necessity, Willard tended to issue comparatively proplanter orders and champion comparatively restrictive work rules.[155]

Willard's relative conservatism colored his *Burgess* concurrence. Although he agreed with Justice Wright that Henry Burgess was not a servant, he disagreed with the breadth of Wright's reasoning. Willard argued

149. Ibid.

150. Woody, "Jonathan Jasper, Wright" 117.

151. Ibid., 120; "The Men Who Rule South Carolina," *New York Herald*, June 7, 1874, 11.

152. John S. Reynolds, Esq., "Chief Justice Amiel J. Willard," in *South Carolina Bench and Bar*, vol. I, ed. Ulysses R. Brooks (Columbia, SC: State Company, 1908), 36; William J. Cooper, *The Conservative Regime: South Carolina, 1877–1890* (Columbia: University of South Carolina Press, 2005), 50; Woody, "Jonathan Jasper Wright," 118.

153. Quoted in Gergel and Gergel, "To Vindicate," 40.

154. Taylor, "Wright, Jonathan Jasper," 669.

155. Schmidt, "'A Full-Fledged Government of Men,'" 237.

that Henry Burgess was not a "servant," because Burgess was a sharecropper. The sharecropping contract meant that "the master" (a term that Wright avoided but Willard invoked) "has not an entire interest in the services of his laborer," for the fruits of the worker's labor were to be divided among several parties to a contract, including the injured worker. "In this respect," Willard wrote, "the relation [of landowner to sharecropper] is not such as can warrant the application of the rule of the common law [of master and servant] contended for in this case." Willard, however, quickly qualified the implications of his concurrence. Although sharecroppers were not servants, he explained, other workers, including other agricultural workers, might be: "I do not regard the present case as rendering any expression . . . as to whether that rule [of master and servant] is applicable in this country to a case of hiring for wages." As for the egalitarian rhetoric that Wright sprinkled throughout his ruling—by which he pronounced that the white landowner "sustained the same relation to Henry Burgess that Henry Burgess did to him" and "neither [was] the servant of the other"—Willard included nothing of the sort.[156]

By a two-to-one margin, Wright's sweeping ruling carried the day.[157] It conferred costs as well as benefits upon landless Black workers. In some circumstances, hierarchical "master and servant" law arguably would have benefited some agricultural laborers—for example, by shifting liability for their negligence to their "masters." But in Wright's mind, that benefit was not worth the cost. He was determined to use the law to reinforce the egalitarian norms that he had helped write into the Constitution of 1868, whereby all South Carolina men were theoretically equal. With *Burgess*, this norm would extend beyond the ballot box and courtroom to encompass the work done in the state's vast green fields.

Retreat from *Burgess*

Burgess v. Carpenter (1870) represented a high-water mark for the South Carolina Supreme Court's racial and labor egalitarianism. In this book's pages, it represents a pivot point. Within a few years, South Carolina's high

156. Burgess v. Carpenter.
157. Ibid.

court had reembraced master-servant hierarchies;[158] South Carolina Republicans, including Justice Wright, had been bullied from office; and the state's Democrats had hammered down civil rights in South Carolina, though not to preemancipation levels.

An early post-*Burgess* case that weakened Justice Wright's handiwork by applying "master and servant" logic to nondomestic work came from Justice Wright's own pen. In *Redding v. South Carolina Railroad Company* (1871),[159] as in *Burgess* (1870), Wright sought egalitarian ends. But whereas in *Burgess* he pursued racial equality by withholding the "servant" label from a nondomestic worker, in *Redding* he pursued it by attaching that label to a nondomestic worker.

The "servant" in *Redding*, Charles Wollen, was a white railroad employee who, among other things, supervised a railroad depot's sitting parlor for "lady passengers." Early in 1870, Wollen allegedly injured the plaintiff, Julia Redding, by "throwing her with violence to the floor upon her face (she being then pregnant)"[160] and forcibly ejecting her from this room. Wollen assumed that Redding was a "negro" (which she denied) and that the railroad reserved that room for whites (which the railroad denied). Wollen apparently acted on his own. "I gave no instructions to keep colored persons out of the parlors," testified Wollen's boss. The parlor had been reserved for whites in previous years, but "that ceased to be as soon as the Civil Rights Bill had passed." After the passage of that bill, Wollen's boss testified, "We never interfered with colored persons going in there."[161]

Rather than suing Wollen, who had little money, Redding sued the South Carolina Railroad Company, which had plenty. The railroad sought a nonsuit on grounds that Wollen was a rogue employee. Wollen alone was responsible for Redding's injuries, the railroad argued, for he had acted contrary to his employer's instructions.[162] The trial court sided with the railroad and granted a nonsuit, reasoning that Wollen alone had committed the tort.[163]

Redding appealed, and the South Carolina Supreme Court reinstated her case against the railroad. Writing for the Court, Justice Wright invoked

158. Daniel v. Swearengen.

159. Redding v. South Carolina Railroad Company, 3 S.C. 1 (1871).

160. Redding v. S.C. R. Co., 3 S.C. 1, 2 (1871).

161. Redding v. S.C. R. Co., Testimony of J. B. Martin, 2.

162. Ibid.

163. Redding v. S.C. R. Co., 6.

the labels "master" and "servant," which he had recently rejected in *Burgess*. "The master is liable for the tortious acts of his servant, when done in the course of his employment, although they may be done in disobedience of the master's orders," Wright stated.[164] His use of the terms "master" and "servant" in *Redding* helped him to achieve procivil rights result. Future employers, he may well have reasoned, would now work harder to prevent rogue employees from ad-libbing in a racist fashion. *Redding*, however, seemingly contradicted Wright's own recent efforts to confine master-and-servant logic to domestic-labor settings. The justice may have reasoned that *Redding* did not undermine *Burgess* because it dealt with different work contexts (railroad versus agriculture) and different legal circumstances (an employer's liability for the misdeeds of an employee rather than an employer's ability to recover damages from a third party who interfered with his employee's labor). Nonetheless, Wright's reembrace of "master and servant" so soon after *Burgess* was notable.

The next stage in *Burgess*'s demise was more damaging: a string of "labor enticement" cases heard in nearby states' courts in the first half of the 1870s. Those courts could have joined Wright by refusing to call white landowners "masters" or Black farmworkers "servants." Consistently, however, they rejected Wright's reasoning.

The cases in question typically began when one white farmer sued another for luring away his under-contract workers. Courts in neighboring states unhesitatingly applied the term "master" to white agrarian employers and "servant" to their workers. The rulings that resulted were in line with labor law nationally[165] but arguably meant something different in the South, where the doctrine of master and servant was less advanced, and where the history of slavery made "master" a loaded term.

Salter v. Howard (Georgia, 1871) began late in 1865, when John Howard, a white landowner in Georgia, hired a number of Black sharecroppers for the entirety of 1866. Like other southern landowners, Howard was desperate for workers. Nearby white planter Samuel Salter was equally desperate. In mid-January 1866, Salter sent a wagon to Howard's place, hoping to lure some of his hands away. Howard indignantly returned the wagon "with

---

164. Ibid.

165. Tomlins, *Law, Labor, and Ideology*, 280–83; Nelson, *Americanization of the Common Law*, 125–26; Boston Glass Manufactory v. Binney, 4 Pick. 425 (Mass., 1827).

a note stating that the negroes were in his employment."[166] Before long, however, "the negroes left and were found on [Salter's] plantation."[167] Rather than suing the penniless workers for breach of contract, Howard sued Salter for "enticing servants out of his employ."[168] He won substantial damages at trial. Salter appealed, and the Georgia Supreme Court reversed, but only on the grounds that the damage award had been wrongly calculated. As for "master and servant" law, the Georgia court unhesitatingly invoked it. If "servants" are under contract with one person, the court wrote, anyone "intruding upon the rights of the master by enticing them away is liable in an action of damages."[169] *Salter*, in other words, ignored *Burgess*. So did another agricultural labor enticement case from Georgia, *Jones & Jeter v. Stephen Blocker* (1871).[170]

Haskins v. Royster (North Carolina, 1874) went one step further. Like the Georgia cases before it, *Haskins* affirmed the applicability of "master and servant" doctrine to agricultural employment. Unlike the Georgia cases, *Haskins* also explicitly rejected *Burgess*. The case began in early 1871, when John Haskins hired two men, "one white and the other colored,"[171] to labor on his farm throughout the year. In March, the two laborers left Haskins's employ to work for F. A. Royster. Haskins sued Royster, arguing that labor enticement of this sort was actionable under the law of master and servant. Haskins lost at trial but won on appeal. Justice William Rodman's majority opinion for the North Carolina Supreme Court demonstrated an awareness that, in the aftermath of slavery, some egalitarians might feel uncomfortable calling agrarian employers "masters." But Rodman dismissed these objections. "Master" simply meant employer, he argued, and "servant" employee. The principle that masters could recover damages from those who knowingly enticed away their contracted "servants" was a "familiar and well[-]established doctrine,"[172] one that applied to "all" types of labor contracts, including sharecropping, Rodman held.[173] "It need scarcely be said," he added, as if anticipating criticism from Justice

166. Salter v. Howard, 43 Ga. 601–02, 604 (1871).
167. Ibid.
168. Ibid., 603.
169. Ibid.
170. Ibid., 331.
171. Haskins v. Royster, 70 N.C. 601, 618 (1874).
172. Ibid., 606.
173. Ibid., 607.

Wright and his antislavery ilk, "that there is nothing in this principle inconsistent with personal freedom."[174] Labor-enticement rules were "not derived from any idea of property by the one party in the other"—that is, slavery. Rather, Rodman wrote, labor enticement was actionable because it constituted malicious interference with "the obligation of a contract freely made."[175] Rodman further sought to distance antienticement principles from slave law by noting that these principles existed not just in the South but also in "the laws of the freest and most enlightened States in the world,"[176] a claim that he substantiated by citing master-servant precedents from England and the North.[177]

As for *Burgess v. Carpenter* (1870), Justice Wright's egalitarian ruling, Rodman explicitly rejected it. He first cited *Salter* and *Jones*, the Georgia cases described above, in support of the proposition that the antienticement principles of "master and servant" law applied to agricultural employment.[178] "The only case to the contrary that we are aware of," Rodman wrote, "is *Burgess v. Carpenter*." But the Pennsylvania pilings upon which Wright had constructed his ruling struck Rodman as thoroughly wobbly. "The authorities relied on in that case," Rodman dismissively wrote, "seem to us not in point."[179] Thus, Rodman's North Carolina decision both embraced "master and servant" law and repudiated *Burgess*.

Haskins was not unanimous. Justice Edwin Reade dissented.[180] Like Wright in *Burgess*, Reade passionately warned about the social implications of applying the labels "master" and "servant" to agricultural labor. Legally speaking, some sorts of workers certainly qualified as servants and others did not. Domestic workers were servants, for their employment inherently entailed "duty, subjection and allegiance."[181] Apprentices were another species of servant, for "service and subjection" were inherent to their condition.[182] But agricultural laborers were neither domestics nor apprentices.

174. Ibid., 605.

175. Ibid., 601.

176. Ibid., 605.

177. These included Walker v. Cronin, 107 Mass. 555 (1871), and Lumley v. Gye, 2 E & B 216 (Queen's Bench, 1853).

178. Haskins v. Royster, 607.

179. Ibid., 607–8.

180. Ibid., 612.

181. Ibid., 613.

182. Ibid., 613–14.

"How then," Reade rhetorically asked, "can the relation in this case be that of master and servant?"[183] Like Justice Wright before him, Justice Reade worried about the social implications of labor law. "There is no greater danger in any community," Reade ominously warned, "than a dependent class upon whom is the hand of oppression bearing hard, and who have nowhere to look for relief."[184]

Reade's 1874 dissent and Schouler's 1870 treatise show that Justice Wright was not alone in resisting the spread of master-servant doctrine in the Age of Emancipation. But the prevailing tide flowed the other way. As Reade feared, the majority ruling in *Haskins* influenced other courts. Scores of subsequent cases would cite Rodman's majority opinion.[185] Reade's dissent, like *Burgess* before it, evaporated.

Beyond courtroom walls, history's tide was also turning against *Burgess*-style egalitarianism. The sputtering southern economy did not help. The price of cotton fell consistently throughout the postwar decade, squeezing southern stomachs.[186] The Panic of 1873, a transatlantic economic collapse, spread desperation and undermined northern support for Reconstruction.[187]

The political underpinnings of Reconstruction also weakened. Scandal and factionalism weakened the Republican Party nationally. In the South, Democrats retook state after state. Republicans maintained control in South Carolina longer than in most southern states, thanks to its Black voting majority, but their power weakened.[188] During the early years of Recon-

---

183. Ibid., 614.

184. Ibid., 618.

185. Sixty-one subsequent cases cited Rodman's majority opinion, WestLawNext, https://1-next-westlaw-com.proxy048.nclive.org/Search/Home.html?rs=IWLN1.0&vr=3.0&sp=003422628-2100&transitionType=Default&contextData=(sc.Default)&bhab=0&bhav=&bhqs=1#sk=1.tarFBw.

186. See US Bureau of the Census, *Historical Statistics of the United States, Colonial Time to 1957* (Washington, DC: n.p., 1960), 123, E101–112; Woodman, *New South—New Law: The Legal Foundations of Credit and Labor Relations in the Postbellum Agricultural South New South* (Baton Rouge: Louisiana State University Press, 1995); Roger Ransom and Richard Sutch, *One Kind of Freedom: The Economic Consequences of Emancipation* (Cambridge: Cambridge University Press, 1977), 126–70.

187. Foner, *Reconstruction*, 512–63.

188. Walter Edgar, *South Carolina*, 394–406; Foner, *Reconstruction*, 346–92, 535–87; Holt, *Black over White*; Hyman Rubin, *South Carolina Scalawags* (Columbia: University of South Carolina Press, 2006); Michael R. Hyman, "Taxation, Public Policy, and Political Dissent:

struction, at least some white South Carolinians had joined with freedmen and white migrants from the North to form a formidable Republican coalition. As the 1870s advanced, however, most white South Carolinians, rich and poor, embraced "white-line" politics under the leadership of the Democratic Party and vowed to retake power, by violent means if necessary.[189]

The number of white Republicans in the state shrank,[190] but the Republican Party's decline was not fast enough to suit Democratic militants, who concluded that, because the Palmetto State was majority Black, white dominance and electoral democracy were incompatible. As long as elections were fair, Black South Carolinians would retain a political voice. So white supremacists embraced dirty schemes, including the "Edgefield Plan," named after the unruly district in western South Carolina where the plan originated, to defeat democracy through violence and intimidation. Paramilitary groups intimidated Black voters, suppressed Republican turnout, and violently rocked Reconstruction back on its heels.[191]

Daniel v. Swearengen

These ominous economic and political winds prompted the South Carolina Supreme Court to trim its sails. Amid the Panic of 1873, as the region struggled to feed itself, the strong labor-enticement protections offered by "master and servant" doctrine might have seemed like a prudent way of keeping workers in the fields. "The loss of agricultural labor, for even a few days, might often prove of irreparable injury to the crop," the Court would note

---

Yeoman Dissatisfaction in the Post-Reconstruction Lower South," *Journal of Southern History* 55, no. 1 (Feb. 1989): 49–76; and Richard Zuczek, *State of Rebellion: Reconstruction in South Carolina* (Columbia: University of South Carolina Press, 1996).

189. Foner, *Reconstruction*, 548–49; Steven Hahn, *The Roots of Southern Populism: Yeoman Farmers and the Transformation of the Georgia Upcountry, 1850–1890* (New York: Oxford University Press, 1983), 222–23; David Jaynes, *Branches without Roots: Genesis of the Black Working Class in the American South, 1862-1882* (New York: Oxford University Press, 1986), 191–93; W. Scott Poole, *Never Surrender: Confederate Memory and Conservatism in the South Carolina Upcountry* (Athens: University of Georgia Press, 2004), 176; D. Wyatt Aiken, "The Patrons of Husbandry," *Rural Carolinian* 3, no. 9 (June 1872).

190. See chart in Holt, *Black over White*, 97.

191. Edgar, *South Carolina*, 402–3; Foner, 570–72; Stephen Kantrowitz, *Ben Tillman and the Reconstruction of White Supremacy* (Chapel Hill: University of North Carolina Press, 2000).

in 1875.[192] With judicial elections approaching in the state legislature in 1876, the members of the South Carolina Supreme Court backed away from *Burgess*-style egalitarianism.

In 1875, a new case, *Daniel v. Swearengen*, offered the Court an opportunity to revisit the *Burgess* question: whether, as a matter of law, agricultural employers were "masters" and their workers "servants." Both parties in the case, Thomas Daniel and Ansel Swearengen, were white farmers. Swearengen's money was older. Prior to the war, he had enslaved dozens of laborers. Daniel, by contrast, was a mere overseer, but he hustled, acquired land, plowed the earth, and yanked hard upward on his bootstraps.[193] On New Year's Day, 1872, Daniel verbally hired, for the full year, two Black men to work his fields and one Black woman to serve "as a domestic and house servant."[194] By Valentine's Day, they were gone, enticed away by Ansel Swearengen's sweeter terms. Daniel invoked master-servant law and sued Swearengen. An Abbeville County jury awarded him $600 in damages.[195]

Swearengen appealed, citing *Burgess v. Carpenter* on behalf of the proposition that "the domestic relation of master and servant does not exist" in South Carolina, and therefore labor enticement was not actionable.[196] Although Swearengen himself was a rich former enslaver, his lawyer enthusiastically embraced Justice Wright's antislavery reasoning. Channeling *Burgess*, Swearengen's brief argued that "the word master implies authority, control, command, the right to exact service," while the word "servant implies obedience, subjection to the will of another."[197] Put the two together and you effectively get "property in another"—slavery.[198] If slavery still existed in South Carolina, Swearengen conceded, "masters" such as Thomas Daniel certainly would retain the power to recover damages from those who deprived them of the labor of their human possessions. But slavery no

192. Daniel v. Swearengen, 303.

193. See *U.S. Census, 1860,* South Carolina: Abbeville County, series M653, roll 1212, p. 136; *U.S. Census Slave Schedule, 1850,* series M432, reel 861; *U.S. Census Slave Schedule, 1860,* series M653, reel 1229. Note that Ansel's son James Swearengen was a named coparty to the suit.

194. Daniel v. Swearengen, 297.

195. Ibid.

196. Ibid., 301.

197. Ibid., 300.

198. Ibid.

longer existed.[199] Labor relations in South Carolina were now based on voluntary labor contracts, Swearengen noted. And unlike slavery, a voluntary labor contract "confers no control of the [workers'] will, no subjection to [the employer's] authority." Workers were free to stay on the job or leave, being responsible for the consequences of their decisions.[200] The proper legal remedy for jilted employers was to sue faithless workers for breach of contract, not to sue subsequent employers for "enticement."[201] The trial judge, therefore, should have nonsuited the case before it reached the jury, Swearengen argued, on grounds that the relation of master and servant no longer existed in the state, and therefore an original employer "cannot maintain an action" against a subsequent employer for "causing a laborer . . . to leave his service."[202] (Or, if the two male agricultural workers were not "servants" but the female domestic worker was one, then a new trial should be granted on that basis.[203])

Daniel countered by citing English cases and South Carolina statutes in support of the proposition that "the relation of master and servant at common law . . . has long been recognized, and now exists, in South Carolina."[204] Daniel's lawyer cited neither southern nor northern precedents, even though, as we have seen, several existed. Instead, the lawyer, who was an immigrant from Scotland,[205] relied on English cases, with which he may have been more familiar.[206]

Had this case arisen in 1870, just after Justice Wright wrote his opinion in *Burgess*, it likely would have been an easy victory for Swearengen, at least with respect to the two agricultural workers. *Burgess* distinguished sharply between domestic workers, whom Justice Wright's original ruling considered legally to be "servants," and agricultural workers, whom he did not consider to be servants. The key difference was that domestic workers were

199. Ibid. 298–99.

200. Ibid., 300.

201. Ibid.

202. Ibid., 301.

203. Ibid., 300.

204. Ibid.

205. *U.S. Census 1860*; Census Place: Abbeville, South Carolina, Family History Library Film 805212, roll M653 1212, p. 24.

206. Cases cited: Blake v. Lanyon, 6 Term. R., 221; Lawley [*sic*] v. Gye, 20 Engl. Law and Equity Rep., 168; and Hart v. Aldridge, Cowpen, 56.

effectively "part of a man's family"[207] and therefore could be presumed to be "subjected to the coercion of the master."[208] Agricultural workers, by contrast, being "exclusively concerned in the cultivation of the soil," and therefore having "no domestic cast within the nature of [their] service," did "not fall within the class to which the term 'servant' can, in any sense, be applied."[209] Under *Burgess*, the female domestic worker would have been deemed a "servant," allowing Daniel to recover damages from Swearengen for enticing her away from his domestic employ. But the two agricultural workers would not have been found to be "servants."

Chief Justice Franklin J. Moses Sr., however, ignored *Burgess* when he wrote *Daniel v. Swearengen* five years later. Moses was the third member of the Supreme Court of South Carolina during Reconstruction, along with Wright and Willard. All three were members in 1870, when Wright penned the unanimous *Burgess* ruling; all three remained members as of 1875, when Moses overturned it, in *Daniel*.

The Chief Justice began with some South Carolina legal history. Prior to emancipation, Moses wrote, slavery dominated the state's labor law. But the master-slave labor relation was not alone. "Another relation was recognized, arising from the employment of one free man by another." This was the relation of "master and servant."[210] Master-servant relations had existed before emancipation and persisted following emancipation. Ansel Swearengen's claim, based on *Burgess*, that "the relation of master and servant does not exist in South Carolina," was simply incorrect.[211]

Moses also asserted that labor enticement had long been actionable in South Carolina and remained so. "It cannot be questioned," he wrote, "that an action of the character of the one before us, where the party employed was a free person, was maintainable while slavery actually existed in the State," and continued to be maintainable despite slavery's demise.[212] Swearengen's lawyer had argued that the proper remedy in such cases would be for employers to sue fickle employees for breach of contract.[213] Moses

207. Burgess v. Carpenter, 10, quoting *Ex parte Measan*, 5 Binn., 167.

208. Burgess v. Carpenter, 9.

209. Ibid., 10.

210. Daniel v. Swearengen, 302.

211. Ibid.

212. Ibid., 302.

213. Citing S.C. Rev. Stat., §12, 4916 S.C. 297, 299, 1875 WL 5401 (S.C.), 2.

disagreed. He acknowledged that labor contracts established mutual obligations, but insisted that, in cases of labor enticement, the action should lie against "those who by their . . . interference have induced" the workers to betray their obligations, not the laborers themselves.[214] Obtaining relief with breach-of-contract suits was unworkable. South Carolina laborers were simply too poor. If such suits were the jilted employer's only remedy, Moses reasoned, "in most instances, his reparation would fall far below the actual damage he has suffered."[215] In practice, Moses concluded, only labor-enticement claims under master-servant law, not failure-to-perform claims under contract law, would achieve justice.

With considerable understatement, Moses admitted that *Burgess v. Carpenter*, an opinion that he himself had joined five years previously, "may be somewhat in conflict with the views which dispose of the case before us." Moses craftily sought to reconcile the two decisions by focusing on Justice Willard's weak *Burgess* concurrence, not Justice Wright's strong majority ruling. Paraphrasing Willard's concurrence, Moses noted that Henry Burgess, being a sharecropper, arguably "did not occupy the relation of servant to . . . W. R. Burgess" because "he was a co-worker with him in the crop, each contributing the means necessary to its production." The two were "partners." Moses claimed that this distinguished *Burgess* from *Daniel*, which involved farm laborers, not sharecroppers.[216] Moses's misleading focus on Willard's concurrence rather than Wright's majority opinion in *Burgess* masked *Daniel*'s wholesale reversal of the earlier ruling.[217]

Justice Wright's silence in *Daniel* spoke as loudly as the Chief Justice's ruling. During Wright's heady early days on the Court, when Reconstruction was in full bloom, he spoke his mind. His ruling in *Burgess* (1870) showed how important he considered agricultural labor relations to be and how committed he was to racial equality in the world of work. White landowner W. R. Burgess was not a "master," Wright had insisted, and Black sharecropper Henry Burgess was not a servant. In the law's eyes, the two were equal, connected horizontally by a voluntary labor contract, not vertically by the master-servant relationship. After all, Wright had written,

---

214. Daniel v. Swearengen, 302.

215. Ibid., 302.

216. Ibid., 304.

217. Ibid.

Henry Burgess was "a free man."[218] Now, in 1875, as anti-Reconstruction winds howled, Justice Wright sat mum. Even though the Chief Justice's opinion eviscerated *Burgess*, Wright did not respond. He wrote no fiery dissent. He wrote no separate concurrence. Instead, he quietly joined the majority, as if tacitly recognizing the bitter truth that the egalitarian dreams of Reconstruction were dying.[219]

Epilogue

One year after *Daniel*, voters went to the polls in the "Bloody South Carolina Election of 1876,"[220] the most tumultuous in state history.[221] Irregularities occurred on both sides but were egregious among Democrats.[222] For months prior to Election Day, Democratic "Red Shirts" had used violence and intimidation to discourage Republican and Black turnout.[223] During

218. Ibid.

219. Despite the significance of the shift in South Carolina law from *Burgess* to *Daniel*, historians have all but ignored it. Even some first-rate explorations of state-level labor law in the post–Civil War South overlook *Burgess* and *Daniel* entirely. See Woodman, *New South*; Harold D. Woodman, "Post-Civil War Southern Agriculture and the Law," *Agricultural History* 53, no. 1 (January 1979): 319–37; Suresh Naidu, "Recruitment Restrictions and Labor Markets: Evidence from the Post-Bellum U.S. South," *Journal of Labor Economics* 28, no. 2 (2010): 413–45; and William Cohen, *At Freedom's Edge: Black Mobility and the Southern Quest for Racial Control, 1861–1915* (Baton Rouge: Louisiana State University Press, 1991): 20–32. Other works mention the two cases but place them in the same category, without distinction. See "Maliciously Inducing a Breach of Contract: *Lumley v. Gye*," *Michigan Law Review* 2, no. 4 (Jan. 1904): 309. Still others recognize that differences separated the two cases but fail to analyze those differences and do not situate those differences within the broader history of Reconstruction. G. R. R. Jr. and F.H.B. Jr., "The Action for Loss of Services and the Measure of Damages to Be Applied," *University of Pennsylvania Law Review* 69, no. 2 (Jan. 1921): 161; Laura Edwards, "The Problem of Dependency: African Americans, Labor Relations, and the Law in the Nineteenth-Century South," *Agricultural History* 72 (Spring 1998): 336, note 32.

220. Jerry L. West, *The Bloody* South Carolina *Election of* 1876*: Wade Hampton III, the Red Shirt Campaign for Governor and the End of Reconstruction* (Jefferson, NC: McFarland, 2011).

221. Foner, *Reconstruction*, 573.

222. Ibid., 573–74.

223. See ibid.; and Richard Zuczek, "The Last Campaign of the Civil War: South Carolina and the Revolution of 1876," *Civil War History* 42, no. 1 (March 1996): 18–31.

the elections themselves, Democrats, as they later proudly admitted, engaged in ballot-box stuffing, repeat voting, and having Georgia Democrats cross state lines to vote.[224] (Edgefield County, in western South Carolina, infamously returned two thousand more votes than it had voters.[225])

Republican Governor D. H. Chamberlain and his Democratic challenger, Wade Hampton, both claimed victory. So did rival state legislatures.[226] The two parties set up competing governments in Columbia. Fraud and uncertainty likewise marred the presidential contest between Republican Rutherford B. Hayes and Democrat Samuel Tilden. National attention in that neck-and-neck race focused on disputed results in three southern states, including South Carolina.[227] Party leaders in Washington resolved the electoral dispute by striking an informal compromise, whereby the Republican Hayes got the White House in exchange for his party's agreement to pull Northern troops out of the South, ending Reconstruction. The withdrawal of federal troops from South Carolina in April of 1877 doomed Republican prospects there. The Democrats assumed complete control of the state.[228]

Justice Jonathan Jasper Wright could not escape the tumult. A temperamental moderate,[229] he tried to keep his head down, as evidenced by his silence in *Daniel v. Swearengen*. But controversy ensnared him. The disputed gubernatorial race wound up in the state Supreme Court, putting Justice Wright in the crossfire. Both parties put tremendous pressure on him.[230] When Wright questioned some of Hampton's legal claims, Democrats, whose blood was up, began efforts to eject Wright from office.[231] The state House appointed an impeachment committee, which mounted questionable charges of drunkenness against the Black jurist. In June of 1877,

224. "Election of 1876," in Edgar, *The South Carolina Encyclopedia*, 293.

225. Melinda Meek Hennessey, "Racial Violence during Reconstruction: The 1876 Riots in Charleston and Cainhoy," *South Carolina Historical Magazine*, vol. 86, no. 2, April 1985, 110.

226. Coleman, "Wright, Jonathan Jasper," 831.

227. Foner, *Reconstruction*, 570.

228. Edgar, *South Carolina*, 402–6; and Foner, *Reconstruction*, 565–86.

229. Caleb A. Jaffe, "Obligations Impaired: Justice Jonathan Jasper Wright and the Failure of Reconstruction in South Carolina," *Michigan Journal of Race and Law* 8, no. 2 (2003): 471–501.

230. Coleman, "Wright, Jonathan Jasper," 832; R. H. Woody, "Jonathan Jasper Wright, 125.

231. Coleman, "Wright, Jonathan Jasper," 1051.

the full House voted to impeach.[232] Two months later, before the State Senate could rule, Justice Wright, aware that the legislature was forcing other Republicans from office, resigned.[233]

Wright ended his career practicing law in Charleston, battling disease, and training the state's next generation of Black lawyers. In 1885, Wright died in obscurity.[234] No African American would again ascend to any state's top court until 1955.[235]

Wright's ruling in *Burgess v. Carpenter* (1870) preceded him in death. Recall that several decisions in the 1870s, including *Daniel v. Swearengen* (1875), had seriously wounded the precedent. In 1877, the same year in which Wright was toppled from South Carolina's high bench, H. G. Wood of the New York bar buried *Burgess* in an influential work called *A Treatise on the Law of Master and Servant*.[236] Wright's *Burgess* opinion had drawn a bright line between domestic workers, who were "servants," and agricultural workers, who were not. By contrast, Wood's treatise declared that "no such distinction exists." "All who are in the employ of another, in whatever capacity," Wood flatly stated, "are regarded in law as servants."[237] Wood's treatise likewise presented *Haskins v. Royster* (North Carolina, 1874), "a case quite similar in principle [to *Burgess*]," as having gotten right what *Burgess* got wrong. Wood wrote that "there can be no question" that all employers were masters, all employees servants.[238]

---

232. Coleman, 832; Richard Gergel and Belinda Gergel, "'To Vindicate the Cause of the Downtrodden,': Associate Justice Jonathan Jasper Wright and Reconstruction in South Carolina," in *At Freedom's Door*, 65.

233. Frederic D. Schwarz, "The Reluctant Judge," *American Legacy* 10, no. 3 (Fall 2004): 18; Gergel and Gergel, 65.

234. Gergel and Gergel, "To Vindicate," 67–71; and Underwood and Burke, *At Freedom's Door*; "Another Witness: How the State of South Carolina was Robbed," *News and Herald* (Winnsboro, SC), August 29, 1878.

235. Mireya Navarro, "Judge Harold Stevens, 83, Dies; First Black on Court of Appeals," *New York Times*, Nov. 11, 1990, 40; "First Black Judges on the State Supreme Courts," Ballotpedia, accessed Aug. 28, 2022, https://ballotpedia.org/First_black_judges_on_the_state_supreme_courts.

236. Wood, *A Treatise on the Law*; "Death of Horace G. Wood," *New York Times* (Jan. 10, 1893): 5; *The Employment Relationship in Anglo-American Law: A Historical Perspective* (Westport, Ct: Greenwood Press, 1989), 144.

237. Wood, *A Treatise on the Law of Master and Servant, Covering the Relation, Duties, and Liabilities of Employers and Employees*, 2nd ed. (San Francisco: Bancroft-Whitney, 1886), 4.

238. Ibid., 4, 402–4. Note that, while *Burgess* undoubtedly lost out in the short run, it has interestingly undergone somewhat of "resurrection" in the modern era. At its most basic level, *Burgess* dealt with the issue of an employee injured by a third party. Numerous cases

South Carolina's high court would soon shovel additional dirt on *Burgess*. In *Huff v. Watkins* (1881), the court's three new justices, all Democrats, confronted a labor-enticement case involving a sharecropper, Jordan Butler. They held that "the manner in which compensation is to be made ought not to have any effect in determining the nature of the relation."[239] Wage earner versus cropper was a distinction without a difference, the Court held. The common law of master and servant governed both.[240] In subsequent South Carolina cases, this doctrinal shift stuck. The sharecropper exception disappeared. All agricultural workers in South Carolina were servants; all had masters.[241]

Huff v. Watkins illustrates the racial masking accomplished by master and servant law. Unlike "slave," the legal category of "servant" was not racially specific. It applied to white and Black employees alike. Thus, *Huff v. Watkins* mentioned the names but not the races of participants. It merely described a tug-of-war between two landowners, Huff and Watkins, over the services of a sharecropper. But the races of the participants are not difficult to guess. Both landowners were white; the sharecropper, Jordan Butler, was Black.[242] Although *Huff* discouraged "labor enticement" and thereby hurt South Carolina's overwhelmingly Black agricultural workforce, it did so in a facially neutral way. It quietly aided in the construction of an oppressive system of debt-peonage.[243] South Carolina's system of agrarian labor relations was heavily racialized, but it was de facto, not de jure, making it legally impervious to equal protection challenge.

From afar, South Carolina's post-*Burgess* embrace of master and servant doctrine might appear as nothing more than a lagging state's belated acceptance of modernizing transatlantic trends. It was in England, after all, the cradle of industrialization, where the common law courts first stretched the

---

have cited it on that point. See Frank Horton & Co., Inc. v. Diggs, 544 S.W.2d 313 (Mo. 1976); Offshore Rental Co. v. Continental Oil Co., 22 Cal.3d. 157 (1978); Risdon Enterprises, Inc. v. Colemill Enterprises, Inc., 172 Ga. App. 902 (1984); I. J. Weinrot & Son, Inc. v. Jackson, 40 Cal. 3d 327 (1985); and Simmons v. Robinson, 303 S.C. 201 (1990).

239. Huff v. Watkins, 15 S.C. 82, 85 (1881); *Edgefield Advertiser*, April 14, 1881.

240. When *Huff* reappeared in the Supreme Court in 1883, the Justices saw no new reason to change their minds. Huff v. Watkins, 18 S.C. 510 (1883).

241. Carpenter v. Strickland, 20 S.C. 1 (1883); Duckett v. Pool, 33 S.C. 238 (1890); and Duckett v. Pool, 34 S.C. 311 (1891).

242. United States Federal Census, South Carolina, 1880.

243. Douglas A. Blackmon, *Slavery by Another Name: The Re-enslavement of Black Americans from the Civil War to World War II* (New York: Anchor Books, 2008).

edges of "master and servant" beyond domestic employment, until they covered all work relations. The US North followed, both economically and legally. Now, following emancipation, it was the New South's turn.

A quick glance at our comparative data from New York and South Carolina initially appears consistent with this narrative. In the years leading up to the Civil War, master and servant cases accounted for a comparatively large and growing percentage of total reported cases in industrializing New York, but a comparatively small—and, indeed, declining—share of total reported cases in slavery-based South Carolina. South Carolina's decline reversed following the war, however. Starting immediately after 1865, the year of emancipation, master and servant cases accounted for a growing share of South Carolina's total caseload, though South Carolina's percentages still lagged New York's.[244]

The delayed-industrialization explanation is not entirely wrong. A closer look at the numbers, however, suggests that other factors were more important. Agricultural disputes, not industrial disputes, drove the South Carolina story. In antebellum New York, agricultural labor cases had accounted for an insignificant share (less than 5 percent) of master-servant cases. In postemancipation South Carolina, agricultural cases accounted for half of master-servant cases. Admittedly, railroad cases and, to a lesser extent, manufacturing cases were also part of the South Carolina mix. But agricultural disputes accounted for the lion's share. In other words, whereas the spread of master and servant law in the North was driven by industrialization, in the South, it can be primarily understood as a legal replacement for master-slave relations in the fields.[245]

Most of South Carolina's postbellum master-servant cases involving farm labor concerned labor enticement. These cases reestablished the norm that agricultural employers enjoyed quasi-ownership stakes in their workers' labor. The result was not exactly slavery but not exactly freedom either. One of the main goals of these cases was to discourage worker movement. This was a newly urgent concern. Prior to emancipation, most South Carolina workers could not leave because they were chained to the land. Planters

244. "'Master and Servant' Cases/Total Reported Cases, South Carolina and New York, 1801–1900," (table). Data and methodological discussion in author's possession and available upon request. Coauthor William Mogen performed this research.

245. Ibid.

knew that the toilers whom they forced to sow would also be available to reap. Emancipation broke those chains, freeing workers to move. Postwar landowners feared that their newly unshackled laborers would flee, leaving crops untended and profits unearned. Every winter, starting in 1865–1866, landowners scrambled to sign yearlong labor contracts with as many workers as they could afford. Their biggest threat was competition from each other. Unaccustomed to competing for Black labor, planters turned to the law, hoping to make the free-labor market a bit less free.[246] Successful labor-enticement cases empowered jilted employers to recover monetary damages from enticing employers. The threat of such litigation made landowners think twice before hiring away workers suspected of being under contract elsewhere. This was true even in the absence of written contracts, for courts held that an oral understanding was sufficient to bind a worker to an employer in a legally actionable way.[247] The result, for workers, was fewer job offers, less bargaining leverage, and less freedom.

Outside of the agrarian sector, master and servant cases in the appellate courts of South Carolina did not focus on labor enticement. They focused on other employment-law staples such as compensation disputes,[248] masters' liability for servants' negligence,[249] and masters' liability for servants' workplace injuries or deaths.[250] Inside the agrarian sector, however, labor-enticement cases dominated. Labor-enticement litigation can be best understood not as a legal offshoot of industrialization but rather as a racially neutral legal device that southern landowners used during the Jim Crow era to bolster their economic power and ensure a cheap and semicaptive workforce. Justice Wright sought to avoid these ends in *Burgess* (1870) by finding that employers could not recover damages from third parties who deprived them of their workers' labor. Had *Burgess* prevailed, labor enticement cases

---

246. Suresh Naidu, "Recruitment Restrictions and Labor Markets: Evidence from the Post-Bellum U.S. South," *Journal of Labor Economics* 28, no. 2 (2010): 416.

247. Daniel v. Swearengen.

248. Mitchell v. Toale, 25 S.C. 238 (1886).

249. Conlin v. City Council of Charleston, 15 Rich. 201, Court of Appeals of Law of South Carolina (1868).

250. *Ex parte Johnson*, 19 S.C. 492 (1883); Coleman v. Wilmington, C. & A. R. Co., 25 S.C. 446 (1886); Bridger v. Asheville & S.R. Co., 27 S.C. 456 (1887); Parker v. South Carolina & G. Ry. Co., 48 S.C. 364 (1897).

involving agricultural workers presumably would not have been possible.[251] But *Burgess*, like Reconstruction itself, was quickly overturned, and labor-enticement cases bloomed.

As Jim Crow hardened in the late-nineteenth century, South Carolina further undermined the bargaining position of farmworkers, most of whom were Black people. In 1880, South Carolina recriminalized labor enticement. (Labor enticement had briefly been criminalized under the state's post–Civil War Black Code.)[252] Labor enticers already could be sued privately; after 1880, they also risked criminal prosecution.[253] Thomas Miller, a Black Republican who briefly represented South Carolina in the US House of Representatives, described the law's effect during a congressional debate in 1891. Miller invoked a hypothetical case in which a South Carolina landowner forced a worker to toil without pay—in other words, reimposed a form of slavery. "In my State," Miller said, "if the employer states verbally that the unpaid laborer of his plantation contracted to work for the year[,] no other farmer dares employ the man . . . [for] it is a misdemeanor so to do, the penalty is heavy, and the farmer who employs the unpaid, starving laborer of his neighbor is the victim of the court."[254] South Carolina was hardly alone. Virtually all southern states adopted criminal labor-enticement statutes. Most of these laws remained on the books until World War II.[255]

In 1891, South Carolina, fearing an exodus of farmworkers, adopted a law designed to obstruct out-of-state labor recruitment. The law required "emigrant agents" (as out-of-state labor recruiters were known) to acquire $1000 annual licenses for every county in which they wished to recruit.

251. Burgess v. Carpenter, 10.

252. Punishments for the criminal labor enticement in the Black Codes were fines of from twenty dollars to $200 and imprisonment or hard labor of up to sixty days. See "An Act to Establish and Regulate the Domestic Relations of Persons of Color and to Amend the Law in Relation to Paupers and Vagrancy, Act No. 4733," in *The Statutes at Large of South Carolina*, vol. 12: *Containing the Acts from December 1861 to December 1866*. (Columbia, SC: Republican Printing, 1875), 276, South Carolina Department of Archives and History, Columbia, South Carolina.

253. "Labor in South Carolina," *New York Times*, Feb. 23, 1880, 2; "Legislating against Exodus Agents," *Baltimore Sun*, Feb. 28, 1880, 2.

254. Thomas E. Miller, Representative from South Carolina, an African American Republican, *Congressional Record*, 22 (February 14, 1891), 2693.

255. William Cohen, "Negro Involuntary Servitude in the South, 1865–1940: A Preliminary Analysis," *Journal of Southern History* 42, no. 1 (Feb. 1976): 35–36.

With each new county (South Carolina had thirty-five at the time), and each new year, agents had to pony up another grand. Unlicensed recruiters faced fines of $500 to $5,000, or imprisonment for four months to two years, for "each and every offence."[256] Even though the emigrant-agent statute, like master-servant law generally, was racially neutral, everyone understood its racially specific intent. One commentator complained that the state's politically dominant agrarians "refuse[d] to allow the negroes to leave."[257] Another described the bill as placing "a prohibitory duty" on recruiters who "carry off the colored population" to out-of-state jobs.[258] It "ought to flatter the colored citizen," this commentator quipped, "to know that he is so much wanted that obstruction is made to his emigration."[259]

All of these legal devices—the emigrant agent law, the criminalization of labor enticement, the labor-enticement civil suits—shackled the "free" labor market. They were facially neutral, which shielded them from equal-protection attack, but widely understood to target Black South Carolinians. They undergirded the Jim Crow era's repressive labor system, known variously as "peonage," "involuntary servitude," "the new dependency," and "neo-slavery."[260]

Justice Jonathan Jasper Wright envisioned a fairer South Carolina. He sought to use free-market means to achieve egalitarian ends. In coming decades, free-market means would migrate from the progressive left to the probusiness right.[261] Wright's egalitarian ends remain elusive.

---

256. "Emigrant Agents to Pay Licenses," *The State*, Dec. 23, 1891, 1; Act of Dec. 24, 1891, no. 697, 3, 1891 S.C. Acts 1084, 1084. For more on laws of this sort, see David E. Bernstein, "The Law and Economics of Post-Civil War Restrictions on Interstate Migration by African Americans," *Texas Law Review* 76, no. 4 (Mar. 1998): 781–847.

257. "The Gates Shut," *The State*, Dec. 23, 1891, 4.

258. "The State's Survey," *The State*, Dec. 11, 1891, 4.

259. Ibid.

260. See, for example, Leon F. Litwack, *Been in the Storm So Long: The Aftermath of Slavery* (New York: Alfred A. Knopf, 1979); Leon F. Litwack, *Trouble in Mind: Black Southerners in the Age of Jim Crow* (New York: Vintage Books, 1998); Pete Daniel, *The Shadow of Slavery: Peonage in the South, 1901–1969* (Champaign: University of Illinois Press, 1990); Blackmon, *Slavery by Another Name*; Foner, *Reconstruction*, 593.

261. Godcharles v. Wigeman, 113 Pa. 431 (1886) [striking down a state law that required mining and manufacturing companies to pay wages in cash: "An attempt has been made by the legislature to do what, in this country, cannot be done; that is, prevent persons who are sui juris from making their own contracts"]; Arthur M. Schlesinger Jr., *The Age of Jackson* (Bos-

The precipitous decline of Wright's dream, like its heady rise, shows how weak the law can be in the face of brute force. Back in 1860, slave law in South Carolina seemed an impregnable fortress. Ten years and a massive war later, it was no more, and Wright, the son of an enslaved person, sat on South Carolina's highest bench. He used his position to construct a new employment law for the state, in which consensual labor contracts theoretically established horizontal relations between employers and employees, not vertical relations between masters and servants. Though carefully chiseled, Wright's doctrine was a handsome ice sculpture in a South Carolina summer, destined to melt away. Before long, South Carolina "slaves" became "servants." Masters remained masters.

And yet, the fall from Reconstruction's heights did not return South Carolina to prewar depths. Emancipation held, as did many other bedrock legal achievements of Reconstruction. Black education, albeit on a separate-and-unequal basis, remained a constitutional mandate. The right of Blacks to marry, move about, own property, practice law, sue, be sued, make contracts, testify in court, hold public office, vote, and serve on juries were among Reconstruction's legacies. Although, as we shall see, some of those rights were smothered during the Jim Crow era, none was extinguished entirely. Legal guardrails, both institutional and ideological, forged during Reconstruction, mattered. They constrained white supremacy, somewhat, through Jim Crow and beyond.

---

ton: Little, Brown, 1946), 315–17; Morton J. Horwitz, *The Transformation of American Law, 1870–1960: The Crisis of Legal Orthodoxy* (New York: Oxford University Press, 1992); Daniel T. Rodgers, *Age of Fracture* (Cambridge, MA: Harvard University Press, 2011), 41–76.

CHAPTER FOUR

Tucker v. Blease: Jim Crow Schools[1]

On January 24, 1913, the trustees of the Dalcho School, an all-white public school in Dillon County, South Carolina, expelled Dudley, Eugene, and Herbert Kirby, ages ten, twelve, and fourteen, respectively. According to subsequent testimony, the Kirby boys were "good pupils" who "never . . . exercise[ed] any bad influence in school."[2] Moreover, the boys' overwhelmingly white ancestry, in the words of the South Carolina Supreme Court, technically "entitled [them] to be classified as white."[3] They seemingly qualified in every way to attend the segregated Dalcho School. Nevertheless, because white locals believed that the Kirbys were "not of pure Caucasian blood," and that therefore their removal was in the school's best interest, the court, in *Tucker v. Blease* (South Carolina, 1914), upheld their dismissal.[4]

This chapter uses the Kirbys' story to examine public school segregation, a topic that, thanks to *Brown v. Board of Education* (US, 1954), would come, for a time, to symbolize the entire Jim Crow system that prevailed in the US South from the late-nineteenth through the mid-twentieth century. The two chapters that follow discuss two other components of Jim Crow: jury service (chapter 5) and lynching (chapter 6). Together, these three chapters add texture to our understanding of how white supremacy operated in the post-Reconstruction South. They depict abuse after abuse, as well as occasional glimmers of justice. They also challenge the conventional wisdom that Jim Crow marked the nadir, or low point, of African American history.

---

1. Harper Addison, Jessica Bradshaw, Allyson Cobb, E. Dudley Colhoun, Samuel Diamant, Andrew Gilbert, Jeffrey Higgs, Nicholas Skipper, and John Wertheimer coauthored this chapter. A version of this chapter appeared in the *Law and History Review* 29, no. 2 (2011): 471–95.

2. Tucker v. Blease, 81 S.E. 668, 669–70 (S.C. 1914).

3. Ibid., 675.

4. Ibid.

Howard University historian Rayford Logan provided the classic expression of this notion in his seminal 1954 book *The Negro in American Life and Thought: The Nadir*. "The last decade of the nineteenth century and the opening of the twentieth century," Logan wrote, "marked the nadir of the Negro's status in American society."[5] Subsequent generations of historians have likewise referred to the Jim Crow era as "the nadir of the negro,"[6] "the nadir of U.S. race relations,"[7] "the nadir of African American history,"[8] or simply "the nadir."[9]

Unquestionably, the twisting plunge from Reconstruction's heights was brutal for Black southerners, marked, as it was, by disfranchisement, peonage, separate-and-unequal opportunities, and lynching, all undergirded by an unapologetic, militant ideology of white supremacy. Hard-won constitu-

---

5. Rayford W. Logan, *The Negro in American Life and Thought: The Nadir, 1877–1901* (New York: Dial Press, 1954), 52.

6. "Nadir of the Negro," in *Jim Crow: A Historical Encyclopedia of the American Mosaic*, eds. Nikki L. M. Brown and Barry M. Stentiford (Santa Barbara, CA: Greenwood Press, 2014), 295.

7. Jolene Hubbs, "Goophering Jim Crow: Charles Chestnutt's 1890s America," *American Literary Realism* 46, no. 1 (Fall 2013): 12; David Brown and Clive Webb, *Race in the American South: From Slavery to Civil Rights* (Edinburgh: Edinburgh University Press, 2007), 180; Martha Jones, *All Bound Up Together: The Woman Question in African American Public Culture, 1830–1900* (Chapel Hill: University of North Carolina Press, 2007), 174; Rachel D. Godsil, "The Politics of Law in the Jim Crow Era," *Michigan Law Review* 105, no. 3 (Dec. 2006): 538; Steven Hoelscher, "Making Place, Making Race: Performances of Whiteness in the Jim Crow South," *Annals of the Association of American Geographers* 93, no. 3 (Sept. 2003): 675.

8. Leon Litwack, *Trouble in Mind: Black Southerners in the Age of Jim Crow* (New York: Vintage Books, 1999), xiv; Glenda Elizabeth Gilmore, "'Somewhere' in the Nadir of African American History, 1890–1920," National Humanities Center, accessed Aug. 29, 2022, http://nationalhumanitiescenter.org/tserve/freedom/1865-1917/essays/nadir.htm; Brian Kelly, "Labor, Race, and the Search for a Central Theme in the History of the Jim Crow South," *Irish Journal of American Studies* 10 (2001): 61; Jay Winston Driskell, *Schooling Jim Crow: The Fight for Atlanta's Booker T. Washington High School and the Roots of Black Protest Politics* (Charlottesville: University of Virginia Press, 2014), 26 ("the nadir of black history").

9. Angela M. Hornsby, "Gender and Class in Post-Emancipation Black Communities," in *A Companion to African American History*, ed. Alton Hornsby Jr. (Malden, MA: Blackwell Publishing, 2005), 381; Leon F. Litwack, "Jim Crow Blues," *OAH Magazine of History*, vol. 18, no. 2, Jan. 2004, 7; Gerald Ianovici, "'A Living Death': Gothic Signification and the Nadir in 'The Marrow of Tradition,'" *MELUS* 27, no. 4 (2002): 34; Charles E. Wynes, "The Evolution of Jim Crow Laws in Twentieth Century Virginia," *Phylon* 28, no. 4 (1967): 416; James Smethurst, *The African American Roots of Modernism* (Chapel Hill: University of North Carolina Press, 2011), 102.

tional rights were ripped away from Black arms, by force, violence, and law. United States Senator "Pitchfork" Ben Tillman, South Carolina's leading turn-of the-century politician, acknowledged in 1906 that the law theoretically gave "Negroes" the same rights as it gave "the Caucasians" but vowed that Black southerners would "never have those rights," for "the white people of the south," on whose behalf he claimed to speak, regarded the Fourteenth and Fifteenth Amendments as "mere pieces of paper and a bit [of] wasted ink."[10] With South Carolina in mind, Tillman figured that there were enough Black Republicans "to outvote the whites . . . if they [Black Republicans] were allowed to vote." Fortunately, he said, there were enough "shotguns . . . to carry the elections for the Democrats."[11] During the Jim Crow era, Tillman and company relegated Black southerners to a demeaning form of second-class citizenship. Northerners, including the Republican Party, acquiesced.

And yet, although the status of Black southerners undeniably plummeted in the decades surrounding 1900, it never approached the depths of slavery. Separate-and-unequal Jim Crow schooling was indefensible, but not as indefensible as the criminalization of education under slavery. During Jim Crow, few Black South Carolinians were able to vote or serve on juries, despite what the US Constitution said. During slavery, no Black South Carolinians, free or enslaved, were permitted to vote or serve on juries, precisely because of what the state constitution said. If Jim Crow "marked the nadir of the Negro's status in American society,"[12] what did the era of slavery mark?

Admittedly, lynching was a Jim Crow–era horror with no exact antebellum correlate. Slavers had a powerful profit motive not to kill enslaved workers so wantonly. But lynching, a lethal, quasi-public form of racial terror, was, in a way, a Jim Crow–era replacement for the usually nonlethal, private form of racial terror that prevailed during slavery. Lynching can also be seen as a white supremacist response to Black advances. Lynching rates rose as interracial economic competition increased.[13]

It might also be noted that many Reconstruction-era advances persisted

---

10. "Tillman Says War Amendments Are Mere Bits of Wasted Paper," *New York Age*, Sept. 6, 1906, 5.

11. Ibid.

12. Logan, *The Negro in American Life*, 52.

13. Sarah A. Soule, "Populism and Black Lynching in Georgia, 1890–1900," *Social Forces* 71, no. 2 (Dec. 1992): 431–49.

through the Jim Crow years. As the present chapter shows, nonwhite South Carolinians continued to have access to public education. Jim Crow public schools were segregated, of course, but so were most Reconstruction-era schools.[14] Unquestionably, the "equal" in "separate but equal" never ceased to be a cruel joke. Funding disparities favoring white public schools were huge at the dawn of Jim Crow. Then they increased.[15] "Separate but equal" logic, however, occasionally raised the floor for Black education. For example, the same Constitution of 1895 that effectively disfranchised Black South Carolinians also ordered the establishment of the state's first publicly funded land-grant college for "colored" students, with "representation to be given" in the selection of "professors and instructors" to "the men and women of the negro race."[16] Black illiteracy in South Carolina—an estimated 95 percent before emancipation[17] and almost 80 percent following Reconstruction[18]—declined steadily during Jim Crow: to roughly 50 percent in 1900,[19] 40 percent in 1910,[20] and 30 percent in 1920.[21] By 1940, racial gaps in school-attendance rates were modest: 51 percent of young Black South Carolinians attended school, as did 56 percent of young white

---

14. Walter Edgar, *South Carolina: A History* (Columbia: University of South Carolina Press, 1998), 390.

15. Ibid., 448.

16. S.C. Const. art. XI, § 8 (1895). The state already funded whites-only Clemson, Winthrop, and the University of South Carolina. It risked losing federal "land grant" funding unless it either admitted Black students to its existing land-grant colleges or opened an alternative for nonwhite students. The so-called Second Morrill Act (Agricultural College Act of 1890 [26 Stat. 417, 7 U.S.C. § 321 et seq.]), which the US Congress adopted in 1890, ordered states that, on racial grounds, denied Black applicants admission to federally funded land-grant colleges to provide separate institutions for nonwhite students. The constitutional convention chose the latter course. It ordered the State Assembly to establish a land-grant college for "colored" students. That university is known today as South Carolina State University. William C. Hine, *South Carolina State University: A Black Land-Grant College in Jim Crow America* (Columbia: University of South Carolina Press, 2018).

17. Edgar, *South Carolina*, 299.

18. The actual figure was 78.5 percent. Ibid., 421.

19. The actual figure was 52.8 percent. *Thirteenth Census of the United States, Taken in the Year 1910*, vol. 3, Population, 1910 (Washington, DC: Government Printing Office, 1913), 655.

20. The actual figure was 38.7 percent. Ibid.

21. The actual figure was 29.3 percent. "Illiteracy, for the State, Urban and Rural, 1930 and 1920," in *Fifteenth Census of the United States, 1930: Population*, vol. 3, table (Washington, DC: Government Printing Office, 1932), 780.

South Carolinians.[22] Nonwhite schools, including historically Black colleges, remained an important legacy of Reconstruction, funding disparities notwithstanding.

Another Reconstruction-era advance that persisted despite white supremacist opposition was the freedom of Black people to migrate legally, an option unavailable to enslaved people. Industrial jobs pulled Black South Carolinians northward, especially when European immigration slowed during and after World War I. Southern atrocities, meanwhile, pushed them. Sympathetic observers noted that repeated "outrages upon Negro men and women" committed by "South Carolina mobs," along with the state's "double standard of justice as between black and white," furnished a powerful "impetus to migration."[23] (One curious northerner took to asking Black migrants about their decisions to leave the South. "Aren't you afraid it will be too cold for you in this part of the country?" Migrants typically replied, "I'd rather take my chance of freezing to death up here than run the risk of being roasted alive, tied to a stake down South."[24]) During the Jim Crow era, millions of Black southerners voted with their feet in this way. The South Carolina population was 60 percent Black in 1890, but only 46 percent Black in 1930.[25]

Chapters 5 and 6 illustrate the persistence, through the Jim Crow years, of another important legacy of Reconstruction: the continued ability of Black South Carolinians to litigate in the state's courts, sometimes represented by Black lawyers.[26]

---

22. "School Attendance by Age, Race, and Sex, for the State, Urban and Rural: 1940 and 1930," in *Sixteenth Census of the United States, 1940: Population*, vol. 2: *Characteristics of the Population*, table (Washington, DC: Government Printing Office, 1943), 357.

23. "The Mockery of Justice in the Southern States," *Negro World* (New York), June 14, 1924, 2.

24. "The Negro Migration," *New York Age*, Oct. 20, 1923, 7.

25. "Population of States, by Sex, Race, Urban-Rural Residence, and Age: 1790–1970," *Historical Statistics of the United States: Colonial Times to 1970*, (Washington, DC: US Department of Commerce, Bureau of the Census, 1975), 34, 195–209.

26. For more on Blacks as litigants and lawyers in the Jim Crow South, see Myisha S. Eatmon, "Public Wrongs, Private Rights: African Americans, Private Law, and White Violence during Jim Crow" (PhD diss., Northwestern University, 2020); Melissa L. Milewski, *Litigating across the Color Line: Civil Cases between Black and White Southerners from the End of Slavery to Civil Rights* (New York: Oxford University Press, 2018); and William Lewis Burke, *All for Civil Rights: African American Lawyers in South Carolina, 1868–1968* (Athens: University of Georgia Press, 2017).

Even the cornerstone of Jim Crow law in South Carolina, the disfranchising Constitution of 1895, demonstrates the persistence of some Reconstruction-era protections. That constitution's universally understood goal was, as one contemporary pundit wrote, to "disfranchise the negro."[27] As chapter 5 demonstrates, the new constitution went far toward achieving this goal, using such indirect devices as literacy tests, "understanding" clauses, and poll taxes.[28] These indirect devices had the residual effect of disfranchising some poor white voters. White supremacists would have preferred a more direct route: white-only voting rights, such as had existed prior to emancipation. But Reconstruction-era laws constrained them. As one white advocate of Black disfranchisement put it at the 1895 constitutional convention, the challenge was to "get around the Chinese wall, the impassable bulwark which the Fifteenth Amendment throws around the negroes."[29]

The resulting indirect disfranchisement schemes did not please everyone. The few Black delegates at the convention "asked and obtained permission to be excused from signing the Constitution."[30] Some white delegates, including some advocates of white supremacy, also opposed the new constitution's disfranchisement schemes. J. W. Gray, a white delegate, voted against the suffrage provisions at the convention because, in addition to disfranchising some white voters, which he opposed, the provisions would open the convention to charges that it had mounted a "conspiracy to defraud a certain class of American citizens in the exercise of the elective franchise." Gray, a lawyer, "greatly fear[ed that] this charge may be sustained in the United States Supreme Court."[31] I. Harleston Read, another white delegate, likewise opposed the constitution's vague "understanding clause" because it "open[ed] the door for fraud" in the voter registration process and was likely "to be upset if tested" in the federal courts.[32] Their worries were misplaced. The federal courts did almost nothing to protect Black voting rights

27. D.D. Wallace, "The South Carolina Constitutional Convention of 1895," *Sewanee Review* 4, no. 3 (May 1896): 350–51.

28. S.C. Const. art. II, § 4 (1895).

29. *Journal of the Constitutional Convention of the State of South Carolina* (Columbia, SC: Charles A. Calvo Jr., 1895), 468.

30. Ibid., 727.

31. Ibid., 518.

32. Ibid., 727.

during these years.[33] Yet Jim Crow–era white supremacists were clearly aware that some legal legacies of Reconstruction had not been fully erased.

The white-supremacist impulse raged so intensely at the 1895 constitutional convention that modern observers might easily overlook how encumbered white supremacists of the time imagined themselves to be. Ben Tillman's older brother George addressed the convention at its close. He praised the convention's handiwork—the disfranchising constitution—as the best that could be achieved given the day's constraints. But he rued those constraints, which, he said, Republicans had clapped around the white South's wrists during Reconstruction and which still restricted white southerners in the exercise of the dominance that was their racial birthright. The new constitution was "not such an instrument as we would have made if we had been a free people," Tillman said, with reference to white South Carolinians. "We are not a free people. We have not been since the war. . . . If we were free, instead of having negro suffrage, we would have negro slavery."[34]

Racial hierarchy anchored George Tillman's worldview. "I have an abiding faith in the Anglo-Saxon race," he declared, "as there has never been a considerable number of them together anywhere that they did not dominate any race with which they came into contact." "Whatever may happen," Tillman told the assembled delegates, "I have faith that they [Anglo-Saxons] will rule."[35] George Tillman was no pariah. His convention-closing remarks stirred "prolonged applause."[36]

The present chapter is a case study of *Tucker v. Blease*, the school-segregation case described above, in which school leaders, Board of Education officials, and ultimately the South Carolina Supreme Court had to decide which public school a group of mixed-race siblings should attend. The chapter highlights South Carolina's continued obsession with racial categories.[37] The way the government treated its citizens—even during

---

33. Michael J. Klarman, *From Jim Crow to Civil Rights: The Supreme Court and the Struggle for Racial Equality* (New York: Oxford University Press, 2004), 37. Things changed slightly in the Progressive Era. See Guinn v. United States, 238 U.S. 347 (1915); and Myers v. Anderson, 238 U.S. 368 (1915).

34. G. D. Tillman, *Journal of the Constitutional Convention*, 731.

35. Ibid., 734.

36. Ibid., 734.

37. Charles Black, "The Lawfulness of the Segregation Decisions," *Yale Law Journal* 69 (1960): 424.

childhood, even in their home communities—depended entirely upon their perceived racial classifications. That was true under slavery. It remained true under Jim Crow, though the stakes were lower.

The chapter also demonstrates how fuzzy legal lines could be at the racial margins. In South Carolina, the law of racial determination was characterized by relatively weak legislative guidelines, a relatively strong tradition of local community control, dogged white determination to patrol the boundaries of whiteness, and an appellate judiciary powerful enough to rewrite even constitutionally mandated rules.

Tucker also highlights the centrality of state-level legal systems to the so-called Black-white paradigm—the misleading notion that America's racial palette historically contained only two colors. The *Tucker* ruling conceptualized South Carolina as a place containing just two sorts of people: "those with and those without negro blood."[38] Hidden beneath the surface of the published opinion in the case, however, was a fact that previous scholars have overlooked.[39] The Kirby boys were not alleged to have "negro" ancestry, and their neighbors did not seek to send them to "negro" schools. Instead, the siblings were alleged to have Croatan Indian ancestry, and their neighbors sought to send them to Indian schools. The legal system, however, filtered out this complexity. By the time the South Carolina Supreme Court ruled, the dispute's multicultural features had all but disappeared. Subsequent journalists, law reporters, lawyers, and scholars would all assume, wrongly, that the case involved only Black people and white people. In *Tucker v. Blease*, the judicial process served as a primitive camera, turning America's multicolored rainbow into grainy Black and white.[40]

---

38. Tucker v. Blease, 81 S.E. 668, 673 (1914).

39. Dudley O. McGovney, "Naturalization of the Mixed-Blood: A Dictum," *California Law Review* 22, no. 4 (May, 1934): 377–91; Joseph S. Ransmeier, "The Fourteenth Amendment and the 'Separate but Equal' Doctrine," *Michigan Law Review* 50, no. 2 (Dec. 1951): 203–60; Daniel J. Sharfstein, "Crossing the Color Line: Racial Migration and the One-Drop Rule, 1600–1860," *Minnesota Law Review* 91 (2007): 592–656; J. Anthony Paredes, ed., *Indians of the Southeastern United States in the Late Twentieth Century* (Tuscaloosa: University of Alabama Press, 1992), 82; Frank W. Sweet, *Legal History of the Color Line* (Palm Coast, FL: Backintyme, 2005), 403–4.

40. For an expanded discussion of this theme, see John W. Wertheimer, Jessica Bradshaw, Allyson Cobb, Harper Addison, E. Dudley Colhoun, Samuel Diamant, Andrew Gilbert, Jeffrey Higgs, and Nicholas Skipper, "'The Law Recognizes Racial Instinct': *Tucker v. Blease* and the Black-White Paradigm in the Jim Crow South," *Law and History Review* 29, no. 2 (May 2011): 473-76.

The Croatan Indians of Dillon County

Dillon County lies in northeastern South Carolina,[41] across state line from Robeson County, a famously triracial North Carolina county whose population historically divided into three groups of roughly equal size: Indians, whites, and Blacks. Robeson County is the traditional home of the Native American group known today as the Lumbee Tribe. In 1885, North Carolina officially recognized this group as the "Croatan Indians of Robeson County." The state renamed them "Indians of Robeson County" in 1911, "Cherokee Indians of Robeson County" in 1913, and "Lumbee Indians" in 1953.[42] According to the 1910 census, the Croatans were the seventh largest Indian tribe in the nation, with an official population of about six thousand. Most Croatans lived in North Carolina's Robeson County, which, since the 1880s, had maintained three-way school segregation: white, Black, and Indian. Over the years, the Croatan population slowly spread to surrounding counties. Three-way segregation spread too.[43]

Dillon County, South Carolina, was among the surrounding counties that contained small pockets of Croatans.[44] The US census for 1910 reported that Dillon County contained over eleven thousand "negros," just under eleven thousand white people, and seventy-seven "Indians,"[45] many of

41. Thomas Hunter McEaddy, "The Creation of Dillon County" (Columbia: University of South Carolina, 1971), held at the Dillon County Library.

42. See Adolph L. Dial and David K. Eliades, *The Only Land I Know: A History of the Lumbee Indians* (Syracuse, NY: Syracuse University Press, 1975); "30,000 North Carolinians Vote Themselves a Name," *Carolina Indian Voice*, Dec. 14, 1978, 9, reprinted from *The State* (Columbia, SC), Jan. 26, 1952.

43. Department of Commerce, Bureau of Census, *Indian Population in the United States and Alaska, 1910* (Washington, DC: Government Printing Office, 1915), 17–21; "Report on Tribal Rights of Croatans," *Charlotte Observer*, May 18, 1915, 12; *Laws and Resolutions of the State of North Carolina, 1885*, Public Laws, ch. 51; E. Dale Davis, "The Lumbee Indians of Robeson County, North Carolina, and Their Schools," paper presented at the National Conference of Christians and Jews, Pembroke, NC, Dec. 19, 1986, 1–4; V. Ray Thompson, "A History of the Education of the Lumbee Indians of Robeson County, North Carolina from 1885 to 1970," (EdD diss., University of Miami, 1973), 39–43; Adolph L. Dial, *The Lumbee* (New York: Chelsea House, 1993), 57–61; "Legislature's Dull Day," *Charlotte Observer*, Jan. 19, 1907, 1; and John Wertheimer, *Law and Society in the South: A History of North Carolina Court Cases* (Lexington: University Press of Kentucky, 2009), 165–89.

44. "Report on Tribal Rights of Croatans," *Charlotte Observer*, May 18, 1915, 12.

45. *Thirteenth Census of the United States*, 660.

whom had migrated from North Carolina.[46] The county's "Indian" population was larger than reported; many Indians appeared in the census as "mulattos," not Indians, a common practice nationally.[47]

Locally, Dillon County's "Croatans" were a recognized social group. Newspapers routinely affixed that label in stories. One 1911 article described an altercation in Dillon County involving "Pierce Allen, white," "Dave Allen, a negro," and "Esau Locklear, a Croatan."[48] Another story from Dillon County introduced John Miller as "an old Croatan."[49] A third reported that Ed Chavis, "a Croatan," had shot and seriously wounded Bob Locklear, "Croatan."[50]

North Carolina officially mandated three-way school segregation in areas where Croatans were numerous. At the statewide level, at least, South Carolina, with a much smaller Croatan population, employed just two-way school segregation. At the 1895 Constitutional Convention, South Carolina Governor John Gary Evans declared that "experience has proved the wisdom of separate education for the races." Although he urged that public schools be "liberally supported by taxation," given that education was a prerequisite to citizenship and therefore "the most serious" issue that state government handled, he insisted that districts provide separate "white and colored school[s],"[51] implicitly recognizing that Black South Carolinians were citizens of the state and therefore deserving of state-funded education, albeit in segregated form. The 1895 constitution implemented this racial binary, mandating that the state provide separate schools "for children of the white and colored races," respectively, and stipulating that "no child of

---

46. One sample of twenty-four Dillon County "Indians" listed in the 1910 census contained thirteen who had been born in North Carolina. Many of these Dillon County Indians had surnames that, despite unusual spellings, Robeson County residents would, to this day, recognize as "Lumbee"; e.g., Oxendine, Locklayer, Chavas, Dials. *United States Census*, Dillon County, South Carolina, 1910, HeritageQuest Online, https://www.ancestryheritagequest.com/search/categories/usfedcen/.

47. Ariela Gross, "'Of Portuguese Origin': Litigating Identity and Citizenship among the 'Little Races' in Nineteenth-Century America," *Law and History Review* 25, no. 3 (Fall 2007): 478.

48. "Negro Badly Beaten," *The State*, July 18, 1911, 3.

49. "Further Details of Berry Killing: Many Rumors Conflict with Accepted Version," *The State*, Mar. 8, 1911, 9.

50. "Shot in Family Row: Bob Locklear Seriously Wounded by Ed Chavis," *The State*, May 30, 1911, 12.

51. *Journal of the Constitutional Convention*, 12.

either race shall ever be permitted to attend a school provided for children of the other race."[52] (The two-way segregation could have been even more complete. At the 1895 convention, white delegate J. P. Derham of Horry County proposed that counties segregate not just their schools, but also their school taxes. "There shall be two funds in each County," Derham explained, "one for the support of the public schools for the whites" and another "for the support of the school[s] for the negroes." Individual taxpayers would designate the fund to which they wanted their school taxes to go. The measure failed.[53]) In line with these binary racial norms, Dillon County officials listed just two sorts of schools there: "White" and "Negro."[54]

At the local level, however, some South Carolina communities quietly maintained three-way school segregation, with separate schools for "whites," "negroes," and "Indians," respectively. Dillon County's Oakland District No. 5, for instance, supported "a white school, a negro school, and a school for the descendants of the Indian race."[55] Where it existed, this localized, three-way school segregation appears to have resulted both from anti-Croatan racism among whites and from anti-Black racism among Croatans.[56] The apparent Croatan disinclination to attend "negro" schools may also have reflected their awareness that Black schools were dreadfully under-funded. Statewide, per-student spending in South Carolina was substantially higher for white people than for Black people. The racial funding gap had grown since the 1880s, reflecting the consolidation of Jim Crow.[57] In few places was the funding gap larger than in Dillon County. Around the time of the Kirby boys' expulsion, Dillon County spent twenty-five dollars and fifty-six cents per white student per year. The comparable figure for "negro" students: one dollar and twenty-eight cents. Croatan families may have rightly concluded that educational opportunities in the "negro" schools were not robust.[58]

---

52. S.C. Const. art. XI, § 7 (1895).

53. *Journal of the Constitutional Convention*, 93.

54. "Public Schools of Dillon County, S.C.," *State Department of Education Bulletin*, Oct. 1915; and "What the Schools Cost," *Dillon Herald*, Nov. 6, 1913, 7.

55. "Well Meant Criticisms and Timely Suggestions," *Dillon Herald*, April 23, 1914, 1.

56. "Croatan Case Was Decided," *The State*, June 12, 1908, 11; and *Charlotte Observer*, Sept. 11, 1902, 4.

57. Edgar, *South Carolina*, 448.

58. "What the Schools Cost," *Dillon Herald*, Nov. 6, 1913, 7.

The Kirbys

John and Annie Kirby, the parents of Dudley, Eugene, and Herbert, had always lived as "white," as had their eight children. The Kirbys attended white churches. Their children attended white schools. The census classified them as white.[59] The family associated with whites.[60] By local standards, the Kirbys were well-to-do. At a time when land-renters (tenant farmers, sharecroppers) outnumbered landowners in rural Dillon County by almost three to one, the Kirbys owned hundreds of acres.[61]

Beginning in 1909, however, a series of tragedies buffeted the family. In June of that year, John Kirby, the children's father, was shot and killed by a local physician following an altercation.[62] A few months later, seventeen-year-old daughter Lucy died.[63] The 1910 census, taken locally in May, lists the widowed Annie Kirby, white, living with her seven surviving and still-unmarried children, all white, on a Dillon County farm that she owned outright (no mortgage).[64] Although Annie Kirby could neither read nor write, her five school-aged children could. Six months later, Annie Kirby died, orphaning her seven children. The still-visible epitaph on her headstone in Mt. Holly Cemetery (a historically whites-only graveyard in Dillon County) evoked the suffering of the entire Kirby family: "How many hopes lie buried here."[65]

---

59. *1900 United States Census, Dillon County, South Carolina*, roll 1535, 154; *1910 United States Census, Dillon County, South Carolina*, roll 1458, 171. HeritageQuest, https://www.ancestryheritagequest.com/search/categories/usfedcen/.

60. Tucker v. Blease, 671.

61. *Thirteenth Census of the United States*, vol. 7: *Agriculture* (Washington, DC: Government Printing Office, 1913). For evidence of the Kirbys' landownership, see Tucker v. Blease, 81 S.E. 668, 669 (1914).

62. "Physician Shoots, Perhaps Kills: Dr. H.A. Edwards and John Kirby of Dillon Fight," *The State*, June 16, 1909, 1; "John Kirby Succumbs to his Many Wounds," *The State*, June 18, 1909, 1.

63. Lucy Kirby died on November 16, 1909, just days before her eighteenth birthday. Headstone, Mt. Holly Cemetery, Dillon County.

64. The children were: Eddie, 15; Lila, 10; Herbert, 9; Eugene, 8; Dudley, 7; Dessie, 5; and John C, 3. United States Census of 1910, South Carolina, Dillon County, Manning Township, Supervisor's District no. 60, Enumeration District No. 68, sheet no. 17B, HeritageQuest, https://www.ancestryheritagequest.com/search/categories/usfedcen/.

65. Annie Kirby died on November 11, 1910. Headstone, Mt. Holly Cemetery, Dillon County, South Carolina. Mt. Holly Cemetery appears to have been historically for white people, as suggested by the burial there of several white Confederate Civil War veterans. See

The Kirby children moved in with their mother's sister, Sarah Tucker, in Dillon County's Bethea Township. Sarah and her husband George were in their early forties. Years previously, they had lost their only child, two-year old daughter Mary, a loss that may have predisposed them to respond sympathetically to the Kirbys' misfortunes. George Tucker was "an industrious and successful farmer." He and Sarah were consistently known as white people.[66]

The Tuckers lived in the Dalcho School District. For a time, Dalcho, one of Dillon County's Croatan population pockets, maintained separate public schools for white students, "negro" students, and Indian students, respectively.[67] The Indian school, however, failed to retain its teachers and closed. By the time the Kirby children moved to the area, only white and "negro" schools remained.

Herbert, Eugene, and Dudley Kirby chose the white option, as they had throughout their lives.[68] In Dalcho, that meant the Dalcho School. As southern-born legal scholar Charles Black later remarked of Jim Crow school-naming practices, "When you are in Leeville and hear someone say 'Leeville High,' you know he has reference to the white high school." Schools for nonwhite students had other names.[69] So it was in Dalcho. The Kirby boys enrolled in the all-white, highly regarded Dalcho School.[70] Before they could graduate, however, the school's trustees expelled them on account of their race.

"Graves Vandalized at Mt. Holly Cemetery," *Dillon Herald*, Oct. 6, 2014, http://www.dillonheraldonline.com/2014/10/06/graves-vandalized-at-mt-holly-cemetery/.

66. "Death Notices," *The State*, Mar. 3, 1916; Tucker v. Blease, 670–72; *Thirteenth Census of the United States* (1910), South Carolina, Dillon County, Bethea Township; and Tucker family headstones, Catfish Creek Baptist Church Cemetery, Latta, South Carolina.

67. Dillon County had at least one other Native American School at that time: the Sardis Indian School. See Durward T. Stokes, *The History of Dillon County, South Carolina* (Columbia: University of South Carolina Press, 1978), 150. The Sardis Indian School continued to operate until 1952. See J. Anthony Paredes, ed., *Indians of the Southeastern United States in the Late Twentieth Century* (Tuscaloosa: University of Alabama Press, 1992), 82.

68. Tucker v. Blease, 669.

69. Charles Black, "The Lawfulness of the Segregation Decisions," *Yale Law Journal* 69 (1960): 425.

70. Stokes, *The History of Dillon County*, 146.

Expulsion

The Kirbys' expulsion from the Dalcho School reveals how uncertain racial definitions were at the time. Different sources of legal authority competed to define racial identity. Unlike, say, the centralized and professionalized system of racial determination that prevailed decades later in Nazi Germany,[71] racial determination in early-twentieth-century South Carolina had a notably grassroots feel.

The racial expulsion of the Kirby children occurred during their third year at the Dalcho School. It was initiated not by state officials or even local school administrators, but rather by crusading white neighbors. Sam Edwards, a Dalcho School parent, "dictated and circulated"[72] a petition demanding the dismissal of all nonwhite students. Although the petition did not name Dudley, Eugene, or Herbert, everyone understood that the Kirby boys were, in fact, its targets. Bad blood existed between the Edwardses and the Kirbys. Sam Edwards's brother was the local physician who, four years previously, had killed John Kirby, the boys' father, following an altercation. Sam Edwards's insistent denial at a subsequent hearing that his petition had "anything to do with the killing of John Kirby" reveals local suspicion that a connection may have existed.[73] (It also raises the possibility that a dispute over racial reputation may have had something to do with the killing of John Kirby.)

Many Dalcho School parents and some others signed Sam Edwards's petition, which Edwards then delivered to the school's board of trustees.[74] Trustee chair John D. Coleman was familiar with local doubts about the Kirbys' whiteness. Questions had arisen when the light-skinned Kirby orphans first applied for admission to Dalcho, Coleman later testified. Nonetheless, out of respect for George Tucker, the boys' highly regarded (and indisputably "white") uncle, the trustees "thought it a business thing to

71. Thomas Pegelow Kaplan, "'In the Interest of the *Volk* . . .': Nazi-German Paternity Suits and Racial Recategorization in the Munich Superior Courts, 1938–1945," *Law and History Review* 29 (2011): 523–48.

72. Tucker v. Blease, 670.

73. Sam Edwards was the brother of H. A. Edwards, the doctor who killed John Kirby. Tucker v. Blease, 670; "Physician Shoots, Perhaps Kills: Dr. H. A. Edwards and John Kirby of Dillon Fight," *The State*, June 16, 1909, 1; "John Kirby Succumbs to His Many Wounds," *The State*, June 18, 1909, 1.

74. Tucker v. Blease, 670.

do" to let them attend Dalcho.[75] The trustees vowed to reconsider their offer of admission, however, should the boys' attendance "in some way become detrimental" to the school.[76]

Subsequent events persuaded the trustees to reconsider. Following the Kirbys' matriculation, four other allegedly mixed-race children, "some of whom were a good deal darker" than the Kirbys, sought to enroll. That, plus Edwards's petition, convinced the board to dismiss the Kirbys (and, presumably, the other allegedly mixed-race children). These students' continued attendance at Dalcho was not in the school's best interest, the trustees reasoned. After all, parents of the school's other pupils demonstrably did "not want their children raised up with" their kind.[77] On January 24, 1913, the trustees dismissed Dudley, Eugene, and Herbert Kirby. They then "had a talk . . . with Mr. Tucker," and explained why the boys had been dismissed: they "were not white."[78]

When determining the Kirby boys' racial identity, parents and trustees alike ignored the racial formulas in the South Carolina Constitution of 1895. The constitution's marital provisions considered anyone with "one-eighth or more negro blood" to be Black.[79] Although the constitution was ostensibly the state's supreme law, the Dalcho School's trustees ignored its one-eighth rule entirely. Nor did they rely on their eyes. The children's appearance and behavior seemed unimportant. Instead, trustees relied on their ears. The boys' community reputation would determine their racial identity. "In dismissing them," trustee chair Coleman later explained, "we did not investigate what mixture of blood was in them." Instead, Coleman based his vote on "what [he had] heard people say."[80] Trustee J. F. Williams reported that the board "did not act from appearance" but rather from "reputation and petition."[81] Trustee L. E. Dew explained that the Kirbys were dismissed "because they had the reputation of not being pure-blooded."[82]

George Tucker appealed his nephews' expulsion. Much like the trustees, he based his racial arguments on local reputation, not ancestral arithmetic,

75. Ibid., 669.
76. Ibid.
77. Ibid.
78. Ibid., 669, 672.
79. S.C. Const. art III, § 33.
80. Tucker v. Blease, 669.
81. Ibid.
82. Ibid.

the eyeball test, or state law. The Kirby children, he insisted, had "never been considered anything but white."[83] On February 24, 1913, a month after the dismissals, the Dillon County Board of Education conducted a hearing.[84] The most explicit testimony about the Kirby children's racial identity alleged that they were Croatan Indian. Dalcho resident G. F. Bethea testified that the late John Kirby, the children's father, "was considered a Croatan."[85] A school trustee stated that the children were "neither white nor black, but were Croatan."[86]

Describing someone as "Croatan" raised as many genealogical questions as it answered. According to the 1910 census, only about 8 percent of Croatans were "full blooded" Indians. The rest were "mixed blood." No Indian tribe in the country had a higher proportion of "mixed blooded" members. Although most Croatans mixed Indian with white lineage, an estimated 12 percent, according to the 1910 census, had partial "negro" ancestry.[87] If the testimony at the Kirby hearing is to be believed, however, the Kirbys were not among the minority of Croatans who had "negro" ancestry. No witness alleged that the Kirbys had any "negro" blood.[88]

The testimony offered at the board of education hearing demonstrates that school officials imagined a three-way local racial divide and placed the Kirby children in the Croatan category. At the time, the Dalcho School District contained approximately eighty white students and one hundred and twenty "negro" students.[89] Yet trustee Coleman stated that the Kirbys belonged to a third racial classification, one whose school-age cohort in the district numbered just "10 or 12." He meant the Croatans. The school to which the trustees proposed sending the Kirbys provides additional evidence of the trustees' intent. As of 1913, the Dalcho district operated one "white" school (the Dalcho School) and two "negro" schools. Yet when considering where the expelled Kirbys might study, the trustees admitted that the district operated no schools for "children of this class"—Croatans. Years

83. Ibid.

84. Ibid., 668.

85. Ibid., 668, 670–71.

86. Ibid, 669.

87. Department of Commerce, Bureau of Census, *Indian Population in the United States and Alaska, 1910* (Washington: Government Printing Office, 1915), 36–38.

88. Tucker v. Blease.

89. *Annual Records of the South Carolina State Superintendent of Education* (1912), Dillon County, 325, table 3, South Caroliniana Library, University of South Carolina.

previously, trustee Coleman stated, the district had "established a separate school" for "children of this class," who were neither Black nor white. Unable to retain a sufficient number of teachers, however, the school closed, leaving no local educational options for "children of this class."[90] He meant Croatans.

The Legal System Imposes the Black-White Paradigm

The further the case traveled from Dalcho, up through the South Carolina appeals process, the more the boys' alleged Croatan ancestry faded, and the more the case resembled a binary (Black-white) racial quarrel involving the one-drop-of-"negro"-blood rule. Although neither the one-drop rule nor any allegations of "negro blood" figured in the factual record of the Kirby case, the South Carolina courts invoked it because it was useful to the statewide administration of Jim Crow.

The Board of Education Hearing

The attorneys for both sides were from the local area, and thus were familiar with local segregation of Croatans. Both legal teams, however, had extensive statewide legal experience and thus understood how state-level legal elites thought. James Gibson, the lawyer who represented George Tucker, was both a leading member of the Dillon County bar and a familiar presence in the State Supreme Court.[91] Lanneau D. Lide, who represented school officials, was from neighboring Marion County. He also had a statewide professional portfolio.[92]

The only known surviving record of the Dillon County Board of Educa-

---

90. Tucker v. Blease, 669. Trustee Chair Coleman further distinguished the Kirbys' "class" from "negroes" when adding that "people of this [the Kirbys'] class had a space set apart for them in Catfish Baptist church, as did also the negroes." Ibid.

91. Yates Snowden, ed., *History of South Carolina*, vol. 4 (Chicago: Lewis Publishing, 1920), 141.

92. Snowden, *History of South Carolina*, 133; "Memory Hold the Door," University of South Carolina Law Library, accessed June 10, 2009, http://law.sc.edu/memory/1958/lideld.shtml.

tion hearing reports no lawyer questions—only witness testimony. [93] Nonetheless, the synopsis strongly suggests that lawyers' questions guided witness testimony. This is evident both from the substance of the witnesses' remarks and from references to "cross-examination" and "redirect examination."[94] Guided by lawyers' questions, witnesses played down the case's locally distinctive triracialism and played up the Black-white binary. Few witnesses provided positive declarations about the Kirbys' alleged Croatan identity. The assertion that the Kirbys were "neither white nor black, but were Croatan" was an outlier.[95] Instead, guided by lawyers' questions, witnesses tended to testify in negative terms that fit the Black-white paradigm: the Kirbys were "not white,"[96] "not clear-blooded,"[97] "not pure white,"[98] and "not [of] pure Caucasian blood."[99] Some witnesses who did make positive declarations about the Kirbys' racial identity did so in a guarded way, referring to the Kirbys as "mixed"[100] or "colored."[101] No witnesses claimed that the Kirbys were "negroes" or had any "negro blood."

The influence of lawyers was even more conspicuous in a series of questions about the Kirby family's interactions with other racial groups. Even though local expulsion advocates considered the Kirby children to be part Croatan, lawyers, being familiar with statewide legal norms, repeatedly asked witnesses to comment on the extent to which the boys associated with "negroes," but not Croatans. "I never heard of her . . . associating with negroes," S. T. Godbolt testified in apparent response to a lawyer's query about the Kirby boys' mother.[102] Other witnesses stated that neither the boys' father[103] nor the boys themselves had associated with "negroes."[104]

Lawyers appear similarly to have asked witnesses to discuss the Kirbys'

---

93. The case began with a Dillon County Board of Education hearing, proceeded to a South Carolina Board of Education appeal, and ended in the state Supreme Court. Tucker v. Blease; "Former Students Get Scholarship," *The State*, Aug. 29, 1913, 12.

94. Tucker v. Blease, 669.

95. Ibid., 669.

96. Ibid., 670.

97. Ibid.

98. Ibid.

99. Ibid., 669.

100. Ibid., 669–71.

101. Ibid.

102. Ibid., 670.

103. Ibid., 671.

104. Ibid., 669.

interactions with white people. John Sellers had heard that the Kirbys attended white churches and schools.[105] J. E. Henry and John Hayes reported that John Kirby "associated with white people in a business way."[106]

When considered in the context of the Dalcho School District, this line of questioning, especially as it pertained to the Kirbys' associations with "negroes," seems irrelevant. Expulsion advocates, after all, considered the boys part Croatan, not part "negro," and sought their removal to a Croatan school, not a "negro" school. Yet no witness seems to have been asked to comment about the Kirbys' associations with Croatans. Statewide, and indeed nationwide, association with "negroes" was a standard feature of racial determination cases; association with Croatans was not. The lawyers' awareness of this broader legal culture apparently led them to generate a factual record in this triracial dispute that would fit comfortably within the biracial legal paradigm that Jim Crow supporters were working to consolidate.

The South Carolina Supreme Court

In the spring of 1914, following losses in the Dillon County Board of Education and the South Carolina Board of Education, George Tucker appealed his nephews' expulsions to the South Carolina Supreme Court. He fared no better there. Chief Justice Eugene Gary's ruling upheld the boys' dismissals and steered South Carolina racial determination law away from the state constitution's one-eighth rule and toward the one-drop rule. Justice Gary's decision also furthered the process, begun below, of filtering out evidence of the boys' allegedly Croatan heritage. He analyzed the case in strictly Black-and-white terms.

Two factors help explain the *Tucker* court's imposition of the Black-white paradigm. The first looks backward, to legal precedent. Much of the prevailing law at the time—constitutional law, statutory law, and case law—emphasized a Black-white racial binary. Chief Justice Gary quoted the school-segregation provision of the South Carolina Constitution of 1895.[107] That provision divided the state's children into two groups, "white and col-

105. Ibid., 671.

106. Ibid., 670.

107. Edgar, *South Carolina*, 443–48.

ored," and declared, in binary terms, that "no child of either race shall ever be permitted to attend a school provided for children of the other race."[108] Gary also quoted South Carolina's legal bans on interracial marriages, which specified the degree (one-eighth or more) of "negro blood" that would prevent someone from marrying a white person in the state.[109] In addition, Gary invoked classic segregationist precedents such as *Plessy v. Ferguson*,[110] as well as passages from previous South Carolina racial determination cases that contained phrases such as the "admixture of negro blood"[111] and degrees of "African stock."[112] The judicial impulse to discuss new facts in terms of old authorities surely influenced Gary's binary, Black-white analysis.

But when Chief Justice Gary folded under the irregular, Croatan edges of the *Tucker* case so that it would fit within the Black-white paradigm, he was also looking forward, to the precedent he hoped to set. Gary was a committed promoter of Jim Crow, in the tradition of his mentor, South Carolina Senator "Pitchfork" Ben Tillman. Gary owed his public career to his association with Tillman. In 1890, when Tillman first ran for South Carolina governor, Gary was his running mate, as Democratic candidate for lieutenant governor.[113]

The South Carolina Democratic Party's campaign that year was overtly white supremacist. "White supremacy is the bulwark of our civilization," their platform proclaimed. The platform denounced a federal proposal to protect Black voting rights. It championed segregated, Jim Crow education and urged that school districts be drawn so as to allow "one white and one colored" school per district, "separate and distinct." It urged a constitutional convention to replace what Gary's stump speeches repeatedly denounced as the "carpet-bagger" Constitution of 1868. The Tillman-Gary ticket swept to victory.[114]

---

108. S.C. Const. art. III, § 7 (1895), quoted in Tucker v. Blease, 673.

109. S.C. Const. art. III, § 33, quoted in Tucker v. Blease, 673.

110. 163 U.S. 537 (1896), cited in Tucker v. Blease, 674.

111. State v. Cantey, 20 S.C.L. 614 (1835), cited in Tucker v. Blease, 673.

112. White v. Tax Collector, 37 S.C.L. 136 (1846), cited in Tucker v. Blease, 673.

113. U. R. Brooks, "Associate Justice Eugene B. Gary," in *South Carolina Bench and Bar*, vol. 1 (Columbia, SC: State, 1908), 78–80, 78.

114. "South Carolina Democrats: Nominate Tillman for Governor—The Platform," *Springfield [MA] Republican*, Sept. 12, 1890, 5. Gary's stump speeches against the 1868 constitution are reported in "All Efforts to Harmonize Have Failed," *The State*, Jul. 29, 1895, 1;

In 1893, Tillman appointed Gary to the South Carolina Supreme Court, prompting rumors that the governor was hatching a "Plot to Change the State Judiciary" by packing it with "Subservient Judges."[115] Critics, underwhelmed by Gary's legal credentials, attributed his rise to his tight grip on Tillman's coattails. Gary "caught on early" to those coattails, critics sneered, "and . . . never let go."[116] Subsequent commentators referred to Gary as a "Tillmanite"[117] judge. Governor Tillman himself infuriated critics by allegedly "taking it for granted and advertising to the world" that Justice Gary would "do what B. R. Tillman want[ed] him to do" on the bench.[118] In 1912, Gary rose to the position of Chief Justice.[119]

Tucker v. Blease presented Chief Justice Gary with an opportunity to sharpen the color line separating white people from Black people. South Carolina did not yet follow the one-drop rule. It followed the one-eighth rule, as articulated in the marital provision of the 1895 Constitution, which made it unlawful for a white person to marry anyone "who shall have one-eighth or more negro blood."[120] White supremacists objected to the one-eighth rule because they believed that it legitimated racial mixing. As Chief Justice Gary recognized in *Tucker*, the one-eighth rule entitled "the child of parents, where one of them was a white person, and the other had *less* than one-eighth of negro blood, to be classed as a white person."[121] Under South Carolina law, in other words, some people with "negro blood" technically counted as white people and could marry, and have children with, whites. To the committed white supremacist, this prospect was anathema. Gary sought to close this loophole.

Chief Justice Gary candidly acknowledged that the one-eighth rule, if applied in *Tucker*, would compel the children's reinstatement. Even if the so-called nonwhite "blood" in question had been "negro," not Croatan, its

---

"South Carolina: Tillman and the Regular Democrats Carry Off Everything," *Omaha (NE) Morning World-Herald*, Nov. 5, 1890, 1; Kantrowitz, *Ben Tillman and the Reconstruction of White Supremacy*, 143.

115. "Want Subservient Judges: An Alleged Plot to Change the State Judiciary," *The State*, October 2, 1893, 6.

116. "The New and the Old," *The State*, Dec. 2, 1893, 4.

117. "Latest Dispatches," *Savannah (GA) Tribune*, Aug. 4, 1894.

118. "The Imperial Ukase," *The State*, July 23, 1894, 4.

119. Snowden, *History of South Carolina*, 3.

120. S.C. Const. art. III, § 33 (1895).

121. Tucker v. Blease, 673. Emphasis in original.

proportion in the Kirby children's veins was far less than one-eighth. Only one witness at the Dillon County Board of Education hearing, John Sellers, offered specific testimony regarding the racial makeup of the Kirby children. Sellers, an authority on local history and genealogy, traced the Kirby family tree and found that the fraction of nonwhite blood in the Kirby children's veins was "one-thirty-second"—well below the one-eighth threshold.[122] No witness challenged Sellers's findings. The clarity of this testimony led Chief Justice Gary to a conclusion that was as inescapable as it was (to him) disagreeable: as a technical legal matter, the Kirby boys were "entitled to be classed as white."[123]

But Gary would not leave it at that. He chose to overlook the constitution and its one-eighth rule, even though it was the supreme law of his state. Instead, in tones reminiscent of the day's sociological jurisprudence, he suggested that good legal thinkers should occasionally get their noses out of law books and consider the real world. "The law recognizes that there is a social element," he reasoned, "arising from racial instinct." Chief Justice Gary was not the first Jim Crow–era jurist to invoke the concept of a "racial instinct." The US Supreme Court previously did so in *Plessy v. Ferguson.*[124] In Gary's mind, a "racial instinct" arose naturally "between those with and those without negro blood." With this phrasing—the divide between "those with and those without negro blood"—Gary overrode the state constitution's one-eighth rule. He held that a child of a mixed marriage, whose nonwhite parent had less than one-eighth "negro" blood, was entitled to "exercise all the legal rights of a white person, except those arising from a proper classification, when equal accommodations are afforded."[125] Gary thus legitimated the white parents' complaints about the Kirby children's continued presence at the Dalcho School, complaints that, he implied, had naturally arisen due to the "racial instinct" that divided "those with" from "those without negro blood." The Chief Justice invoked this "negro blood" factor even though the record in *Tucker* contained no evidence that the Kirby children had any "negro blood."

Gary concluded that the Kirbys' dismissals were justified. He cited a

122. Ibid., 671.

123. Ibid., 675.

124. "Legislation is powerless to eradicate racial instincts, or to abolish distinctions based upon physical differences, and the attempt to do so can only result in accentuating the difficulties of the present situation." Plessy v. Ferguson, 163 U.S. 537, 551 (1896).

125. Tucker v. Blease, 97 S.C. 326 (1914). Emphasis added.

1912 South Carolina law authorizing public school trustees "to dismiss pupils, when the best interest of the schools" warranted it.[126] "The decided majority of the [parents] would refuse to send their children to the Dalcho school if the Kirby children were allowed to continue in attendance," Gary asserted. "Tested by the maxim, 'The greatest good to the largest number,' it would seem to be far better that the children in question should be segregated than that the large majority of the children attending that school should be denied educational advantages." As long as the Kirby children and others of "their class" were provided separate-but-equal accommodations, he reasoned, their exclusion from Dalcho School was legal, even though the state constitution's one-eighth rule technically entitled them "to be classed as white" and attend that school.

One of Chief Justice Gary's Supreme Court colleagues appears to have rejected his reasoning, at least initially. In April of 1914, when the *Tucker* ruling first appeared, newspapers reported that Associate Justice George W. Gage had dissented. Gage was a newcomer to the court[127] who appears to have been more racially liberal than the Tillmanite chief justice.[128] Presumably believing that the 1895 Constitution's one-eighth rule settled the matter, Gage apparently opposed Gary's judicial imposition of the one-drop rule. "If these [Kirby] children are white and are 'entitled to be classed as white,'" Gage reportedly argued, "then they may not be rightfully excluded from schools made up of white children."[129] For reasons unknown, however, Gage subsequently withdrew his dissent.[130] The published opinion itself contains no evidence of a dissenting opinion.[131]

126. Subdivision 3 of section 1761, *South Carolina Code of Laws 1912*, providing that public schools' boards of trustees "shall . . . have authority . . . to dismiss pupils, when the best interest of the schools make it necessary."

127. "The Lawmakers of South Carolina: Gage Gets Promotion," *The State*, Jan. 16, 1914, 9; "Judge Gage's Election," *The State*, Jan. 17, 1914, 4.

128. "No Verdict Yet in Risinger Case," *The State*, Sept. 24, 1910, 2; "Judge Censures Lexington," *The State*, Sept. 25, 1910, 1; "No Aid for Negroes," *The State*, Feb. 14, 1916, 5; "The Risinger Case," *The State*, Sept. 26, 1910, 4; and "Iguorance [*sic*] Cause of Crime: Judge Gage Charges Grand Jury to See that Good School Houses and Teachers Abound," *The State*, Mar. 2, 1911, 8.

129. "Sustains Ruling of State Board: Supreme Court Decides the Dalcho School Case," *The State*, Apr. 22, 1914.

130. "South Carolina Supreme Court: Synopses of Opinions in the Highest Tribunal," The State, Jul. 15, 1914, 15.

131. Tucker v. Blease.

Officially, then, a unanimous South Carolina Supreme Court used a case concerning Croatan students—not Black students—to sharpen the line between "those with and those without negro blood."

The Case Lives On

Chief Justice Gary's ruling achieved its desired effect. It imposed the one-drop rule and a binary conception of race upon state law.[132] Newspaper reporting on the case accepted the Black-white paradigm. Press coverage mentioned nothing about the Kirbys' alleged Croatan origins or segregated Indian schooling. Instead, it emphasized the case's implications for Black-white relations. In the state capital, the *Columbia Record* described *Tucker v. Blease* as "an illuminating commentary on the social condition of the negro in this State and generally throughout the South."[133] Papers across the region followed suit.[134]

Legal scholars have generally written about the case in similar terms. A 1934 piece in the *California Law Review* invoked *Tucker* while discussing the proposition that "the least ascertainable trace of negro blood" might control in some areas, such as school segregation, even if other standards for racial determination applied in other areas, such as marriage.[135] A 1951 piece in the *Michigan Law Review* cited *Tucker* to argue that even white-seeming children might legally be barred from white schools "if there were a solitary distant Negro forebear."[136] Recent scholarship continues to invoke *Tucker* when discussing Jim Crow–era legal treatment of "whites with African ancestry."[137]

---

132. Sharfstein, "Crossing the Color Line," 654.

133. "Three Children Are Prohibited in School Rooms," *Columbia (SC) Record*, April 22, 1914, 5.

134. See "Supreme Court Bars Children of Caucasian Blood," *Greenville (SC) Daily News* (South Carolina), April 23, 1914, 8; "These Children Must Quit School for Whites," *News and Courier* (Charleston, SC), April 22, 1914, 3; "Barred from White School," *Charlotte (NC) Observer*, 22 Apr., 1914, 9. For a more neutral write-up of the ruling, one that does not mention the "condition of the negro," see "Sustains Ruling of State Board: Supreme Court Decides the Dalcho School Case," *The State*, April 22, 1914, 14.

135. Dudley O. McGovney, "Naturalization of the Mixed-Blood: A Dictum," *California Law Review* 22, no. 4 (May 1934): 386.

136. Joseph S. Ransmeier, "The Fourteenth Amendment and the 'Separate but Equal' Doctrine," *Michigan Law Review* 50, no. 2 (Dec. 1951): 254.

137. Sharfstein, "Crossing the Color Line," 655. See also J. Anthony Paredes, ed., *Indians of*

Three subsequent appellate rulings cited *Tucker*. All three discussed the case in racially binary terms. Johnson v. Board of Ed*ucation*, a 1914 school segregation ruling from North Carolina, described *Tucker v. Blease*, then just months old, as a case whose "facts [were] practically the same as those in this record," even though *Johnson*, unlike *Tucker*, specified that the children in question had "partial Negro parentage."[138] The 1920 Oklahoma school segregation case Jelsma v. Butler included *Tucker* in a long list of cases establishing, in racially binary terms, the constitutionality of segregating Blacks and whites "by requiring separate schools for each and prohibiting members of either race from attending the school provided for the other."[139] Perhaps most intriguing is *Gong Lum v. Rice*, a 1927 case from the United States Supreme Court. Martha Lum was a Chinese student who wanted to attend an all-white public school, rather than the "colored" school that Mississippi had ordered her to attend. "Colored," her lawyers argued, "describes only one race, and that is the negro." In defense of this proposition, her lawyers cited, ironically, *Tucker v. Blease*.[140]

Late in the twentieth century, legal indexers at the influential LexisNexis corporation prepared a "Case Summary" of *Tucker v. Blease* for inclusion in its widely used electronic database of US legal opinions.[141] The LexisNexis synopsis eclipsed even Chief Justice Gary's original opinion in its reinforcement of the Black-white paradigm. Recall that Gary's 1914 ruling masked testimony alleging that the Kirbys were part Croatan and implied, though did not explicitly assert, that the children were part "negro." LexisNexis was not so guarded. Its "Case Summary" reported that the Kirbys were dismissed from school "because they were allegedly part black."[142]

---

the Southeastern United States in the Late Twentieth Century (Tuscaloosa: University of Alabama Press, 1992), 82. For a different, but also inaccurate, take on *Tucker*, see Frank W. Sweet, *Legal History of the Color Line* (Palm Coast, FL: Backintyme, 2005), 403–4.

138. Johnson v. Board of Ed., 166 N.C. 468, 475 (1914).

139. Jelsma v. Butler, 80 Okla. 46; 194 P. 436, 438 (1920).

140. Gong Lum v. Rice, 275 U.S. 78 (1927).

141. Around the turn of the twenty-first century, LexisNexis was reportedly the "world's largest online electronic library of legal opinions." "Lexis-Nexis Founder Don Wilson Dies," UPI.com, Dec. 1, 2006, https://www.upi.com/Top_News/2006/12/01/Lexis-Nexis-founder-Don-Wilson-dies/UPI-36121164992489/.

142. "Case Summary," Tucker v. Blease, 8801, Supreme Court of South Carolina, 97 S.C. 303; 81 S.E. 668; 1914 S.C. LEXIS 189 (April 21, 1914), Decided. The "late twentieth century" date of this blurb's creation is based on discussions with LexisNexis representatives, reported in Susanna Boylston to John Wertheimer, email message, August 19, 2008.

Conclusion

Tucker shows how salient race was during the Jim Crow era. As the Kirby boys learned, one's official racial classification affected one's life prospects greatly, from childhood on. White South Carolinians enjoyed disproportionate power to police racial lines. They vigilantly did so, both from the bottom up, as in the parents' petition urging the Kirbys' expulsion from the all-white Dalcho School, and from the top down, as in the South Carolina Supreme Court's validating recognition of a "racial instinct" that supposedly divided people based on the presence or absence of "negro blood."

The actual record in *Tucker v. Blease* challenges the Black-white paradigm. The United States—even in the Deep South, even during the Jim Crow era—was always more multicultural and multiethnic than the paradigm suggests. The case also illuminates the role that state-level legal systems played in the paradigm's spread. The *Tucker* court consciously filtered out evidence of multiethnic complexity and described Dillon County's social world in Black-and-white terms. Thereafter, journalists, scholars, lawyers, judges, and legal indexers all discussed the case (and surely others like it) in ways that reinforced an inaccurate, racially binary understanding of southern society.

Tucker also highlights the extraordinary indeterminacy of racial classification law in Progressive Era South Carolina. Three different legal rules, springing from as many sources, struggled for supremacy. The first and most obvious source of racial determination law was the South Carolina Constitution of 1895, which employed a "one-eighth" rule for classifying persons as "negro or mulatto."[143] Although the state constitution is theoretically supreme, this rule proved to be the weakest of the three.

The second source of law was local opinion. In *Tucker*, neighbors sought to remove the Kirby children from an all-white public school on grounds that they were not seen as white people, even though the Kirbys technically qualified as white people under the state constitution. After verifying that neighbors regarded the Kirbys as nonwhite people, the public school agreed to expel them, a decision upheld by education officials at the county and state levels. All of these education administrators ignored the constitution's one-eighth rule and substituted a locally managed "community reputation" test for racial determination.

---

143. S.C. Const. art. III, § 33 (1895).

The third source of law was the South Carolina Supreme Court itself. In one way, the high court favored local over statewide control of racial determination. Chief Justice Gary's decision upheld the school's decision to ignore the state constitution and expel technically white children from an all-white school. In another way, however, Gary's ruling represented a dramatic assertion of judicial power. The chief justice used that power to eviscerate the constitution's one-eighth rule and to put the one-drop rule in its place. Moreover, he consciously obscured the three-way segregation that was locally at issue, writing as if the case concerned just two classes of people: "those with and those without negro blood." Appellate judges in South Carolina had tremendous power to make law. Gary used that power aggressively in furtherance of a two-tiered, segregated, white supremacist society.

As for the Kirbys, the three brothers, though deemed insufficiently white for the Dalcho School, nonetheless joined "white" military units during World War I where, in Uncle Sam's racially divided ranks, they answered segregationist president Woodrow Wilson's call to make the world safe for democracy.[144]

144. 1920 Census, Cameron County, Texas, roll 1784, 178, HeritageQuest Online, https://www.ancestryheritagequest.com/search/categories/usfedcen/; Sharfstein, "Crossing the Color Line," 655; "Address of President Wilson to Joint Session of Congress, April 2, 1917," Woodrow Wilson Papers, Manuscript Division, Library of Congress, https://www.loc.gov/exhibitions/world-war-i-american-experiences/about-this-exhibition/arguing-over-war/for-or-against-war/wilson-before-congress/. Regarding Wilson's support for Jim Crow, see Kenneth O'Reilly, "The Jim Crow Policies of Woodrow Wilson," *Journal of Blacks in Higher Education* 17 (Autumn 1997): 117–21.

CHAPTER 5

State v. Sanders: Jim Crow Juries[1]

On June 11, 1915, a white man named R. L. Bailey took a seat in the Richland County Courthouse in Columbia, South Carolina, to undergo questioning for jury selection. If chosen, he would join a jury that would decide whether or not a Black man named James "Bogus" Sanders was guilty of murdering a white man named Charles Ellers. Defense counsel asked Bailey whether anything might prevent him from ruling fairly in this racially charged case. Bailey admitted that his "natural resentment" against Black people "might prejudice [him] in rendering a verdict." Despite this explicit admission of bias, the court deemed Bailey fit for jury service.[2]

State v. Sanders highlights the legal system's blatant failure to provide racial justice during the Jim Crow era. At the same time, however, it suggests something quite different: that the legal system was an unusually open forum within which Black people and their defenders could challenge racism. Occasionally, as in *Sanders*, they won.

Scholars have paid comparatively little attention to Jim Crow juries. Other legal pillars of white supremacy during this period—electoral disfranchisement, separate and unequal facilities, lynching—have received closer inspection. Some top-notch scholarship does explore the statutes and judicial rulings that putatively governed jury composition during the Jim Crow era.[3] This scholarship, however, reveals little about how juries actually

1. Gerardo Alvarez Sottil, Katy Boyle, Peter Bruton, Katie Burwick, Bridget Flynn Kastner, Daniel Guenther, Katherine Herold, Andrew Jones, William Mahler, Emily May, Kayla McCann, Alexander Merritt, Lee Mimms, Everett Muzzy, Robin Malloch, Cameron Parker, Rex Salisbury, Alex Sineath, CT Talevi, Lawrence Wall, David Warren, and John Wertheimer coauthored this chapter.

2. State v. Sanders, 103 S.C. 216, 220 (1916).

3. Michael J. Klarman, *From Jim Crow to Civil Rights* (New York: Oxford University, 2004),

worked. Legal historian Kermit Hall's observation that we know "tantalizingly little" about jury selection during the antebellum years also applies to the Jim Crow era.[4]

In the absence of close studies of Jim Crow juries, three general assumptions predominate. *First*, scholars assume that jury composition was merely a subset of the larger (and admittedly more important) matter of electoral disfranchisement. To be eligible for jury service, after all, a citizen, by law, first had to be eligible to vote. The purging of Black names from voter-registration lists, this assumption holds, explains their corresponding disappearance from jury lists. In one historian's words, "The elimination of the Negro as a voter served also to remove him from the jury bench."[5] "As whites suppressed black voting," another writes, "blacks disappeared from juries."[6] The assumption that the jury composition story was really a voter registration story may have discouraged research into the history of juries.

Second, scholars generally assume that Jim Crow juries were entirely white. Standard accounts assert that Black southerners were "systematically excluded"[7] under Jim Crow. Some scholars hedge a bit, carefully calling the elimination of Black jurors in the South "*virtually* total," [8] asserting that the "elimination of Negroes from *practically* all jury service was complete" by the early twentieth century,[9] or saying that Black people remained "*almost* universally excluded from southern juries until after World War II."[10] Most scholars, however, do not hedge. "In the South," at the dawn of the twentieth century, one writes, "no blacks served on the jury."[11] Black jurors

---

39–43, 55–57; Charles S. Mangum Jr., *The Legal Status of the Negro* (Chapel Hill: University of North Carolina Press, 1940), 308–42.

4. Kermit Hall, *The Magic Mirror: Law in American History* (New York: Oxford University Press, 1989), 173.

5. Vernon L. Wharton, *The Negro in Mississippi, 1865–1890* (Chapel Hill: University of North Carolina Press, 1947), 137.

6. Klarman, *From Jim Crow*, 39.

7. Mark Curriden and Leroy Phillips Jr., *Contempt of Court: The Turn-of-the-Century Lynching that Launched 100 Years of Federalism* (New York: Anchor Books, 1999), 132.

8. Benno C. Schmidt Jr., "Juries, Jurisdiction, and Race Discrimination: The Lost Promise of *Strauder v. West Virginia*," *Texas Law Review* 61 (May 1983): 1407. Emphasis added.

9. George Brown Tindall, *South Carolina Negroes, 1877–1900* (Columbia: University of South Carolina Press, 1952), 264. Emphasis added.

10. Klarman, *From Jim Crow*, 55. Emphasis added.

11. Lawrence M. Friedman, *American Law in the Twentieth Century* (New Haven, CT: Yale University Press, 2002), 264.

"vanished."[12] They "disappeared."[13] They were "universally excluded from southern juries."[14] Southern states secured the "complete elimination"[15] of Black people from juries. Those states "excluded blacks from sitting on juries altogether,"[16] leaving "all-white juries" "throughout the South."[17] The assumption that the needle was stuck on zero may likewise have discouraged detailed historical research.

The *third* assumption underlies the first two. It is the assumption that the proper question to ask about Jim Crow juries is a quantitative one: What percentage of southern jurors during the Jim Crow era were Black? How many Black people served?

All of these assumptions contain more than a kernel of truth. To embrace them is to know the basic story. But all three invite refinement. This chapter seeks to refine them.

Regarding the *first* point, voter registration indeed directly affected jury composition. The widespread, deliberate purging of Black names from southern voting rolls in the years surrounding 1900 drastically reduced the pool of Black people eligible to serve on juries. But voter registration and jury selection were distinct though related processes. They might best be understood as sequential sieves. The voter-registration process filtered out many Black people. Thereafter, jury commissioners and trial courts applied an even finer weave and filtered out more. This chapter illuminates these twin processes.

Second, although the removal of Black people from southern juries during the Jim Crow years was breathtakingly widespread, it was not as total as many assume. Small but discernible numbers of Black jurors sat on juries throughout the period, at least in some southern jurisdictions. The jury service of Black southerners during the Jim Crow years was never proportionate, or close to proportionate, to their share of the population, but it was not flatlined on zero. Rather, it fluctuated from place to place and year to year, even during the nadir of Jim Crow. To point this out is not to downplay

12. Donald G. Nieman, "Black Political Power and Criminal Justice: Washington County, Texas, 1868–1884," *Journal of Southern History* 55, no. 3 (Aug. 1989): 420.

13. Klarman, *From Jim Crow*, 39.

14. Klarman, 43.

15. Wharton, *The Negro in Mississippi*, 137.

16. Vikram David Amar, "Jury Service as Political Participation Akin to Voting," *Cornell Law Review* 80 (Jan. 1995): 203.

17. Curriden and Phillips, *Contempt of Court*, 132–33.

conflict over Black jury service. To the contrary, it calls new attention to the existence of conflict. Jury composition generated ample debate, thanks to the persistent efforts of advocates of inclusion, including Black lawyers. These advocates won occasional victories. Although the conventional story of the "lily-white"[18] jury is not exactly wrong, we zoom in and capture missing details.

Finally, although quantitative measures of Black jury service are vitally important—indeed, this chapter produces plenty of them—the history of Jim Crow juries also contains an important qualitative dimension, one that is too often overlooked. The main question in *State v. Sanders* did not involve the jurors' *race*. It involved the jurors' *racism*. R. L. Bailey admitted that racial prejudice might skew his verdict. Defense lawyers in this case, and in several others like it, fought hard for the right to interrogate prospective jurors about their racial views and to exclude those who admitted to explicit racism. Their efforts improved the prospects of individual Black litigants. They also made a broader point: that racism was incompatible with justice. Indeed, the jury-selection process was among the few—and surely among the best—spaces in the Jim Crow South wherein racism could be openly and effectively challenged.

The Crime

Many residents of Columbia, South Carolina, relaxed on their front porches as the sun sank on Tuesday, May 25, 1915. A lazy breeze from the southwest provided welcome relief. It had reached ninety-one degrees that day.[19]

Charles Ellers, his brother-in-law George Ruff, and a friend named John Crouch strolled in the southern part of the city. The three white men had enjoyed an after-work beer and were now meandering back in the direction of Olympia Mill Village, the textile town where Ellers and Crouch lived and worked.[20]

In Columbia, and across the southern piedmont, textiles were booming.

18. Jeffrey Abramson, *We, the Jury: The Jury System and the Ideal of Democracy* (New York: Basic Books, 1994), 109.

19. "Weather Bureau: U.S. Department of Agriculture, 144th Day of 1915," *The State* (Columbia, SC), May 25, 1915, 10.

20. The State v. Bogus Sanders, Charles Ellers Inquest, witness testimonies by E. J. Crouch and George Ruff, South Carolina Department of Archives and History, 12–16. Hereafter cited as SCDAH.

As recently as 1880, just fourteen textile mills operated in South Carolina. By 1910, 167 did. Each new factory spilled additional millworkers into the streets in the early evenings, following twelve-hour shifts.[21] The mammoth Olympia Mills contributed more than its share. When it opened in Columbia in 1900, it was heralded as "the world's largest cotton mill under one roof."[22]

Although southern textile workers received low wages by national standards, they enjoyed some compensating benefits. Textile companies claimed to "take care of their own" by providing workers with housing, schools, churches, recreation, and health facilities.[23] Partly in order to discourage unionization, the owners of Olympia Mills provided unusually good living conditions.[24] Mill-village life provided residents with a sense of community and identity. And because textile jobs were largely closed to Black people, white mill workers such as Ellers and Crouch absorbed a powerful sense of racial privilege.[25] Textile work was obsessively segregated. A 1907 survey asked 152 southern textile mills if they employed any Black workers on the factory floor. Zero did. Only a handful of mills employed Black workers for even menial "outdoor" jobs.[26] White supremacist politicians encouraged white textile workers' sense of racial superiority.[27] In 1915, South Carolina adopted a law prohibiting textile firms from mixing Black and white workers in the same room. As a practical matter, this ensured the perpetuation of the all-white textile factory.[28]

The sense of privilege that policies like this one urged white millhands

21. Jennifer F. Martin, Nicholas G. Theos, Sarah A. Woodard, "Olympia Mill and Village: Upper Richland County, South Carolina Historical and Architectural Inventory," Edwards-Pitman Environmental, Inc., June 2002, 10, http://nationalregister.sc.gov/SurveyReports/Olympia2002SM-2.pdf.

22. Walter Edgar, ed., "Olympia Cotton Mill," in *The South Carolina Encyclopedia* (Columbia: University of South Carolina Press, 2006), 683; Martin et al., "Olympia Mill and Village," 13–15; Edgar, "Olympia Cotton Mill," 256.

23. Martin et al., "Olympia Mill and Village," 15–17; Jacquelyn Down Hall, James L. Leloudis, Robert Rodgers Korstad, Mary Murphy, Lu Ann Jones, and Christopher B. Daly, *Like a Family: The Making of a Southern Cotton Mill World* (Chapel Hill: University of North Carolina Press, 1987).

24. Edgar, "Olympia Cotton Mill," 683.

25. I. A. Newby, *Black Carolinians: A History of Blacks in South Carolina from 1895 to 1968* (Columbia: University of South Carolina Press, 1973), 134.

26. Patrick Huber, *Linthead Stomp: The Creation of County Music in the Piedmont South* (Chapel Hill: University of North Carolina Press, 2008), 13.

27. Bryant Simon, *A Fabric of Defeat: The Politics of South Carolina Millhands, 1910–1948* (Chapel Hill: University of North Carolina Press, 1998).

28. Huber, *Linthead Stomp*, 13.

to feel surfaced that sticky evening in May, when Ellers and company wandered homeward through a predominantly Black section of Columbia.[29] Heading south on Gadsden Street, the men passed a Black woman named Ada Sanders, a basket on her arm, heading north. She was walking to her nearby house, where her husband Bogus waited.[30] An ugly encounter ensued. Details are disputed, but at the very least, the men harassed Ms. Sanders with sexually suggestive language. She later claimed that they also laid hands on her, a story corroborated by at least one witness.[31]

A long history of sexual abuse of Black women by white men underlay this encounter. In the antebellum era, white men routinely took sexual advantage of Black women, often fathering their children. It was common for white men to lose their virginity to enslaved Black women, gaining sexual release without threatening the "purity" of white women.[32] No matter how abusive these encounters, the victims, because of their race and status, could not easily complain.

The Civil War ended slavery but not the sexual mistreatment of Black women by white men. One of the many facets of the white, Democratic "redemption" of the South following Reconstruction was the sexual terrorizing of Black women by white men. The Ku Klux Klan and other militant opponents of Reconstruction infamously brutalized Black men; less well known were the multiple rapes and assaults they committed against Black women.[33] Although the problem of white male abuse of Black women received little public notice, it festered through the Jim Crow era.[34]

This long history provided an ominous soundtrack when Ada Sanders encountered Ellers, Ruff, and Crouch on the streets of Columbia that evening. Charles Ellers, beer on his breath, confronted Ada Sanders and asked, "Do you want to go and grind around on the bed?"[35]

---

29. City Directory, the Walsh Directory Company, Columbia, South Carolina, 1915.

30. We will refer to her as Ada Sanders, even though she appears variously in print as Ada, Ada Lee, Adlee, Adelaide, and Addie.

31. The State v. Bogus Sanders, 12–13.

32. Bertram Wyatt-Brown, *Honor and Violence in the Old South* (Oxford: Oxford University Press, 1986), 99.

33. Lisa Cardyn, "Sexualized Racism/Gendered Violence: Outraging the Body Politic in the Reconstruction South," *Michigan Law Review* 100 (2002): 813–16.

34. Al-Tony Gilmore, "Black Southerner's Response to the Southern System of Race Relations: 1900 to Post World War II," in *The Age of Segregation: Race Relations in the South, 1890–1945* (Jackson: University Press of Mississippi, 1978), 70.

35. *State v. Bogus Sanders*, 12-13.

The Jim Crow code called for Ada Sanders to lower her eyes and walk on. Her fury made that impossible. Ellers's words constituted a verbal assault. They also attacked her ladyhood. National and regional mores at the time were obsessively protective of the presumed virtue and innocence of respectable women. Some off-color male behavior, completely legal with no women present, turned criminal in the presence of women.[36] In the Jim Crow era, however, the term "lady" was generally understood to apply white women only. Women of color were denied its privileges.[37] Some Black women pushed back, demanding the respect afforded to ladies.[38] Ada Sanders was among them. She responded indignantly to Ellers's harassment, dashed one block to her home, and urgently told her husband what had happened.[39]

Bogus's anger matched Ada's. His reaction blended two cultural traditions. The first was the code of southern male honor. This code deemed an insult directed at a man's wife to be an attack on his manhood. The code demanded fierce retaliation.[40] Like its southern-ladyhood counterpart, the southern code of male honor was generally understood to apply to white men only. This racialized understanding of southern (white) male honor was seared into the national consciousness in D. W. Griffith's *The Birth of a Nation*, the KKK glorifying film that had opened just three months earlier, in February of 1915. Nevertheless, some southern Black men embraced this code of honor, in implicit challenge to white supremacy.[41] Bogus Sanders reached for his pistol.

The second and related cultural tradition that underlay Bogus's reaction was violence. The South was a peculiarly bloody place. Charleston (second only to Memphis) and other southern cities were the nation's "most murderous," the press reported in 1915. By contrast, New York City, despite its "enormous population," was a "peaceful, law-abiding place."[42] In 1906, South Carolina's homicide total (243) dwarfed Chicago's (143), even though Chicago's population of 1.9 million people was substantially larger than

36. Redd v. State, 7 Ga. App. 575 (1910).

37. Barbara K. Welke, *Recasting American Liberty: Gender, Race, Law, and the Railroad Revolution, 1865–1920* (New York: Cambridge University Press, 2001).

38. Ibid.

39. *The State v. Bogus Sanders*, 12–13.

40. Wyatt-Brown, *Honor and Violence*, 36.

41. Newby, *Black Carolinians*, 17.

42. "Southern Cities Most Murderous," *The State*, Dec. 27, 1915, 9.

South Carolina's 1.4 million. As one Palmetto State judge lamented, "South Carolinians hold human life very cheap."[43]

Bogus Sanders took his pistol and joined his wife's search for the three white men. Although Bogus and Ada Sanders's thirst for retribution is easy to understand, their actions would have been difficult to recommend, given the time and place. Prudence counseled silent acceptance. But years of suppressed outrage prevailed. The couple tracked down the men on Gadsden Street, about a block away.[44] Accounts vary on what happened next. Bogus confronted them. "What were you talking about down this road?" he reportedly asked.[45] Charles Ellers replied defiantly, "Not anything that I could not say again."[46] A brick—a rock?—flew. Or not. It hit, or missed, Bogus Sanders.[47] Ruff and Crouch may or may not have advanced, flashing open knives.[48] Ada Sanders may or may not have "urged her husband on to emptying his pistol." Without question, Bogus's pulse raced. Flustered, fearful, and fuming, Bogus fumbled for his Smith & Wesson. He "kinder dropped his gun and caught it again," an eyewitness reported. Then "he went to shooting."[49] Five bullets sprayed wildly. Only one hit home, penetrating Charles Ellers's flesh.[50] Columbia Police Officer W. F. Hicks heard the shots and came running. He found Ellers on the ground and Bogus Sanders "walking off."[51] Officer Hicks apprehended Bogus Sanders without a struggle. Bogus quickly admitted the shooting and explained his motivations. "[Sanders] stated to me," Officer Hicks reported, "that a white man had insulted his wife and that is why he did the shooting."[52]

Two things stand out about the way people tried to make sense of this highly publicized case. First, everyone involved viewed the events through thick racial lenses. Bogus did not tell Officer Hicks that a "man" had insulted

43. Newby, *Black Carolinians*, 50-2; and Al-Tony Gilmore, "The Black Southerner's Response," 70. The judge's quotation appears on 52.

44. "Bogus Sanders on Trial Again," *The State*, May 25, 1916, 6.

45. The State v. Bogus Sanders, 13

46. Ibid.

47. "Plea of Negroes Is Self-Defense: Sanders Says White Men Attacked Him," *The State* June 12, 1915, 10.

48. Ibid.

49. The State v. Bogus Sanders, 6.

50. "White Man Was Badly Wounded by a Negro," *Columbia (SC) Record*, May 26, 1915, 6.

51. The State v. Bogus Sanders, 3.

52. Ibid., 4.

his wife. He told him that a "white man" had done so.[53] The press's extensive coverage was entirely racialized, as indicated by headlines such as "White Man Was Badly Wounded by a Negro"[54] and "White Man Whom Negro Shot Is Dead of Wound."[55] Newspaper descriptions of Bogus Sanders highlighted racial signifiers (e.g., "His hair is conspicuously bushy and kinky, his lips and nose correspondingly thick and broad").[56] White witnesses in the subsequent trial used racial language to explain what happened, as when Officer Hicks told the court that he had arrested not the shooter but "the darkey."[57] Lawyers framed questions racially when examining witnesses, as when asking, "Did the negro man say which one of the white men . . . made the remark?"[58] Lawyers also occasionally joined witnesses in referring to Bogus Sanders, in court, as a "darkey," as in the phrase, "What were the exact words this darkey used?"[59] From start to finish, race framed people's understandings of *State v. Sanders*.

A second noteworthy feature of the case was the inability of some white southerners to imagine that a Black man could possibly be motivated by the code of honor that was understood naturally to motivate the actions of southern white men. Not all white southerners would have approved of an honor killing whereby a white husband intemperately slayed his wife's insulter, but all white southerners would have understood what was going on. This was not so when the shooter was a Black man. Even though Bogus Sanders immediately admitted responsibility and frankly explained his motivations in classic "honor-killing" terms (he had pulled the trigger to avenge a vulgar insult to his wife), the coroner could make no sense of Ellers's death. "Coroner Scott," the press reported, had explored the case, but "had been unable to discover any motive for the shooting."[60]

53. Ibid. In another report, Bogus provided a plural but nonetheless racialized description of the insulters, saying that a "party of white men" was responsible. "White Man Was Badly Wounded by a Negro," 6.

54. Ibid., 6.

55. "White Man Whom Negro Shot Is Dead of Wound," 10.

56. "Bogus Sanders Is on Trial Second Time for Murder," *Columbia Record*, May 24, 1916, 12.

57. The State v. Bogus Sanders, 3.

58. Ibid.

59. Ibid., 5.

60. "Sanders and Wife Held by Coroner," *The State*, May 29, 1915, 8.

The Trial

By later standards, the 1915 prosecution of Bogus and Ada Sanders flew at supersonic speed. Bogus shot Charles Ellers on May 25. Ellers died two days later, on May 27. The very next day, May 28, a coroner's jury investigated. The very *next* day, May 29—a Saturday!—a grand jury indicted both Sanderses for murder. The couple was arraigned and pleaded not guilty on June 5. Their capital trial for murder began late on the afternoon of June 10—two weeks to the day after Ellers's death. It ended just two days thereafter, on June 12, 1915.[61]

Several factors fueled the proceedings' rocket-like flight. For one thing, criminal trials generally raced. Defendants lacked many of the constitutional protections that would later gum prosecutorial gears.

Even by the standards of 1915, however, *State v. Sanders* sped. In part, this was a fluke of timing. The Richland County criminal court met only a few times per year, and each session lasted just a few weeks. As luck would have it, Sanders shot Ellers on May 25, just as the first criminal court session since January began.[62] The state could either prosecute immediately or wait until the September session. Waiting would mean keeping Ada and Bogus Sanders locked up for several months, at taxpayer expense.[63]

The racial dynamics of *State v. Sanders* gave officials an additional reason to fast-track it: fear of lynching. Had they not been worried about a lynching, they might well have decided to hold *Sanders* until September. The three-week spring term was already clogged by the time of the Sanders incident. "With more than 90 indictments ready to hand to the grand jury when it convenes this morning," *The State* reported on May 24, the day before the Ellers shooting, the caseload was already shaping up to be "the largest docket of new cases" that the Columbia solicitor had ever seen.[64] All other things being equal, postponement of *Sanders* would have made sense. Officials routinely postponed cases. Indeed, twenty prosecutions from the

---

61. "White Man Whom Negro Shot Is Dead of Wound," 10; "Sanders and Wife Held by Coroner," 8; "59 Cases Taken from Docket in One Week Court," *Columbia Record*, May 30, 1915, 11; "Record for Week Fifty-Nine Cases," *The State*, May 30, 1915, 2; "Many Cases Tried in Criminal Court," *The State*, June 6, 1915, 11.

62. "Heaviest Docket He Has Handled," *The State*, May 24, 1915, 8.

63. "Sanders and Wife Held by Coroner," 8.

64. "Heaviest Docket He Has Handled," 8.

January 1915 term were carried forward to May–June.[65] In turn, a "number of cases" from the crammed spring term would be held over until September.[66] Given its recent origin and its high stakes as a capital murder trial, *State v. Sanders* would seem a good candidate for delay. Instead, officials accelerated, likely fearing a lynching.

The threat of lynching always loomed when Black people were suspected of committing serious crimes against whites.[67] Murder certainly qualified as a lynchable offense. Whenever a "negro" killed "a good white man," a white South Carolinian had declared a few years earlier, a lynching should follow, for it was "a waste of time and money to put the machinery of the law in motion."[68] Southern officials believed that expedited justice was one of the best safeguards against vigilantism. Every delay, they thought, increased the odds of a lynching. Some officials even called criminal courts into special session, hoping to keep lynch mobs at bay.[69] Southern champions of the rule of law trumpeted a "Remedy for Lynching" that would have come as cold comfort to Black criminal defendants: "A Quick Trial and Prompt Execution."[70] Had Bogus's trial been postponed, officials likely reasoned, a lynch mob might have prevented him from seeing September. Had that happened, Richland County would have faced criticism for having allowed a lynching to occur within its borders. (The county could also have been liable in exemplary damages, as detailed in the following chapter.[71])

Consequently, *State v. Sanders* was conducted at a sprint, highlighting a conundrum of crime and punishment in the Jim Crow era: in the name of advancing the rule of law—that is, avoiding lynching—South Carolina wound up compromising it through haste. The breakneck pace denied defense counsel adequate time to prepare. Rushed proceedings also meant that the community passions stirred by the Ellers shooting had not yet

65. Ibid.

66. "Many New Cases for Grand Jury," *The State*, Sept. 4, 1915, 8.

67. Michael J. Pfeifer, *The Roots of Rough Justice* (Champaign: University of Illinois Press, 2011), 41; Christopher Waldrep, ed., *Lynching in America* (New York: New York University Press, 2006), xviii.

68. "Justice to the Negro" *The State*, April 22, 1906, 16.

69. "A Remedy for Lynching and to Check Rapine: A Quick Trial and Prompt Execution," *The State*, Sept. 10, 1894, 6.

70. Ibid. See also "The Shame of the State," *The State*, Dec. 9, 1895, 2; Bob Davis Eludes Avenging Mobs," *The State*, Aug. 16, 1906, 1; "Officials File Report on Recent Lynching," *The State*, Nov. 29, 1910, 3.

71. S.C. Const. art. VI, §6 (1895).

cooled when the capital murder trial began. The Sanderses' defense lawyers quite reasonably requested a continuance—that is, a delay—arguing that they needed more time to prepare the sort of defense that justice demanded in a capital trial. The court said no.[72] The trial would begin as scheduled, on June 10, 1915. Charles Ellers had been dead exactly two weeks. "Justice delayed is justice denied," an old maxim holds. Justice rushed is no better.

The Sanderses' lawyers, Nathaniel Frederick and Jacob Moorer, filed some additional pretrial motions. Among other things, they asked the court to start over with entirely new grand jurors and petit jurors, on grounds that, the defendants, "being negroes[,] should have had race representation in the two bodies."[73] Trial Judge Hayne P. Rice refused. All sixteen grand jurors, and all twelve petit jurors, were white men.[74]

The press predicted that *State v. Sanders* was "destined to be the feature [case] of the present term."[75] And so it was. The courtroom "filled to its capacity."[76] Interest ran so high that trial Judge Rice feared losing control. He issued "special instructions limiting the spectators to the number that could be seated in the court room proper." Sheriff's deputies guarded the doors.[77]

The prosecution's case ranged from credible to far-fetched. Physicians presented gruesome testimony about the bullet that had perforated Charles Ellers's intestines in six places, causing death.[78] The testimony of E. J. Crouch, one of the friends who was walking with Ellers when the fatal incident occurred, was less credible. He claimed that Ellers had not directed the offending words at Ada Sanders at all. Crouch blamed the incident on bad timing. As the three men strolled near the Sanders house on Gadsden Street, Crouch testified, Ellers happened to be relating a story about a "pretty young thing" whom he had propositioned years before by asking, "Do you want to go and grind around on the bed?" By chance, Crouch claimed, unconvincingly, Ada Sanders happened to pass the men at exactly that moment and wrongly assumed that the words were directed at her.[79]

72. "Negro and Wife Placed on Trial," *The State*, June 11, 1915, 5.

73. Ibid.; "Trial of Sanders Has Begun with New Features," *Columbia Record*, June 10, 1915, 2.

74. "Crowded Room at Sanders Trial," *Columbia Record*, June 11, 1915, 8.

75. "Trial of Sanders Has Begun with New Features," 2.

76. "Crowded Room at Sanders Trial," 8.

77. Ibid.

78. "Negro and Wife Placed on Trial," 5.

79. State v. Bogus Sanders, 12–13.

Other prosecution testimony was more credible, though the defense still disputed it. Prosecution witnesses testified that the white men were not drunk, did not lay hands on Ada, and did not rush at Bogus with knives or hurl anything at him prior to the shooting. They also claimed that Ada commanded Bogus to shoot and, thereafter, asked a neighbor to testify falsely on her behalf.[80]

Both Ada and Bogus Sanders testified in their own defense. Some other eyewitnesses joined them. Although Ada's perspective would seem highly relevant, reporters failed to mention her testimony, focusing exclusively on her husband's. In doing so, they seemingly replicated the public silencing that Black women often suffered during this era. The essence of Bogus's testimony was that he had shot in self-defense. He claimed that he followed the white men for a block, then confronted them. Charles Ellers temporarily calmed things by assuring Bogus that "no insult had been given his wife." Satisfied, Bogus "turned back." There the confrontation would have ended, Bogus said, had the white men let it lie. Instead, according to Bogus, the men cursed him, threw a brick that hit his shoulder, and approached him "with open knives." Terrified, Bogus reflexively shot. Ellers fell.

Interestingly, the emphasis of Bogus Sanders's testimony had shifted since the time of his arrest. On the night of the shooting, although he did mention that one of the white men had drawn a knife, the main thrust of his statement to Officer Hicks was that he had shot to avenge the insult to Ada.[81] Bogus's courtroom testimony differed. He now played down the honor-killing element, perhaps fearing that white jurors would not look kindly upon a Black man who invoked such a masculine (and traditionally white) code of behavior. Bogus no longer stated that he shot to avenge the insult to his wife. He now claimed that Ellers had assured him that no insult had been given, and that this assurance had satisfied him, causing him to turn back toward his home. Only when "one of the white men . . . threw a brick" and two of the men rushed him "with open knives" did he fire.[82] Reflexive self-defense, not assertive masculine honor, moved him to shoot. Playing to a jury of white men, Bogus portrayed himself in as passive and unthreatening a light as possible.

Jury deliberations sped as quickly as the trial's other phases. The jury got

80. Ibid.; "Plea of Negroes Is Self-Defense," *The State*, June 12, 1915, 10.

81. The State v. Bogus Sanders, 4.

82. "Plea of Negroes Is Self-Defense," 10.

the case at 1:00 p.m. Before the clock struck two, it returned both verdicts. Jurors acquitted Ada Sanders but found Bogus Sanders guilty of murder in the first degree, with no recommendation of mercy. That meant one sentencing option: death.[83]

Judge Rice told Bogus to stand. "Without apparent fear or the least nervousness," the press reported, "the young negro faced the judge."[84] "Bogus," the judge intoned, perhaps trying to convince himself as much as anyone else, "you have been given a fair trial, just as fair as if you had been the most prominent white man in the State, and I think you were justly convicted. You are sentenced to be electrocuted within the walls of the State penitentiary on Friday, July 16." Total time from shooting to scheduled electrocution: less than two months.

Judge Rice asked Sanders if he had anything to say about why the sentence of death should not be imposed upon him. Sanders remained silent.[85] The judge then offered Sanders some final words: "My advice to you is to prepare for death and make your peace with your God. . . . May God have mercy on your soul!"[86]

The Lawyers

Nathaniel J. Frederick and Jacob A. Moorer, attorneys at law, had tried hard to win acquittals for Ada and Bogus Sanders. They went one for two. After Bogus's conviction, they worked even harder, for their goal was bigger. In addition to saving Bogus's life, they now sought to use his case to make the law fairer for all South Carolinians. Their goal was to make South Carolina juries more representative and less racist. When Judge Rice refused to grant their motion for a new trial, claiming that the proceedings in Bogus's case had been perfectly fair, Frederick and Moorer announced their intent to appeal—if necessary, all the way to the Supreme Court of the United States.[87]

---

83. "Bogus Sanders Is Found Guilty of Murder of Ellers," *Columbia Record*, July 12, 1915, 2.

84. "Negro Sentenced to Death; Killed White Man Here," *Columbia Record*, June 13, 1915, 1.

85. Ibid.

86. "Orders Sanders to Death Chair," *The State*, June 13, 1915, 2; "Bogus Sanders Is Found Guilty of Murder of Ellers," 2.

87. "Orders Sanders to Death Chair," 2; "Negro Sentenced to Death," 1.

Frederick and Moorer were members of a tiny fraternity: Black lawyers in the Jim Crow South. Only a handful of Black lawyers practiced anywhere in the United States at the time.[88] In South Carolina, as of 1900, Black people constituted a majority of the population, but just twenty-nine Black lawyers practiced there, alongside 818 white lawyers. For the next four decades in South Carolina, the number of white lawyers increased while the number of Black lawyers declined.[89]

Aspiring southern Black lawyers faced daunting challenges.[90] Segregation limited their educational prospects, from grade school through law school. White law offices would not accept Black lawyers as apprentices, much less colleagues. The American Bar Association and state bar associations raised educational requirements and other barriers to entry to the legal profession. Given the educational disabilities imposed by Jim Crow, these bar-imposed requirements constituted imposing obstacles to aspiring Black lawyers.[91]

The job market for Black lawyers was anemic. White firms would not hire them. White clients were similarly disinclined. Black lawyers necessarily relied on Black clients, who tended to have shallow pockets. The arena within which they worked, the court system, was completely dominated by white men. "The profession of law is the most difficult one a colored man can follow in the South," one observer noted in 1909, "because he must deal with white judges, white jurors, [and] white lawyers."[92] Many Black litigants preferred to hire white lawyers, fearing that Black legal counsel, however good, would rub white jurors and judges the wrong way.[93] "The colored

88. Gilbert T. Stephenson, *Race Distinctions in American Law* (New York: D. Appleton, 1910), 240.

89. W. Lewis Burke, *All for Civil Rights: African American Lawyers in South Carolina, 1868–1968* (Athens: University of Georgia Press, 2017), 242.

90. Stephenson, *Race Distinctions*, 240.

91. Carter Goodwin Woodson, *The Negro Professional Man and the Community: with Special Emphasis on the Physician and the Lawyer* (Washington, DC: Association for the Study of Negro Life and History, 1934), 184–86; Maxwell Bloomfield, "From Deference to Confrontation: The Early Black Lawyers of Galveston Texas, 1895–1920," in *The New High Priests: Lawyers in Post-Civil War America*, ed. Gerard W. Gawalt (Westport, CT: Greenwood Press, 1984), 151–70; J. R Oldfield, "A High and Honorable Calling," *Journal of American Studies* 23, no 3 (1989): 395–406.

92. *The Emmanuele Magazine*, July 3, 1909, quoted in Stephenson, *Race Distinctions*, 241.

93. David Kenneth Pye, "An African-American Attorney Navigates Jim Crow Atlanta," *Georgia Historical Quarterly* 91, no. 4 (2007): 453–77; Oldfield, "A High and Honorable Call-

preacher has no competition in the white minister," one white observer explained. "The same is true of the colored teacher in the South. With the negro lawyer it is different. For legal advice and direction, his people . . . are accustomed to going to the white attorney."[94] Moreover, many Black lawyers faced quiet hostility—and sometimes noisy protest—from white people who objected to Black people holding positions of power.[95]

Admission to the bar, thus, did not promise wealth to Black lawyers. It would seem, however, to have positioned them well to fight for civil rights. Many historians assert that Black lawyers of the Jim Crow era were not so inclined. These writers claim that Black lawyers were, on the whole, self-interested accommodationists. Given the risks associated with civil rights activism, these scholars assert, Black lawyers were reluctant to challenge white supremacy in court.[96]

"Self-interested accommodationist" may describe some Jim Crow-era Black lawyers, but not Frederick and Moorer. Both were outspoken, effective civil rights crusaders.[97] Far from avoiding controversial civil rights cases, Nathaniel Frederick sought them out. As he explained in a letter to NAACP head Walter White, "I am destined to be involved in cases where human rights are at a low discount. Though financially they mean a loss to me. . . . I get quite a kick out of trying to help the poor and unfortunate, especially since I belong to th[is] group."[98]

Frederick appeared regularly in Columbia-area trial courts and argued over thirty cases in the South Carolina Supreme Court. He was equally active in the community. He helped found the Columbia chapter of the

---

ing"; Melissa Milewski, "From Slave to Litigant: African Americans in Court in the Post-war South, 1865–1920" (PhD diss., New York University, 2011), 732–33; "Afro-American Council Emphasizes Its Cowardice," *Washington (DC) Bee*, Sept. 12, 1903, 4.

94. Burke, *All for Civil Rights*, 219–20; James Underwood and William Lewis Burke, *At Freedom's Door: African American Founding Fathers and Lawyers in Reconstruction South Carolina* (Columbia: University of South Carolina Press, 2005), 119–20.

95. J. Clay Smith Jr., *Emancipation: The Making of the Black Lawyer, 1844-1944* (Philadelphia: University of Pennsylvania Press, 1993), 8–16; Pye, "Complex Relations," 455.

96. Bloomfield, "Deference to Confrontation," 151–52; Oldfield, "A High and Honorable Calling."

97. They were not alone. For other examples, see R. Volney Riser, *Defying Disfranchisement: Black Voting Rights Activism in the Jim Crow South* (Baton Rouge: Louisiana State University Press, 2010); and Burke, *All for Civil Rights*.

98. Winfred B. Moore Jr. and Orville V. Burton, eds., *Toward the Meeting of the Waters* (Columbia: University of South Carolina Press, 2008), 76–77.

NAACP. He was an educational leader, serving for a time as principal of the all-Black Howard School and as a member of the South Carolina State Teachers Association.[99] He was a journalistic leader, founding and editing newspapers that denounced lynching, promoted Black education, decried second-class Black citizenship, and championed a procivil rights legislative agenda. One piece, "The Black Touch," juxtaposed the fabled Midas touch, which turned everything suddenly to gold, with what Frederick called the "black touch," wherein everything related to the Black community was suddenly held in lower esteem.[100] Frederick saw his crusade as part of a long-term struggle, one that required patience and persistence. "Let us wait and bide our time," he counseled readers. "Right will eventually win."[101]

Jacob Moorer also fought passionately for civil rights.[102] He gained admission to the South Carolina Bar in 1896, the year after the state's disfranchising constitution went into effect.[103] As of the early twentieth century, he was apparently "the only negro at the Orangeburg [SC] bar."[104] He was a leader of the local Black community and an outspoken champion of civil rights. From the 1890s through the 1910s, he chaired the local Republican Party, ran for the state legislature on the Republican ticket, and attended local Republican Party conventions.[105] He was active in religious affairs, embracing the social gospel. Once, at a Colored Baptist State Convention, a white Presbyterian minister counseled Black Baptist ministers to "preach for saving souls, not about material" things. Moorer objected, insisting that ministers "must" attend to "some of the material things on

99. Oldfield, "A High and Honorable Calling," 404; Damon L. Fordham, "Nathaniel Frederick: The Crusading Lawyer," in *True Stories of Black South Carolina* (Charleston: History Press, 2008), 96–101.

100. "The Black Touch," *Southern Indicator* (Columbia, SC), Feb. 15, 1913.

101. "Smith-Lever Bill," *Southern Indicator*, June 6, 1914.

102. Moorer's wife, Lizeila Moorer, was a poet who voiced the frustration that the couple felt as, in her words, "victim[s] to the inconvenience of prejudice." Lizeila A. J. Moorer, *Prejudice Unveiled: And Other Poems* (Boston: Roxburgh Publishing, 1907), 5.

103. Burke, *All for Civil Rights*, 26.

104. "Kept on His Coat While Others Were Cool: Negro Lawyer for Jacobs in Contest Case," *The State*, July 16, 1905, 9.

105. "On the Edisto," *The State*, Nov. 2, 1896, 3; "Republicans in Orangeburg: Delegates to the Seventh District Convention Elected," *The State*, Oct. 16, 1902, 2; "Instruct for Taft," *The State*, March 29, 1912, 3.

earth."[106] In the area of education, Moorer teamed with Frederick to fight for enhanced educational opportunities for Black Americans, including education at the highest levels, contrary to the views of Booker T. Washington and other Black accommodationists.[107]

Moorer doggedly championed voting rights.[108] He waged a one-man crusade against the disfranchising provisions of the 1895 constitution. Following the 1900 elections, he went to Columbia to protest a congressional race in which a white Democrat had defeated a Black Republican (whom the white press had dubbed the "Old Darkey from Orangeburg").[109] Moorer decried severe undercounting in heavily Black districts and other irregularities.[110] His protest had no impact, other than to steel his own determination to fight. Every two years thereafter, for the next decade or so, one could count on three things: disfranchisement would suppress the Black vote, Republicans would lose South Carolina congressional elections, and Jacob Moorer would travel to Washington, DC, to protest electoral irregularities. Although Moorer was often "the only negro present"[111] at these congressional hearings, he pulled no punches. He argued that "the registration laws of South Carolina are unconstitutional."[112] He attacked the unfair administration of those laws, whereby "negroes were not allowed to register while white people were."[113] And he did so with wit. In 1906, he "was very earnest in his plea that the negro in South Carolina is denied justice at the ballot box, or rather before he gets to the ballot box."[114] A Pennsylvania representative pressed Moorer about race discrimination in South Carolina generally, beyond the particulars of this election. "Well sir," the *Columbia State*, using the demeaning spelling that it reserved for Black speakers, reported Moorer as replying, "I'm jes' tryin' to tell you about the discriminations which affect this particular case. If you want me to tell you about all the

106. "Colored Baptist in Session," *The State*, Dec. 8, 1904, 5.

107. "Educating the Negro: Discussion of the Subject at Orangeburg," *The State*, Sept. 7, 1898, 2.

108. R. Volney Riser, *Defying Disfranchisement: Black Voting Rights Activism in the Jim Crow South, 1890–1908* (Louisiana: Louisiana State University Press, 2010), 248.

109. "Wants to Go to Congress on Republican Ticket: Dantzler the Old Darkey from Orangeburg County," *The State*, March 1, 1901, 5.

110. Ibid.

111. "Kept on His Coat While Others Were Cool," *The State*, July 16, 1905, 9.

112. "Negro Contests Mr. Lever's Seat," *The State*, Dec. 20, 1908, 9.

113. "A Negro Lawyer on Race Problem," *The State*, March 6, 1906, 1.

114. Ibid.

cases of discrimination against the colored men down there, I'm afraid I wouldn't have time."[115]

South Carolina's white press mercilessly derided Moorer and his voting rights activism. Reporters portrayed him as a pompous ignoramus who did not realize how much amusement he unwittingly provided white audiences. "The house elections committee considered the race problem today," the Columbia *State* reported in 1906. "They had lots of fun, though Jacob Moorer, a negro lawyer from Orangeburg, insisted that this was a serious question. Jacob Moorer, however, was the one who caused all the fun."[116] Reporters especially delighted in lampooning his clothing. When Moorer donned a fancy coat for a congressional hearing in the summer of 1905, *The State* portrayed him as a strutting peacock who did not understand appropriate attire for a summertime congressional hearing. *The State's* headline for an article ostensibly about voting rights was: "Kept on his Coat while Others Were Cool."[117]

Moorer was also interested in jury composition. In *Franklin v. State* (US, 1910), he challenged the murder conviction of a Black man in Orangeburg County, South Carolina, on the grounds that the county had deliberately—and unconstitutionally—excluded Black men from the grand jury.[118] Moorer pointed out that jurors were chosen from the pool of registered voters. Thus, the discriminatory voting rules established under South Carolina's Constitution of 1895 had an unconstitutional secondary effect (Black exclusion from juries) to go along with its unconstitutional primary effect (Black disfranchisement). The United States Supreme Court disagreed, ruling that the appellants had failed to show that Black men were excluded from juries "because of their race or color."[119] Although he lost the case, Moorer had succeeded in calling attention to the unfairness of South Carolina's voting and jury rules.[120]

Both Frederick and Moorer, thus, had backbones. Defenders of white

115. Ibid.

116. Ibid.

117. "Kept on His Coat While Others Were Cool," 9.

118. Pink Franklin v. State of South Carolina, 218 U.S. 161 (1910).

119. Ibid.

120. See "South Carolina Supreme Court," *The State*, April 1, 1908, 10; "Two Negro Lawyers not Gen. Bonaparte Are Responsible for Case of Pink Franklin Coming to Supreme Court," *Macon (GA) Daily Telegraph*, April 7, 1910, 9; "Franklin Case Heard by Court," *The State*, April 22, 1910, 1; "Pink Franklin to Hang," *The State*, Sept. 7, 1910, 1.

supremacy bristled at such men operating within the legal system. Critics resented their ability to leverage the rule-of-law ideal against white supremacy. Such resentment appears to have surfaced in 1915, when a white constable struck Frederick with the palm of his hand and drew a pistol. Unbowed, Frederick pressed charges.[121] The hot-tempered constable was convicted of assault and battery on May 25, 1915. Later that day, Bogus Sanders shot Charles Ellers.

Bogus and Ada Sanders hired Frederick and Moorer to defend them against charges of murder. The lawyers got Ada off, but not Bogus, who was convicted and sentenced to die in the electric chair. Frederick and Moorer immediately appealed.[122] They had their work cut out for them.

On July 15, 1915, one day before Bogus's scheduled electrocution, the South Carolina Supreme Court granted the appeal and stayed the execution.[123]

Juries

The jury system, upon which Frederick and Moorer focused their appeal, was an ancient feature of Anglo-American law. It evolved from the inquest, a legal procedure in medieval England wherein royal officials summoned local men to answer questions about matters of interest to the crown. Juries became a regular part of royal justice in the second half of the twelfth century. The Magna Carta (1215) solidified the jury's position in English law.[124]

Trial by jury was a fundamental part of the common-law system that English settlers transported across the Atlantic in the seventeenth century. Soon, the jury was as entrenched in the colonies as in England. One of the injuries and usurpations cited in the Declaration of Independence of 1776 was that King George III had "depriv[ed colonists] in many cases, of the benefits of Trial by Jury."[125] When the Constitution of the United States

121. "Constable Fined for an Assault," *The State*, May 26, 1915, 10.

122. "An Appeal Stays the Execution of Negro Manslayer," *Columbia Record*, July 16, 1915, 6.

123. Ibid.

124. Leonard W. Levy, *The Palladium of Justice: Origins of Trial by Jury* (Chicago: Ivan R. Dee, 1999), 7–16.

125. "Declaration of Independence," transcript, National Archives, accessed Sept. 29, 2022, https://www.archives.gov/founding-docs/declaration-transcript .

appeared eleven years later, it guaranteed the right to trial by jury in federal criminal trials.[126] Antifederalists complained that this was insufficient. The Bill of Rights (1791) strengthened requirements for jury trials in criminal[127] and civil cases.[128] South Carolina, like other newly independent states, also embraced trial by jury. This was as true following the Civil War as it had been during the colonial era. The "Reconstruction Constitution" of 1868 affirmed that the right of trial by jury "shall remain inviolate" in the Palmetto State.[129] A companion measure, "An Act to Regulate the Manner of Drawing Juries," spelled out the procedures by which South Carolina jurors were to be chosen. It required local officials to draw between 5 and 10 percent of the names on the local voting rolls each year. The statute further specified that all of the people whose names were drawn for jury service should be of "good moral character," of "sound judgment," and "free from all legal exceptions."[130]

Under the 1868 South Carolina Constitution, every male citizen of the United States who was at least twenty-one years of age and a resident of South Carolina was eligible to vote and, therefore, to serve on a jury.[131] In theory, racially representative juries should have emerged naturally under these rules. But South Carolina lawmakers, early in Reconstruction, did not trust theory. They adopted two additional measures in 1868 that, they hoped, would guarantee fairness in jury composition. The first provision limited the discretionary power of local officials by requiring that the list of potential jurors be posted in two public places in the given jurisdiction for at least ten days. That list would then be "submitted for revision and acceptance" before an open meeting, during which people could make changes, "adding the names of any person liable to serve, or striking any names therefrom." Only after this revised list was approved would the names be placed in a box for periodic selection, as needed, throughout the year. The hope was that this public oversight would prevent abusive officials from distorting the jury-selection process.[132]

---

126. US Const. art. III, § 2.

127. US Const. amend. V and VI. Initially, at least, Bill of Rights protections applied to federal but not state trials.

128. US Const. amend. VII.

129. S.C. Const. art. I, § 11 (1868).

130. "An Act to Regulate the Manner of Drawing Juries," § 4 (South Carolina, 1868).

131. S.C. Const. (1868).

132. "An Act to Regulate the Manner of Drawing Juries," § 5.

A second provision adopted in 1868 further limited the discretion of local officials. It mandated that the annual lists of potential jurors that local officials compiled maintain the same proportion of white names to "colored" names as existed on the lists of registered voters "in the township, city, or County" in question. These laws were designed to prevent jury registrars from using their discretion to skew the racial balance of South Carolina jury pools.[133]

These egalitarian rules were a flower's petals. By the 1890s, they had wilted, Reconstruction was a fading memory, and a bellicose white supremacist movement dominated state politics. South Carolina Democrats, led by "Pitchfork" Ben Tillman, called a constitutional convention in 1895 with the explicit purpose of restricting Black voting. "The question of suffrage . . . is the sole cause of our being here," Tillman told the convention. He explained that the Reconstruction-era Constitution of 1868 had established "the rule of the negro over the Anglo-Saxon."[134] Whatever the race of the winning candidates, he explained, the very fact that Black people voted served to delegitimate those Reconstruction-era elections. "The negroes put the little pieces of paper in the box," he argued. They "blindly followed like sheep wherever their black and white leaders told them to go," they "voted unanimously every time for the Republican ticket during that dark period [Reconstruction]," and these horrible things were possible "solely . . . by reason of the ballot being in the hands of such cattle."[135]

White South Carolinians heroically suffered the indignities of Reconstruction for eight long years, Tillman explained, until "life became worthless." South Carolina Democrats tried to overcome the Republicans' electoral advantages "by honest methods," but in a majority-Black state, that was "a mathematical impossibility."[136] How did white South Carolinians finally "recover [their] liberty?" Pitchfork Ben asked. "By fraud and violence," he proudly explained to the 1895 convention. But, "Is the danger

---

133. An Act to Amend an Act Entitled "An Act to Regulate the Manner of Drawing Juries," S.C. Stat. at L. No. 155in *The Constitution of South Carolina, Adopted April 16, 1868, and the Acts and Joint Resolutions of the General Assembly Passed at the Special Session of 1868, Together with the Military Orders Therein Re-Enacted* (Columbia, SC: John W. Denny, 1868), 236.

134. *Journal of the Constitutional Convention of the State of South Carolina* (Columbia, SC: Charles A. Calvo Jr., 1895), 443–45.

135. Ibid., 463–64.

136. Ibid., 463.

gone? No." The Black vote was "like the viper that is asleep." It could be "warmed into life again and sting . . . whenever some more white rascals . . . mobilize[d] the ignorant blacks." Therefore, Tillman declared, in the presence of Black as well as white convention delegates, "the only thing we [whites] can do as patriots and as statesmen is to take from them [Blacks] every ballot that we can under the laws of our national government."[137]

The 1895 constitution put Tillman's playbook into action. It used tools such as a literacy test, an "understanding" clause, poll taxes, and disqualification based on criminal records to restrict suffrage.[138] Although these provisions were racially neutral on the surface, they were, as Tillman admitted, purposefully designed to disfranchise as many Blacks and as few whites as possible.[139] A key mechanism was to vest local white officials with maximum discretion and then trust them to implement literacy and "understanding" tests unfairly.[140] Tillman opposed more objective suffrage restrictions, such as property qualifications, because they would disfranchise poor white people, which, Tillman explained, would have been "contrary to all my ideas of principle, fairness and right," given that some poor white people were "the most intelligent of . . . citizens." The genius of the literacy test was its reliance on official discretion. "If you put it in here [in the Constitution's suffrage provisions] that a man must understand, and you vest the right to judge whether he understands in an officer, it is a constitutional act," Tillman explained. "That officer is responsible to his conscience and his God, [but] he is responsible to nobody else. There is no particle of fraud or illegality in it. It is just simply showing partiality, perhaps, [laughter] or discriminating."[141]

This laughter did not come from Black people, who saw Tillman's suffrage proposals as tragedy, not comedy. According to press reports, Black South Carolinians were "up in arms" against Tillman's suffrage plan and vowed to "fight it to the end."[142] At the convention, all six Black delegates in attendance, among 154 white delegates, "pleaded eloquently against the

137. Ibid., 463–64.

138. S.C. Const. art. II, § 4 (1895).

139. James Lowell Underwood, *The Constitution of South Carolina: The Struggle for Political Equality* (Columbia: University of South Carolina Press, 1986), 109–13.

140. Tindall, *South Carolina Negroes*, 233; S.C. Const. (1895).

141. *Journal of the Constitutional Convention of the State of South Carolina*, 469.

142. "Colored Men Protest," *Philadelphia Inquirer*, Oct. 27, 1895, 3.

adoption of the [suffrage] article."[143] William J. Whipper, a Black delegate from Beaufort County, reminded fellow delegates that, though the proposal was racially neutral on its face, "its authors declared" prior to the convention "that it was necessary in order to disfranchise the negro without disfranchising a single white man" so as to "establish white supremacy."[144] The "negro" had emerged from slavery, Whipper told his white colleagues at the convention. "You meet him now as a man, and you would strip him of his manhood."[145] A white South Carolina paper tipped its cap to Whipper's eloquence. "Viewed in any light, the speech was a powerful one and did credit to the coal black man who delivered it."[146]

Robert Smalls, another Black delegate, also decried the convention's suffrage proposals. "This convention has been called for no other purpose than the disfranchisement of the negro. . . . On behalf of . . . negro voters, all that I demand is that a fair and honest election law be passed. We care not what the qualifications imposed are; all that we ask is that they be fair and honest."[147]

Another Black delegate, Thomas Miller, charged that the "evident purpose" of the pending suffrage measure was "to trample upon all the political rights of the colored man in South Carolina, and rob him of his franchise." As "an American citizen," Miller implored the convention "to give the negro the equal political rights to which he was justly entitled." Observers complimented Miller's "strong and forcible" argument but suspected, rightly, that he was "talking to the wind."[148]

A few white delegates joined these Black delegates in voting "nay," though for less principled reasons. One white planter worried that the infinitely vague "understanding clause" was vulnerable to US Supreme Court review and, in any event, was "unnecessary, inasmuch as other provisions in the [suffrage] Article, which are beyond suspicion of unfairness, will accomplish the desired end, i.e., securing white supremacy."[149] Another white delegate likewise feared that the suffrage article's arbitrariness was too blatant:

143. Ibid.

144. Quoted in "Negro Rule! No Danger of it in South Carolina at All," *Knoxville (TN) Journal*, Oct. 27, 1895, 9; and "'Nigger' Spelt with Two G's: Grates Harshly on Negroes' Ears," *Daily Charlotte Observer*, Oct. 27, 1895, 1.

145. Ibid.

146. "Smalls and Whipper: Voices from the Past Raised in the Constitutional Convention," *The State*, Oct. 27, 1895, 1.

147. Quoted in "Negro Rule!," 9; and "'Nigger' Spelt with Two G's," 1.

148. "Blacks Fight for Franchise," *Columbus (GA) Daily Enquirer*, Oct. 27, 1895, 4.

149. *Journal of the Constitutional Convention*, 727.

"White supremacy may be secured without resorting to the perhaps questionable means adopted by the Convention."[150]

These white opponents worried that the new constitution's discriminatory, though facially neutral, voting rules might prompt the North to interfere in South Carolina's business. Disfranchisers knew better. "They are going to let us alone," Pitchfork Ben's brother G. D. Tillman predicted, "and if we don't pile on too much . . . they will let us have considerable elbow room."[151] He was right.

Jim Crow Juries

By 1915, when jurors were chosen for the Sanders case, the voting rolls in South Carolina were much, much whiter than they had been during Reconstruction. That mattered. Voting rolls were the seas in which local jury commissioners fished. Moreover, these officials enjoyed substantially more discretionary power than had their Reconstruction-era predecessors. No longer did local communities—or anybody else—exercise any meaningful oversight. And no longer were jury commissioners statutorily obliged to assemble juries whose racial ratios mirrored those of voting roles.

Although jury commissioners enjoyed wide discretion in practice, on paper they were constrained by meticulously detailed procedures. South Carolina guarded against the prospect of a lone official going rogue by dividing the power to choose juries among three people. In each county, three local officials—the county treasurer, the county auditor, and the clerk of the court of common pleas—jointly served as jury commissioners.[152] Each local trio had to follow an intricate, four-step jury-selection process:

1. *Voting list*: Jury commissioners began the jury-selection process by acquiring their county's voter-registration list of eligible "electors." By law, everyone on that list was male, met residency requirements, had paid a poll tax, was over twenty-one, and either had passed a literacy test or owned more than $300 in property. Depending on the year and county in question, this "voting list" might already be overwhelmingly white.

150. Ibid., 517.

151. G. D. Tillman, quoted in *Journal of the Constitutional Convention*, 732–33.

152. S.C. Stat. at L. No. 578 (1902).

2. *Jury list:* Every December, jury commissioners in each county compiled the following year's "jury list" by selecting "not less than one from every three" (this ratio changed over time) of the names that appeared on their county's voting list. Not all registered voters qualified for inclusion on jury lists. Some failed on objective grounds. For example, jurors faced more restrictive age requirements than voters did. Although jurors, like voters, had to be at least twenty-one years of age, jurors additionally could be no more than sixty-five, an age ceiling that did not apply to voters.[153]

   Other restricting criteria, however, were more subjective. By law, jury commissioners were to select only people who, in their judgment, were of "good moral character" and "sound judgment."[154] This reflected the then-prevalent notion that serving on a jury was akin to holding public office. It was a civic duty too important, and too complicated, to be entrusted to just anyone. The ideal was the "blue-ribbon jury," containing only men of unquestioned intelligence, morality, and character.[155] Jury commissioners alone were to determine who qualified. Clearly, much room for conscious or unconscious discrimination existed. Appellate courts were reluctant to second-guess the subjective judgments of jury commissioners regarding "good moral character."[156]
3. *Jury panel:* Jury commissioners next assembled jury panels. They began by copying all of the names from their annual jury lists, one-by-one, onto slips of paper. They were to prepare these slips of paper "so as to resemble each other as much as possible and so folded that the name written thereon shall not be visible on the outside."[157] The identical-looking slips of paper were then placed in a "strong and

---

153. Ibid.

154. S.C. Rev. Stat., § 3 (1873); Gen. Stat., § 2236 (1882); Civ. Code, § 2911 (1902); Civ. Code art. 1, § 4017 (1912); Code of Civ. Pro. art. 2, § 2 (1922); Code of Civ. Pro. (1942).

155. Abramson, *We the Jury*, 99.

156. S.C. Stat. at L. No. 578, § 2 (1902). For a discussion of subsequent judicial scrutiny of "good moral character" and "sound judgment" requirements, see Randall Kennedy, *Race, Crime, and the Law* (New York: Pantheon Books, 1997), 182.

157. S.C. Stat. at L. No. 578, § 3 (1902). In a later revision, commissioners in counties with large cities additionally had to insert each slip of paper into an individual "opaque capsule, or container, uniform in size, shape, and color"—yet another step designed to create the appearance of blindfolded fairness. S.C. act 321, §3 (1933).

substantial" compartment that was equipped with three different locks,[158] with each of the three corresponding keys being held by a different jury commissioner so that the lockbox could be opened only if all three commissioners were present.[159] Throughout the year, whenever local courts were in session, judges would tell jury commissioners how many jurors they needed. The commissioner trio would then convene, open the triple-locked compartment, and randomly draw that number of names. A group of prospective jurors drawn in this way was known as a "jury panel." For a twelve-member trial jury, also known as a petit jury, commissioners might assemble a jury panel of thirty-six names.[160]

4. *Actual juries:* The final stage in the process was the selection of actual juries. Everyone on a jury panel—that is, everyone whose name was drawn from a lockbox (and not immediately discarded by jury commissioners)—was summoned to court on a given date. At this late stage, the jury-selection process left the hands of jury commissioners and entered the domain of judges and lawyers. Judges decided whether or not to excuse would-be jurors who claimed illness or other legitimate factors. Remaining people were made available for service on either grand juries or petit juries. Grand juries heard quick-and-dirty versions of prosecutorial evidence in criminal cases. If prosecutors presented reasonable-sounding unilateral cases, grand juries would issue indictments and the suspects in question would be held for trial.

Panelists not called to serve on grand juries were eligible to serve on petit juries. Petit juries sat during actual criminal and civil trials. Before being seated, however, they had to pass through voir dire, the final step in

---

158. S.C. Stat. at L. No. 578, §3 (1902).

159. A later legal reform allowed any two of the three to open the box in order to draw names.

160. South Carolina jury books include many names clustered into groups of thirty-six, representing jury panels. See also "Trials and Tribulations of Honest Jury Commissioners," *The State*, Oct. 20, 1909, 2. In addition, a "tales box" containing the names of between one hundred and four hundred qualified potential jurors who resided within five miles of the courthouse was to be kept inside the lockbox. These individuals were available to serve as emergency jurors in the "case of deficiencies arising from any cause or emergency during the sitting of the court." S.C. Stat. at L. No. 578, §3 (1902).

the jury-selection process. During voir dire, judges and lawyers questioned potential jurors and excluded some. Those who survived voir dire sat in jury boxes and heard trials.

On rare occasions, popular pressures directly affected southern jury selection. In 1888, jury commissioners in Dodge County, Georgia, where the rules were roughly similar to those of South Carolina, received a petition from local "colored citizens," asking that some Black names be placed in the jury lockbox. The commissioners agreed and added the names of fifty Black men to the pool from which jurors would be chosen. Local whites were outraged. They smashed open the lockbox and burned its contents.[161] But this was not the norm. Most jury commissioners acted beyond the reach of public scrutiny, petitions, or torches.

On paper, these elaborate procedures should have made it nearly impossible to exclude Black jurors due to their race. Apparent protections existed throughout the process. The Fifteenth Amendment to the US Constitution barred states from disfranchising citizens "on account of race, color, or previous condition of servitude," seemingly assuring fair voting lists at the start.[162] The Civil Rights Act of 1875 extended similar protections to the jury-selection process. It prohibited discrimination in jury construction on "account of race, color, or previous condition of servitude."[163] The US Supreme Court endorsed this ideal in *Strauder v. West Virginia* (1879), which barred states from excluding Black people from juries on account of their race.[164] And South Carolina's elaborate jury-selection procedures, far from discriminating on the basis of race, appeared to provide triple-locked guarantees of fairness.

Frederick and Moorer, however, understood that the law lives in action, not in books. They understood how much discretion the law left in the hands of jury commissioners and how common it was for commissioners to abuse their power by unfairly filtering Black people out of jury pools. In *State v. Sanders*, the two lawyers confronted the Jim Crow jury.

---

161. "Opposed to Negro Jurors," *Augusta (GA) Chronicle*, Aug. 25, 1888, 1.
162. U.S. Const. amend. XV, § 1 (1870).
163. Stephenson, *Race Distinctions*, 247–48.
164. Strauder v. West Virginia, 100 U.S. 303 (1879).

The Quantitative Approach: The Exclusion of Black People from Juries

Frederick and Moorer opened their South Carolina Supreme Court brief in *State v. Sanders* by attacking the unfair exclusion of Black men from juries. They argued that both the grand jury that indicted Sanders and the petit jury that convicted him were "unlawfully constituted, in that, in the formation of the same, discrimination was made against the negro race because of race and color."[165] They had a point. Black residents constituted a majority in Richland County at the time. Both juries were all white.[166]

Frederick and Moorer were not pioneers. For years, lawyers representing Black criminal defendants in the South had attacked the exclusion of Black men from grand and petit juries.[167] In 1910, a legal scholar wrote, "A custom seems to have grown up among some lawyers, particularly in the South, to move to quash the indictment whenever a Negro is on trial for a crime and there are no Negroes on the grand jury."[168] Occasionally, these lawyers won. In 1901, a Texas appellate court reversed and remanded the case of John Kipper, "a negro who was given a life sentence for the murder of a police officer," on the grounds that "there were no negro jurors on the grand or petit jury."[169]

Such claims, however, were hard to substantiate. The case-law at the time required lawyers to demonstrate not just that Black jurors were absent but that their absence resulted from overt and intentional racial exclusion. In *Strauder v. West Virginia* (US, 1879), that was the case. A West Virginia statute explicitly barred Black people from juries. Strauder won.[170] In *Franklin v. State of South Carolina* (US, 1910), by contrast, no such policy existed.

165. State v. Sanders, 103 S.C. 216, 218 (1915).

166. "Bogus Sanders Is on Trial Second Time for Murder," 12; "Richland Jurors: Panels Drawn for two Weeks of Criminal Court," *The State*, May 19, 1915, 10.

167. "Colored Jurors," *People's Advocate* (Washington, DC), June 12, 1880, 1; "Obstruction of Justice," *Daily Picayune* (New Orleans, LA), Nov. 27, 1894, 4; "No Negro Jurors," *Jonesboro (AR) Evening Sun*, Mar. 10, 1908, 1; "Negro Civil Rights," *Dallas Morning News*, Mar. 14, 1896, 7; "African-American Council Emphasizes Its Cowardice," *Washington Bee*, Sept. 12, 1903, 4.

168. Stephenson, *Race Distinctions*, 250.

169. "Verdict Reversed Because a Negro Was Tried by a White Jury," *Daily Charlotte Observer*, April 11, 1901, 1.

170. Strauder v. West Virginia.

Jacob Moorer knew *Franklin* well, having litigated it. In *Franklin*, the absence of Black jurors resulted not from explicit racial bars but from supposedly nonracial criteria such as "good moral character." Franklin lost.[171]

Given these precedents, litigants who alleged jury-composition discrimination faced long odds. Frederick and Moorer understood this. Their decision to make these arguments anyway suggests that they may have sought political as well as legal gains. Their original jury challenge in *Sanders* took the form of a pretrial motion, which was heavily covered in the local press. They called two of Richland County's jury commissioners into court at the outset of the high-profile Sanders trial "to answer questions relating to the drawing of the jury." Regardless of its legal impact, this move forced jury commissioners to defend their actions under oath and it called public attention to the issue of racial discrimination. An optimist might have hoped that the experience of publicly defending their actions against charges of racial discrimination might have had the subtle effect of making jury commissioners more aware of subconscious biases and therefore less likely to discriminate in the future. Legally, however, the move was feeble. The press reported that the jury commissioners "denied in direct terms that there had been discrimination on account of race." They had chosen jurors, they said, on the basis of "merit and morality," not race.[172] "The only reasons for exercising their personal choice in drawing the jury," they testified, was "to obtain worthy men as members of the jury."[173]

In later years, lawyers seeking to prove discrimination in the absence of explicit racial preferences would invoke a sort of evidence not available to Frederick and Moorer in 1915: population statistics. Later generations of civil rights lawyers would use such evidence, analyzed by methods derived from probability theory, to attack racially biased jury-selection policies.[174] Frederick and Moorer did not attempt this. Compiling data would have taken more time and money than the lawyers had, especially given the accelerated pace of *Sanders*. Had Frederick and Moorer asked to see jury books, commissioners might well have said no, citing *State v. Merriman* (SC, 1891), a South Carolina precedent authorizing jury commissioners to

---

171. Pink Franklin v. State of South Carolina, 218 U.S. 161 (1910).

172. "Negro and Wife Placed on Trial," 5.

173. "Trial of Sanders Has Begun with New Features," *Columbia Record*, June 10, 1915, 2.

174. See Michael McGovern, "Just in Numbers? Statistics and Civil Rights in the Cold War United States" (PhD diss., Princeton University, forthcoming).

work secretly.[175] Frederick and Moorer's only hint in this direction was a request that the trial judge admit into evidence the Richland County voter-registration list, which the lawyers sought to use to demonstrate that "colored" voters' names were marked with the letter "C." or "Col.," making it possible for jury commissioners to discriminate systematically. The trial judge in *Sanders* refused to admit this evidence.[176]

Nonetheless, quantitative evidence, though not a part of the *Sanders* record, is worth hearing now.[177] Historians of the Jim Crow jury have done little quantitative research. Most simply assume that Blacks were "universally excluded from southern juries" and leave it at that.[178] As a rhetorical matter, this is probably good enough. As a historical matter, it is not. A closer look reveals a somewhat more nuanced story.

Scholars may have avoided statistical analysis of the Jim Crow jury because it is a methodological minefield. The naïve scholar dashes in, imagining the truth about jury composition to be a Sleeping Beauty, needing only the kiss of a dauntless researcher to restore it to life. Almost immediately, however, thorny research challenges humble even the most intrepid explorer. Archival records are spotty and inconsistent. Voter-registration lists exist for some counties in some years; jury lists exist for other counties in other years. Some archived tomes clearly label jury lists, jury panels, and actual jurors. Others simply list page after page of names, daring researchers to guess. Some commissioners had excellent handwriting; others did not. Some consistently listed dates. Others did not. All seemed to mark "colored" names with "C." or "Col.," but perhaps some did not. Either way, the responsible researcher must cross-reference jury and voter names—one by one, slowly, deliberately—with names appearing in census reports or other records from the time that categorized people by race. This process is quicksand—slow and treacherous. Scribes frequently used initials rather than first or middle names, creating ambiguities. Many names appear on jury lists but not census reports. Perhaps they moved before the end of the decade. Or died. Perhaps their names are spelled incorrectly in one place.

175. State v. Merriman, 34 S.C. 16, 24, 12 S.E. 619, 624 (S.C. 1891).

176. State v. Sanders, 219.

177. For a discussion of "common-sense quantification" in the practice of legal history, see John Wertheimer, "Counting as a Tool of Legal History," in *Making Legal History: Essays in Honor of William E Nelson*, ed. Daniel J. Hubebosch and R. B. Bernstein (New York: New York University Press, 2013), 162–78.

178. Klarman, *From Jim Crow*, 39, 43.

Or the other. Or both. Other names on jury lists could be any of several people listed in the census, some Black, some white. Then—hark!—a jury name perfectly matches a census listing, and all is well. The researcher confidently records the person's listed race, ignoring a troubling truth: the two names may or may not represent the same person. Racially identifying jury and voting lists is so laborious that the researcher must resort to sampling—that is, choosing only some names from some tomes to cross-reference in the census. But might commissioners, due to geographical clustering or other reasons, have grouped white—or Black—names on sampled pages rather than distributing them evenly throughout the tome? The researcher hopes not, but fears so. At the end of the day—or year—the humbled researcher, realizing why so few have previously attempted this sort of research, hopes only to have made reasonable and consistent decisions. Sleeping Beauty will never really be revived.

We did our best. We analyzed select South Carolina counties, in select years, from Reconstruction to the 1920s.[179] We determined, as accurately as our sources allowed, the racial compositions of the counties' populations generally and of the voter-registration and jury records that we sampled.[180] Our findings are more suggestive than conclusive. Undeniably, different research samples and methods would produce different conclusions. We invite others to improve upon our efforts.

We arrived at three general conclusions: (1) levels of Black jury service varied substantially from county to county, (2) successive stages in the jury-selection process filtered out Black names gradually, and (3) the numbers of Black people who served on southern juries fluctuated dramatically over time.

1. County-by-county variation

Although a uniform set of rules governed jury selection statewide during the Jim Crow years, Black representation on juries varied from county to

179. Our data come from Abbeville, Aiken, Berkeley, Charleston, Clarendon, Florence, Georgetown, Newberry, Richland, Spartanburg, and Union Counties in South Carolina.

180. Data on the racial makeup of each county came from the US census. Voting data came from record books maintained by county clerks. Data on jury panels and jury boxes came from civil, criminal, and common pleas journals maintained by each of the counties. Unlike the voter registration books, these journals did not necessarily differentiate between white and nonwhite individuals, so names that appeared in these documents were checked in the census.

county. This reflected not only demographic differences but also the unchecked discretionary power of local officials. Jury commissioners in some counties interpreted "good moral character and sound judgment" one way; their counterparts elsewhere interpreted it differently. Some officials considered Blackness to be a priori proof of lack of "good moral character and sound judgment." Others disagreed. To an extent, a Black man's prospects for serving on a jury depended on his address.

Variation existed in federal as well as state courts. Prior to 1948, federal statutes required federal juries to follow the same eligibility criteria used by state juries in the same jurisdictions. This allowed state-level disfranchisement to limit Black service on federal juries. Yet federal jury-selection officials also enjoyed a fair amount of discretion.[181] Following emancipation, some federal courts empaneled Black jurors years before state courts in the same areas would do so. Black people, for example, had "served for years" as federal jurors in Baltimore, Maryland, and Richmond, Virginia, before appearing on city- or state-court juries there.[182] Federal courts varied in their openness to Black jurors, however. In the 1890s, the Black community in Savannah, Georgia, where "colored" federal jurors were "a rarity," looked with envy upon the federal court in Atlanta, which reportedly "never fail[ed] to have a considerable number of colored citizens on its grand and petit juries."[183]

State courts varied even more.[184] In 1910, southern legal scholar Gilbert T. Stephenson polled clerks of court across the region.[185] Their replies reveal huge county-to-county variation. Most clerks reported systematic exclusion of Black people because of their race. A North Carolina clerk of court proudly reported: "Negroes do not serve on the jury in this county and have not since we, the white people, got the government in our hands."[186] A Missouri official unashamedly reported: "As far as I am informed, no Negroes

181. "An Analysis of Alternative Constructions of the Requirement That Federal Jurors Be Competent under State Law," *Yale Law Journal* 64, no. 7 (June 1955): 1059.

182. "Negro Jurors: Summoned for the First Time in Virginia," *Philadelphia Inquirer*, Mar. 27, 1880, 1; "Colored Jurors in Baltimore," *Cincinnati Daily Gazette*, May 12, 1880, 5.

183. "The United States Court at Atlanta," *Savannah Tribune*, April 27, 1895: 2.

184. "Negroes as Jurors," *Dallas Morning News*, June 2, 1907, 25; "Judge Foraker and the South," *Cincinnati Commercial Tribune*, Sept. 7, 1885, 2; "Piling on the Agony," *Macon (GA) Telegraph and Messenger*, Mar. 18, 1880, 2.

185. Stephenson, *Race Distinctions*.

186. Ibid., 265–66.

have served as jurors . . . in this county." According to that Missouri official, the white residents of his county would not have had it any other way. "While probably under our laws Negroes would be legal jurors, the county court . . . will not draw them as jurors, and the Sheriff, when he has to get jurors, will not summon them. And I do not believe our lawyers here would permit a Negro to remain on a jury before which they would have to try a case. Further, I am sure that no white man here would serve on a jury with a Negro, even though his refusal to so serve would subject him to a jail sentence."[187]

Elsewhere, however, Black jurors were common. A Louisiana official wrote in 1910: "In this Parish, Negroes have served on both our grand and petit juries ever since the Civil War. . . . They usually constitute about one-half of the panel on the petit jury and on the grand jury they are always represented. . . . They render very good service."[188] A North Carolina clerk reported that "Negroes occasionally serve[d] on juries in [this] county."[189] A Missouri commissioner reported that Black jury service was fairly common there. Just the previous week, two "Negroes" had served on a jury. No lawyer objected, and the "other [white] jurors did not seem to feel any antipathy."[190] A Mississippi clerk of court wrote that his judicial district contained five counties, "in three of which Negroes serve[d] upon juries in about the proportion that they [were] qualified [to vote] under the law."[191] A Texas clerk estimated that Black jurors were about one-tenth of the total in his county's court system, "and they [were] rarely ever discriminated against."[192] A second Texas clerk estimated that "colored jurors" accounted for about 25 percent of the jurors in his county.[193] A third Texas clerk bucked the trend: "We do not use Negro jurors," he explained.[194] Some clerks reported a recent increase in Black jurors; others reported a recent decrease. The picture was anything but uniform.

Although officials from just five South Carolina counties responded to Stephenson's 1910 query, even this small sample spanned a wide spectrum.

187. Ibid., 263–64.
188. Ibid., 259.
189. Ibid., 265–66.
190. Ibid., 264.
191. Ibid., 260–61.
192. Ibid., 268.
193. Ibid., 269.
194. Ibid., 269.

One Palmetto State clerk reported including "a good many negroes on juries."[195] Another reported that "no Negroes serve[d] on the jury in the county courts."[196] Stephenson did not identify the home counties of any quoted clerks, so we do not know if any represented Richland County, home to Columbia and Bogus Sanders. Evidence suggests, however, that Richland County was unfavorable to Black jury service. In 1905, the *Southern Sun*, a Black newspaper published in Columbia, protested: "We wonder what excuse our jury commissioners can give for not putting some . . . negroes on the jury in this county?"[197] A decade later, all of the jurors in the Bogus Sanders trial were white.

These textual documents suggest that Black jury participation varied from county to county during the Jim Crow era. Our quantitative study reinforces this conclusion. Although our sampled counties differed only modestly in terms of the racial composition of the population as a whole, they differed more in the racial composition of registered voters and more still in the racial composition of jurors. The discretion that the law left in the hands of county-level officials explains these county-to-county variations.

2. Gradual filtration

In addition to assuming that southern Black jurors "vanished"[198] during the Jim Crow era, most scholars assume that they know why: electoral disfranchisement. Jury lists, after all, were subsets of voting lists. The conventional wisdom seems perfectly logical: "As whites suppressed black voting, blacks disappeared from juries."[199] This conventional wisdom is not so much wrong as incomplete. Disfranchisement undeniably filtered out Black jurors. But it was not the only, or even the most important, filter. Each phase of the elaborate jury-construction process, our research suggests, was a sieve of progressively finer weave. Electoral disfranchisement was an important but not uniquely exclusionary part of the process.

In order to assess the relative impact of the different stages of the jury-selection process, we aggregated our eleven-county data over our entire time period: 1869 to 1926. We aggregated our numbers because we lacked

195. Ibid., 267.

196. Ibid., 268.

197. Quoted in "No Negroes on Juries," *The State*, Sept. 7, 1905, 4.

198. Nieman, "Black Political Power and Criminal Justice," 420.

199. Klarman, *From Jim Crow*, 39.

complete data sets (voting lists, jury lists, jury panels, and actual jurors) from any one county and during any one year. Admittedly, given how widely counties varied from each other, and how dramatically things such as voter registration levels changed over time, this is not an ideal methodology. But it seemed to be the best available way to assess the relative impact of the various stages of the jury-selection process. Our results make intuitive sense, suggesting that they are not wildly inaccurate. We invite others to challenge our findings.

Undeniably, voter registration profoundly affected Black availability for jury service. Black people constituted about 60 percent of the overall population in our sampled counties during the half-century under study. Early in our time period, during Reconstruction, Black and white residents registered to vote at roughly comparable levels. Later in our time period, South Carolina's disfranchisement measures dramatically reduced Black voter registration relative to white voter registration. The overall average Black share of registered voters in our eleven-county sample, from 1869 to 1926, was 31.8 percent. This meant that the voter registration process alone reduced the Black share of the potential jury pool from about 60 percent (the Black share of the population as a whole in sampled counties) to 31.8 percent. Between 1869 and 1926, in other words, the voter-registration process filtered out almost half of the Black men who would otherwise have been eligible for jury service.

The next stage in the jury-selection process had an even greater impact. This was the phase during which jury commissioners compiled annual "jury lists" by selecting a fraction of the names from their counties' voting lists. This part of the process had proportionally the greatest discriminatory effect of all. As noted, Black names constituted 31.8 percent of the whole on the voter registration lists that we sampled. By contrast, Black names constituted just 9.5 percent of the names on sampled jury lists.

Two lists from the same county—an 1896 voter registration list and a 1902 jury list, both from Clarendon County, South Carolina—afford us a rare opportunity to observe jury commissioners at work. Admittedly, two lists from the same year would have been preferable. But the whims of the archives did not allow that. In this case, the lists, though compiled six years apart, provide an instructive glimpse. Both were created after the adoption of the disfranchising state constitution of 1895. As far as we know, nothing dramatic changed in the intervening years.

To burrow into these two lists is to marvel at how much discretion jury commissioners exercised. Creating a jury list was hardly a random process. Take the issue of age. As noted above, jurors faced age restrictions that voters did not. Although both voters and jurors had to be at least twenty-one, jurors, unlike voters, could not exceed sixty-five. Jury commissioners, therefore, scrupulously avoided adding elderly "electors" (registered voters) to their jury lists. The demographic profiles of the two lists, thus, differed at the upper end of the age spectrum. Men sixty years of age and older constituted over 7 percent of the 1896 voter list but just 1.4 percent of the 1902 jury list.

The astonishing fact about ages, however, is this: despite the statutory bar on jurors over sixty-five, and despite the presence of aged electors—William Buddin, age seventy-four; Wash Burgess, age eighty-two—the average prospective juror was actually older (41.7 years) than the average registered voter (37.8 years). The explanation lies at the youngest end of the spectrum. Men under thirty accounted for about 30 percent of names on the voter list but only about 11 percent of names on the jury list. Apparently, jury commissioners consciously avoided selecting twenty-somethings, presumably because they associated "good moral character" and "sound judgment"[200] with more advanced age. Jury commissioners themselves tended to be older than the average voter, which may have influenced their thinking. The three jury commissioners in Richland County who chose the jurors for *State v. Sanders* in 1915 were all in their sixties.[201]

Jury commissioners, thus, did not select randomly from voting lists. They carefully picked and chose. They favored property owners over renters.[202] They favored farmers over others.[203] Most importantly, and most disproportionately, they favored white people over Black people. Approximately 30 percent of registered voters in our 1896 voting list sample from Clarendon County (thirty-four of 112 positively identified names) were nonwhites. By contrast, less than 1 percent of the names on the 1902 jury list from the same county (one out of 161 identified names) appear to have

200. S.C. Rev. Stat. § 3 (1873); Gen. Stat. § 2236 (1882); Civil Code § 2911 (1902), Civil Code art. 1, § 4017 (1912); Code of Civil Prod. art. 2, § 2 (1922); Code of Civil Prod. (1942).

201. Richland County Jury Commissioners in 1915 were Belin C. DuPre, age sixty-four; Prescott B. Spigner Sr., age sixty; and J. Frost Walker, age sixty-two.

202. Property owners accounted for 63 percent of Clarendon County's registered voters in 1896 but 70 percent of the names on that county's 1902 jury list.

203. Farmers accounted for 71 percent of Clarendon County's registered voters in 1896 but 84 percent of the names on that county's 1902 jury list.

been nonwhite. Clarendon was therefore one of those southern counties where Black jurors, at least for a time, essentially "vanished." But this was not due simply to disfranchisement, as commonly believed. Rather, it resulted, above all, from the deliberate actions of jury commissioners.

The remaining two steps in the jury-selection process—from jury list to jury panel and from jury panel through voir dire to jury service—had more modest effects. They reduced the percentage of Black names in the pool, but only slightly. Qualitative evidence suggests, however, that both of those steps could be used in particular instances to filter out Black people.

The "jury-panel" stage, during which jury commissioners randomly drew names from triple-locked compartments, conveys the image of utter fairness. But jury commissioners sometimes manipulated results at this stage. "If . . . improper names find their way into the general box it is never too late to correct such error," a Richland County jury commissioner admitted in 1909, six years before he would help compose the jury in the Bogus Sanders case, "and this duty is exercised by the Richland commissioners at almost every drawing."[204] Commissioners were permitted to do all of this secretly, beyond the gaze of lawyers and others who, during Reconstruction, had enjoyed the right to witness this stage of the jury-selection process. The South Carolina Supreme Court defended the Jim Crow procedure's new secrecy. Because the law now required jury commissioners to exclude persons who were not of "good moral character" and "sound judgment," the court reasoned in 1891, "it might greatly embarrass the board of jury commissioners"—not to mention the people they discussed—if deliberations were open to the public.[205] For similar reasons, jury commissioners were not obliged to explain their reasons for discarding names. Nor were they obliged to release copies of the jury panels that they drew.[206]

Frederick and Moorer, Bogus Sanders's lawyers, were aware that legal challenges to commissioner discretion at this stage of the jury-selection process faced tall odds. Just a few years earlier, in *State v. Cunningham* (SC 1911), a white lawyer representing a "mixed"-race man convicted of murder appealed to the South Carolina Supreme Court on the grounds that jury commissioners had illegitimately discarded three would-be jurors whose names had been drawn. The jury commissioners explained that one of the discarded would-be jurors was mentally unfit, another was not known to

204. "Trials and Tribulations of Honest Jury Commissioners," *The State*, Oct. 20, 1909, 2.

205. State v. Merriman, 34 S.C. 16, 24, 12 S.E. 619, 624 (S.C. 1891).

206. Ibid.

them personally (and might have moved out of the county), and the third was reportedly a drunkard. The attorney did not explicitly accuse the jury commissioners of racial discrimination, even though Blacks accounted for at least one, and perhaps all three, of the excluded names. Rather, the lawyer argued that jury commissioners had illegitimately discarded duly drawn names. The state supreme court rejected this argument, ruling that the jury commissioners had legally exercised their discretion and that any irregularities were "not such as to render the [jury-selection process] illegal."[207]

During the final stage, voir dire, the jury-selection process moved into the open, to courthouses, where criminal and civil jury trials were held. Lawyers and judges took jury panels—groups of thirty-six names, which jury commissioners previously had drawn from their triple-locked compartments—and whittled them down to twelve-person juries. Juror names were randomly chosen, one by one. Attorneys and judges interrogated each would-be juror in turn. Lawyers could "strike" (request the removal of) unwanted jurors in two different ways. First, if a prospective juror arguably would be unable to rule fairly in the case, a lawyer could request removal "for cause." A prospective juror's close family connection to one of the litigants, for example, would justify a "for-cause" strike. So would the prospective juror's recent experience as a victim of a traumatic crime similar to the one in the case to be tried. If the trial judge agreed that the prospective juror would be unable to rule fairly, he (all judges were male) would dismiss him (all jurors were male) "for cause."

Lawyers for each side also could strike a limited number of prospective jurors without providing any justification. These were called "peremptory strikes." Lawyers treasured them. In murder cases, the prosecution could use up to five peremptory strikes and the defense up to ten. Peremptory strikes were powerful chisels that lawyers could use, if so inclined, to shape the racial composition of juries. Some lawyers indeed used their discretionary strikes deliberately to remove Black people. Perhaps predictably, Jim Crow–era prosecutors sometimes struck would-be Black jurors in cases involving Black criminal defendants. Perhaps less predictably, in some other cases with Black criminal defendants, it was defense lawyers, not prosecutors, who sought to keep Black men off juries, presumably acting on

207. State v. Cunningham, 87 S.C. 453, 69 S.E. 1093, 1094 (1911). This decision was in line with previous rulings in which South Carolina's high court had similarly rejected challenges to alleged irregularities committed by jury commissioners. Rhodes v. Railroad, 68 S. C. 494, 47 S. E. 689 (1904); State v. Smalls, 73 S.C. 519, 53 S.E. 976 (1906); Hutto v. Railroad, 75 S. C. 295, 55 S. E. 445 (1906); and State v. Smith, 77 S. C. 248, 57 S. E. 868 (1907).

the oft-repeated belief from the time, as one judge put it in the 1880s, that "negroes [were] much severer on one another than white jurors [were] on negroes."[208] A Black newspaper in Alabama reported in 1883 that the jury in a criminal trial of a Black man would be all white, after "five colored jurors" had been "challenged by the defendant."[209] Likewise, at jury selection in an 1880 case, a Black murder suspect in Georgia reportedly struck a Black juror because he "wanted no 'nigger' to try him for his life."[210]

Lawyers defending white criminal defendants likewise sought on occasion to manipulate the racial composition of juries. Some defense lawyers with white clients sought to keep Black men off juries.[211] Others sought more, not fewer, Black jurors. Louisiana lawyers representing two white men accused of a gruesome murder in 1871 challenged every white juror on the panel, purportedly "with the hope that they could influence more easily a jury made up entirely of colored men."[212] The resulting all-Black jury wound up convicting their clients anyway. When asked why the sentence of death should not be passed upon him, one of the white convicts complained that the twelve "colored" jurors in his case had been ignorant, "not one of them being able to read or write, and three of them not even knowing what was capital punishment."[213] The trial judge was unsympathetic: "If that jury could not read or write, it was not the fault of the State. It was your fault. There were plenty of white, intelligent jurors, but you have refused every one. The jury, however, which tried your case were impartial, and there was plenty of evidence to convict you."[214]

Because the voir dire phase of jury selection was conducted in open court, observers may have overestimated its importance. Our quantitative analysis suggests that the voir dire process played a comparatively modest

208. "Objecting to Colored Jurors," *Baltimore Sun*, Dec. 11, 1884, 3.

209. "Circuit Court," *Huntsville (AL) Gazette*, Feb. 24, 1883, 3. The assertion that Selleck Moore was Black is based on an exact match of his name, found in the United States Census (1900), Census Place: Triana, Madison, Alabama, p. 12; Enumeration District 0108; FHL microfilm 1240028. Another possible match from the US Census, that of a man listed under "Sellick" (not "Selleck") Moore, is also listed as a Black man. United States Census (1880), Census Place: Madison, Alabama, roll 21, p. 111A, Enumeration District 205.

210. Quoted in "The Colored Juror," *Patriot* (Harrisburg, PA), July 8, 1880, 1.

211. "The Jury Selected in the Shedd Case," *Augusta (GA) Chronicle*, May 6, 1913, 1.

212. "The Colored Jurors," *Weekly Louisianian* (New Orleans), June 25, 1871, 2.

213. "Garvey and Earle, Convicted of Murder, Sentenced: Remarks of the Accused," *New Orleans Republican*, Aug. 24, 1871, 5.

214. Ibid.

role in preventing Black jury service. In select South Carolina counties between 1869 and 1926. Black people accounted for about 60 percent of the total populations in sampled counties, 32 percent of the names on sampled voting lists, 9.5 percent of the names on sampled jury lists, 8.7 percent of the names on sampled jury panels, and 8.3 percent of the names of sampled jurors who actually served. Each filter whitened juries to one degree or another. Together, in sequence, the effect was formidable.

The third major finding of our quantitative analysis, following county-by-county variation and sequential filtration, is volatile fluctuation over time. Many scholars assume a flat line of all-white juries throughout the Jim Crow era. Our closer look reveals a needle that jumped around as history unspooled.

Prior to the Civil War, Black jury service was, at most, sporadic in the North and presumably nonexistent in the South, in part due to near-universal disfranchisement. Black men in northern states occasionally, in the words of journalists, sat "cheek by jowl in the jury box" with white men.[215] But this was unusual. For the most part, in places such as Providence, Rhode Island, and Brooklyn, New York, whenever a "colored man's name was drawn" for possible jury service, the custom apparently was "to pass it over."[216]

The Civil War, emancipation, and Reconstruction changed everything, at least for a time. Black men drawn for jury service in the North were "called and empaneled," causing "considerable remark."[217] Some northern whites protested.[218] In 1871, a white Philadelphian refused to serve on a racially mixed jury. The trial judge granted his wish; he fined him and sent him packing.[219] Many other white northerners, however, accepted the new state of affairs. Journalist Horace Greely commented in 1866 that "a colored juror had been impaneled in Brooklyn," and "the sun did not fail to set or the moon to rise in consequence."[220] Black activists optimistically believed that integrated jury service would "do much to break down the barriers"

215. "A Black Juror," *Boston Evening Transcript*, Sept. 15, 1843, 2; "A Colored Juror," *Frederick Douglass' Paper*, Aug. 24, 1855, 3.

216. "A Black Juror," *San Francisco Bulletin*, April 11, 1865, 3.

217. "A Colored Juror," *New York Tribune*, Sept. 19, 1865, 5.

218. "A Negro Juror Rejected," *Columbus Daily Enquirer*, Nov. 4, 1865, 1.

219. "The Man Who Objected to Serve with a Negro Juror," *Cincinnati Commercial Tribune*, April 15, 1871, 4.

220. Quoted in "Progress in Texas," *Flake's Bulletin* (Galveston, TX), June 19, 1867, 6.

that they were "struggling to surmount."[221] They had reason to hope. Some white northerners were pleasantly surprised to find that trailblazing Black jurors "appeared to act quite intelligently"[222] and "acquitted [themselves] very creditably."[223] A Black juror in Maryland "received many compliments from his fellow-jurors for the faithful discharge of his duties."[224] More promising still were reports that avoided all fanfare and simply observed, as did one report from the early 1870s, that the jury, "white and colored, presented a good appearance."[225]

In the South, Black jury service following emancipation was both more controversial and more consequential. Southern white opponents of Reconstruction resented what they saw as the federal imposition of Black jury service on their region,[226] indignantly grumbling that any southern judge who refused to seat Black jurors "would be pricked from his bench by the bayonet."[227] They also rued what South Carolina's first post-Civil War governor James Orr called the "ruinous results"[228] that they imagined Black jury service would produce. The demographic concentration of Black people in the South meant that Black jury service at anything like proportional levels would have an infinitely greater impact there than in the North. White South Carolinians did the math and shuddered: "In Charleston, eight colored to four whites; in Columbia, nine colored to four whites."[229] And the absence of literacy tests for voting under Reconstruction constitutions, combined with nearly universal Black illiteracy under slavery, meant that most southern Black jurors were virtually guaranteed to lack formal education. Opponents of Reconstruction conjured nightmarish images of jury boxes containing twelve Black "plantation hands, not one of whom

221. "Colored Jurors," *Boston Paper*, reprinted in *People's Advocate* (Washington, DC), March 20, 1880, 2.

222. Ibid.

223. "General News Items," *(Windsor) Vermont Journal*, Nov. 17, 1866, 1.

224. "Letter from Annapolis," *Baltimore Sun*, Oct. 29, 1880, 4.

225. "Colored Jurors Summoned," *San Francisco Evening Bulletin*, Feb. 12, 1872, 3.

226. "The New Military Order," *Flake's Bulletin*, May 1867, 10; "The Negro Juror Order," *Macon Weekly Telegraph*, Aug. 30, 1867, 1; "Colored Jurors in South Carolina," *Philadelphia Inquirer*, Sept. 17, 1867, 1.

227. Quoted in "A Negro Juror," *Weekly Patriot and Union* (Harrisburg, PA), Feb. 6, 1868, 3

228. "Beauties of the Negro-loving System in the South," *Cincinnati Daily Enquirer*, Oct. 21, 1867, 3.

229. Ibid.

[could] read or spell his name—not one of whom knows anything beyond the rules of a cotton field."[230] They asked: With such "ignorant and unwise" jurors as military orders compelled, "will not the effort to administer justice be a mockery?"[231]

As time passed, however, Black jurors ceased to be a spectacle. From the late 1860s through the mid-1880s, in at least some parts of the South, they were routine. The press took to reporting without comment that one southern jury "consists of five white, and seven colored jurors,"[232] and that another "was composed of six white and six colored jurors."[233] In Georgia in 1880, a Black juror served with eleven "well known white citizens"—and was made foreman.[234] (White Georgians did not appear to object. According to a widely reprinted news story about this case, "the addition of the names of intelligent colored men" to jury lists in the state court was "generally approved."[235]) In 1883, an Alabama newspaper revealed how much progress had been made when it deemed it noteworthy enough to report that a jury in one local criminal case was "exclusively white."[236]

White ridicule and resentment of Black jury service did not cease,[237] but it abated, thanks in part to the reputation that Black jurors gained for treating members of their own race sternly.[238] In 1870, an all-Black North Carolina jury proved "their willingness to do justice to a criminal as black as themselves" by convicting a Black man for a raping a white woman. ("Would twelve *white* men of North Carolina have consigned to the gallows a man of *their* color for committing a similar outrage upon a negro woman?" a northern newspaper rhetorically asked. "Doubted."[239])

All was not peace and harmony. Integrated juries sometimes rubbed against segregationist habits. When it appeared that a Black man might be

230. "The New Military Order," 10.

231. "Beauties of the Negro-loving System in the South," 3.

232. "The Rainey Murder Case," *Weekly Louisianian*, Nov. 30, 1871, 2.

233. "Latest News by Telegraph," *Daily Nebraska Press* (Nebraska City), July 22, 1869, 1.

234. "The Colored Juror," *Patriot*, July 8, 1880, 1.

235. "The First Colored Juror," *Galveston Weekly News*, July 15, 1880, 2.

236. "Circuit Court," *Huntsville Gazette*, Feb. 24, 1883, 3.

237. "Negro Jurors," *Eastern Argus* (Portland, ME), Jan. 19, 1871, 1; "A North Carolina Colored Juror," *Cincinnati Daily Enquirer*, Sept. 23, 1871, 3; "Unadulterated Eloquence," *Pomeroy's Democrat* (Chicago, IL), Jan. 3, 1874, 1; "The Indicted Political Refugees from South Carolina," *Baltimore Sun*, Oct. 6, 1877, 1.

238. "Colored Jurors in Texas," *New York Herald*, Nov. 19, 1870, 11.

239. "Brief Topics," *Jamestown (New York) Journal*, Nov. 25, 1870, 4.

added to a Missouri jury in 1905, one white juror, during voir dire questioning, said that "he didn't believe he could serve on the same jury with a negro and be impartial," and "did not think it was right . . . to ask him to serve" on an integrated jury. Other white jurors nodded in assent. The trial judge spinelessly excused the Black juror, who "took his hat and left the courtroom, and further trouble was averted."[240] In the 1880s, a federal judge in Arkansas showed more backbone when a racially mixed jury sought breakfast in an elegant hotel restaurant in Little Rock. The restaurant refused service because the jury included a Black member. The judge ordered a US marshal to accompany the body, and "for the first time a negro enjoyed his repast at the leading hotel in the state and among white people."[241]

Some southern whites defended Black jury service. "The instinct of fair play revolts against" those who would deny the right of Black men to serve on juries, declared an editorial in *The State* of Columbia, South Carolina, in 1894. "The records of the courts show that negro jurymen rarely if ever draw the color line, and a dozen years of observation ha[ve] satisfied us that the negro on a jury is ready to convict his fellow on any satisfactory evidence."[242] In 1878, a white Louisianan, the foreman of a recent trial jury, assessed the performance of the "colored jurors" with whom he served: "Throughout the whole trial their conduct and demeanor, as regards civility and propriety, did not differ from that of their fellow jurors, and, as a result, we were harmonious and not an unkind word did I hear spoken one to the other. Under the law, and in the position of jurors, we were equals—all distinctions leveled."[243]

The Civil Rights Act of 1875 sought to cement such gains into place. Section four stipulated that no citizens possessing all other legal qualifications "shall be disqualified for service as grand or petit jurors" in any state or federal court "on account of race, color or previous condition of servitude." It was supposed to have teeth. Any public official who excluded or failed to summon would-be jurors on account of their race could be found guilty of a misdemeanor and fined up to $500.[244] Per-

240. "Negro Juror Is Excused," *Kansas City (Missouri) Star*, Jan. 27, 1905, 1.

241. "A Negro Juror," *(Cleveland) Plain Dealer*, Nov. 8, 1886, 2.

242. "The State's Survey," *The State*, Oct. 5, 1894, 4.

243. "City News: A Readable Document from the Foreman of the Anderson Jury," *Daily Picayune*, March 2, 1878, 2.

244. "Communicated. Our Jury Commissioners," *Savannah Colored Tribune*, June 3, 1876, 2.

haps the most noteworthy feature of section four's reception was how little controversy it stirred.

Section four of the Civil Rights Act of 1875, like previous orders to this effect, was not implemented vigorously. In many counties, North and South, it was a dead letter.[245] But by the end of the 1870s, when federal authorities indicted a dozen or so Virginia state judges for "unlawful discrimination against duly qualified colored citizens in the selection of grand and petit jurors,"[246] there was no question that things had dramatically changed in recent years. "Had a novelist a generation ago depicted a fictitious trial scene in a Southern court in which the fate of a white prisoner was in the hands of colored jurors," one writer marveled in 1889, while reporting on the criminal trial of a prominent white man in Charleston, South Carolina, before a majority-Black jury, "the production would have been criticized as absurdly improbable. Had a statesman prior to the war predicted that the jury box would be thrown open throughout the South to blacks before the close of this century he would have been voted a fanatic dreaming of Utopia."[247]

By the end of the 1880s, then, "mixed juries in the South," as one reporter noted, were "no novelty."[248] At least occasionally, this made a substantive difference. In 1888, a coroner's jury in Kansas split along racial lines in a lynching case. All four white jurors wanted to report that the Black lynching victims had perished "at the hands of parties unknown." The eight Black jurors countered that the names of over one hundred of the mob were known. They wanted the coroner's verdict to charge the responsible parties by name and "refused to consent to a verdict otherwise."[249]

Our quantitative analysis reveals thorough jury integration in South Carolina during this period. For several years following the Civil War, Black men served on South Carolina juries in rough proportion to their share of the population. In 1872, 64 percent of racially identifiable jurors for criminal cases in Richland County were Black men, essentially the same as the Black share of the county's 1870 population: 66 percent.[250] Abbeville County

245. Ibid.; "The Jury Box," *Savannah Colored Tribune*, June 10, 1876, 2.

246. "Discrimination against Colored Jurors," *Boston Evening Journal*, Oct. 17, 1879, 4; "Colored Jurors," *Boston Daily Advertiser*, Oct. 17, 1879, 1.

247. "Black Jurors in the South," *New York Herald*, June 26, 1889, 6.

248. Ibid.

249. "A Jury Disagrees," *Augusta Chronicle*, June 30, 1888, 2.

250. Richland County Criminal Journals, SCDAH US Federal Census Collection, Rich-

was 65 percent Black in 1870; its percentage of Black jurors in 1873 was precisely the same: 65 percent. All told, between 1865 and 1879, the percentage of Black jurors serving in our sampled South Carolina counties was 58 percent, almost identical to the counties' 60 percent Black population.

Starting in the 1880s, Black jury service in South Carolina slumped. Then it plummeted. The century's end was a tumultuous time for Black southerners. The federal government retreated from Reconstruction. Black rights withered. Lynchings increased. White supremacist leaders urged Black disfranchisement and Jim Crow segregation laws across the South. In South Carolina, as we have seen, "Pitchfork" Ben Tillman stoked fear of "negro domination" and worked to eviscerate Black political rights. The 1895 constitution made it more difficult for Black men to become voters and, hence, jurors.[251]

White supremacist attitudes influenced jury commissioners, suppressing Black jury participation well beyond the effects of electoral disfranchisement alone. A closely watched criminal trial in South Carolina in 1894 brought this issue to the surface. Two Black men were accused of breaking into a railroad freight car. Evidence was murky. On the one hand, some of the stolen goods were reportedly found in the suspects' possession. On the other, "several witnesses" testified that the suspects were elsewhere at the time of the break-in. The jury's eleven white members favored conviction; its lone Black member favored acquittal.[252] When the trial judge asked why the jury was taking so long, the foreman pointed to the hold-out. The judge fumed. If Black jurors refused to convict Black suspects, he said, it would "necessarily lead to the jury commissioners excluding colored people" from juries, "which they [had] a perfect right to do under the law." The judge ordered the clerk to "excuse the colored juror and strike his name from the roll." Although the Black juror appears genuinely to have believed that the defendant was not guilty, the judge cut him no slack. He publicly declared that such action as this Black juror displayed "would justify the jury commissioners in excluding all colored men's names" from the jury-selection process.[253]

---

land County, South Carolina (1870), Heritage Quest, https://www.ancestryheritagequest.com/search/categories/usfedcen/.

251. Francis Butler Simkins, *Pitchfork Ben Tillman, South Carolinian* (Columbia: University of South Carolina Press, 2002); Stephen Kantrowitz, *Ben Tillman & the Reconstruction of White Supremacy* (Chapel Hill: University of North Carolina Press, 2000).

252. "The Color Line in Court," *The State*, Oct. 4, 1894, 8.

253. Ibid. For a principled critique of the judge's actions in this case, see "The State's Survey," *The State*, Oct. 5, 1894, 4.

Black jury service in South Carolina plunged in the years bracketing 1900. In many counties, it ended, at least for a time. Between 1890 and 1903, although the Black share of Clarendon County's overall population remained over 70 percent, the presence of Black jurors fell from 21 percent to, it seems, zero.[254]

Observing this late-century decline, some historians contend that Black men were "universally excluded from southern juries" during the entire period.[255] This is wrong. Although the decline in Black presence on juries was precipitous, it was not complete. After about 1900, Black jury participation rebounded, albeit slightly. Some counties saw notable shifts. Although the Black share of Berkeley County's population declined by almost 10 percent between 1900 and 1920, the percentage of Black jurors increased from 5 percent in 1908 to 20 percent in 1919, according to our samples. Georgetown County's Black population declined from 79 percent to 67 percent between 1900 and 1920, but the percentage of Black jurors in the county increased from under 3 percent in 1900 to 20 percent in 1916. All told, between 1906 and 1930, Black jurors constituted just over 8 percent of our sampled South Carolina total. This approximately doubled the percentage of Black jurors who served between 1890 and 1905. Black jury participation in South Carolina from Reconstruction through the 1920s, thus, traced a swooping curve: way up, way down, and slightly back up. Our figures come from jury books held at the South Carolina Department of Archives and History. The numbers are in the table on the following page.

Several factors may explain the slight rebound in Black jury service that began early in the new century. Legislative change is not among them. Jury-selection laws remained essentially unchanged.[256]

The inefficiency of Jim Crow may have played a role. In terms of jury service, the greater the exclusion of Black men, the greater the burden on whites. Where Blacks were in the majority, the jury-service burden borne by the white minority was substantial. Some white men quietly resisted by securing exemptions from jury duty, fibbing their way off juries,[257] and even "refrain[ing] from taking out [voter] registration papers so as to avoid jury

254. The percentage for Reconstruction–era decades (~1860–1880) considered a total of seventy-seven names from two counties. The percentage of Black jurors serving between 1880 and 1905 considers a total of 323 names from four different counties.

255. Klarman, *From Jim Crow*, 43.

256. Civil Code (1912); Code of Civil Prod. (1922).

257. "In Terror of the Law," *The State*, Oct. 28, 1896, 5.

County	Year	Black share of county population (census year)	Black jury participation
Richland	1872	66% (1870)	64%
Abbeville	1873	65% (1870)	65%
Clarendon	1890	70% (1890)	21%
Georgetown	1900	79% (1900)	3%
Clarendon	1903	75% (1900)	0%
Berkeley	1908	81% (1900)	5%
Berkeley	1916	78% (1910)	7%
Georgetown	1916	72% (1910)	20%
Berkeley	1919	72% (1920)	20%
Georgetown	1926	67% (1920)	14%

duty."[258] According to a 1907 report, white men did such things because jury duty was an "irksome," "disagreeable . . . sacrifice."[259] Year after year, South Carolina jury commissioners struggled to fill their large quotas. "It is a problem which makes us commissioners sweat," one complained in 1909.[260] Commissioners grumbled about the large number of professions (e.g., ministers, bank tellers, newspaper workers) that had won dubious exemptions from jury service. Commissioners complained that the "good moral character" requirement made it especially hard to meet their quotas. "Should [conscientious jury commissioners] find upon the registration books the names of only 900 citizens who are personally known to them to be of 'good moral character,'" one mused, "and should they be required to place 1,800 names into the box, then . . . they would seem to have no option but to comply with the law and place the names" of nine-hundred others of unknown moral character in the box.[261] One South Carolina jury commissioner even wondered whether it might make sense to open up eligibility so that jurors could be chosen from "the population at large," whether registered to vote or not, and whatever their moral character.[262] Given these frustrations, jury commissioners in some counties appear to have been willing to invite limited numbers of Black electors to share the burden of jury service.

258. "Shirking Jury Duty: Men Evade This Service Who Should Be Compelled to Act," *Newberry Observer*, quoted in *The State*, Sept. 29, 1907.

259. Ibid.

260. "Trials and Tribulations of Honest Jury Commissioners," *The State*, Oct. 20, 1909, 2.

261. Ibid.

262. Ibid.

Additionally, some white elites worried aloud that discrimination against Black jurors threatened the rule of law. Too often, they complained, all-white juries ruled by pigment, not evidence. "Race prejudice too often settles a verdict of not guilty when a white man has taken the life of his brother in black," one white member of the South Carolina legal elite worried in 1904.[263] He also perceived a connection between Jim Crow juries and lynching, speculating that all-white juries provided "training" in racialized injustice that encouraged a "contempt" for the legal system that, in turn, was "conducive to mob law."[264] Similarly, an editorial in the Columbia *State* lamented that white juries too often "refuse[d] to find a verdict against a white man," even in "cases where the proof [against him] appear[ed] to be conclusive," perhaps fearing, the *State* speculated, that "to convict a white man [was] to put him down on the level with a negro."[265]

Alongside these concerns of white legal reformers, Black activists and lawyers of both races fought doggedly for fairer jury selection. Lawyers for Black criminal defendants routinely moved to quash indictments that emerged from all-white grand juries on the grounds of unfair grand-jury-selection procedures.[266] Activists and lawyers, including Frederick and Moorer, kept the issue of Black jury underrepresentation burning through Jim Crow's coldest winters.[267] When the harshest storms passed, their arguments achieved some traction. At least some white southerners were sensitive to charges that their region mistreated Black people. South Carolina "gets mad," a Philadelphian noted at the dawn of the Jim Crow era, "when charges are made against her record of lawlessness."[268] Elite white southerners also may have been concerned about the Black labor migration out of the region that began in earnest around the time of World War I. They may have reasoned that allowing a few more Black jurors might mute northern accusations of racism while also dissuading some Black southerners from leaving. Black elites similarly suggested that more Black jury service might increase Black respect for the rule of law, reducing Black criminality.[269]

263. G. Duncan Bellinger, "The Reign of Lawlessness," *The State*, Jan. 7, 1904.

264. Ibid.

265. "Race Prejudice and Crime," *The State*, July 20, 1907, 4, reprinted from the *Newberry (SC) Observer*.

266. Stephenson, *Race Distinctions*, 262.

267. See State v. Brownfield, 60 S.C. 509, 39 S.E. 2 (1901).

268. "The Acquittal of Dr. McDow," *Augusta Chronicle*, July 3, 1889, 4.

269. "Colored Men on Juries," *Savannah Tribune*, Feb. 12, 1921, 4.

Notwithstanding this modest uptick early in the century, Black representation on southern juries remained tiny. It was far from proportional, far from just, and far from the levels attained both previously and subsequently. Nonetheless, in some counties, in South Carolina and elsewhere in the South, Black jurors did occasionally sit. Amid the relentless indignities of Jim Crow, the presence of even a single Black juror carried large symbolic weight. It meant that exclusion was not universal, that the fight was not hopeless. "We were very pleasantly surprised," a Black southerner wrote following World War I, "to find a Negro citizen serving his state this week and functioning as a real citizen by doing jury duty." This happy news left the writer wanting more: "There are many other men, similarly fitted and capable, to do this service and to exercise this prerogative of the good citizen, if only the orderly processes would cast the lot upon them."[270] If only.

When Frederick and Moorer appealed Bogus Sanders's 1915 conviction on the grounds that the jury-selection process had been racially discriminatory, they lacked the sort of quantitative evidence that we have assembled here. Indeed, they presented almost no evidence at all. They did not demonstrate, as we have tried to do, that South Carolina counties varied arbitrarily in their openness to Black jurors. They did not show, as we have tried to do, that the state's jury-selection process operated as a series of sieves that systematically filtered out Black names, with jury commissioners' discretion doing the bulk of the damage. When an elections official testified in the Bogus Sanders trial that about fifteen hundred "negroes" were registered to vote in Richland County (about 27 percent of registered voters),[271] Frederick and Moorer could not counter, as we can, that in Clarendon County, early in the century, Black residents accounted for about 30 percent of registered voters but 0 percent of jurors. Nor could the lawyers demonstrate numerically that Black jury service had fallen (or, more accurately, had been hurled) off a cliff in the closing years of the nineteenth century.

Given the state of the law at the time, however, even the best quantitative evidence about jury composition would likely have failed. Fortunately for Bogus Sanders, Frederick and Moorer had some qualitative arguments that were even stronger.

---

270. Ibid.

271. "Negro and Wife Placed on Trial," 5.

The Qualitative Approach: Juror Racism

Frederick and Moorer's first three arguments in the Bogus Sanders appeal charged that jury and voting commissioners, while compiling voter lists, jury lists, and jury panels, had unlawfully discriminated against Black people. Their fourth argument was different. Rather than highlighting the absence of Black jurors, it highlighted the biases of white ones. And rather than challenging the actions of electoral officials or jury commissioners during the early stages of the jury-selection process, it challenged the actions of lawyers and judges during the final stage: the courtroom voir dire. During voir dire, lawyers and judges questioned prospective jurors and sought to remove any whose prejudices would prevent them from ruling fairly. Frederick and Moorer complained that the trial judge in the *Sanders* case had wrongly allowed a prejudiced white man to join the jury, despite that man's admission that his racism might sway his judgment.

Ever since emancipation, defenders of civil rights had realized that juror racism threatened the rule of law. Reformers hoped that voir dire questioning would facilitate the removal from jury pools of the most virulent racists. At first, lawyers representing Black clients relied on general, catchall questions about bias to ferret out explicit racism. "Have you any bias or prejudice resting upon your mind either for or against the prisoner at the bar?" a lawyer might ask. Occasionally, prospective jurors were honest enough to say, "Yes." During voir dire in the late 1870s, an unusually forthright prospective juror responded to this question by turning to the bench and saying, "Judge, I'm agin the nigger." The trial proceeded without him.[272]

Late-nineteenth-century lawyers who sought to supplement catchall questions about juror bias with specific questions about racial prejudice, however, often butted up against rules that limited what they could ask. In some states, statutes prescribed both the questions that could be asked and the answers that would be deemed acceptable during voir dire.[273] In other states, statutes were silent but trial judges prevented lawyers from asking potential jurors about their racial views.[274]

Around the turn of the century, as Jim Crow–era racism intensified and

272. "A Conscientious Juror," *Macon Telegraph and Messenger*, July 2, 1882, 1.

273. "Woolfolk Must Choke!" *Macon Telegraph*, July 29, 1890, 1.

274. See Frederick v. The State, 39 Tex. Crim. 147, 45 S.W. 589 (1898); and "Judge Moise Cuts Off Some Latitude," *Daily Picayune*, June 16, 1897, 11.

juries whitened, the dangers posed by explicitly racist jurors increased. Lawyers representing Black clients, no longer able to rely on racially representative juries, sought at least to keep avowed racists off juries. Many, though not all, southern courts granted lawyers greater leeway to use voir dire questioning to identify and remove explicitly racist jurors. Prosecutors contributed to this trend. When white people were accused of committing crimes against Black people, prosecutors feared that racist white jurors might refuse to convict. In some of these cases, prosecutors grilled would-be jurors about their racial views. Louisiana prosecutors asked such questions in 1900, while preparing to try two white suspects for the murder of a Black man. As reported in the *Daily Picayune*, "The state, by its questioning of the [white] jurors in their voir dire, asked particularly if any prejudice existed in their minds on account of color."[275] Questioned thus, some would-be jurors admitted that "prejudices against the negro race" might "prevent them from bringing in a verdict of guilty." Prosecutors struck such jurors for cause.[276]

Criminal defense lawyers pushed even harder for the right to question jurors about racial biases in cases involving Black defendants and white victims. They often succeeded. In 1901, Louisiana accused three Black men of murdering a white man. The case's voir dire process wowed observers. "On the part of the defense," newspapers reported, "the cross-examination of the jurors on their voir dire was extraordinary, to say the least, being entirely different from any ever held in the criminal court before." Among the many questions that defense counsel put to would-be jurors in this racially charged case were: "Have you any prejudices against the negro race?" "Do you believe negroes your equal?" "If not socially, do you believe them equals in law?" "According to the golden rule, put yourself in the place of a negro, and if you were a negro would you be willing to be tried by white people?" "Do you think there is any race prejudice existing among the white people against negroes?" "According to the constitution of the United States . . . the negroes are equal. Do you believe that?" And, "Do you think the accused would have a good chance with a white jury?"[277] Would-be jurors in this and like cases had to answer such questions under oath. In theory, those who answered untruthfully could be arrested and charged with perjury.[278]

275. "The First of the Riot Murder Trials," *Daily Picayune*, Oct. 25, 1900, 14.

276. "Michael Biri on Trial for Murder," *Daily Picayune*, Dec. 14, 1900, 11.

277. "Charles' Friends on Trial for Murder," *Daily Picayune*, May 14, 1901, 13.

278. "The Southern States," *Daily Picayune*, May 24, 1893, 8.

In South Carolina, around the time of the Bogus Sanders case, trial judges enjoyed considerable discretion over whether to allow such questions during voir dire. State law provided that "the [trial] court shall, on motion of either party," examine any would-be juror "to know whether he is related to either party, or has any interest in the cause, or has expressed or formed any opinion, or is sensible of any bias or prejudice therein." If such questioning conveyed the impression that "the juror [was] not indifferent in the cause," then that juror would "be placed aside as to the trial . . . and another [would] be called."[279] This procedure invited lawyers to request extra questioning but empowered trial judges to allow or deny such requests as they saw fit.[280]

Some judges allowed lawyers free rein. In 1909, during a racially charged prosecution of four white men for whipping a Black man to death, a South Carolina judge announced that, "in addition to the usual questions," lawyers could ask would-be jurors "any additional questions." The solicitor promptly asked jurors "if it would make any difference . . . if one of the parties were white and the other colored." Defense counsel objected, but the judge allowed the question.[281]

Other South Carolina trial judges, however, did not allow lawyers to grill prospective jurors about their racial ideologies. During a 1909 South Carolina criminal trial, a lawyer representing a Black defendant requested permission to ask potential jurors whether "the fact that the defendant at the bar [was] a negro" would bias them. The court refused to allow the question. "You can't go into that sea," the judge told the lawyer. "It might swamp us all." Following conviction, the defense appealed. The South Carolina Supreme Court upheld the conviction, ruling that trial judges could determine what sorts of questions were allowed at voir dire.[282]

Lawyers in racially charged cases hoped that questioning jurors about racial bias would accomplish three things. First and foremost, they sought to prevent open racists from serving on juries. Weeding out racists would improve their clients' prospects. Second, lawyers' questions about racist views sent subtle message to all jurors about the importance of open-mindedness. This, too, would improve their clients' prospects. Like "push-

279. S.C. Civil Code § 2944, quoted in State v. Bethune, 67 S.E. 466, 468 (S.C. S. Ct. 1910).

280. State v. Bethune, 75 S.E. 281, 282 (S.C. S. Ct. 1912).

281. "Trying Accused Gilchrist Slayers," *The State*, Oct. 29, 1909, 1.

282. State v. Bethune, 86 S.C. 143, 67 S.E. 466 (1910); "South Carolina Supreme Court: Synopses of Opinions of the Tribunal of Last Resort," *The State*, April 28, 1910, 9.

pollers" years later, early-twentieth-century lawyers realized that well-phrased questions could influence thought. "According to the [C]onstitution of the United States . . . negroes are equal. Do you believe that?"[283] Jurors who answered in the negative would likely be struck. Those who answered in the affirmative, and others present, may have subconsciously wound up being more likely to give Black litigants a fair shake.

Third, lawyers may have aimed beyond jurors to all within earshot. This may have been especially true in the case of lawyers, such as Frederick and Moorer, who were also civil rights activists. They realized that local courtrooms were more than venues for resolving disputes. They also were forums for establishing community values. They were public theaters where community morality was enacted.[284] When lawyers asked jurors whether they could weigh the evidence fairly, regardless of race, there was only one right answer, and everyone knew it. The juror who answered incorrectly would, in theory, not be allowed to serve. The exclusion of explicitly racist jurors sent a powerful message to the community: overt, extreme racial bias was incompatible with the rule of law and thus was unacceptable in court. Thanks to the efforts of lawyers such as Frederick and Moorer, courtrooms may have outdistanced all other mixed-race venues in the South in their openness to questions about racial prejudice and in their rhetorical commitment to equality.

For all its breakneck speed, the trial of Bogus and Ada Sanders did have one slow, deliberate phase: jury selection. Defense lawyers set the pace. "The trial is proceeding slowly," the press reported, "and the drawing of the jury will probably require all the afternoon, as the prospective jurors are being put on their voir dire at the request of the defense."[285] The Sanders trial began at 12:30 p.m. By the time the jury was sworn in, it was 5:30.[286]

Judge Rice, prosecution lawyers, and defense lawyers all scrutinized potential jurors. It being a murder case, the prosecution was granted five

283. "Charles' Friends on Trial for Murder," 13.

284. Robert P. Burns, *The Death of the American Trial* (Chicago: University of Chicago Press, 2009) 63, 71; Jon-Christian Suggs, *Whispered Consolations: Law and Narrative in African American Life* (Ann Arbor: University of Michigan Press, 2000), 7; Robert L. Griswold, "Divorce and Legal Redefinition of Victorian Manhood," in *Meanings for Manhood: Constructions of Masculinity in Victorian America*, ed. Mark C. Carnes and Clyde Griffen (Chicago: University of Chicago Press, 1990), 96–110.

285. "Trial of Sanders Has Begun with New Features," *Columbia Record*, June 10, 1915, 2.

286. "Negro and Wife Placed on Trial," 5.

peremptory strikes and the defense ten, meaning they could eliminate up to that number of jurors without any justification.[287] In addition, the court, often at the invitation of one side or the other, could strike an infinite number "for cause" upon a showing of unacceptable bias.

Neither the court nor the prosecution was particularly active during voir dire. Judge Rice struck one juror for opposing capital punishment. The prosecution successfully struck one juror for cause. By contrast, the defense lawyers were extremely active. Newspapers reported that Frederick and Moorer "thoroughly" explored the "question of bias or prejudice against the negro race."[288] In particular, the Black attorneys, anticipating the specifics of the upcoming trial, asked every prospective juror "if he considered that a negro had the same right under the law to resent an insult, if there was any, against his wife as a white man."[289] Apparently, many would-be jurors did not think so. Frederick and Moorer struck an astonishing eighteen jurors for cause while also exhausting their ten peremptory challenges.[290]

To get a sense of how unusual it was for one case to generate twenty strikes for cause (eighteen for the defense, one each for the court and the prosecution), we sampled forty-eight cases from Richland County between 1893 and 1924.[291] Two factors seemed to correlate with high numbers of for-cause strikes. First, strikes for cause tended to be more numerous in cases involving serious crimes, such as murder, than in cases involving less serious crimes, such as burglary. Second, cases involving Black defendants and white victims tended to generate more strikes for cause than other sorts of cases, all other things being equal.[292]

State v. Sanders contained both factors. It involved murder, a serious crime. It also featured a Black defendant (Bogus Sanders) and a white victim (Charles Ellers). A healthy number of for-cause strikes was to be expected. But *Sanders* was still an outlier. Total strikes "for cause" averaged just three in less serious cases and 4.4 in capital cases. *Sanders* was in another league, with twenty. Strikes for cause averaged 4.1 in cases involv-

---

287. "Right of Challenge," *Code of Laws of South Carolina, 1912*, vol. 2 (Charlottesville, VA: Michie Company, 1912), 236; State v. Tidwell, 100 S.C. 248, 84 S.E. 778 (1915).

288. "Negro and Wife Placed on Trial," 5.

289. Ibid.

290. Ibid.

291. Richland County indictment records, SCDAH, 1893–1894, 1896–1897, 1914–1915, 1916, 1917, and 1924–1925.

292. Ibid.

ing white defendants and white victims and 5.3 in cases involving Black defendants and white victims. In *Sanders*, the number was twenty. One likely explanation for this exceptional number of for-cause strikes in *Sanders* is the determination of the defense lawyers, who were also civil rights activists, to take full advantage of the voir dire process, for legal and rhetorical effect.

Although Frederick and Moorer managed to convince the court to strike eighteen jurors for cause, they argued—persuasively—that the court should have struck more. They complained that jury selection in *Sanders* was unjust because they were forced to exhaust two of their precious peremptory challenges on potential jurors, R. L. Bailey and T. D. Murtiashaw, whom the court should have struck for cause. While no evidence remains about the questioning of Murtiashaw, the defense's case regarding Bailey was powerful. Bailey candidly shared his racist views with the crowded courtroom during voir dire. When Judge Rice asked him a proforma question about bias for or against the defendants in the case, Bailey opened up. "It is not exactly bias, your Honor; but I feel a resentment in this particular case, which might prejudice me in rendering a verdict."[293]

Judge Rice should have struck him right then. Instead, he pressed on, asking Bailey if he thought his "feeling would have any effect upon any verdict [he] might render after [he] hear[d] the evidence and the law?" Bailey indicated that he "[believed he] could render a verdict based on the law and evidence," but qualified his statement by saying, "But, as I stated, I feel a prejudice in this particular case." Judge Rice stubbornly continued, "I will ask you again, Mr. Bailey . . . can you give these defendants and the State a fair and impartial trial in this case?" Bailey supposed that he could.[294]

When the judge rested, Frederick and Moorer, surely dismayed by Judge Rice's tolerance of overt racism, pounced. "How did you get the feeling that you spoke of a while ago?" they asked Bailey. The juror retorted, "I am listening to it." The white would-be juror looked one of the Black defense lawyers in the eye and explained that he felt a "natural resentment" against "one of [their] race pleading to a jury that [he was] on."[295]

Bailey's racial bias was open and notorious. It was not, however, enough

293. State v. Sanders, 220.

294. Ibid.

295. Ibid.

to persuade Judge Rice to strike him for cause, even though he had admitted that his views "might prejudice me in rendering a verdict."[296] Overruling defense objections, Rice found Bailey fit for jury service. Something about Bailey had distinguished him from the other eighteen jurors that the defense had succeeded in convincing the court to strike for cause. Perhaps the others had admitted bias against the Black defendants, whereas Bailey had "only" admitted to bias against Black lawyers. Perhaps Rice worried that his jury pool was rapidly evaporating. The typical jury panel numbered thirty-six. With twenty strikes for cause, plus the defense's ten peremptory strikes, plus the need to seat twelve jurors, *State v. Sanders* was already in the red. Whatever the reason, Judge Rice's refusal to strike Bailey for cause publicly validated Bailey's views by finding them compatible with jury service.

Bailey took advantage of the legal theater to publicly proclaim his racism. The condescending theatricality of his response, "I am listening to it," illustrates the drama that courtrooms can foster. Bailey's responses reaffirmed racial hierarchy as a central component of southern life. Judge Rice coaxed Bailey to walk back his answers by affirming that he could act fairly during the trial.[297] Even though Rice agreed to strike twenty other jurors for cause, his decision not to remove Bailey conveyed the message that at least some forms of explicit racial bias were permissible in court.[298] Frederick and Moorer objected and appealed.

Chief Justice Gary's Ruling

Frederick and Moorer's appeal on behalf of Bogus Sanders reached the South Carolina Supreme Court early in 1916.[299] In retrospect, their prospects might appear to have been slim. Southern courts from this era are not known as citadels of justice, especially in cases such as Bogus Sanders's. "Guilt or innocence," one historian has written, "was often beside the point when southern blacks were accused of killing white men."[300] Another histo-

296. Ibid.

297. State v. Sanders.

298. "Negro and Wife Placed on Trial," 5.

299. The decision came on Feb. 26, 1916. State v. Sanders.

300. Klarman, *From Jim Crow*, 118.

rian asserts that the "entire machinery of justice—the lawyers, the judges, the juries" reinforced "in every possible way the subordination of black men and women of all classes and ages."[301] Frederick and Moorer had their work cut out for them.

Chief Justice Eugene B. Gary delivered the unanimous opinion in *State v. Sanders*.[302] We last saw Gary in the previous chapter, reading the one-drop rule about "negro blood" into a school segregation case about suspected Croatan Indians. Chief Justice Gary's résumé contained little that would have improved Bogus Sanders's odds. He had learned the law at the knee of his uncle, Major General Martin Gary, a Confederate officer and a leader of the movement to "redeem" South Carolina from "Negro domination" in 1876.[303] Young Gary became a prominent South Carolina lawyer and a leader in the state's Democratic party. He was an early supporter of the "Straightout" Democrats, a movement that urged white supremacy and Black disfranchisement.[304] In 1890, as we have seen, gubernatorial candidate "Pitchfork" Ben Tillman tapped Gary to be his running mate. White supremacist rhetoric filled their campaign. Militant former "red shirts,"[305] frustrated by the results of Reconstruction, contributed muscle to the Tillman-Gary campaign.[306] Gary's stump speeches trumpeted the supposed need to protect white privilege against Black threats. He advocated railroad segregation, asking, "What white man . . . wants his wife or sister sandwiched between a big bully buck[?]"[307] The ticket won handily. In 1893, Tillman shoehorned Gary onto the state supreme court, where critics expected him "to do whatever Governor Tillman told him to do."[308] Gary

301. Leon F. Litwack, *Trouble in Mind: Black Southerners in the Age of Jim Crow* (New York: Alfred A. Knopf, 1998), 247–48.

302. The other justices were D. E. Hydrick, R. C. Watts, T. B. Fraser, and G.W. Gage. South Carolina Supreme Court et al., *Reports of Cases Heard and Determined by the Supreme Court of South Carolina*, vol. 103 (Columbia: R. L. Bryan, 1916).

303. *Cyclopedia of Eminent and Representative Men of the Carolinas of the Nineteenth Century*, vol. 1 (Madison: Brant & Fuller, 1892), 203.

304. N. Louise Bailey et al., *Biographical Directory of the South Carolina Senate 1776–1985*, vol. 1 (Columbia: University of South Carolina Press, 1986), 551.

305. Eric Foner, *Reconstruction: America's Unfinished Revolution, 1863–1877* (New York: Harper & Row, 1988), 574.

306. Kantrowitz, *Ben Tillman*, 143.

307. Gary, quoted in Kantrowitz, 143.

308. "Closing Up the Campaign," *The State*, Aug. 28, 1892, 1; "An Extra Session Called," *The State*, Sept. 7, 1894, 8.

remained on the bench for decades, becoming Chief Justice in 1912.[309] Among his rulings was *Tucker v. Blease*, which espoused the notion of "racial instinct," the "one-drop rule," and the naturalness of school segregation.[310] Had stereotypes held, Bogus Sanders would have stood little chance in Chief Justice Gary's court.

Frederick and Moorer opened their appeal with "quantitative" arguments about the unlawful exclusion of Black grand and petit jurors. These could have been powerful arguments. Black people at the time constituted a majority of Richland County's population but, it seems, zero percent of the *Sanders* jurors. But absent any showing of racist intent on the part of jury commissioners, these arguments stood no chance. They fared no better on appeal than they had at trial.[311]

The qualitative argument, however, was harder to dismiss. Frederick and Moorer powerfully argued that the trial judge had erred by not setting aside the avowedly racist R. L. Bailey for cause, even though, during voir dire, Bailey admitted that his prejudices might affect his judgment.[312] Chief Justice Gary quoted at length from the voir dire questioning, including the part where Bailey testified that his racial resentment "might prejudice [him] in rendering a verdict."[313] That was too much for Gary. He declared that the trial judge had "erroneously exercised his discretion, in ruling that the juror [Bailey] was competent."[314] On that basis, the South Carolina Supreme Court reversed Bogus Sanders's conviction and ordered a new trial.[315]

Gary's ruling highlights his judicial professionalism. Like many other southern appellate justices, he was willing to defend the rule of law against egregious abuses, even if that meant siding with Black litigants.[316] The politics of the South tended to isolate appellate judges from popular control, affording them space in which to hand down such rulings.[317] Elite jurists

309. "Eugene B. Gary Is Chief Justice," *The State*, Jan. 11, 1912, 1.

310. Tucker v. Blease, 81 S.E. 668, 97 S.C. 303 (S.C. 1914).

311. State v. Sanders, 218–19.

312. Ibid., 219. Frederick and Moorer also complained about a second juror, in addition to Bailey.

313. Ibid., 220.

314. Ibid., 221.

315. Ibid., 222.

316. Klarman, *From Jim Crow*, 118; Joseph A. Ranney, *In the Wake of Slavery: Civil War, Civil Rights, and the Reconstruction of Southern Law* (Westport: Praeger, 2006), 156.

317. Hall, "The 'Route to Hell' Retraced," 232.

such as Gary were committed to a standardized, rule-based approach to legal reasoning designed to promote legal stability and fairness.[318] They also bristled at South Carolina's reputation for lawlessness. They issued rulings that, they hoped, would mute such charges. Consequently, southern appellate courts were surprisingly hospitable to Black litigants. Between 1865 and 1920, Black people litigated against white people in hundreds of civil appeals in southern state courts. Black litigants won more of these cases than they lost.[319]

Gary's fair-minded ruling in *Sanders* contrasts starkly with pronouncements he gave while off the bench. In a 1917 speech, Gary decried Reconstruction as a crime "unexcelled in the history of the world" in which the federal government placed "a portion of its own white citizens, under the political heel of an inferior race."[320] Gary's off-the-bench description of Black people as "inferior" paralleled the white supremacist views of juror Bailey. When robed and on the bench, however, Gary appears to have abided by different set of rules. He muted his personal racism in deference to the rule of law.

The substance of Gary's ruling was egalitarian: racial prejudice is incompatible with justice. The ruling's matter-of-fact form, however, muted that message. When Gary wrote opinions that promoted segregation, his rhetoric soared. "The law recognizes that there is a social element, arising from racial instinct, to be taken into consideration between those with and those without negro blood," he had rhapsodized in the prosegregation *Tucker* ruling two years earlier.[321] *Sanders* contained no such lines about the importance of jury fairness, the rule of law, or any such thing. The key line disposing of the case in Sanders's favor was buried unceremoniously within a no-frills, matter-of-fact decision. Frederick and Moorer, however, would take it. So would Bogus Sanders. It saved his life.

---

318. Ranney, *In the Wake of Slavery*, 18–28, 126–28, 154–156.

319. Melissa Milewski, *Litigating Across the Color Line: Civil Cases Between Black and White Southerners from the End of Slavery to Civil Rights* (New York: Oxford University Press, 2017).

320. Eugene B. Gary, *A Vindication of the South* (Abbeville, SC: Press and Banner, 1917), 14.

321. Tucker v. Blease, 673.

Retrial

Bogus Sanders's retrial began on May 24, 1916, just one day shy of the one-year anniversary of his shooting of Charles Ellers. Interest in the case remained high. The courtroom was "packed" on the retrial's first day[322] and remained crowded throughout the four-day trial, despite a heat wave that baked Columbia.[323] Once again, the courtroom was a public theater. The moralistic drama unfolded before a mixed house. According to press reports, "[a]bout an even number of white people and negroes" watched, "possibly a few more blacks."[324]

Some of the problematic features of the original trial persisted. Frederick and Moorer filed another pretrial motion complaining of "discrimination against the negro race" in jury selection.[325] As before, all of the jurors were white.[326] As before, the court did not care.

In other ways, however, the retrial looked different, suggesting that at least some learning had occurred. During voir dire, the prosecution struck just one juror for cause in the first trial and just two this time; not much changed there. The trial judge, however, was much more vigilant this time around. During the first trial, Judge Rice excused just one juror for cause, the cause being opposition to capital punishment. This time, once again, a single juror spoke out against capital punishment. The new trial judge, M. L. Smith, removed that juror but did not stop there. In all, he struck six. This six-fold increase in court-initiated strikes suggests that Judge Smith worked harder than his predecessor to remove bias from the jury.[327]

Frederick and Moorer struck ten jurors for cause this time, down from eighteen in the first trial. They had grown no less vigilant. The decline likely

322. "Bogus Sanders Is on Trial Second Time for Murder," 12.

323. "Sanders Was Given Life in Prison; Jury Merciful," *Columbia Record*, May 28, 1916, 28.

324. "Bogus Sanders Is on Trial Second Time for Murder," 12.

325. "Bogus Sanders on Trial Again," 6.

326. "Bogus Sanders Is on Trial Second Time for Murder," 12. Using press reports, census reports from 1910 and 1920, and the 1916 Columbia city directory, we have identified the race of eight of the twelve petit jurors in Bogus Sanders's retrial. All eight were white. The press did not identify the race of any of these jurors, which suggests that all were white.

327. "Bogus Sanders Is on Trial Second Time for Murder," 12; "Bogus Sanders on Trial Again," 6.

mirrors the trial judge's increase. Because Judge Smith removed more questionable jurors than his predecessor did, Frederick and Moorer had less work to do. In addition, the decline in defense strikes may reflect juror learning. The lessons of the first *Sanders* case—probably reinforced by instructions from the bench—may have taught would-be jurors that open declarations of racism were not appropriate in a courtroom setting. Racist thoughts did not disappear. Indeed, one potential juror was excused from the Sanders retrial because of his "high regard for the Anglo-Saxon race over the African."[328] But the drop in "for-cause" defense strikes from eighteen to ten suggests that the number of jurors willing to express racist thoughts openly may have diminished.[329]

Once the trial began, state officials, aware of how quick Frederick and Moorer were to appeal, tried to avoid giving them any reason to complain. Solicitor Cobb reasoned that "an absolutely fair trial" would prevent a costly and time-consuming appeal and retrial. Cobb granted the defense "ample opportunity" at the trial's outset "to present concrete evidence" in support of their claim that the all-white grand jury that indicted Sanders in 1915 was unconstitutional.[330] Once testimony began, Cobb, "desiring that the defendant have an absolutely fair trial," claimed to cede to the defense "the advantage of every opportunity." He did not object when the defense took every opportunity throughout the trial to discuss "the race aspect of the situation."[331] When the defense called questionable witnesses to provide testimony that, in Cobb's view, should not have been admissible, Cobb did not object.[332]

Cobb's leniency, combined with greater preparation time, allowed the defense to present more evidence than in the original trial. Defense witnesses asserted many new points that favored Bogus Sanders. They testified that Charles Ellers and his white companions were "in a drunken condition" at the time of the shooting, so intoxicated that one of them had to support another; "they carried a quart bottle" of whiskey;[333] Ada Sanders

328. "Bogus Sanders Is on Trial Second Time for Murder," 12.

329. Ibid.; "Bogus Sanders on Trial Again," 6.

330. "Bogus Sanders is on Trial Second Time for Murder," 12.

331. "Fate of Sanders Rests with Jury; Strong Arguments," *Columbia Record*, May 26, 1916, 2.

332. "Sanders Was Given Life in Prison; Jury Merciful," *Columbia Record*, May 28, 1916, 28.

333. "Bogus Sanders Pleads Defense in Circuit Court," *Columbia Record*, May 25, 1916, 9.

"went out of her way in order to keep from passing the white men, who, however, caught up with her"; the men grabbed her, saying, "Look here, don't you do business?"; when she said, "No," they "said they would assault her"; when she broke away and hurried home, the men followed; when she got home she was crying and disheveled;[334] Bogus, "having worked all day," was "getting ready to take a bath when his wife arrived in a very excited frame of mind"; he "had one shoe off at the time"; he donned his shoe, a hat, and a coat, and "made his way down to the white men," whom he told "they should be more careful about talking to women";[335] he had turned to leave when the men threatened him with knives and threw a rock; he "began firing at the men when they started at him with their knives";[336] and he "wasn't shooting to kill any one particularly, just to keep them off of [him]."[337]

All of this new testimony made a difference, especially when heard by a jury newly mindful of the need for fairness. The first time around, the jury took less than an hour to rule on the case.[338] This time, the jury was out for twenty hours. The original jury found Sanders guilty of murder with no recommendation of mercy, which resulted in a death sentence. The new jury found Sanders "guilty of murder with recommendation to mercy," resulting in a life sentence.[339]

Life in a South Carolina prison was not attractive, but it beat the alternative. Frederick and Moorer had done their jobs.

Conclusion: Clemency

Advocates of jury fairness during the Jim Crow era had three main concerns. First, they sought fairer trials, especially criminal trials involving Black defendants. All people have the right to be tried by juries of their

334. "DePass & DePass to His Excellency, Governor Robt. A. Cooper, Nov. 12, 1920," in "Petition for Clemency," Richland County, James Sanders (Colored), filed Nov. 13, 1920, SCDAH; "Bogus Sanders Pleads Defense in Circuit Court," 9; "Begin Argument in Sanders Case," *The State*, May 1916, 10.

335. "Bogus Sanders Pleads Defense in Circuit Court," 9.

336. Ibid.

337. "Begin Argument in Sanders Case," 10.

338. "Bogus Sanders Is Found Guilty of Murder of Ellers," 2.

339. "Sanders Was Given Life in Prison," *Columbia Record*, May 1916, 28.

peers, they insisted.[340] Excluding Blacks from juries compromised this right.[341] So did including avowedly racist whites. Fairer juries would produce greater justice for all.[342] Second, Black advocates realized that citizenship entailed obligations as well as benefits. Among the most important and public of those obligations was jury duty.[343] In the South, jury service had long been associated with male honor.[344] Ben Tillman and other white supremacists had this in mind when alleging that the "sacred dut[ies] of the citizen" were "beyond the capacity" of most Blacks.[345] Frederick, Moorer, and others begged to differ.

Third, advocates of racial justice opposed the exclusion of Black jurors because they opposed racial discrimination generally. To keep Blacks off juries systematically, they argued, was to withhold "the full and equal benefit of laws . . . as are enjoyed by white persons."[346] Their legal ideal was color-blindness. In their experience, all racial distinctions were invidious. All worked to the disadvantage of Black people. As one Black commentator observed, at the dawn of the Jim Crow era, "Any drawing of the race or color line in matters of public concern is injurious."[347] Another argued that "any discrimination founded upon the race or color of the citizen [was] unjust and cruel."[348] Excluding otherwise qualified people from juries "because they are negroes" violated the equal protection of the law and was unjust.[349]

Our close inspection of *State v. Sanders* and the Jim Crow jury has revealed several things. Voter registration and juror selection were distinct processes. Both contributed to the suppression of Black jury service. The

340. "Thompson's Weekly Review," *The Freeman*, July 21, 1906, 1.

341. "A New Legal Departure," *Wheeling (WV) Register*, Aug. 26, 1895; "Negro Loses Case: Murderer Alleged He Was Discriminated Against on Trial, but Supreme Court Finds Differently," *Duluth News-Tribune*, March 10, 1903, 10.

342. "Negroes Will Object to Jim Crow Laws!" *Plaindealer* (Topeka, KS), Nov. 30, 1906, 1.

343. "The Negro Question so far as Judicially Adjudicated," *Times-Picayune*, June 21, 1903, 6.

344. Ariela Gross, *Double Character: Slavery and Mastery in the Antebellum Southern Courtroom* (Princeton, NJ: Princeton University Press, 2000).

345. "Gov. Tillman's Appeal," *Plaindealer* (Detroit, MI), Dec. 12, 1890, 1.

346. "Negro Civil Rights: The Attorneys for Frank Davis, Colored, Want Negro Jurors," *Dallas Morning News*, March 14, 1896, 7.

347. *New Orleans Crusader*, quoted in "The Press on the League," *New York Age*, Feb. 1, 1890, 1.

348. "Settled Once and for All," *Plaindealer*, Oct. 17, 1890, 1.

349. "Legislative Acts/Legal Proceedings," *Washington Bee*, June 24, 1905, 8.

removal of Black men from southern juries during these years, though massive, was not total. Jim Crow-era lawyers established jury composition as an important civil rights battleground. The legal system provided them space to attack racism. Although they failed to democratize juries very much during their day, their ability to wage such battles marks this period as a steppingstone between the era of slavery, where no such battles were imaginable; Reconstruction, when no such battles were necessary; and post–Jim Crow eras, during which jury-selection processes, though not perfectly neutral,[350] grew dramatically fairer.[351] Finally, quantitative measures of Black jury service, though crucial, are not the only way of analyzing Jim Crow juries. Juror racism, as well as juror race, mattered. The decisive issue in the *Sanders* appeal—the issue that saved Bogus Sanders's life—was the incompatibility of openly expressed juror racism with the rule of law.

Late in 1920, a white Columbia law firm filed a clemency petition on behalf of James "Bogus" Sanders, who, by then, had spent about five years in prison. Perhaps Ada Sanders, Frederick and Moorer, or someone else hired the firm. Perhaps the lawyers acted on their own.[352] Whatever their motivations, they presented a powerful case. They told South Carolina governor Robert Cooper that Bogus Sanders's "record prior to the time of the killing had been good."[353] They described the events of the killing in ways sympathetic to Bogus's perspective.[354] And they pointed out that Sanders had already served about five and a half years in prison.[355]

They supplemented their letter with several supporting documents. M. L. Smith, the (white) trial judge who sentenced Sanders to life in prison in 1916, submitted a letter recommending that Sander be paroled. Five years of punishment was sufficient, he argued.[356] W. A. Banks, the (white) captain of the Richland County chain gang upon which Sanders served while incar-

350. Hiroshi Fukurai, Edgar W. Butler, and Richard Krooth, "Where Did Black Jurors Go? A Theoretical Synthesis of Racial Disfranchisement in the Jury System and Jury Selection," *Journal of Black Studies* 22, no. 2 (Dec. 1991), 196–215.

351. Roger G. Dunham, Geoffrey P. Alpert, and Darrell J. Connors, "Black Representation on Juries in Miami," *Justice System Journal* 11, no. 1 (Spring, 1986): 79–88.

352. For an example of A. C. DePass's paternalistic generosity, see "'Liberty Acres' for his Tenants: A. C. DePass Enlists Negroes for Bond Sales," *The State*, April 13, 1918, 10.

353. "Petition for Clemency," 3.

354. Ibid.

355. DePass & DePass to His Excellency, Governor Robt. A. Cooper, Nov. 12, 1920, in ibid.

356. Mendel L. Smith to Hon. R. A. Cooper, Dec. 13, 1920, in ibid.

cerated, told Governor Cooper what an "exemplary prisoner in every way" Sanders was and "very heartily" endorsed the petition for clemency. "The facts in his case would seem to me to warrant a pardon for him," the chain gang captain wrote.[357]

S. H. Owens, the (white) Richland County supervisor, "voluntarily" added his two cents. "I am familiar with the testimony that was presented to the Jury," Owens wrote, "and I am satisfied that this man shot Mr. Ellers in defense of his wife's honor, . . . that he and his wife are both decent and respectable people, and that he was fully justified in shooting Ellers. I most heartily and earnestly recommend a pardon for him, and I believe that if more negroes would show a decent resect for the sanctity of their homes that we would have a better citizenship among our negro population."[358]

Most impressively of all, eight of the twelve (white) jurors who voted to convict Sanders in 1916 signed the pardon petition. A ninth, unable to write, signaled his agreement with an X. "Whereas we are of the opinion that this man has been punished sufficiently" for an act that, though technically a crime, was one "for which there was a great deal of justification," the jurors wrote, "and because we think this man committed the act in defense of his home, we petition your Excellency [the governor] to grant him a pardon."[359]

The State Board of Pardons (all white) recommended Sanders's release, "in the light of the fact that the prisoner was only guilty of manslaughter, if that, and of the fact that he has been in prison since 1915."[360]

On June 1, 1921, Governor Cooper paroled James "Bogus" Sanders.[361] Free again, he returned to Ada. We last see them in 1940, still in Columbia, still together, in a home that they owned.[362]

Fittingly, given this chapter's focus, the last word goes to the jurors. As mentioned, nine members of the all-white jury that convicted Sanders

357. W.A. Banks to His Excellency Governor Cooper, in ibid.

358. S.H. Owens to His Excellency, Governor Robt. A. Cooper, Oct. 25, 1920, in ibid.

359. To His Excellency, Governor Robert A. Cooper, and the Board of Pardons, from nine jurors, in ibid.

360. "Petition for Clemency," 3.

361. Ibid.

362. Bogus worked in a cafeteria as a dishwasher; the Sanders's home reportedly was worth $3,000. United States Census, 1940 Population Schedule, South Carolina, Richland County, Columbia City, Ward 7, block 165, sheet no. 2A.

later signed a petition, urging his release.[363] Three others failed to sign. One had joined the US Navy and was unavailable. One was dead. The third was Hosier M. Lee. Lee would never sign, the others said, because he was a died-in-the-wool racist. Apparently, Lee had calculated that, in light of Chief Justice Gary's appellate ruling in *Sanders*, the only way he could get on the jury for the retrial was to mask his racial views. So he dissimulated during voir dire. Once the jury began secret deliberations, however, Lee, according to the petition for clemency, "announced in the Jury room" his unshakable conviction that "any colored man who killed a white man should be electrocuted," regardless of the circumstances.[364] It was Lee whose holdout for a murder conviction had caused the jury to stay out twenty hours, even though others were reluctant to send a man to the chair for a killing that, while technically a crime, was one for which, the other jurors thought, "there was a great deal of justification."[365] The jury finally compromised on "Guilty with recommendation to Mercy," placating Lee's insistence on a murder conviction while still sparing Sanders's life.[366] Apparently, juror Lee refused to don the blindfold of justice, instead slipping it down over his own mouth during voir dire. His jury-mates acted quite differently. It seems that this Jim Crow jury, despite being all-white, contained a rainbow of perspectives.

363. "Petition for Clemency," 3.

364. "DePass & DePass to His Excellency, Governor Robt. A. Cooper, Nov. 12, 1920, in ibid.

365. Ibid.

366. Ibid.

CHAPTER SIX

Tessie Earle v. Greenville County: Lynching and Antilynching[1]

In 2019, during the polarized and racially charged presidency of Donald Trump,[2] the *New York Times* republished a seventy-two-year-old photograph of a South Carolina courtroom scene.[3] The photo depicted a group of jubilant white people celebrating the mass acquittal of twenty-eight white men who had been charged with lynching a Black man named Willie Earle. Although most of the accused previously had confessed to participating in the lynching, an all-white jury acquitted them on all counts. The celebratory acquittal picture was first published in 1947, at the time of the trial.[4] Seven decades later, as concern for racial justice intensified among progressives,[5] and as interest in lynching history spiked,[6] the image achieved

1. Jess Bradshaw, Kathryn Finnigan, Joe Harvey, Charles Horwitz, Randall McLeod, Sam Morris, Madeline Stough, Gabrielle Jones, EJ Canny, Francis Scalia Carroll, Hannah Cohen, Olivia Coral Daniels, Cassandra M. Harding, Stephanie Jefferis, William Stuart Kaskay II, Emilee Lord, Nate MacKenzie, Bryce Simmons, Ellen M. G. Spearing, Seth W. Stancil, and John Wertheimer coauthored this chapter.

2. Alan Abromowitz and Jennifer McCoy, "United States: Racial Resentment, Negative Partisanship, and Polarization in Donald Trump's America," *Annals of the American Academy* (Jan. 2019): 137–56, https://journals.sagepub.com/doi/pdf/10.1177/0002716218811309.

3. Jamelle Bouie, "Donald Trump's 'Lynching,'" *New York Times*, Oct. 25, 2019, https://www.nytimes.com/2019/10/25/opinion/trump-graham-lynching.html.

4. "South Carolina: Twelve Men," *Time*, June 2, 1947, 27; "Lynch Trial Makes Southern History," *Life*, June 2, 1947, 27.

5. Erik Kaufman, "Americans Are Divided by their Views on Race, Not Race Itself," *New York Times*, March 18, 2019; Thomas B. Edsall, "The Democrats' Left Turn Is Not an Illusion," *New York Times*, Oct. 18, 2018; and David Brooks, "How White Democrats Moved Left: Racial Equity Has Become the Defining Issue of the Moment," *New York Times*, July 25, 2019.

6. Natasha Bertrand, "There Were Way More Lynchings in America than Anyone

new prominence as a haunting tableau of white supremacy swamping the rule of law.[7]

The republished photograph powerfully conveys three common assumptions about the legal history of lynching during the Jim Crow era. First, the picture symbolizes the utter failure of the legal system to provide justice to lynching victims or their families. Few lynchers faced charges. Fewer still were convicted. As observers noted in 1947, the sur-

Thought," *Business Insider*, Feb. 10, 2015; *Lynching in America: Confronting the Legacy of Racial Terror* (Montgomery, AL: Equal Justice Initiative, 2015); Campbell Robertson, "A Lynching Memorial Is Opening," *New York Times*, April 25, 2018.

7. The photo reproduced here did not accompany the print version of a long *New Yorker* article about the Willie Earle trial that appeared in 1947 but was added to the online version of the same piece that appeared years later on Newyorker.com. Rebecca West, "Opera in Greenville," *New Yorker*, June 14, 1947, https://www.newyorker.com/magazine/1947/06/14/opera-in-greenville. The same photo also appeared recently in Seth Ferranti, "The Horrific Story of a Mob of White Cab Drivers Getting away with Murder," Vice, March 18, 2019, https://www.vice.com/en_us/article/gya9v3/the-horrific-story-of-a-mob-of-white-cab-drivers-getting-away-with-murder.

prising thing about the Willie Earle lynching trial was not that the perpetrators were acquitted. It was that South Carolina prosecuted them in the first place.[8]

Second, the photograph emphasizes the extent to which the legal history of lynching, though central to Black history, was dominated by white people. In the "Opera in Greenville"—the *New Yorker*'s 1947 nickname for the dramatic Willie Earle lynching trial[9]—all of the singing roles went to white performers. The judge was white. The lawyers were white. All of the more than two-dozen defendants were white. So were all of the jurors and witnesses. The "Opera" had only two Black cast members: Willie Earle, the lifeless victim; and Mabel Nickles, a blind courthouse concessionaire, brought in during jury selection to draw names from a box.[10] In fact, some Black spectators and journalists were present. But they sat beyond the photo's frame—upstairs, in the segregated courtroom's balcony.[11]

Third, the acquittal shot powerfully suggests how tightly lynching interwove with white supremacy during the Jim Crow era. Lynching was a bloody means; white domination was the end. Black children quickly learned that white power was undergirded by an ever-present threat of violence. "Yes, yes, they [our parents] warned us," a childhood friend of Willie Earle recalled years later. "They warned us: 'Don't mess around because they [white people] will lynch . . . they'll kill you.' And they would."[12] Black leaders saw the Willie Earle tragedy as yet another instance of Jim Crow discrimination, along with disfranchisement and state-mandated racial segregation.[13] Lynching was

---

8. Romney Wheeler, "As Historic Lynch Trial Ends, Grim Satisfaction Greets Acquittals," *Charlotte [NC] Observer*, May 23, 1947, 1; "Lynch Trial Makes Southern History," *Life*, June 2, 1947, 27; and "Mass Lynch Trial Seen as Progress," [Little Rock] *Arkansas State Press*, May 30, 1947, 1.

9. West, "Opera in Greenville."

10. William Gravely to John Wertheimer, email message, Dec. 13, 2019.

11. Robert Bird, "Fair Procedure," *New York Herald Tribune*, May 18, 1947, discussed in William B. Gravely, *They Stole Him Out of Jail: Willie Earle, South Carolina's Last Lynching Victim* (Columbia: University of South Carolina Press, 2019), 137.

12. Acquillious Jackson, interview in Easley, South Carolina, by Cassandra M. Harding, Stephanie Jefferis, Francis Scalia Carroll, and Thomas Espenschied, July 18, 2018. Recording available upon request.

13. "AME Bishops Denounce South Carolina Lynching," *Norfolk Journal and Guide*, March 1, 1947, 1.

wrong not just because it denied due process to individual victims but because it buttressed an unjust system of racial hierarchy.[14]

The acquittal photograph thus captures several truths about lynching's legal history. But it excludes others. This chapter explores some of these other truths both by highlighting underlit features of the Willie Earle lynchers' criminal case and by exploring a subsequent civil case: *Tessie Earle v. Greenville County*.[15]

The chapter reconsiders all three of the assumptions described above. *First*, panning the camera from the criminal prosecution described above to Tessie Earle's subsequent civil suit makes the justice system look slightly less unjust. To be sure, criminal prosecutions of lynchers, including Willie Earle's murderers, consistently failed to provide justice. But *Tessie Earle v. Greenville County* was not a criminal case. It was a civil suit, filed under a South Carolina law that allowed family members to sue the counties in which their relatives were lynched. This law was designed to discourage lynching and to redress its injustices. It did neither, at least not well enough. But it was not the total failure that criminal prosecution was. Indeed, despite the day's extreme racism, several surviving relatives of lynching victims invoked this law in court. Usually, they won.

Second, Black people were not as marginal to the legal history of lynching as the all-white acquittal photograph suggests.[16] Black people pushed hard to get South Carolina to prosecute Willie Earle's murderers. After the mass acquittals, an all-star Black legal team helped Tessie Earle recover civil damages under South Carolina's antilynching law, a legal provision that Black lawmakers helped create. By the time Tessie Earle filed suit in the late 1940s, a long line of Black South Carolinians had already recovered damages under this law. The acquittal photograph, in other words, misleadingly implies that Black people other than victims were absent from the legal history of lynching.

Finally, the deep history of *Tessie Earle v. Greenville County* complicates the assumption that white supremacy and lynching were joined at the hip. Unquestionably, lynching in the Jim Crow South must be understood in a

14. "The National Memorial for Peace and Justice," Equal Justice Initiative, accessed Sept. 3, 2022, https://museumandmemorial.eji.org/memorial.

15. Earle v. Greenville County, et al., 215 S.C. 539 (1949).

16. For recent account of lynching history and historical memory that foregrounds Black perspectives, see Karlos K. Hill, *Beyond the Rope: The Impact of Lynching on Black Culture and Memory* (New York: Cambridge University Press, 2016).

white supremacist context. Racialized violence buttressed racial hierarchy. The South Carolinians who condoned lynching, such as the jubilant white people depicted in the acquittal shot, also favored white supremacy. And many lynching opponents, such as the Black spectators who fell beyond the photo's frame, also opposed white supremacy. But this simple formulation overlooks an important group, arguably the region's most powerful: elite whites who opposed lynching but supported Jim Crow. Yet from the 1890s through the Willie Earle case in the 1940s, South Carolina's most influential whites usually opposed lynching, even while supporting segregation and disfranchisement. They realized that lynching was a regional embarrassment that threatened to delegitimate the entire Jim Crow system. By opposing, or at least claiming to oppose, lynching, they sought to deny rhetorical ammunition to their critics and prove to themselves as well as to others that white supremacy was compatible with the rule of law and capable of good governance. These elite white supremacists sought to weaken lynching as a way of strengthening Jim Crow.

Willie Earle and Thomas Brown

Willie Earle was not the only victim of the tragedy that bears his name. A white man named Thomas Watson Brown died a senseless, violent death within hours and miles of Earle.

Earle was a twenty-four-year-old Black man from a tenant-farming family in upstate South Carolina.[17] Relatives and friends described him as quiet, hardworking, and loving toward his six younger siblings.[18] "Willie would always be the one that would go out and buy some . . . toy or something for us to play with," recalled a childhood friend from a nearby farm. "He was kind of like a big brother to us."[19] Willie's mother Tessie later recalled that a teenaged Willie, following his father's death, sought to be "a financial aid to the family, because he was the oldest."[20]

17. "Lynch Victim Oldest of Seven Children," *Norfolk Journal and Guide*, March 1, 1947, A1; B. M. Phillips, "Mob Victim's Mother Sobs Out Tale of Woe," *Baltimore Afro-American*, March 1, 1947, 1; Gravely, *They Stole Him Out of Jail*, 90, 93.

18. Gravely, 93.

19. Acquillious Jackson, interviewed by Frank Carroll, Thomas Espenschied, Cassandra Harding, and Stevie Jefferis, Easley, South Carolina, July 23, 2018.

20. Phillips, "Mob Victim's Mother Sobs Out Tale of Woe," 2.

In many ways, Willie Earle was unlucky. He suffered from epilepsy.[21] He was a "slow" student, as some people later put it, and dropped out of school after the fifth grade.[22] As he grew into adulthood, he started drinking and had a few nonviolent run-ins with the law. He struggled to hold a job. At the time of his death, he lived in Greenville, South Carolina, and worked for that city's sanitation department.[23]

The incident's other victim was Thomas Brown, a forty-eight-year-old white cab driver, married, with adult children. Cabbies were a tight bunch. When Brown had bad weeks, other drivers steered good fares his way. When fellow drivers were down on their luck, Brown would pitch in and help. This code of reciprocity was good for cabbies but bad for anyone who crossed them. [24]

According to police allegations, Earle's and Brown's paths crossed on Saturday evening, February 15, 1947. The events of that chilly, almost moonless night[25] remain shadowy to this day. The Yellow Cab Company reported that Brown picked up "two negro fares"[26] in Greenville between nine and ten o'clock.[27] This was not unusual. Taxi driving in Greenville was virtually all white.[28] Ridership, by contrast, was mixed. "Ninety per cent of the Negroes of the town ride in taxicabs," a Black Greenvillian explained, there being "no good bus service in most colored districts."[29] One city resi-

21. Ibid.

22. Gravely, *They Stole Him Out of Jail*, 93; Phillips, "Mob Victim's Mother Sobs Out Tale of Woe," 2.

23. Phillips, "Mob Victim's Mother Sobs Out Tale of Woe," 1–2; Gravely, *They Stole Him Out of Jail*, 90, 93.

24. Ruth Clardy, interviewed by William Gravely, June 20, 1990, William Gravely Oral History Collection on the Lynching of Willie Earle, University of South Carolina, https://digital.tcl.sc.edu/digital/collection/gravely/id/3/rec/78; Gravely, *The Stole Him Out of Jail*, 38; West, "Opera in Greenville."

25. "Prisoner Lynched in South Carolina," *New York Times*, Feb. 18, 1947, 9; "Moon Phases 1947," Calendar.com, accessed Sept. 3, 2022, https://www.calendar-12.com/moon_phases/1947.

26. "S.C. Negro, Arrested as Murder Suspect, Slain by Angry Mob," *Charlotte Observer*, Feb. 18, 1947, 10.

27. Gravely, *They Stole Him Out of Jail*, 35–36, 97.

28. At the time of the Willie Earle lynching, Greenville's taxicab fleet was 97 percent white. John N. Popham, "Carolinians Split on Lynch Verdict," *New York Times*, May 23, 1947, 46; Robert S. Bird, "Lynching Town Glad Pressure of Trial Is Off," *New York Herald Tribune*, May 23, 1947, 3.

29. Bird, "Lynching Town Glad Pressure of Trial Is Off," 3.

dent estimated that Black riders accounted for at least half of the local cab-riding total.[30] This made taxis an unusual space in which Black people could tell white people what to do.[31]

Thomas Brown's "two negro fares" told him to drive from Greenville to the tiny town of Liberty, about twenty miles west, in neighboring Pickens County. They never got there. About two miles from Liberty, Brown was robbed and stabbed. A local farmer found him near death, on the ground, near his cab.[32]

At first light the next day, police combed the scene for clues. Investigators claimed that they were able to follow shoeprints—with new heels—between one and two miles, right to the house of Tessie Earle, Willie's mother. Inside, they said, they found Willie's new-heeled shoes and blood-stained jacket. Police inspectors connected the dots: Willie Earle must have taken Brown's cab that Saturday night from his home in Greenville to his mother's home in Liberty. Short on money, and perhaps drunk, he robbed and stabbed Thomas Brown, then walked the rest of the way in new-heeled shoes.

Officers arrested Willie Earle the next day. In his pockets were two dirty one-dollar bills and a "big scout knife"[33] bearing traces of blood.[34] Officers took Earle to the Pickens County jail, confident that they had found Thomas Brown's assailant.

Black people told different stories. Earle denied having taken a cab that night, much less having stabbed Thomas Brown.[35] He did travel from Greenville to Liberty, he said, but by bus, not cab.[36] Tessie Earle told reporters that her son carried no "blood-stained knife" and had no blood on his clothes.[37] Forty dollars, a watch, a ring, and car keys were stolen from Brown on Saturday night,[38] but when the police arrested Earle midday on Sunday,

30. Popham, "Carolinians Split on Lynch Verdict," 46.

31. Bryant Simon, interviewed by William S. Kaskay, April 2018.

32. "S.C. Negro, Arrested," 10; Gravely, *They Stole Him Out of Jail*, 34.

33. "S.C. Negro, Arrested," 10; Gravely, *They Stole Him Out of Jail*, 20 37, 66.

34. Gravely, 36–37, 92.

35. Ibid., 37.

36. Ibid., 93.

37. Phillips, "Mob Victim's Mother Sobs Out Tale of Woe," 2; Gravely, *They Stole Him Out of Jail*, 92–93.

38. "23 Admit Lynching Youth in S.C.," *Plaindealer* (Kansas City, KS), Feb. 28, 1947, 1.

he carried no watch, no ring, no keys, and just two dirty one-dollar bills.[39] The Yellow Cab company reported that Brown drove two people, not one, from Greenville toward Liberty; investigators never tied up that loose end. A wounded Thomas Brown told police that his assailant was a "large, black negro." The press described Willie Earle as "slight."[40] He stood 5'9" and weighed one hundred and fifty pounds.[41] Rumors even swirled in the Black community that "Brown was over in Liberty fooling around." Maybe a romantic rival had stabbed him, the local Black community speculated.[42]

In other words, many South Carolinians were sure that Earle had stabbed Brown,[43] but many others were sure that he had not done so.[44] Courts of law exist to resolve such conflicts. Willie Earle's case never made it that far.

The Lynching

Lynching in the Jim Crow South was a toxic blend of quasi-law, anti-law, and white supremacy. It was quasi-law in that lynchers playacted legal rituals. Mobs identified criminal suspects, faux-adjudicated cases, and imposed punishments. Mobs claimed to administer "lynch law" in "Judge Lynch's Court."[45]

To state the obvious, none of this was legal. Lynch mobs acted under no formal authority, followed no legal procedures, and honored no due-process protections. Instead, they identified suspects impulsively, knew only one verdict (guilty), imposed only one punishment (death), and allowed no appeals. Lynch law was not law. It was the antithesis of law.

Extreme racial bias further tainted "lynch law's" legitimacy. "It is not . . . the immorality or the enormity of the crime itself that arouses

39. "S.C. Negro, Arrested," 10; Gravely, *They Stole Him Out of Jail*, 20 37, 66.

40. "S.C. Negro, Arrested," 10.

41. Gravely, *They Stole Him Out of Jail*, 35.

42. "Earle Family Discussion, 1989, June 6," William Gravely Oral History Collection on the Lynching of Willie Earle, University of South Carolina Library, Columbia, South Carolina.

43. "Participation Is Admitted," *Charlotte Observer*, Feb. 21, 1947, 14; "Lynching Case Inquest Today," *Charlotte Observer*, Feb. 28, 1947, 17.

44. George F. McCray, "The Failure of Southern Justice," *Plaindealer*, May 30, 1947, 7.

45. See Frederick Douglass, "Lynch Law in the South," *North American Review* 155, no. 428 (July 1892): 17–24; "Judge Lynch's Court: Mobs and Violence in Maryland, 1860–1930s," MSA Web, accessed January 8, 2020, http://msaweb/msa/stagser/12159/161/00064/html.

popular wrath," Frederick Douglass observed in 1892, trying to make sense of retribution lynchings, "but the emphasis is put upon the race and color of the parties to it." Douglass thought that the spur to mob action was not "the moral sense" following an alleged crime but rather "the well-known hatred of one class towards another."[46] The record in South Carolina seems consistent with Douglass's observations. From the 1880s to the 1940s, Black people constituted around half of the Palmetto State's population, but 93 percent of its lynch victims.[47] One white South Carolinian at the time referred to lynchings as "crimes committed in the name of white supremacy."[48]

The proliferation of lynching during the high Jim Crow years was possible because a critical mass of white people accepted its quasilegal conceits. Many whites, though more or less law-abiding under most circumstances, willingly joined murderous mobs under other circumstances. The broader white community consistently honored pacts of silence regarding the widely known identities of lynch-mob members. Public officials went along with the charade, chalking up one lynching after another to death "at the hands of persons unknown."[49]

After the 1920s, lynching grew less common and more controversial. But its heart still beat. Its pulse quickened on Sunday, February 16, 1947, when word of Thomas Brown's stabbing ricocheted through Greenville. A cabbie from neighboring Pickens County drove east with news that a Black man was in the Pickens County jail on suspicion of having stabbed Thomas Brown. The Greenville cabbies' atavistic nerves twitched with vows of revenge. Late Sunday night, after hours of telephone calls and whispered plans, dozens of Greenville cabbies liquored up, armed themselves, and headed west.[50]

---

46. Douglass, "Lynch Law in the South," 19.

47. These figures are based on Stewart E. Tolnay and E. M. Beck, "Public Vic List 23 Jan. 2018," in authors' possession. Our thanks to E. M. Beck for his willingness to share data with our research team. See also Stewart E. Tolney and E. M. Beck, *A Festival of Violence: An Analysis of Southern Lynchings, 1882–1930* (Champaign: University of Illinois Press: 1995); and "Lynchings by State and Race, 1882–1968," University of Missouri–Kansas City, accessed January 8, 2020, http://law2.umkc.edu/faculty/projects/ftrials/shipp/lynchingsstate.html.

48. "Murderers without Cause," *Spartanburg Herald*, quoted in *The State* (Columbia, SC), Dec. 16, 1895, 2.

49. Philip Dray, *At the Hands of Persons Unknown: The Lynching of Black America* (New York: Modern Library, 2003).

50. John N. Popham, "'Confessions' Give Lynching Details," *New York Times*, May 15, 1947, 1.

The Pickens County jail could not hold Willie Earle. The problem was not an inability to keep Earle in. It was an inability to keep lynchers out. The cabbies reached the jail at around 4:30 a.m. Without resistance, the white jailer handed over Willie Earle. "They had shotguns and I danced to their music," he later explained.[51] Earle was "frightened into a state of stupefaction."[52]

The lynchers loaded Earle into a cab and headed east, pausing briefly to interrogate him and rough him up. Just after crossing the Pickens County line and entering Greenville County, the caravan stopped. Mob members piled out of their cabs and proceeded to torture, stab, and shoot Willie Earle. They left his lifeless, "knife and shot-ripped body" by the side of the road.[53] An anonymous caller informed a Greenville mortuary of the killing. The coroner found the corpse still warm, the torso "mutilated by . . . knives," the head bearing "gaping shotgun wounds."[54] So badly mutilated was Willie Earle's body that officials identified it by the two dirty dollar bills that they knew to be in his pocket.[55]

Thomas Brown was still alive at the time of the lynching. Hours later, in a Greenville hospital, he succumbed to his stabbing wounds.[56]

In some ways, as one Black newspaper observed, the Willie Earle lynching "followed closely the pattern of most southern lynch atrocities."[57] Like virtually all previous lynchings in the region, it was meant to buttress racial hierarchy. As one Black South Carolinian put it, Willie Earle's killers had acted in the name of "'white supremacy' and 'niggers staying in their place.'"[58]

The Willie Earle lynching also followed historical patterns in its quasi-legal pantomiming. Participants acted as if lynching were a legitimate response to a crime. Ringleaders had no trouble recruiting over thirty oth-

51. "Negro in South Carolina Taken from Jail, Lynched," *News and Observer* (Raleigh, NC), Feb. 18, 1947, 1.

52. Ibid.

53. Ibid.

54. Ibid.

55. "Prisoner Lynched in South Carolina," 9.

56. Gravely, *They Stole Him Out of Jail*, xii.

57. "Mob Leaders Confess to S.C. Lynching," *Chicago Defender*, Feb. 22, 1947, 1. See also "Indian Freedom in '48," *Chicago Bee*, March 9, 1947, 8; and "So. Carolina Man Lynched in Cruel Mob Orgy," *Los Angeles Sentinel*, Feb. 20, 1947, 1.

58. John H. McCray, "The Need for Changing," *Atlanta Daily World*, June 28, 1947, 5.

erwise law-abiding men to commit murder.[59] Feeling no need to hide their identities, they entered the jail unmasked, many still wearing their taxi-driver caps. The jailer seemed to share their presumption of lynching's legitimacy. He surrendered Earle without a struggle and later showed no remorse for having done so.[60] The lynchers briefly suspected that Willie Earle's cellmate, who was also Black, may have joined the attack on Thomas Brown. When the jailer told them otherwise, the mobsters legalistically relented.[61] They wanted the man who had attacked Brown, they said, "and wouldn't harm anybody else."[62]

In their faux-prosecutorial role, the mob worked hard to extract a confession. Willie Earle repeatedly denied having stabbed Thomas Brown.[63] The drivers, however, persisted. One cabbie, a former deputy sheriff, said that he "knew how to get a confession." His technique involved a pocketknife.[64] Finally, after extensive questioning, torture, and threats, Earle supposedly admitted guilt.[65] His reward for confessing: two shotgun blasts to the head. Subsequently, lynchers presented Earle's gun-barrel confession as a justification for their actions.[66]

And yet, in other ways, the Willie Earle story suggests that old lynching patterns were fading. Back in the heyday of lynching, many white people, perhaps most, considered it a socially acceptable civic act. Some lynchings occurred in broad daylight, in town squares, before big crowds. Some were memorialized in photographs and postcards that depicted dangling Black victims, unmasked white perpetrators, and supportive white spectators.[67]

By 1947, however, lynching's social acceptability had waned. Willie Ear-

59. John N. Popham, "Man Named as Lynching Slayer Denies Killing, Admits 'Mistake,'" *New York Times*, May 16, 1947, 1.

60. Gravely, *They Stole Him Out of Jail*, 21.

61. Ibid.

62. Quoted in "S.C. Mob Lynches Prisoner," *Baltimore Afro-American*, Feb. 22, 1947, 1.

63. "23 Taxi Drivers 'Confess' Carolina Lynching: Sheriff Gets Admissions from Suspects, Pickens Officers Say Earle Denied Robbery-Murder," *Atlanta Daily World*, Feb. 22, 1947, 1.

64. "31 Cab Drivers Indicted in S.C.," *Baltimore Afro-American*, March 22, 1947, 1.

65. Ibid.

66. Ibid.; Gravely, *They Stole Him Out of Jail*, 41; "31 Americans on Trial for Lynching a Negro," *Manchester Guardian*, May 13, 1947, 5.

67. Amy Louise Wood, "Lynching Photography and the Visual Reproduction of White Supremacy," *American Nineteenth-Century History* 6, no. 3 (2005): 373–99; James Allen, *Without Sanctuary: Lynching Photography in America* (Santa Fe: Twin Palms, 2000).

le's killers did their work in the dark of night, in the backwoods, with no spectators present. "Somehow," a Black journalist wrote, "[the Willie Earle slaying] doesn't have the earmarks of lynching as it has operated in the South."[68] "True, some 30 or more men executed it, but these men did not represent a community attitude against a Negro. Rather, it was vengeance of a little group of taxi drivers."[69]

The public response revealed even more change than did the lynching itself. Antilynching sentiment was greater than in previous eras. Black people had consistently opposed lynching since its massive upsurge in the late nineteenth century. By 1947, their claims-making ability had increased. The Willie Earle lynching outraged Blacks in South Carolina and beyond.[70] Black clergymen quickly condemned the lynching and attributed it to racial discrimination.[71] Black journalists attacked lynching and Jim Crow. The Palmetto State was already a target of Black editorial scorn, thanks to the US Supreme Court-flouting "South Carolina Plan" of 1944, according to which the state had privatized its primary elections to prevent Black voters from participating.[72] Following the Willie Earle lynching in February of 1947, local and national Black papers blasted South Carolina, the "home of the white primary law and other reactionary forces," for having the "nefarious distinction of ushering in [that] year's first" lynching.[73] Black editors urged state officials to apprehend the mob, though they doubted that this would happen.[74]

The NAACP reacted powerfully to Willie Earle's killing. During the late nineteenth century, lynching's worst years, South Carolina had no NAACP chapter. Indeed, no state did; the organization did not yet exist. By contrast, the NAACP of the 1940s was a leading voice of Black resistance, both statewide and nationally. Much of the group's prestige within the Black community derived from its legal activism. Because disfranchisement had effec-

68. McCray, "The Need for Changing," 6.

69. Ibid.

70. "Lynch Mob Rips Victim's Heart," *New York Amsterdam News*, Feb. 22, 1947, 1.

71. "AME Bishops Denounce South Carolina Lynching," *Norfolk Journal and Guide*, March 1, 1947, 1.

72. William V. Moore, "South Carolina Plan," in Walter Edgar, ed, *The South Carolina Encyclopedia* (Columbia: University of South Carolina Press, 2006), 902.

73. "Year's First Lynching Occurs in SC," *(New York) People's Voice*, Feb. 22, 1947, 1.

74. "The Pickens County Lynching," from the *Lighthouse and Informer* (Columbia, SC), reprinted in *Atlanta Daily World*, Feb. 20, 1947, 6.

tively cut off electoral options in the South, appellate courts loomed large in the Black political imagination. Black communities raised legal defense funds to fight civil rights battles and held out hope that upper-level courts would vindicate their rights. "All that is necessary for Negroes to do to regain their constitutional right to vote is to be able to hear their case in court," Black optimists gushed around the time of the Willie Earle lynching.[75] Somehow, the embers of Reconstruction-era legal egalitarianism still glowed in black historical memory. The NAACP basked in this glow. As one Black paper remarked, the NAACP "took [their] cases . . . when white lawyers refused."[76] In addition to being willing, the NAACP was able. Black commentators praised the organization for having taken twenty-two cases to the US Supreme Court and for having secured "21 victories, the highest number of victories of any other group or lawyer."[77] The association's legal record made it a natural leader of the antilynching crusade. "To whom do Negroes turn for help when a lynching occurs?"[78] one Black journalist rhetorically asked around the time of the Willie Earle case. Answer: the NAACP.

Immediately following the Willie Earle lynching, the South Carolina office of the NAACP sent representatives to Greenville County to help with the crime scene investigation.[79] The national office contacted the mayor of tiny Liberty, South Carolina, to ask about Willie Earle's local reputation.[80] And NAACP leaders fired off telegrams to President Harry S. Truman, members of Congress, the US attorney general, and the governor of South Carolina, demanding "immediate government action" to bring Willie Earle's lynchers to justice.[81]

The NAACP's demand for quick federal action was to be expected. Less expected was the federal government's response: it sprang into action. In

75. "On the White Primary Trail," *Atlanta Daily World*, Feb. 23, 1947, 4.

76. Ibid.

77. Ibid.

78. Ibid.

79. "Demand Investigations of Negro's Lynching," *Charlotte Observer*, Feb. 18, 1947, 10; "Year's First Lynching Occurs in SC," 32; "31 Arrested for Lynching," 1; "So. Carolina Man Lynched in Cruel Mob Orgy," 1.

80. Gravely, *The Stole Him Out of Jail.*

81. "So. Carolina Man Lynched in Cruel Mob Orgy," 1; Oliver W. Harington, "Three Agencies Track Down Lynching Gang," *Norfolk Journal and Guide*, Feb. 22, 1947, A1; "Demand Investigations of Negro's Lynching," 10; "Year's First Lynching Occurs in SC," 32.

the context of the early Cold War, lynching was a diplomatic humiliation. The Truman administration immediately sent the Federal Bureau of Investigation to South Carolina to help find Willie Earle's killers.[82] In short order, thirty-one suspected members of the lynch mob were under arrest. It was the FBI's largest federal-state manhunt to date.[83]

Northern whites cheered. National opinion was aghast at the heavily publicized Willie Earle lynching. World War II had sharpened the nation's civil rights sensibilities, causing at least some Americans to rethink long-accepted injustices. Lynching's decline had also made each new vigilante murder harder to ignore. Back in the 1890s, the pace of lynching in the United States was relentless, with a national average of about three people lynched every week throughout the decade.[84] By the 1940s, lynching had slowed to a trickle. Willie Earle's was the first and, by some counts, only lynching of 1947.[85] It consequently received massive attention.

Calls for quick prosecution of the lynchers rang out coast to coast. Influential northern, white newsman Walter Winchell declared that the Willie Earle lynching would "remain a black blot on the record of justice in th[e] nation until the gang of murderers rounded up by the Justice Department [were] made to pay."[86] The lynching's timing intensified the national reaction. The story broke during the third week of February: national Brotherhood Week, an annual celebration of intergroup harmony. A powerful editorial cartoon in the *New York Times* captured the tragic irony. It depicted a weapon-wielding mob surrounding a lifeless corpse under the title "Brotherhood Week in South Carolina."[87]

More surprising than this national reaction to the Willie Earle murder was the strong antilynching response of influential white southerners. A swell of white southern voices expressed outrage and called for the lynchers to be convicted. The "Brotherhood Week in South Carolina" cartoon that ran in the *New York Times* originated in a white newspaper in Florida. The *Times* published it under the heading "A Southern Comment."[88]

Local Black journalist and activist John H. McCray estimated that the

82. "Mob Leaders Confess to S.C. Lynching," 1; Gravely, *They Stole Him Out of Jail*, 18.

83. "Trial for Lynch Suspects Mon.," *Chicago Bee*, March 9, 1947, 3.

84. "Lynchings: By Year and Race," University of Missouri–Kansas City, Accessed Sept. 3, 2022, http://law2.umkc.edu/faculty/projects/ftrials/shipp/lynchingyear.html.

85. "Yes One Lynching, But," *Atlanta Daily World*, Jan. 6, 1948, 6.

86. "Orchids to Winchell," *New York Age*, March 8, 1947, 6.

87. "Editorial Cartoon 1—No Title," *New York Times*, Feb. 23, 1947, E6.

88. The cartoon originated in the *St. Petersburg (Florida) Times*. "Editorial Cartoon," E6.

majority of white South Carolinians opposed lynching. "Truth is," McCray wrote, "[the] overwhelming number of white people in South Carolina" were "angered by it and sickened by it."[89] This was especially true of elite, white South Carolinians.[90] Although influential white South Carolinians tended to be leery of federal intervention,[91] they deplored the Willie Earle lynching and favored prosecution.[92] This was true of the white press, the white clergy, white lawyers, and white "business men."[93]

Some whites, particularly nonelite whites, however, felt otherwise. Many of them likely felt kinship with the cab-driving lynchers.[94] Following the lynching, while elite whites wailed in dismay, nonelite white Greenvillians remained still. Then they quietly stirred. "Small jars and containers" labeled "Taxi-drivers' Fund" sprouted in shops around town. Coin by coin, the jars filled, adding about $2,000 to the lynchers' defense fund.[95] The coin-clinkers were not the sorts of people who wrote editorials. But they were the sorts of people who served on juries.

On the surface, however, the Willie Earle lynching provoked nearly universal "public wrath"[96] and stirred the government into action.[97] Without hesitation, state officials cooperated with the FBI to arrest the perpetrators. The sheriffs of Pickens County, where Earle was taken from jail, and Greenville County, where he was killed, were both fully on board.[98] "We don't stand for mob violence in South Carolina," declared Greenville Sheriff R. H.

---

89. McCray, "The Need for Changing," 6.

90. John N. Popham, "Civic Courage Shown in Key Carolina Trial," *New York Times*, May 18, 1947, E7; "Lynching at the Bar," *New York Times*, May 13, 1947, 24.

91. Kari Frederickson, "The Slowest State and Most Backward Community: Racial Violence in South Carolina and Federal Civil-Rights Legislation, 19461948," *South Carolina Historical Magazine*, no. 98, 1997, 192–93.

92. The *New York Times* reported that a "strong body of opinion throughout South Carolina" favored "swift action against the mob-killers." "South Carolina Makes a Start," *New York Times*, May 23, 1947, C22; "Carolina Mass Lynching Trial Prompted by Public Wrath," *New York Times*, May 11, 1947, E10.

93. Popham, "Civic Courage Shown in Key Carolina Trial," E7.

94. The nonelite status of the lynch mob is suggested by the educational level of suspected triggerman Roosevelt Carlos Hurd Sr. He left school after the second grade, earlier than Willie Earle. Gravely, *They Stole Him Out of Jail*, 232.

95. "31 Held in Lynching Aided," *New York Herald Tribune*, March 16, 1947, 3.

96. "Carolina Mass Lynching Trial Prompted by Public Wrath," E10; "Negro in South Carolina Taken from Jail," 1.

97. "Carolina Mass Lynching Trial Prompted by Public Wrath," E10; "Negro in South Carolina Taken from Jail," 1.

98. "Armed Men Push Back Jailer, Take Prisoner," *Atlanta Daily World*, Feb. 18, 1947, 1.

Beardon, "and we aren't going to."[99] Strom Thurmond, the state's newly elected governor, ordered the South Carolina Constabulary to aid the local investigation[100] and assigned an all-star prosecutor to the case.[101] "I do not favor lynching," Thurmond announced, "and I shall exert every resource at my command to apprehend all persons who may be involved in such a flagrant violation of the law."[102]

With these antilynching steps, powerful white South Carolinians gave the appearance of turning against Jim Crow. But looks deceived. Although a few white South Carolinians embraced civil rights generally, most remained firmly committed to segregation and disfranchisement. They opposed lynching because it embarrassed the South and undermined the legitimacy of Jim Crow.[103]

Antilynching and white supremacy blended conspicuously in the politics of Govorner Thurmond. The state's newly elected chief executive considered the Willie Earle lynching "a disgrace to the state."[104] "South Carolina today is on trial before the whole world," he declared, days after the lynching. "I want these cases strongly prosecuted.'"[105] If South Carolina failed to act, Govorner Thurmond feared, support for a federal antilynching law would grow. A federal antilynching law, in turn, could pave the way for additional attacks on Jim Crow. Thurmond reasoned that he, his state, and white supremacy generally would benefit from an active pursuit of Earle's killers. The northern press joined local Blacks in praising Thurmond's antilynching stance. They assumed that the governor had "earned the enmity of the purveyors of racial hatred."[106] They misunderstood his

99. "South Carolina Sheriff Will Charge 30 Suspects with Lynching Murder," *(Toronto) Globe and Mail*, Feb. 22, 1947, 1.

100. "S.C. Negro, Arrested," 10; "Armed Men Push Back Jailer, ," 1.

101. The prosecutor was Sam. R. Watt, solicitor in nearby Spartanburg for seventeen years. The previous year, Watt had convicted 471 of the 473 persons he brought to trial. Popham, "Civic Courage Shown in Key Carolina Trial," E7.

102. "Stop Lynching Now," *New York Amsterdam News*, Feb. 22, 1947, 10.

103. "Negro in South Carolina Taken from Jail," 1; "South Carolina Sheriff Will Charge 30 Suspects with Lynching Murder," 1.

104. "Two Men Questioned in Connection with South Carolina Lynching," *Charlotte Observer*, Feb. 19, 1947, 9. See also "31 Greenville Men Held in Lynching of Negro," *Charlotte Observer*, Feb. 22, 1947, 2.

105. "South Carolina Sheriff Will Charge 30 Suspects with Lynching Murder," 1.

106. Popham, "Civic Courage Shown in Key Carolina Trial," E7. For evidence of local

motivations. Within a year, Thurmond would emerge as the public face of Jim Crow.[107]

The Trial

With FBI help, South Carolina quickly rounded up thirty-one suspected lynchers.[108] Twenty-six of them confessed in writing to being part of the mob, though none admitted to firing the shots that killed Willie Earle.[109] The state charged all thirty-one suspects with murder and conspiracy to commit murder. It also charged everyone other than Roosevelt Hurd Sr., whom several cabbies named as the shooter, with being an accessory to murder, both before and after the fact. Hurd, the likely shooter, faced one murder count alone.[110]

Anticipation was keen for what was billed as the largest lynching trial in southern history.[111] The stakes seemed sky high. "The eyes of the nation—more likely the eyes of the world—will be focused . . . on Greenville, S.C.," the *Baltimore Afro-American* declared. "Not only the voice of Willie Earle but also the cries of countless victims . . . will echo through General Sessions Court, crying for justice as the 31 men go on trial."[112]

Black optimists believed that convictions were possible, thanks to the twenty-six signed confessions.[113] Black pessimists—"realists" might be a

---

Black support for Thurmond's actions in the Willie Earle case, see Essie Mae Washington-Williams and William Stadiem, *Dear Senator: A Memoir by the Daughter of Strom Thurmond* (New York: Harper-Collins, 2005), 122, 129.

107. Harlan Trott, "Bolting Democrats in South Form States' Rights Party," *Christian Science Monitor*, July 19, 1948, 1.

108. "FBI Steps out of Earle Case," *Charlotte Observer*, Feb. 24, 1947, 14.

109. "Sidelights on Mass Lynching Trial: No Negro Jurors Likely," *Norfolk Journal and Guide*, May 17, 1947, B1.

110. See Gravely, *They Stole Him Out of Jail*, 143.

111. "31 Americans on Trial for Lynching a Negro," 5; "Sidelights on Mass Lynching Trial," B1; William Gravely, "The Civil Right Not to Be Lynched: State Law, Government, and Citizen Response to the Killing of Willie Earle," 1947, 94, http://www.scpronet.com/modjeskaschool/wp-content/uploads/2016/05/The-Civil-Right-Not-to-be-Lynched.pdf

112. "Wipe Blood from Our Hands," *Baltimore Afro-American*, May 3, 1947, 4.

113. "Stop Lynching Now," 10; "Attack on Two Fronts," *(New York) People's Voice*, March 17, 1947, 16.

better term—expected little more than "a whitewash."[114] "Our experience in the past has shown that local efforts to solve lynchings and bring the perpetrators to justice have been fruitless," the *New York Amsterdam News* wrote.[115] Among other things, Black pessimists knew how southern juries were assembled. Although "qualified Negro voters [were] eligible, technically," the Black press reported, it appeared "unlikely that any Negro [potential jurors] would be called in this trial or selected to serve."[116] Jurors were likely to be neighbors of the lynchers. And "in the past," Black realists knew, lynchers had enjoyed "full protection from their neighbors."[117]

In May of 1947, spectators streamed into the Greenville County Courthouse. White people walked through the front door and onto the fan-cooled courtroom floor. Black people entered through a side door and climbed stairs to a stuffy, segregated gallery. In the bitter words of one Black journalist, it was "strictly a jim crow building."[118] The courthouse's white supremacist configuration symbolized the injustice that it housed. "And [then] it moved . . . to the trial," a childhood friend of Willie Earle later recalled. "And that was the terrible-est trial you'd ever want to hear in your life."[119]

The prosecution's case centered on the written confessions, in which twenty-six suspects admitted participating in the lynching.[120] Many of the confessions had named ringleader Roosevelt Carlos Hurd, Sr., as the triggerman whose shotgun blasts had killed Earle.[121] (According to one statement, Hurd fired two shots into Earle's skull and then "asked for another shell, but nobody gave it to him."[122]) Commentators described this evidence as "unprecedented in the history of Southern lynching cases."[123]

114. "Wipe Blood from Our Hands," 4.

115. "Stop Lynching Now," 10.

116. "Sidelights on Mass Lynching Trial," B1.

117. "The Pickens County Lynching," *Atlanta Daily World*, Feb. 20, 1947, 6, originally published in *Lighthouse and Informer.*

118. "Courthouse of the Lynching Trial," *Norfolk Journal and Guide*, May 24, 1947, A2.

119. Acquillious Jackson, interview by Cassandra M. Harding, Stephanie Jefferis, Francis Scalia Carroll, and Thomas Espenschied, Easley, South Carolina, July 18, 2018. Recording in author's possession, available upon request.

120. Popham, "'Confessions' Give Lynching Details," 1.

121. "31 Cab Drivers Indicted in S.C.," 1; "Sidelights on Mass Lynching Trial," B1; Popham, "'Confessions' Give Lynching Details," 1.

122. Statement of Charles M. Covington, quoted in Popham, "'Confessions' Give Lynching Details," 1.

123. "Own Words Used against the Mob in Lynching Trial," *New York Times*, May 14, 1947, 1;

Defense lawyers called no witnesses. [124] Instead, they attacked the process. They alleged that the police had used threats, intimidation, and deceit to extract confessions from their clients.[125] They denounced FBI meddling in southern affairs and urged jurors to strike a blow against "Federal intervention" by acquitting their clients.[126] Most importantly, defense attorneys, as one white journalist put it, "hammer[ed] away at race prejudice."[127] Defense lawyers compared Earle to a "mad dog" who needed to be put down.[128] They sought to shift the trial's focus away from the killing of Willie Earle and toward the killing of Thomas Brown, the white cabbie. Too much had been said about the lynching victim, defense counsel Thomas Wofford argued, "and not enough of the white cab driver who[m] Earle was accused of stabbing."[129] This tactic assumed the legitimacy of lynching as a response to crimes allegedly committed by Black perpetrators against white victims. Aware that the trial was for Earle's murder, not Brown's, however, Judge J. Robert Martin Jr. worked hard to prevent the jury from hearing these arguments. "I'm not going to allow any racial issue to be injected in this case," he vowed.[130] Nonetheless, defense counsel relentlessly fought for permission to ask questions aimed at showing that "the victim of the lynching had enraged the accused by bringing about the death of a white taxi driver who was their friend."[131] The prosecution repeatedly objected on ground that "there [was] no justification for a lynching"[132] and that therefore questions about "the death of the white man" were inadmissible.[133] Judge Martin repeatedly ordered the jury from the room, hoping to prevent its members from hearing "anything that might tend to inflame their feelings in view of the racial problem in this region."[134]

Judge Martin acted in vain. Racial feeling could not be excluded. Nearly all of the lynchers exercised a right that South Carolina afforded all defendants in capital cases: they had their families sit with them in court. "Many

124. "Defense Hopeful of Acquittal in Greenville Mass Murder Trials; Judge Releases Three Defendants," *New York Age*, May 24, 1947, 1.

125. Popham, "'Confessions' Give Lynching Details," 1.

126. "Defense Hopeful of Acquittal in Greenville Mass Murder Trials," 1.

127. Popham, "Man Named as Lynching Slayer Denies Killing," 1.

128. West, "Opera in Greenville."

129. "Defense Hopeful of Acquittal in Greenville Mass Murder Trials," 1.

130. Ibid.

131. "Own Words Used against the Mob in Lynching Trial," 1.

132. Ibid.

133. Ibid.

134. Ibid.

[defendants] had their wives beside them, young [white] women . . . in bright cotton . . . dresses," the *New Yorker* reported.[135] "A number of these women had brought their children with them; one had five scrambling over her." The presence of these white women and children silently engaged one of Jim Crow's central justifications: the imagined need to defend white women against Black male threats, at all costs. Also on the courtroom's main floor, from which Black spectators were barred, were hundreds of white spectators. According to press accounts, the large white crowd "displayed sympathy for the defendants and tittered with laughter each time the defense counsel made a point."[136]

The twenty-six signed confessions seemed like ironclad evidence for the state. Two acids corroded it. First, Judge Martin ruled that each confession was admissible only against the confessor himself. When the suspects refused to testify against each other in court, and when none admitted to pulling the trigger, prosecutors struggled to prove who had caused Earle's death, despite multiple written statements identifying the triggerman as Roosevelt Carlos Hurd Sr. Not surprisingly, Hurd denied pulling the trigger.[137] Second, the jury, like the mob,[138] was all white, all male, and overwhelmingly working class.[139] No juror shared a racial background with Willie Earle.[140] Although Judge Martin gave the jury "stern directions to ignore all racial issues," it was no use. Racial issues were baked into the proceedings.

The jury acquitted all defendants on all charges.[141]

Black people were not surprised.[142] "Being a Negro . . . has its advantage at times," quipped one Black writer from South Carolina. "And one of the times was when a jury of white men set Scot-free other white men tried for

135. West, "Opera in Greenville."

136. Popham, "Man Named as Lynching Slayer Denies Killing," 1.

137. Ibid.

138. Alleged triggerman R. C. Hurd, for example, was a cabbie with a second-grade education. Gravely, *They Stole Him Out of Jail*, 232.

139. A majority of the jurors were textile workers. "All 28 Win Full Acquittal in South Carolina Lynching," *Boston Globe*, May 22, 1947, 1.

140. "South Carolina Makes a Start," C22.; Gravely, *They Stole Him Out of Jail*, 119–22; West, "Opera in Greenville."

141. "All 28 Win Full Acquittal in South Carolina Lynching," 1.

142. Bird, "Lynching Town Glad Pressure of Trial Is Off," 3; "The South Carolina Lynching Verdict," *Norfolk Journal and Guide*, May 31, 1947, A8.

the Willie Earle lynching." The verdict "was no more than what the Negro . . . expected and predicted. Being thus prepared . . . by years of similar miscarriages of justice, he gritted his teeth a little," then thrust out his face "for another poke on the nose."[143]

The lynchers and their supporters were ecstatic. Hurd, the alleged triggerman, jumped on a chair and shouted, "[I feel] the best I ever felt in my life."[144] Referring both to the lynching and the acquittal, he proclaimed: "Justice was done—both ways."[145] (At that instant, we imagine, a 1940s-era camera snapped the picture with which this chapter began.) Other defendants "walked the streets . . . accepting congratulations."[146] Lyncher Paul Griggs received "many job offers." Lyncher Hendrix Rector clowned that he was going to get drunk in Greenville and then run for sheriff.[147]

Other white southerners, however, did not celebrate. Judge Martin was livid. He "grimly turned his back" on the jury without extending the customary thanks for their service.[148] Governor Strom Thurmond was reportedly "disappointed."[149] A hundred white students from nearby Wofford College protested.[150] "Quite a few people of importance in Greenville" reportedly were "ashamed of the verdict," and said "quite frankly that they will not blame the North for the deluge of criticism" that they expected.[151] Most southern newspapers editorially condemned the outcome.[152] The Columbia *State* wrote that the verdict "[was] not right, [was] not justice."[153] The *Charlotte News* deemed the verdict a "product of an ingrained prejudice."[154] The Atlanta *Journal* called the verdict "a ghastly farce," and "a

143. "Lynching, An Incorporation," *Atlanta Daily World*, June 4, 1947, 6, originally from the *Lighthouse Informer*, a Black paper published in South Carolina.

144. "All 28 Win Full Acquittal in South Carolina Lynching," 1.

145. Bird, "Lynching Town Glad Pressure of Trial Is Off," 3.

146. Popham, "Carolinians Split on Lynch Verdict," 46.

147. Ibid.

148. "South Carolina Makes a Start," C22.

149. Washington-Williams and Stadiem, *Dear Senator*, 123.

150. "How Bush Escaped Mob! Mother of Willie Earle Backs Increased Demand for Anti-Lynch Law," *Norfolk Journal and Guide*, May 31, 1947, 1.

151. Bird, "Lynching Town Glad Pressure of Trial Is Off," 3.

152. Louis Lautier, "Justice Dept. Grows Headachy over Lynchings," *Atlanta Daily World*, May 24, 1947, 1.

153. Quoted in "The South Carolina Lynching Verdict," A8.

154. Quoted in Lautier, "Justice Dept. Grows Headachy over Lynchings," 4.

challenge to all" that was "fair and decent and truly patriotic in the mind and heart of the South." "The law has been lynched."[155]

Public opinion polls showed how closely the nation had followed the trial and how unpopular the verdict was. An astonishing 75 percent of Americans polled nationally in June of 1947, two weeks after the trial's end, had "heard or read about" it.[156] "Do you approve or disapprove of the verdict?" Gallup asked. Approve: 12 percent; disapprove: 70 percent.[157] Even within the South, 62 percent of respondents disagreed with the verdict—not too far below the 70 percent figure nationwide, Gallup reported. Only 21 percent of southern respondents, as opposed to 12 percent nationwide, believed that the lynchers should have been acquitted.[158] The image of white jubilation conveyed in acquittal photographs, in other words, demands an asterisk. According to Gallup, southern critics of the verdict outnumbered southern supporters by a three-to-one margin.

Some of the southerners, white and Black, who opposed the verdict also opposed Jim Crow–style segregation. Most white southerners, however, likely mirrored Strom Thurmond. They opposed lynching but supported the other pillars of Jim Crow.

The Civil Case

The foregoing discussion of the criminal trial following the Willie Earle lynching highlights two frequently overlooked features: Black agency and white supremacist opposition to lynching. Both of these features were even more evident in the next phase of the saga: *Tessie Earle v. Greenville County* (1949),[159] a civil case that Willie's mother Tessie filed following the acquittal of her son's murderers. Tessie Earle based her claim on article VI, section 6,

155. Quoted in "Nation's Press Scores Dixie Lynch Verdict," *Cleveland Call and Post*, May 31, 1947, 1B.

156. Gallup Poll #1947-0398: Politics/Peace Treaty, June 1947, interview dates: June 6–11, 1947, Roper Center at Cornell University, Ithaca, New York.

157. Others either did not care (3 percent) or had no opinion (15 percent). Gallup Poll #1947-0398.

158. "Gallup Poll Reveals 69% Want Federal Lynch Law: Acquittal of 28 S.C. Lynchers Causes Change of Heart; 56% of Southerners Favorable," *Baltimore Afro-American*, July 12, 1947, 15.

159. Earle v. Greenville County.

of the South Carolina Constitution of 1895. The process by which this law came to be, in the 1890s, offers an instructive prequel to the Willie Earle story. It is a backstory worth telling.

The Prequel: "Pitchfork" Ben Tillman and White Supremacist Antilynching

The South Carolina Constitution of 1895, of which article VI, section 6 (the antilynching provision), was a part, was no racially progressive document. Far from it. As we have seen, it was the pièce de résistance of Jim Crow in South Carolina. The 1895 constitution sharpened the legal definition of Blackness, mandated that no child of either race shall "ever" be permitted to attend a school provided for children of the other race, and outlawed interracial marriage. Most importantly, it aimed to disfranchise Black South Carolinians to the maximum extent allowable under federal law. The constitution's chief architect, "Pitchfork" Ben Tillman, was an unapologetic white supremacist. Yet he fought hard, and successfully, for article VI (6). Untangling this seeming paradox sheds light on white supremacy as a governing philosophy during the high Jim Crow years.[160]

Benjamin Ryan Tillman believed that extralegal violence was a symptom of bad governance. The worse the governance, the surer—and more justified—the violence. South Carolina history knew no worse government, thought Tillman, than the Republican administrations that ruled during Reconstruction. In Tillman's view, those biracial governments were so incompetent, so corrupt, that extralegal violence was inevitable. Indeed, it

---

160. Scholars frequently overlook article VI, section 6. Terence Finnegan, *A Deed So Accursed: Lynching in Mississippi and South Carolina, 1881–1940* (Charlottesville: University of Virginia Press, 2013); Stephen Kantrowitz, *Ben Tillman and the Reconstruction of White Supremacy* (Chapel Hill: University of North Carolina Press, 2000). A notable exception is the work of legal historian James Chadbourn, who focuses on the legal mechanisms of the legislation rather than the measure's origins or implementation, as we do. Chadbourn, *Lynching and the Law* (Chapel Hill: University of North Carolina Press, 1933), 50. George Tindall also mentions the provision. Tindall notes that "the issue of lynching was forcefully and repeatedly" pushed "by black delegates" but leaves the final version of the law a tantalizing mystery. "Strangely," he writes, "more stringent anti-lynching proposals were introduced by white delegates." We seek to make this outcome appear less strange to our readers than it appeared to Tindall. Tindall, "The Question of Race in the South Carolina Constitutional Convention of 1895," *Journal of Negro History* 37, no. 3 (1952): 299.

was laudable. Tillman himself joined a paramilitary group called the "Red Shirts" and participated in the bloody Hamburg Massacre of 1876, a key episode in the campaign of South Carolina Democrats to intimidate Black voters and wrest power away from Republicans at the end of Reconstruction—"by fraud and violence," Tillman later boasted.[161]

Tillman's record of extralegal violence did not shame him. Indeed, he boasted about it for the rest of his days. He even displayed his "trusty rifle" from Hamburg in his home parlor.[162] "I proclaim it aloud that I was one of the Hamburg rioters," he declared.[163] (Critics spun it differently: "His hands are red with the blood of murdered Republicans, and he glories in the stain," they said.[164]) Tillman's eventual opposition to lynching, in other words, did not derive from pacifism.

Nor did it derive from egalitarianism. Some Black activists of the day spoke out against lynching because it resulted from, as one put it, "sheer prejudice."[165] Lynching "inculcate[d] the idea that the negro had no rights," observed a Black South Carolinian.[166] These activists opposed lynching because they opposed racism. Not Tillman. He was a racist, loud and proud. He considered Anglo-Saxons to be the world's "superior race"[167] and Black people to be so inferior that they nearly represented "the missing link with the monkey."[168] Whatever progress "the colored race has shown itself capa-

---

161. *Journal of the Constitutional Convention of the State of South Carolina* (Columbia, SC: CA Calvo, Jr. , 1895), 463.

162. "The South Carolina Issue," *Washington Post*, Oct. 31, 1890, 4; "Some Very Frank Talk," *Atlanta Constitution*, Aug. 30, 1888, 1.

163. Quoted in an untitled article, *Worcester Daily Spy*, Sept. 18, 1888, 4. Inconsistencies mark Tillman's stories. He sometimes said that he was ill at the time of the Hamburg Massacre of 1876 and thus lost the chance "to shoot the d—d niggers!" "It Was a Social Revolt," *New York Times*, Sept. 1, 1892, 9. At other times he confessed, "I have never killed a nigger, but I shot at one in Hamburg and tried to kill him, but missed." "Ben and the Blacks: Tillman Interviewed by a Colored Preacher," *The State*, July 3, 1895, 3.

164. "The South Carolina Condition," *(Chicago) Daily Inter Ocean*, Aug. 29, 1890, 4. See also "The Duty of the Negro in the Present Campaign," *Washington Bee*, Oct. 27, 1900, 1.

165. "Suggests the Calling of a Convention," *The (Indianapolis) Freeman*, Oct. 19, 1895, 3.

166. "They Meet in Columbia," *Augusta (GA) Chronicle*, Jan. 3, 1890, 1. See also "Josephine E. Ghant Says We Must Demand Our Rights as American Citizens," *The Freeman*, May 11, 1895, 6.

167. Quoted in Stephen Kantrowitz, *Benjamin Tillman and the Reconstruction of White Supremacy* (Chapel Hill: University of North Carolina Press, 2000), 258. See also "A Plain Statement," *The State*, Feb. 25, 1895, 4.

168. David M. Kennedy and Thomas A. Bailey, *The American Spirit*, 13th ed. (Boston: Cenage Learning, 2016), 392–93.

ble of achieving," he argued, had resulted from the supposedly elevating influence of slavery.[169] Tillman described his victory in the 1890 gubernatorial election as the triumph of "white supremacy over mongrelism."[170] Once in office, he proclaimed that his leadership "mean[t] white supremacy."[171] "We deny . . . that 'all men are created equal,'" Governor Tillman declared in his inaugural address. "It is not true now and it was not true when Jefferson wrote it."[172]

Nor did economic concerns underlie Tillman's antilynching stance. Some advocates of southern industrialization believed that lynching discouraged investment.[173] Lynchings were "injurious to the business interests and progress of the [S]outh," they feared.[174] Tillman, however, was no New South modernizer. He was an agrarian, a rhetorical champion of the small white farmer.[175] Far from wanting the South to industrialize, Tillman claimed to want to emancipate "the masses of white men" from what he called "slavery to corporations, trusts and monopolies."[176]

Thus, the usual antilynching motivations of the day—a distaste for extralegal violence, an aversion to white supremacy, dreams of a modernized Southland—did not move Tillman. His antilynching stance rested upon other bases. At first, Tillman, a political outsider, used antilynching rhetoric to score political points against insiders. In 1890, he ran for South Carolina governor as an antielitist, insurgent, reform candidate within the state's Democratic Party.[177]

Tillman's candidacy tapped into the agrarian populism of the day. He was a farmer from Edgefield County, the mayhem-filled western district where Martin Posey once roamed. Though actually from a fairly wealthy

---

169. Ibid.

170. *Inaugural Address of B. R. Tillman, Governor of South Carolina, Delivered at Columbia, S.C., December 4, 1890* (Columbia, SC: James H. Woodrow, 1890), 4.

171. "Tillman's Talk," *The State*, Aug. 30, 1894, 4.

172. Ibid., 5.

173. These "New South" boosters urged "every one who seeks to promote the South's prosperity" to "rise up and . . . put a stop to [lynching]." "The Butchery at Denmark," *The State*, April 29, 1893, 2. See also "Dastardly and Despicable," *Savannah Tribune*, April 29, 1893, 2.

174. "Lynchings in the South," *The State*, Nov. 19, 1895, 6.

175. Francis Simkins, *The Tillman Movement in South Carolina* (Durham, NC: Duke University Press, 1926): 221; Tindall, "The Campaign for the Disfranchisement of Negroes in South Carolina," *Journal of Southern History* 15, no. 2 (1949): 218.

176. B. R. Tillman, quoted in "Carolina's Cromwell," *The State*, Jan. 23, 1895, 1.

177. "Capt. B. R. Tillman," *Bismark (ND) Tribune*, June 7, 1890, 4; "It Was a Social Revolt," 9.

family, Tillman presented himself as "a poor white small farmer"[178] who would lead an agrarian assault on the corrupt, eastern, "aristocratic"[179] faction of the Democratic Party that had ruled the state since 1876. He also would defend "Anglo-Saxon unity" more vigilantly than the aristocrats did.[180] Tillman followed in the bare-knuckle tradition of Edgefield politics made famous by Preston Brooks, the congressman from Edgefield whose signature act was the caning of an abolitionist senator on the floor of the US Senate in 1856. Observers noted similar frontier rawness in "Farmer Tillman's"[181] political affect. One pundit described him as "a hitter, a hurter and a hustler."[182]

During the 1890 gubernatorial race, Tillman pointed to the state's many lynchings as proof of the incumbents' incompetence. "Bad laws and their inefficient execution have caused the continual recurrence of lynchings," Tillman charged on the campaign trail.[183] Under an inept government, Tillman argued, people inevitably grew "weary of the law's delay" and took matters into their own hands.[184]

Astute observers understood that Tillman's form of antilynching had nothing to do with racial justice. It was simply a convenient cudgel with which to smack his rivals. Tillman wanted to "put a stop to the South Carolina custom of lynching," a Republican paper in Chicago observed, "not because the colored man has a right to be tried by his peers, but because this bloody amusement is likely to bring the State into disrepute."[185]

Tillman's antilynching stance, however, was more than a form of negative campaigning. It also reflected his idealized vision of white supremacy as a governing system. Tillman argued that total white control of govern-

---

178. "It Was a Social Revolt," 9; "Farmers in Revolt," *New York Tribune*, March 10, 1890, 7; and "It Is Farmer Tillman," *Augusta Chronicle*, March 28, 1890, 1.

179. "South Carolina Farmers," *Knoxville Journal*, March 28, 1890, 1.

180. "For 'Anglo-Saxon Unity,'" *Kalamazoo (MI) Gazette*, March 29, 1890, 2.

181. "The Meet at Anderson," *Augusta Chronicle*, May 11, 1890, 1.

182. "B. R. Tillman," *Augusta Chronicle*, March 18, 1890, 4. Another critic described Tillman as possessing "a true demagogue's glib tongue and reckless ambition." Again and again, this critic said, Tillman's impulsive charges of corruption were disproven, "but so impervious were he and his followers to the truth" that these revelations mattered little. "It Was a Social Revolt," 9.

183. "Too Much of Tillman," *Chicago Herald*, July 22, 1890, 8.

184. "Tillman's Strong Words," *Kansas City (MO) Times*, Dec. 5, 1890, 1.

185. "A Bystander's Notes," *Daily Inter Ocean*, Dec. 13, 1890, 4. This critic further noted that Tillman's arguments against lynching revealed an "utter unconsciousness that the colored man has any right, or that murder is an act of any moral significance whatsoever." Ibid.

ment would eliminate lynching, demonstrating, on an ongoing basis, the superiority of white governance.

White supremacy would eradicate lynching in two ways, Tillman figured. First, it would produce superior public administration. "The whites have absolute control," he proclaimed after his election in 1890.[186] And with "all the machinery of law" in white hands, "with every department of the government—Executive, Legislative, and Judicial—held by white men," South Carolinians would no longer feel the need to "resort . . . to lynch law."[187] Lynchings generally occurred when people grew frustrated with the law's technicalities and delays, he argued. Upright white leaders would "make plain and simple the rules of the court," cease "granting continuances and new trials upon technicalities," and guarantee that punishment for crime, "by whomsoever committed," was "prompt and sure." And "with the removal of the cause"—delay and obfuscation—"the effect"—lynching—"[would] disappear."[188]

Second, Tillman thought that white supremacy would eliminate lynching by reducing racial tension. Removing Black South Carolinians from politics and returning them to their natural, subordinate position would restore the instinctive affections that had characterized race relations prior to the twin tragedies of emancipation and enfranchisement, Tillman argued. When Black people were "no longer imbued with the Republican idea"—political equality—"the vexed negro problem [would] be solved."[189] The surest way to end political violence against Black people, he thought, was to remove Blacks from politics.

And yet, although Tillman wished to overturn much of what Reconstruction had accomplished, he knew that he could not overturn it all. Mindful of the Thirteenth Amendment, he did not propose a return to slavery. Mindful of the Fourteenth Amendment, he explicitly promised equal protection of the law to all South Carolinians, though his fingers may have been crossed behind his back. He even supported public education for Black people—something not allowed under slavery—despite saying, "Though I don't see the good it does."[190] His greatest frustration was the Fifteenth Amendment, which obstructed his white supremacist vision by

186. *Inaugural Address of B. R. Tillman, Governor of South Carolina, Delivered at Columbia, South Carolina, December 4, 1890* (Columbia, SC: James H. Woodrow, 1890), 5.

187. Ibid., 6.

188. Ibid., 6.

189. Ibid., 5.

190. Richard Carroll, "Ben and the Blacks," *The State*, July 3, 1895, 3.

preventing states from disfranchising voters on account of their race. Tillman and Jim Crow's other architects responded to these constraints by developing a form of racial subordination for the postslavery era. That meant white acceptance of emancipation, at least rhetorical fealty to the notion of "equal protection under the law,"[191] and the maximum allowable degree of Black disfranchisement.[192] Submissive Black people; magnanimous white people; good government; putatively equal legal protections for Black people, as long as they stayed out of politics; hierarchically harmonious race relations: this was Ben Tillman's Jim Crow fantasy. If it came to pass, he thought, lynching would wither away, and the northern "finger of scorn" would "no longer be pointed" at South Carolina.[193]

Governor Tillman

Candidate Tillman had insisted that lynchings indicated bad governance. Having won the election, Governor Tillman now vowed to prevent them. Sheriffs were key, he thought, for they were responsible for protecting Black prisoners. Some sheriffs were hesitant to stand up to white mobs, however, for fear that outraged white people would either kill them or vote them out of office.[194] This was dereliction of duty, Tillman thought. He asked the state legislature to empower him to fire any sheriff who allowed a prisoner under his watch to be lynched. The legislature refused.[195]

Denied the postlynching power to remove sheriffs from office, Tillman relied on prelynching actions. Shortly after his inauguration, a lynching loomed. The local sheriff sought instructions. "There must be no lynching," Tillman commanded. There was no lynching.[196] Thereafter, he routinely corresponded with sheriffs and, where necessary, called out local militia units to prevent lynchings.[197] Late in 1891, Tillman proudly reported that, during his first year in office, "no person . . . ha[d] been lynched."[198] In the

---

191. *Inaugural Address of B. R. Tillman*, 5.

192. Ibid.

193. Ibid.

194. "Tillman and the Southern Press," *Daily Inter Ocean*, Dec. 10, 1890, 4.

195. *Inaugural Address of B. R. Tillman*, 6; "Tillman and the Southern Press," 4.

196. "A Variety of Things," *Plaindealer*, Jan. 2, 1891, 4; and Jan. 9, 1891, 4.

197. Kantrowitz, *Benjamin Tillman*, 167.

198. Quoted in ibid.

ten years before Tillman became governor, by contrast, South Carolina had averaged between four and five lynchings per year.[199]

The press cheered. South Carolina's leading white papers, though generally critical of Tillman, were uniformly critical of lynching, and therefore complimentary of Tillman's antilynching successes.[200] *The State* newspaper of Columbia frequently criticized "Dictator Tillman"[201] but hailed him as "the man who put a stop to lynchings in South Carolina."[202] Black commentators also approved. Samuel Lee, a Black leader from Charleston, had Tillman's lynching record in mind when noting that the "farmer governor" had "promised less [to Black people] than his predecessors" but had delivered more.[203]

The first recognized lynching under Tillman's watch occurred in December of 1891, over a year after his inauguration.[204] It occurred in Tillman's native Edgefield County.[205] The victim was a Black man, jailed on suspicion of killing a white man. A white Edgefield mob stormed the jail in "broad daylight," cut the prisoner's throat, and "riddled his body with bullets."[206] Tillman was livid. He had instructed the local sheriff to "protect the prisoner at whatever cost"; the sheriff had failed. Tillman ordered a review of the sheriff's performance and offered substantial rewards for the apprehension and conviction of the lynchers.[207]

The Edgefield lynching broke the governor's streak but not his reputation. "Say what you please against Governor Tillman," a Black South Carolina editor wrote in the spring of 1892. "The fact remains that he is the only Democratic Governor of South Carolina since '76 that had the moral courage to oppose lynch law openly, . . . [the result of which] has been the pro-

---

199. Tolnay and Beck, "Public Vic List."

200. "Lynchings in the South," 6.

201. "The Wolf Not Balked of his Prey," *The State*, May 22, 1891, 4, quoting *Marion Star*; "Our Dictatorship," *The State*, April 15, 1891, 4; and "Sic Semper Tyrannis," *The State*, 3 July 1891, 4.

202. "Judged by his Own Mouth," *The State*, Dec. 8, 1891: 4.

203. "A Variety of Things," *Plaindealer*, Jan. 2, 1891, 4.

204. Tolnay and Beck identified what they call a "probable lynching" of an "Unnamed Negro" in August of 1891 in Pickens County, South Carolina. Tolnay and Beck, "Public Vic List." But South Carolina observers, Black and white, at the time believed that the first lynching of Tillman's administration did not occur until December 1891.

205. "The Edgefield Lynchings," *Savannah Tribune*, Dec. 12, 1891, 2.

206. Ibid.

207. Ibid.

duction of but one single case of lynching during his whole term as Governor, for which he was not in the remotest way responsible."[208] Another Black paper noted that lynching had risen to unprecedented national heights in 1891. Thanks to Tillman's leadership, however, lynching numbers in South Carolina, "once a hotbed," had plummeted.[209] No wonder the "colored people of South Carolina" felt "very grateful to Governor Tillman."[210]

As if to avoid a Black embrace from the left, Tillman then dodged right. During his gubernatorial reelection campaign in 1892, he doubled down on his white-populist image, running as the "poor man's Governor," by which he meant the poor white man's governor. He campaigned as the fighting farmer from the state's west who had "whipped" the elitist "cohorts of Charleston and Columbia"[211] and who would defend the little fellow against banks and "double-dealers."[212]

Frontier-style rough justice was part of this politics. Tillman opened his reelection campaign in June of 1892, in Barnwell County, part of a lynching-heavy zone on the state's western fringe.[213] Playing to his antielitist base, Tillman spoke in a grove of trees where, two years previously, eight "lifeless [Black] bodies" had "swung."[214] At this symbolically freighted location, he detonated a rhetorical bombshell that reverberated coast to coast—and echoes still: "I as Governor would head a party to lynch any negro that would rape a white woman."[215]

This was bombast. Tillman never followed through on his "lynching pledge," even when directly asked to do so.[216] Away from the campaign trail,

---

208. "Current Comment," *Plaindealer*, March 18, 1892, 4, quoting *New South*.

209. "Lynch Law in the South," 2.

210. "Political Miscellany," *The State*, April 4, 1892, 7, quoting *(New Beaufort) New South* (colored). See also "Review of the Year," *New York Age*, Jan. 2, 1892, 2.

211. "I Would Lead a Lynching," *The State*, June 8, 1892, 5.

212. Ibid.

213. The three contiguous western counties of Barnwell, Aiken, and Edgefield all ranked in the state's top five for lynching frequency. Tolnay and Beck, "Public Vic List." For more on racial violence in Barnwell County, see "Lynchings in the South,"

214. "Lynched: Judge Lynch Holds High Carnival," *Augusta Chronicle*, Dec. 29, 1889, 1; "Two Views of Lynching," *Washington Post*, June 9, 1892, 6.

215. "The South Carolina Campaign," *Charlotte Observer*, June 8, 1892, 1; "I Would Lead a Lynching," 5; "Two Views of Lynching," 6.

216. "The Irmo Crime: They Want Tillman to Lead the Lynchers," *The State*, July 29, 1892, 8; "How a Mob Was Foiled," *The State*, Aug. 2, 1892), 5; "Ben Tillman and Mayor of Chicago Clash," *Grand Forks (ND) Daily Herald*, Nov. 27, 1906, 1; Kantrowitz, *Benjamin Tillman*, 156.

Governor Tillman quietly continued admonishing sheriffs to prevent lynchings. ("Guard jail. Do your duty. Call on [militia forces] if necessary," Tillman urged an Edgefield sheriff who faced a possible lynching just days after the explosive Barnwell speech.[217]) But the political impact of Tillman's lynching pledge was enormous. Black leaders complained about Tillman's double standard, since he seemed utterly unconcerned about rapes committed by white men. They argued that the governor's "monstrous" failure to dispense equal justice merited impeachment.[218] Elite white Democrats likewise retrieved the antilynching cudgel that Tillman had dropped and bashed the governor for insulting the rule of law and soiling the state's reputation, all "for the sake of perhaps catching a few ignorant voters."[219] "There was a time when South Carolina . . . was the centre of learning, of refinement, gentility, and intellectual achievement," a never-Tillman Democratic sniffed. But thanks to Tillman's celebration of lawlessness, "hers [was] a faded glory."[220]

Elite indignation, Black and white, delighted Tillman's base. Tillmanites showed their delight by adopting their hero's fighting style. Their stump meetings in 1892 routinely degenerated into "rowdyism and violence," the mainstream press disapprovingly reported.[221] This was not happenstance. Tillmanite leaders urged supporters to "knock down any man who approached them to talk Conservative politics."[222] A "mob of Tillmanites"[223] in the South Carolina upcountry did as instructed in the summer of 1892, forcing a prominent Conservative speaker to flee. "I do not blame these

---

217. "In Danger of Lynching: Gov. Tillman Called on to Protect an Alleged Murderer," *New York Times*, June 16, 1892, 1.

218. "Tillman, Governor of South Carolina," *Savannah Tribune*, June 11, 1892, 2. In response to Black criticisms such as this one, Tillman later modified his lynching pledge to make it appear color-blind: "I would lead a mob to lynch any man, white or black, who had ravished any woman, white or black." Quoted in "Tillman and Lynching," *Charlotte Observer*, June 2, 1894, 3. Tillman issued this statement in response to the antilynching activism of Ida B. Wells. For a powerful rebuttal, see "Mob Law in the South," *New York Times*, June 3, 1894, 4.

219. "Violence and Mob Law," *The State*, Aug. 9, 1892, 1; "Leading the Lynchers," *The State*, Aug. 2, 1892, 4.

220. "As Others See Us: The Disgrace Brought upon South Carolina by Tillman," *The State*, Aug. 15, 1892, 7.

221. Ibid.

222. Ibid.

223. Ibid.

deluded men who attacked me," the nimble Conservative mused. "What can you expect of them when the man they have elected Governor . . . confesses that under some circumstances he would lead a lynching party?"[224]

Tillman's provocative "lynching pledge" won for him the enemies he wanted—Black people, the white elite—and may have helped him win reelection in 1892.[225] These benefits, however, came with costs. Lynchings were not popular, and Tillman now owned them, for his pledge appeared to give lynchers a green light. In 1893, Tillman reaped what he sowed. South Carolina lynchings shot up to their highest level since Reconstruction.

The most politically explosive lynching of 1893 occurred in Denmark, South Carolina, a small town in the very county—Barnwell—in which Tillman had uttered his 1892 lynching pledge while on the campaign trail.[226] A white teenaged girl in Denmark reported that "an unknown negro" had assaulted her, with intent to rape.[227] Tillman's response reflected the complexity of his views on lynching. He wrote to a white Barnwell supporter, "Hoping to hear that you have caught and lynched [the Black assailant]." The same letter, however, warned that any lynching should occur before the accused was in custody, for Governor Tillman "would not consider it right" to have a man "caught by process of law," only to have citizens "break the law by killing him."[228]

Local whites suspected a Black man named John Peterson.[229] Terrified, Peterson fled to Columbia and "delivered himself" to the governor, swearing that he was innocent and could prove it. Tillman unwisely ordered Peterson back to Barnwell County for a court investigation.[230] The court failed to find any evidence against Peterson and released him, whereupon a massive white mob, "so frenzied that it could not be restrained," seized him.[231] Peterson convinced the mob to bring him to the young victim. She would tell them whether or not he was her attacker.

224. Ibid.

225. Walter Edgar, *South Carolina A History* (Columbia: University of South Carolina Press, 1998), 440.

226. Denmark today sits in Bamberg County, which was founded in 1897.

227. "Probably Lynched the Wrong Man," *New-York Tribune*, April 26, 1893, 4.

228. Kantrowitz, *Benjamin Tillman*, 175–77.

229. "Probably Lynched the Wrong Man," 4.

230. Stephen Kantrowitz, "Tillman, Benjamin Ryan," in *The South Carolina Encyclopedia*, 962.

231. "Probably Lynched the Wrong Man," 4.

"That don't look like him at all," the teenager said when she saw Peterson. "He is the same color, that's all."[232]

No matter. Five hundred white people "filled [Peterson's] body with bullets while it dangled from a tree."[233]

A "Tidal Wave of Condemnation"[234] crashed down upon "Pitchfork" Ben for the "inconceivable atrocity"[235] at Denmark. "Governor Tillman cannot escape the blame that must attach to him for this horrid crime," critics cried.[236] "It was the duty of the Governor, not only to protect" Peterson against vigilante violence, they charged, "but to protect the dignity and good name of the State" by preventing lawlessness.[237] But instead of doing his duty, Tillman tossed the defenseless Peterson "into the midst of the excited mob,"[238] feeding "its mad fury"[239] and doing more than any other southern governor[240] to place a "foul blot upon the honor" of his state.[241]

The Denmark outrage energized Tillman's natural political enemies: Black people and the white elite. "Indignation meetings" sprouted around the state and beyond.[242] The day after the Denmark lynching, an interracial group of protestors packed the courthouse in Columbia to condemn Tillman for "encouraging lynch law." Black people silently occupied the right-hand side of the courthouse.[243] White people occupied the left side and did all the talking. Speakers decried the "outrage upon law" at Denmark and expressed paternalistic sympathy "for that people [Blacks] who ha[d] been [their] faithful servants for two hundred years and who [were] now [their] wards." As such, it was their duty "to spread . . . protecting wings over them."[244] A white lawyer brought the house down by saying that, if he were

232. "Was an Innocent Man Lynched?" *(Abbeville, SC) Press and Banner*, April 26, 1893, 4.

233. "Probably Lynched the Wrong Man," 4.

234. "Sentiment of the State: The Tidal Wave of Condemnation of the Denmark Murder," *The State*, May 1, 1893, 4.

235. *Richmond Times*, quoted in "Inconceivable Atrocity," *The State*, April 29, 1893, 2.

236. "Sentiment of the State," 4.

237. Ibid.

238. Ibid.

239. Ibid.

240. "Governor Tillman an Accessory," *The State*, April 29, 1893, 2.

241. "The Governor's Course Indefensible," *Camden (SC) Chronicle*, reprinted in *The State*, May 1, 1893, 4.

242. "Condemned in Georgia," *The State*, April 27, 1893, 6.

243. "Gov. Tillman Rebuked," *The State*, April 26, 1893, 8.

244. Ibid.

the solicitor of Barnwell County, he would indict all of the lynchers and "name as accessory before the fact B. R. Tillman, who [was] more responsible than any other for the crime that ha[d] been done."[245] "Almost deafening applause" broke out on both sides of the room, and resolutions condemning the governor passed unanimously.[246]

The following evening, Black protesters returned for a "mammoth" meeting of their own. The courthouse setting symbolized the Jim Crow–era legal system's segregated openness to Black southerners, in sharp contrast to the antebellum world, which excluded them entirely.[247] According to press reports, the estimated crowd of a thousand constituted the "largest gathering of negroes seen in Columbia for years."[248] Speakers "opened their guns on the Tillman administration"[249] and adopted "scorching" antilynching resolutions.[250] The Black meeting's resolutions were more pointed than those prepared by white leaders at the previous meeting. The white resolutions had emphasized the outrageous particulars of the Denmark case.[251] The Black follow-up went further, denouncing lynching's systemic racism. The "frequent lynchings of negroes" and the "refusal of the officers of the law to bring a single lyncher to justice, although the men be known to them," Black protesters charged, "show[ed] official collusion" with lynching and "denied justice to over half of [South Carolina's] citizens."[252]

Antilynching outrage fueled Black political mobilization. "It is time . . . to rise up in our manhood and defend ourselves against mob law," one Black orator declared. "We, as a race . . . allow too many wrong things to be placed upon us; we are too submissive. We do not act enough."[253] But they

245. Ibid.

246. Ibid.

247. For additional examples of the move from exclusion to segregation, see Howard N. Rabinowitz, "From Exclusion to Segregation: Southern Race Relations, 1865–1890," *Journal of American History* 63, no. 2 (Sept. 1976): 325–50.

248. "The Negro Aroused: Denmark Lynching and Gov. Tillman Denounced," *The State*, April 27, 1893, 8; "Condemning Gov. Tillman," *Savannah Tribune*, May 6, 1893, 4.

249. "Condemning Gov. Tillman," 4.

250. "The Negro Aroused," 8.

251. "Gov. Tillman Rebuked," *The State*, April 26, 1893, 8.

252. "The Negro Aroused," 8.

253. Ibid.

would "not be submissive any longer."[254] His remarks touched off "the wildest applause and cheering."[255] Similar protests, elsewhere in South Carolina and beyond, touched on similar themes.[256]

The lynching crisis of 1893 created two problems for Tillman. It spurred Black people to political action, and it made a mockery of his argument that white supremacy was uniquely able to reduce racial tension.[257] Tillman responded to these twin challenges with two silent vows: Black voting must end, and lynching must cease. At the 1895 Constitutional Convention, he pursued both goals.

The 1895 Constitutional Convention

Following the 1894 elections, Ben Tillman moved from the South Carolina governorship to the US Senate, where he would serve until his death in 1918. But he remained a powerful force in South Carolina politics. Indeed, his most consequential contribution to the political history of his state occurred after he had left the governorship: the Constitutional Convention of 1895.[258] The South Carolina convention was part of a regional wave. From Mississippi, in 1890, to Georgia, in 1908, every former Confederate state revised its constitution, with an eye toward disfranchising as many Black people as possible.[259] As the South Carolina convention approached, two things were clear: Tillman would dominate[260] and Black political rights

254. "Condemning Gov. Tillman," 4.

255. "The Negro Aroused," 8.

256. "The Denmark Lynching," *The State*, May 13, 1893, 3; "Carolina at the Capital," *The State*, April 29, 1893, 1.

257. "Notwithstanding the fact that the white people control the entire machinery of justice in the State," Black Charlestonians argued in 1893, in a direct rebuke to Tillmanism, "they [white people] resort to mob violence instead of pursuing the course pr[e]scribed by law." "The Denmark Lynching," 3.

258. Kantrowitz, "Tillman," 962.

259. Paul Brest, *Processes of Constitutional Decisionmaking: Cases and Materials* (New York: Wolters Kluwer, 2018), 430.

260. Tindall, "The Campaign for the Disfranchisement," 218, 229–30; Edgar, *South Carolina*, 44; "A Blackmailing Convention," *The State*, Nov. 1, 1894, 4; "Tillman's Plan Presented," *The State*, Feb. 22, 1895, 1; D. D. Wallace, "The South Carolina Constitutional Convention of 1895," *Sewanee Review* 4, no. 3 (May, 1896): 351.

would suffer. "What are you going to do in the convention?" a Black man asked Tillman in the summer of 1895. "The negroes are alarmed. You are the cause of it."[261]

Tillman's top convention goal was to "disfranchise the negro,"[262] which, he said, would strengthen "white supremacy . . . [and] save [whites] from negro domination."[263] To be sure, by 1895, the specter of "negro domination" was rhetorical only. Rule changes and intimidation had already suppressed the Black vote substantially.[264] But as long as any Blacks remained on the rolls, Tillman feared, unscrupulous whites would be tempted to manipulate Black votes to achieve undeserved power. "I want peace among the white people," Tillman explained prior to the convention, "and we never can have it with [so many] . . . negro votes that dissatisfied white men can buy up and use at will."[265] He sought a new constitution that would disfranchise Black men, though not white men.[266] That was "the only way to ensure white supremacy."[267]

There was nothing secret about this. The press reported that the convention was called "for the unconcealed purpose of disfranchising the negroes as near as possible, under the Federal Constitution." Were it not for this purpose, "the convention would not have been called."[268] Once the convention was underway, white delegates debated "how best to get rid of the mass of negro voters."[269] Holding the reins was Senator Tillman, chair of the convention's powerful Committee on the Rights of Suffrage.[270] Tillman implored competing white factions to unite against "the black cohorts" whom they had come "to reduce and paralyze."[271] Their job, he told white delegates, was "to take from them [Black people] every ballot that [they

261. Carroll, "Ben and the Blacks," 3.

262. "Self-Disfranchisement," *The State*, Jan. 10, 1895, 4.

263. "Tillman's Plan Presented," 1.

264. Tindall, "The Campaign for the Disfranchisement," 216–17.

265. Carroll, "Ben and the Blacks," 3.

266. Tindall, "The Campaign for the Disfranchisement," 224.

267. *Columbia Daily Register*, Oct. 12, 1894, quoted in ibid., 225. The *Daily Register* was a Tillmanite organ.

268. "Suffrage in South Carolina," *The State*, Sept. 23, 1895, 6.

269. "Lynch Law Laid Low," *The State*, Nov. 10, 1895, 1.

270. Tindall, "The Question of Race," 277–82.

271. *Journal of the Constitutional Convention of the State of South*, 468.

could] under the laws of [the] national government"[272] while "saving the right of suffrage for the poor and illiterate white man."[273]

This required some ingenuity. The US Constitution's Fifteenth Amendment (1870) prevented states from abridging the right to vote on account of race, color, or previous condition of servitude. For Tillman, this was a problem. He asked: "[How can we] get around . . . the impassable bulwark which the Fifteenth Amendment throws around the negroes"?[274] He found his answer in the pioneering Mississippi Constitution of 1890, which had mixed together a cocktail of suffrage restrictions that, though race-neutral on their face, combined to suppress Black voting, especially when implemented by racist white officials. Prior to the South Carolina convention, Tillman asked Richard Carroll, a Black preacher from Barnwell County, "Do you know anything about the Mississippi plan? . . . You must pay a heavy poll tax and be able to read the Constitution of the United States and understand it."

"Who is to be the judge?" Carroll inquired.

Tillman: "The supervisor."

Carroll: "And what if he be . . . prejudiced?"

Tillman: "That's another thing; but the United States will not allow us to make a law for the negroes and not have the same law for white people."

Carroll: "But making laws [is one thing] and enforcing them after they are made is another thing."

Tillman: [No reply.][275]

The South Carolina Constitution of 1895 wove a Mississippiesque mesh of property requirements, poll taxes, literacy tests, "understanding" clauses, and felony disfranchisement rules. The Tillmanites' goal was to filter out the maximum number of Black people while waving through the maximum number of white people.[276] Indeed, their stated goal was to disfranchise Black men while taking the vote away from "no white man," however poor or illiterate.[277]

---

272. Ibid., 463–64.

273. Ibid., 468.

274. Ibid., 468.

275. Carroll, "Ben and the Blacks," 3.

276. Ibid, 285–87.

277. "Hypocrisy," *The State*, Oct. 13, 1895, 4; Kantrowitz, *Benjamin Tillman*, 209; and Tindall, "The Campaign for the Disfranchisement of Negroes in South Carolina," 224.

Despite powerful objections from the tiny Black contingent at the convention, Tillman's proposals passed. National headlines blared: "The Negro Disfranchised," "Tillman and His 'White Supremacy' Idea in Full Control."[278] The new suffrage law, though racially neutral, was designed to be administered unequally. "It is presumed that any white man will be able to 'understand' the clauses read to him, so that the [Tillmanite] promise not to disfranchise any white man is kept," a constitutional expert wrote. "Such is the South Carolina suffrage law, under which it is hoped to put negro control of the State beyond possibility and still preserve the suffrage for the illiterate whites."[279]

The new rules disfranchised most Black men and some white men. In 1896, when voters reregistered under the new constitution's terms, fifty-five hundred Black names and fifty thousand white names remained on the rolls. Black people now accounted for 59 percent of the state's population and 10 percent of its electorate. Tillman was proud of his handiwork. "We did not disfranchise the Negroes until 1895," he boasted to his colleagues in the US Senate in 1900. "Then we had a constitutional convention . . . which took the matter up calmly, deliberately, and avowedly with the purpose of disfranchising as many of them as we could under the Fourteenth and Fifteenth Amendments."[280] "All men are not created equal and the niggers are not fit to vote," he explained.[281] The suffrage provisions would remain in effect through World War II.

Article VI, Section 6

After figuring out "how best to get rid of the mass of negro voters,"[282] newspapers reported, the 1895 convention next "took up the matter of lynchings."[283] Black delegates initiated the discussion.[284] Of the convention's

278. "The Negro Disfranchised," *New York Tribune*, Nov. 4, 1895, 5.

279. Wallace, "The South Carolina Constitutional Convention of 1895," 355. For more on the subjectivity and abuse allowed by literacy tests, see John Wertheimer, *Law and Society in the South: A History of North Carolina Court Cases* (Lexington: University Press of Kentucky, 2009), 127–64.

280. Kennedy and Bailey, *The American Spirit*, 392.

281. "Senator Tillman Has No Use for 'Niggers,'" *(Boise) Idaho Statesman*, Aug. 5, 1901, 1.

282. "Lynch Law Laid Low," *The State*, Nov. 10, 1895, 1.

283. Ibid.

284. Tindall, "The Question of Race," 67.

one hundred and sixty delegates, six were Black.[285] (Recall that Black people constituted almost 60 percent of the state's population at the time.) Their promotion of antilynching measures was consistent with national patterns. Much of the Jim Crow era's antilynching legislation was initially sponsored by Black leaders.[286]

At the South Carolina convention, Black delegates proposed a variety of antilynching measures.[287] Their previous fight against disfranchisement had been gallant but utterly fruitless.[288] To oppose disfranchisement in 1895 was to swim against powerful white supremacist tides. The politics of antilynching were different. To oppose lynching, Black delegates found, was to flow with white supremacist currents. At the convention, Black delegates proposed strong antilynching measures. White delegates made them stronger.[289] Black delegate I. R. Reed proposed empowering the governor to fire any official who allowed harm to come to a prisoner in his custody. George Bellinger, the white chairman of the Jurisprudence Committee, took this idea one step further, proposing that negligent officers who allowed lynchings should be removed from office and also banned from future office-holding.[290] With slight modifications, this measure passed.[291]

Ben Tillman approved of the negligent-sheriff provision. But he wanted more. After all, many lynching victims were killed before being taken into police custody. South Carolina needed to change the behavior of mobs, not just the behavior of sheriffs, Tillman thought.[292] As things stood, mobs had little to fear. Although criminal prosecution was theoretically possible, the mobsters' close connections to surrounding white communities effectively made it impossible for prosecutors to secure jury convictions.[293] During

285. Ibid., 60.

286. James H. Chadbourn, *Lynching and the Law* (Chapel Hill: University of North Carolina Press, 1933), 26–27.

287. Tindall, "The Question of Race," 61, 67; *Journal of the Constitutional Convention of the State of South Carolina*, 123, 316.

288. "How They View It," *The State*, Nov. 4, 1895, 1; Tindall, "The Question of Race," 63.

289. Ibid., 67.

290. *Journal of the Constitutional Convention of the State of South Carolina*, 10; "Woman's Suffrage," *The State*, Oct. 29, 1895, 1, 2, 5; "Lynching and the South Carolina Constitution," *Memphis Commercial Appeal*, Nov. 1, 1895; "To Discourage Lynching," *Charleston News and Courier*, Nov. 12, 1895.

291. S.C. Const. art. VI, § 6 (1895).

292. "The Convention on Lynching," *The State*, Nov. 12, 1895, 4.

293. "Lynchings in the South," 6.

Tillman's term as governor, South Carolina prosecuted several suspected lynchers; local juries acquitted them all.[294]

Tillman's response was a proposal to make counties financially liable for lynchings that occurred within their borders. "In all cases of lynching," he proposed, "the County where such lynching takes place shall be liable in exemplary damages."[295] The only way to stop lynching was to "ma[k]e the people pay for it," Tillman reasoned.[296] The press agreed. Making counties liable would "prick the consciences of taxpayers"[297] and cause residents to say: "We cannot afford to lynch because it would increase the taxes."[298]

Debate focused on the details. One delegate suggested specifying that the money should go to "the legal representatives of the party killed."[299] Done. Another delegate proposed specifying that counties would be liable "without regard to the conduct" of public officials. Done. A third delegate suggested allowing trial juries to decide how much or how little particular counties should pay. Tillman disagreed. "If we want to stop lynchings," he exclaimed, "then we ought to make them as . . . costly as possible."[300] But how much money, at a minimum, should offending counties have to pay?

Tillman: "Five thousand [dollars]."

Voice: "One thousand."

Tillman: "Oh, no, life is too cheap now."[301]

The result was a compromise: $2,000.[302] Henceforth, surviving family members would be able to sue the county in which a lynching occurred for a minimum of $2,000, whether or not public officials were involved.[303]

294. Ibid.

295. "Considering Corporations," *The State*, Nov. 12, 1895, 2. This idea reportedly "ha[d] been advanced several times in recent years, but ha[d] never been tested." See "The Convention on Lynching," 4. A county-liability antilynching law failed in Ohio in 1894 but passed there in 1896. *Cleveland (Ohio) Gazette*, March 16, 1907, 2.

296. "Considering Corporations," 1.

297. "The Convention," *Charleston News and Courier*, Nov. 13, 1895.

298. "Considering Corporations," 1.

299. "Considering Corporations," 2.

300. "The Law and the Lynchers," *Charleston News and Courier*, Nov. 12, 1895.

301. Ibid.

302. "Considering Corporations," 1.

303. S.C. Const. art. VI, § 6 (1895): "In all cases of lynching when death ensues, the County where such lynching takes place shall, without regard to the conduct of the officers, be liable in exemplary damages of not less than two thousand dollars to the legal representatives of the person lynched."

Although "Pitchfork" Ben wanted even stronger antilynching provisions,[304] he was satisfied with what he got. Under Article VI, negligent state officials could be punished if they allowed lynchings to occur,[305] and legal representatives of lynching victims could sue to recover a minimum of $2,000 from the South Carolina counties in which their loved ones were lynched, whether or not any public officials were involved.[306]

The public cheered. Black observers, though outraged by the new constitution's suffrage provisions,[307] were pleasantly surprised by Article VI, having never imagined, as one Black editorialist wrote, "that any such liberal provision would have been made" at the convention.[308] South Carolina's white newspapers also applauded. Two papers argued in print about which one deserved more credit for the passage of Article VI.[309] Editorialists declared that the "convention did the right thing" by passing the measure.[310] The "average man hates nothing quite so bitterly as taxes," *The State*

304. Tillman and an ally proposed allowing lynching victims' families to sue "each and every" lynch mob member for $5,000 in damages. Lynchers who were found liable but failed to pay would be imprisoned until they paid in full. Even if only a few families of lynch victims proved willing to sue under this provision, Tillman argued, each case "would act as a scarecrow," discouraging future lynchings. "There were attorneys who took cases on contingent fees," Tillman noted, "who would stand as a menace to this class of lawbreakers." The proposal was too radical for many delegates. Unlike the county-liability provision, this measure would require the naming of names. And imprisonment for debt irked some defenders of the little lyncher. "Mr. Tillman's Lynching Clause" failed by a two-to-one margin. The tiny Black contingent voted unanimously in favor. So did "Pitchfork" Ben, the arch-white supremacist. "To Discourage Lynching"; *Journal of the Constitutional Convention of the State of South Carolina*, 655–56; "The End Draws Nigh," *The State*, Nov. 24, 1895, 1; "The State Survey," *The State*, Nov. 24, 1895, 4; "Going Further," *The State*, Nov. 24, 1895; "Lynching Provision," *Idaho Statesman*, Nov. 24, 1895, 1; "Mr. Tillman's Lynching Clause Rejected," *Washington Post*, Nov. 24, 1895, 12; "The Sign of Weakness," *The State*, July 27, 1892, 5.

305. S.C. Const. art. VI, § 6 (1895).

306. Ibid.

307. "Negroes Protest: Do Not Relish Disfranchisement by Fraud," *The State*, Oct. 12, 1895, 1.

308. "Editorial Survey," *The State*, Dec. 14, 1895, 4, originally published in the *Beaufort New South*, a "colored Republican paper."

309. See the argument between *The State* and the *Anderson People's Advocate*, described in "Vainglorious Boasting," *The State*, Dec. 25, 1895, 4.

310. "The State's Survey," 4.

noted.[311] Make the tax burden heavy enough and "every man would have an interest in being a conservator of the peace."[312] "Five years ago eight negroes were lynched in Barnwell County at one lynching," the *Charleston News and Courier* editorialized. "Possibly John Peterson would not have been lynched at Denmark in the same county two years later had the taxpayers been required to pay $16,000."[313] Even commentators who despised Tillman tipped their caps. "Give the Devil his Due," wrote the *Greenville News*. "This Newspaper is against him. We do not like his politics or his methods, but when he does a good thing"—such as adding antilynching provisions to the new constitution—"he ought to have credit for it."[314] The only criticism came from those who thought that the law did not go far enough to discourage lynching.[315] Still, commentators thought that South Carolina should take a bow. The Palmetto State, "long racked and shamed by bloody and lawless deeds," had "earned the plaudits of civilization." In "one great reform at least," South Carolina had "taken the lead of all her sister States."[316]

Supporters of the law were wildly optimistic about its likely impact. "We have seen the last of" lynching, the white *Charleston News and Courier* predicted. "When the new Constitution goes into effect there will be no more of it."[317] "We say to the colored people," declared the white *Greenville News*, "that the days of lynching in South Carolina are nearly ended." And the paper thought it knew whom to thank: "B. R Tillman."[318] Black observers, too, were optimistic. "By reason of the adoption of [Article VI]," the *Beaufort New South Black Republican* wrote, "the nefarious practice of lynching will be minimized in South Carolina, if not wholly obliterated."[319]

The Tillmanites had many reasons for opposing lynching, but sympathy for lynching victims was not among them. To them, lynching was many bad

---

311. "The Convention on Lynching," 4.

312. Ibid.

313. Editorial, *Charleston News and Courier*, Nov. 25, 1895.

314. "Give the Devil His Due: B. R Tillman to be Thanked for the Anti-Lynching Clauses," *Charleston News and Courier*, Dec. 4, 1895, quoting the *Greenville News*.

315. "To Discourage Lynching"; "South Carolina's Anti-Lynching Law," *Cleveland Gazette*, June 6, 1896.

316. "South Carolina Shamed," *The State*, Dec. 8, 1895, 4.

317. "Give the Devil His Due.".

318. "Give the Devil His Due.".

319. "The Thanks of the Negroes: Solicitor Bellinger Praised for his Anti-Lynching Law," *Charleston News and Courier*, Dec. 4, 1895, quoting the *Beaufort New South Black Republican*.

things, including a political liability, a regional embarrassment, and an affront to their governing authority. As they framed it, however, it was not an offense against human beings. Realizing this makes it easier to reconcile the seemingly disparate aims of the Convention: to "reduce and paralyze"[320] Black people politically and to suppress mob violence against them. Antilynching, Ben Tillman style, was scarcely about Black people at all.

Article VI in Court

In order for Article VI[321] to bend the lynching curve downward, the families of South Carolina lynching victims had to invoke it in court. Black families were quick to do so. They had many opportunities, given the measure's inadequacy as a lynching cure.[322] In January of 1897, just thirteen months after South Carolina's Constitutional Convention adjourned, a lynch mob left the bullet-riddled body of Lawrence Brown hanging from a railroad signal in Orangeburg County. He was the fourth South Carolina lynching victim—all Black men—to perish since Article VI went into effect. Contrary to stereotype, Brown was not accused of raping a white woman or murdering a white man. His alleged offence was barn burning. Officials briefly jailed Brown but released him "on account of a lack of evidence." Brown walked out of jail—and into Judge Lynch's fatal grasp.[323] Brown's murderers were never brought to justice. Officials concluded, unhelpfully but typically, that he had perished at the hands of "parties unknown."[324]

Lawrence Brown's father, Isaac Brown, would not let the matter rest. He took advantage of a right unavailable to enslaved forebears. He sued, seeking

320. *Journal of the Constitutional Convention of the State of South Carolina*, 468.

321. Note that the South Carolina legislature quickly passed legislation that adopted the language of the constitution's Article VI, Section 6, word for word. See Brown v. Orangeburg County, 55 S.C. 45, 32 S.E. 764, 765.

322. An estimated fifty-seven possible, probable, and confirmed lynchings occurred in South Carolina in the ten years prior to the adoption of Article VI, Section 6. In the ten years afterward, the number was virtually identical: sixty. Tolnay and Beck, "Public Vic List."

323. "On the Danger Sign," *The State*, Jan. 7, 1897; "State of County and the Church," *The State*, Feb. 24, 1897, 6.

324. "Parties Unknown," *The State*, Jan. 8, 1897, 5; "The Anti-Lynching Law," *The State*, Sept. 28, 1900, 2.

$10,000 in exemplary damages from Orangeburg County.[325] In court, Brown provided ample evidence of his son's lynching. He introduced a note found at the Orangeburg County scene: "Judge Lynch's court is in session tonight for the protection of our property," it read. "And by the help of God we will convict and execute any man, woman or child that tries to destroy our property with fire. . . . Let this be a warning to others." Signed, "Citizens."[326]

The defendant in the article VI case, Orangeburg County, submitted no testimony. Its lawyers merely asked the judge to direct a verdict for them on the ground that Article VI applied only when "the person lynched was taken from the custody of public officers by the lynchers."[327] At the time of the mob's attack, Lawrence Brown was not in custody.[328]

This was a weak argument, but it impressed the trial judge, James Aldrich. In his decade on the state bench, Aldrich had compiled an impressive antilynching record.[329] Judge Aldrich was "not a man whom lynchers would select to sit in their case," the press thought.[330] But Aldrich disapproved of Article VI. A jurist "of the old school,"[331] he opposed finding the blameless liable. In Isaac Brown's case, Orangeburg County, the defendant, had done nothing wrong. Lawrence Brown was not in police custody when the mob took him. Making the county pay damages was simply unjust, Aldrich thought.

Judge Aldrich attempted to kneecap Article VI. He ignored the provision's clear language and decided that counties should be liable only if public officials were involved in the lynching. If, as in *Brown v. Orangeburg County*, lynching victims were not in custody at the time of their abduction, then counties could not be found liable.[332] Never mind what Article VI said. Aldrich substituted what he thought it should say. On

325. "Black and White," *The State*, Jan. 8, 1897, 4. One article described this case as "without precedent in this State." "For Lynching Brown," *The State*, May 11, 1898, 5. An earlier article, however, suggests that Isaac Brown was not the first South Carolinian to sue under Article VI. *Cleveland Gazette*, May 29, 1897, 2.

326. "The Lynching Clause," *The State*, April 22, 1898, 4.

327. Ibid.

328. Brown v. Orangeburg County, 55 S.C. 45 (1899), 46.

329. "Unnecessary Uneasiness," *The State*, July 17, 1895, 1; "Law in Greenwood," *The State*, Nov. 24, 1897, 1.

330. "Before the Jury: Trial of the Parties Charged with Colleton Lynchings," *The State*, Feb. 21, 1896, 1.

331. "James Aldrich Has Resigned," *The State*, Nov. 27, 1907, 12.

332. "The Lynching Clause," 4.

that shaky basis, he directed a verdict for the defendant, Orangeburg County.[333]

The press realized that Judge Aldrich's ruling, if allowed to stand, would knock "a great, big hole . . . in the [antilynching] law."[334] Isaac Brown would not let it stand. He appealed to the South Carolina Supreme Court, arguing that Judge Aldrich had misread the law.[335] Article VI explicitly stated that counties were liable "in all cases of lynching where death ensue[d] . . . without regard to the conduct" of public officials. Judge Aldrich's interpretation of Article VI was simply wrong, Brown's lawyers argued.

The South Carolina Supreme Court agreed. The opinion was written by Associate Justice Eugene B. Gary, the Jim Crow champion whom we have seen in the previous two chapters. Gary was a Ben Tillman protégé.[336] (By contrast, Judge Aldrich, who sought to hogtie the antilynching provision, was not a Tillmanite.[337]) Like his mentor, Justice Gary was a white supremacist.[338] In *Brown v. Orangeburg County* (1898), he showed that he, like Tillman, was an antilynching white supremacist. Gary rejected Adlrich's misreading of Article VI. He also gave the measure a judicial thumbs-up, calling it "salutary" and noting that it "ma[d]e communities law-abiding" and "render[ed] protection to human life."[339] Siding with Isaac Brown, Justice Gary found that it made no difference whether Brown's son was in police custody or strolling freely when taken by the mob. Judge Aldrich was simply wrong. The Supreme Court reversed and ordered a new trial.[340]

Lynching opponents cheered Isaac Brown's appellate victory. A Pennsylvania newspaper called it "the most encouraging decision with regard to

333. Ibid.

334. Ibid.

335. "Damages for Lynching," *The State*, Jan. 5, 1899, 8.

336. "The State's Survey," 4; "No More Raiding," *Plaindealer*, April 4, 1894, 2; and "The South Carolina Ring," *The State*, Sept. 21, 1894, 4.

337. Unlike most South Carolina judges of the day, Judge James Aldrich took office before Tillman's governorship began. He owed no allegiance to "Pitchfork" Ben. "List of Judges Since the War," *The State*, Feb. 14, 1909, 12; "To Wear the Ermine," *The State*, Dec. 6, 1894, 1; "James Aldridge Has Resigned," *The State*, Nov. 27, 1907, 12; and "Judge Aldrich Passes Away," *The State*, Jan. 24, 1910, 1.

338. See Tucker v. Blease, 81 S.E. 668, 673 (1914), discussed in chapter 4.

339. Brown v. Orangeburg County, 55 S.C. 45, 49 (1899)

340. Ibid., at 48.

lynch law that has ever come from a Southern court."[341] The paper thought that forcing counties to pay exemplary damages, even "in a few instances," would "do more to array the respectable white citizens of a given county against lynch law than all other forces combined."[342]

The celebrations were premature. When the case returned to Orangeburg County, it slipped into a repeating cycle: a Brown loss before a comparatively nonelite jury followed by a Brown victory before a comparatively elite judge. The first retrial took place in the fall of 1899. The plaintiff presented "overwhelming" evidence of Lawrence Brown's lynching in Orangeburg County.[343] The defendant resorted to weak arguments, such as the implausible suggestion that Brown had committed suicide, even though his neck was broken, his hands and feet were tied, and his body was "riddled with bullets."[344] "At this rate," the *Baltimore Afro-American* quipped, "there will soon be a band of upstarts in the Southland arguing that Jesus Christ crucified himself on the cross."[345] Unaccountably, the jury ruled for the defendant, Orangeburg County.[346]

Isaac Brown moved to have this verdict set aside as a miscarriage of justice.[347] The trial judge agreed and ordered a third trial.[348] Again, Isaac Brown presented evidence of his son's lynching in Orangeburg County. Again, the defense offered no testimony.[349] Again, the trial judge issued a plaintiff-friendly charge to the jury[350] but "had no effect."[351] The jury ruled for Orangeburg County, giving Article VI, in the words of one reporter, "another black eye."[352]

After the tireless Isaac Brown moved to have that third verdict set

341. "To Stop Lynching," *Wilkes-Barre (PA) Times*, May 9, 1899, 4.

342. Ibid. See also "Note and Comment," *(Portland) Oregonian*, May 2, 1899, 4.

343. "Verdict for the County," *Baltimore Sun*, Oct. 2, 1899, 9.

344. Ibid; "Anti-Lynching Law," *Augusta Chronicle*, Sept. 28, 1900, 1.

345. "Damages for Lynching," *Baltimore Afro-American*, Oct. 28, 1899, 3.

346. Ibid.; and "Law Not Effective," *The State*, Oct. 2, 1899, 7.

347. "Verdict for the County," 9.

348. "Anti-Lynching Law," 1. Note that the trial judge, George W. Gage, voted with Tillman on Article VI questions at the 1895 constitutional convention. *Journal of the Constitutional Convention of the State of South Carolina*, 528.

349. "Anti-Lynch Law No Good," *Charlotte Observer*, Sept. 28, 1900, 1.

350. Ibid.

351. Ibid.

352. "Anti-Lynching Law," 1.

aside,[353] the paper trail fades. Perhaps Brown's Sisyphean struggle ended in an out-of-court settlement. Perhaps he gave up. Perhaps he was coerced into silence. In any event, the press drew a bleak conclusion: "South Carolina's Anti-Lynch Law Does Not Work."[354]

Isaac Brown's pioneering case, however, was not a total dud. A northern Black newspaper in Philadelphia cheered Brown's "test case" and reported that relatives of other South Carolina lynching victims were following Brown's lead and "preparing to file suits."[355] The paper also speculated that the mere threat of tax increases would dissuade Palmetto State lynchings, even if specific litigants came up empty. "As a Southerner's aversion to paying higher taxes is strong, lynching in South Carolina will probably be less frequent," the paper predicted.[356] A white Minnesotan similarly observed in 1899 that, even though South Carolina's Article VI had "thus far" proven to be a "dead letter" in court, it was recognized nationally as "the only enactment on this subject which provides a practical and enforceable penalty."[357] A couple of years later, a Massachusetts paper reported that South Carolina's county-liability law had "proved effective."[358] Such optimism was not confined to northerners. The *Augusta Chronicle*, a white paper in Georgia, likewise noted that, even though Article VI remained "a dead failure" in court, "it ha[d] been largely successful" in its broader aim: "the suppression of lynching."[359] Critics, too, appeared to believe that Article VI was having an impact. At least three times in the measure's early years, opponents tried unsuccessfully to repeal it.[360]

Many of the notes struck in *Brown v. Orangeburg County*, the first known Article VI case, echoed in the second known case: *Harris v. Anderson County*. Elbert Harris, a young Black man, was lynched in Anderson County in 1898. Like Lawrence Brown before him, Harris was suspected not of rape but of burning down a building—in Harris's case, a ginhouse

353. "The Anti-Lynching Law," 2.

354. "Counties Won: South Carolina's Anti-Lynch Law Does Not Work," *The Age Herald* (Birmingham, AL), Sept. 28, 1900, 8; "Anti-Lynch Law No Good," 1.

355. "Must Pay for Lynchings," *Cleveland Gazette*, May 13, 1899, 2.

356. Ibid.

357. [No title], *Duluth [MN] News Tribune*, April 25, 1899, 4.

358. "Lynching No Bar to Crime," *Worcester (MA) Daily Spy*, Aug. 27, 1901, 6.

359. "Anti-Lynching Law," 1.

360. "Last Week's Work in the Legislature," *The State*, Feb. 5, 1900, 1.

where cotton was processed.[361] Unlike Brown, however, Harris was in state custody when the mob took him. A constable was escorting Harris to jail on suspicion of arson when a pistol-waving white mob appeared, whisked Harris into the woods, tied him to a tree, and whipped him. He died of injuries to his back and stomach. "Several" members of the coroner's jury realized that the stomach abrasions "were caused by the negro being tied to a tree" while his back was whipped. Horrifyingly, they had "seen such effects before."[362]

As usual, the criminal law proved worthless, despite the best efforts of a "very indignant" circuit judge who ordered a grand jury to remain on the job past its planned discharge date so as to undertake a "rigid examination" of the Harris lynching.[363] Grand jurors found "plenty of evidence" that Harris had been lynched, but no one would name names. Although the judge "excoriat[ed] without mercy" the tight-lipped witnesses,[364] the grand jury still blamed Harris's death on "unknown parties."[365]

Harris's mother sued Anderson County for $10,000 under what the press called "the celebrated lynching law."[366] In the fall of 1900, an Anderson County jury found the county not liable, despite clear evidence of Harris's death from lynching there. The trial judge indignantly "set aside the verdict and ordered another trial."[367] Once again, the jury ruled for the county, the judge declared a mistrial, and the paper trail inconclusively dissipated.[368]

Brown and *Harris* are the two best-documented Article VI cases from the early years, but they were not alone. According to the press, family members sued "several" South Carolina counties in these early years but "without success in one single instance."[369] The facts did not matter. The law did not matter. The indignation of elite judges did not matter. This persistent jury nullification frustrated those who hoped that Article VI would reduce lynchings. Commentators perceived "a sort of tacit understanding"

361. "Confessed and Was 'Whipped,'" *The State*, May 26, 1898, 5.

362. "'Severely Whipped': Death Was the Result," *The State*, May 26, 1898, 5.

363. "The Anderson Whipping Case," *The State*, July 6, 1898, 3.

364. Ibid.

365. "'Severely Whipped,'" 5.

366. "Anderson County Sued for Price of a Lynching," *The State*, March 9, 1901, 1.

367. Ibid.

368. "South Carolina News and Gossip: That Anderson Lynching Case," *The State*, Nov. 29, 1901, 5.

369. "Lawlessness in South Carolina," *The State*, Dec. 25, 1904, 7.

among white jurors "to nullify the law by refusing to find verdicts in lynching cases against the defendant county."[370] The antilynching law, pundits concluded, was "good in theory" but worthless in practice.[371]

The case that broke this losing streak concerned a 1913 lynching in Clarendon County. The victim, a Black seventeen-year-old named Marion Cantey, was accused of assault and battery against a young white man.[372] While a constable escorted Cantey to jail, a masked white mob stole the prisoner away and shot him to death.[373] The victim's father, Madison Cantey, sued Clarendon County for $2,000, the statutory minimum.[374]

There was not much for the jury to decide in this "closely watched" trial.[375] To rule in favor of the victim's father, the jury merely had to find that he was his son's legal representative and that his son had died by lynching in Clarendon County. Trial testimony conclusively demonstrated both things. After deliberating "for many hours," the jury found the county liable.[376] The county appealed but lost.[377]

Cantey v. Clarendon County was a turning point. Thereafter, Article VI plaintiffs fared consistently well. Four factors underlay this trend. *First*, as lynching grew less socially acceptable, jury behavior changed. South Carolinians no longer favored lynch law, a commentator asserted in 1915, citing, among other things, the *Cantey* case. "In Clarendon County lately, a jury gave to the family of a victim of lynching compensatory damages and the [state] Supreme Court sustained the verdict. . . . Lynching is, in truth, on the decline."[378] Successful Article VI cases both resulted from and reinforced this trend.[379]

---

370. "Must Rest on Public Sentiment," *The State*, Oct. 5, 1899, 6.

371. "The Morrison Lynching," *Yorkville Enquirer*, quoted in *The State*, Oct. 14, 1905, 4.

372. "Young Negro Boy Lynched in S.C.," *Augusta Chronicle*, Feb. 24, 1913, 10.

373. Ibid.

374. "County Must Pay for Mob's Actions," *The State*, Oct. 1, 1914, 11.

375. Ibid.

376. Ibid.

377. The county argued that the trial judge had erroneously defined the word "mob." Cantey v. Clarendon County, 101 S.C. 141, 143 (1915); "Doings of the Race," *Cleveland Gazette*, May 29, 1915, 2. In addition, a state senator from Clarendon unsuccessfully proposed deleting the county-liability provisions from Article VI. "Would Amend Law as to Lynchings," *The State*, Jan. 29, 1915, 6.

378. "The Counsels of Despair," *The State*, June 21, 1915, 4.

379. On the legal system's power to influence local views regarding lynching's legitimacy, see William D. Carrigan, *The Making of a Lynching Culture: Violence and Vigilantism in Central Texas, 1836–1916* (Urbana and Chicago: University of Illinois Press, 2004).

Second, favorable appellate rulings from the State Supreme Court, including *Brown* and *Cantey*, gradually reduced legal wiggle room. Juries had a harder time ruling against plaintiffs.

Third, plaintiffs learned that tempering their demands increased their chances of success. Article VI prescribed a $2,000 floor for damage awards but no ceiling. Early plaintiffs generally sought $10,000 or more. As far as the record reveals, they consistently lost.[380] Beginning with *Cantey*, plaintiffs and their lawyers requested less—often just the $2000 minimum—but won more.

Finally, some trial judges began directing verdicts in favor of plaintiffs. *Sims v. York County* set that precedent. In the summer of 1917, amid the hyperpatriotism surrounding US involvement in World War I, W. T. Sims, a Black preacher, spoke out against the military draft. He also made "allegedly disparaging remarks about a woman."[381] A "score or more" of furious residents silenced Sims forever. Three white people and two Black people were tried for Sims's murder. All five were acquitted.[382] Shortly thereafter, counsel for Mary Sims, the preacher's widow, proposed an out-of-court settlement to the York County Board of Commissioners. If the Board refused, she would sue under Article VI.[383] The county, being "opposed to paying the money,"[384] rolled the dice and litigated. At first, this seemed like the right call. York County juries, like others before them, twice found the county not liable.[385] Both times trial judges set aside the verdicts as being "contrary to the greater weight of the evidence."[386] The third time, the trial judge decided to direct a verdict for $2,000 in favor of Mary Sims.[387] In doing so, he set a precedent that many subsequent trial judges would follow. By the mid-1920s, according to press reports, directed verdicts that ordered counties to pay surviving family members $2000 were "customarily

380. The lone known white plaintiff to sue under Article VI fared particularly badly. In addition to receiving zero of the $50,000 that he sought, he was ordered to pay $350 in court costs. "South Carolina Supreme Court," *The State*, July 27, 1906, 3; "Noted Lynching Case Dismissed by Courts," *The State*, April 30, 1907, 1; Castles v. Lancaster, 74 S.C. 512 (1906).

381. "Verdict of Acquittal in York Lynching Trial," *Augusta Chronicle*, Nov. 30, 1917, 4.

382. [No Title], *Charlotte Observer*, Aug. 31, 1917, 10; "Verdict of Acquittal in York Lynching Trial,"4.

383. "To Sue York County for Death of Sims," *The State*, Feb. 7, 1918, 2.

384. Ibid.

385. "York Colored Woman Sues for Damages for Lynching of Husband," *Augusta Chronicle*, July 24, 1918, 3.

386. "Widow of Victim Awarded Verdict," *The State*, Dec. 6, 1919, 2.

387. Ibid.

given."[388] By then, Article VI plaintiffs consistently won at trial—often by directed verdict.[389]

Surviving family members of lynch victims also fared well on appeal. A total of eight Article VI cases reached the South Carolina Supreme Court. Surviving family members won five of them. Even the three losses did not constitute substantive defeats. In *Green v. West* (1931), for example, the widow of a Black lynching victim sued the county where her husband was slain.[390] She won at trial and was awarded $2,000 in exemplary damages. After the county claimed that it was unable to pay, the plaintiff asked the South Carolina Supreme Court to compel the county to levy a special tax so that it could pay the judgment. The Supreme Court refused on the ground that it lacked the power to compel counties to levy taxes. Notwithstanding this victory on appeal, however, the county still owed the plaintiff $2,000, plus interest.[391]

By the time of Willie Earle's lynching in 1947, thus, surviving family members of lynch victims had worn deep paths to courtroom doors. More often than not, they had won civil damages under Article VI. Tessie Earle, Willie Earle's mother, was next.

Tessie's Earle's Civil Suit

"Study this face," the *Baltimore Afro-American* instructed readers, following the mass acquittal of Willie Earle's lynchers in May of 1947. There, in grainy black and white, was Tessie Earle. "We ask you to study this mother's face and look beyond the . . . deep-set lines that anguish has written there. . . . Read in her eyes the helpless query, 'Why should my boy have been lynched in a land of freedom and democracy?'" Editors hauntingly reminded readers: "It Could Have Been Your Son."[392]

The Willie Earle lynching and trial shocked the nation. Advocates of a federal antilynching law hoped that the episode might change people's minds. A group called the National Negro Day Committee thought that

388. "May Sue County for Lynching of 3," *New York Times*, Nov. 14, 1926, 27.

389. See Kirkland v. Allendale County, 128 S.C. 541 (1924); Green v. Greenville County, 176 S.C. 433 (1935).

390. "Aged Man Seized," *Negro World* (New York, NY), May 10, 1930, 8; "Southern Editors Concede Innocent Man Was Lynched," *Plaindealer*, Nov. 14, 1930, 1.

391. Green v. West, 161 S.C. 161 (1931).

392. "Opinion: It Could Have Been Your Son," *Baltimore Afro-American*, May 24, 1947, 4.

public sympathy for Willie's mother Tessie might change people's hearts.[393] In late May of 1947, immediately after the Greenville trial ended, the Committee invited Earle's grieving mother Tessie to New York City. It was her first time there.[394] Tessie Earle was uncomfortable in the spotlight[395] but decided to add her voice to the call for a federal antilynching law in order "to see that other mothers [were] protected against what happened to [her]."[396] "If they [are] going to keep lynching people," she added, "they might as well close up the jails and have no law.'"[397]

The National Negro Day Committee knew that South Carolina allowed family members of lynch victims to recover damages but was fuzzy on the legal details. With considerable fanfare, before thousands of spectators at a Manhattan rally, the Committee announced its intent to help Tessie Earle file two $250,000 civil suits: one against the City of Greenville, the other against lynchers themselves. Any money recovered in these suits would go not to Earle but to "Negro educational societies in the South."[398]

The high point of Earle's New York stay was supposed to be a "Negro Freedom Rally" at Madison Square Garden in mid-June. Publicity posters for the event advertised such "Brilliant Speakers" as "Militant Congressman" Adam Clayton Powell Jr. and a "Star Studded Program" of entertainers, including Bill "Bojangles" Robinson.[399] The event also would include a "Special Presentation" from Tessie Earle: "a mother's reaction" to lynching, as "only the mother of a mob victim" could provide.[400] A collection for Tessie Earle would be taken up at the event.

The big day came; big crowds did not. Factionalism on the Black left

393. The National Negro Day Committee was an advisory committee of Black community leaders led by newspaperman Chandler Owen. It spearheaded an effort to set aside a separate day for Black people—Negro Day—at the Chicago World's Fair of 1933. Cheryl R. Ganz, *The 1933 Chicago World's Fair: A Century of Progress* (Champaign: University of Illinois Press, 2008), 113; Christopher Robert Reed, "A Century of Progress," University of Virginia, accessed March 7, 2009, http://xroads.virginia.edu/~UG00/3on1/worldfair/plantsho.htm.

394. "Mother Can't Talk about Lynched Son," *New York Herald Tribune*, May 26, 1947, 13.

395. Ibid.

396. "How Bush Escaped Mob! Mother of Willie Earle Backs Increased Demand for Anti-Lynch Law," *Norfolk Journal and Guide*, May 31, 1947, 1.

397. "Mother Can't Talk about Lynched Son," 13.

398. "Mother Will Sue in Son's Lynching," *New York Times*, May 28, 1947, 20; "Mother Will Sue County," *New Journal and Guide*, June 7, 1947, 2.

399. Advertisement, "Lynching Must Stop!" *(New York) People's Voice*, May 31, 1947, 20.

400. "Mob Victim's Mother to Urge Lynch Law," *Atlanta Daily World*, May 28, 1947, 1.

resulted in low turnout and rival-group picketing outside. Madison Square Garden could hold twenty-thousand people. Sponsors hoped for ten thousand. Perhaps three thousand showed up—Adam Clayton Powell and Bill Robinson not among them.[401] In the words of one Black weekly, the rally was "a pitiable fizzle . . . the people stayed away in droves."[402] Adding injury to insult, much of the money collected in Tessie Earle's name wound up in other people's pockets.[403] Like so many other small-town sheep, Tessie Earle surely left the Big Apple feeling as though she had been fleeced.

There was an upside, however. During Earle's Manhattan stay, her hosts took her to the headquarters of the NAACP, seeking litigation advice.[404] NAACP officials were intrigued, but when it came to litigation, they preferred to fly solo. They did not want to partner with the National Negro Day Committee,[405] which, as an internal NAACP memo warned, seemed "about to exploit Mrs. Earle for their purpose."[406] Soon, however, Tessie Earle broke with the National Negro Day Committee and agreed to work with the NAACP. NAACP lawyers Thurgood Marshall, Franklin Williams, Constance Baker Motley, and Harold Boulware would represent her.[407]

Several aspects of Tessie Earle's Article VI case appealed to the NAACP. Up until that era, antilynching had been the group's top priority.[408] The

---

401. Julius J. Adams, "Fight over Freedom Rally Cash," *New York Amsterdam News*, June 21, 1947, 1.

402. "D. A. Intervenes: Mrs. Earle Gets $645 Check from Freedom Rally Collection," *People's Voice*, June 28, 1947, 2.

403. Adams, "Fight over Freedom Rally Cash," 1. The district attorney helped Tessie Earle recover most of the money collected in her name. "D. A. Intervenes," *People's Voice*, June 28, 1947, 2.

404. Memorandum to Mr. [Roy] Wilkins from Franklin H. Williams, In re: Willie Earle, deceased, June 5, 1947, copy in author's possession and available upon request.

405. According to historian Kenneth Janken, the NAACP "as a rule would not get involved . . . [with other civil rights organizations] as junior partners." Janken adds that NAACP attorneys had little regard for attorneys who were not in the NAACP. Kenneth Janken, interviewed by Olivia Daniels, University of North Carolina, Chapel Hill, April 13, 2018.

406. Correspondence from/to Walter White, undated, NAACP correspondence, NAACP Papers, copy in author's possession and available upon request.

407. Earle v. Greenville County.

408. Walter White, *Rope and Faggot: A Biography of Judge Lynch* (Notre Dame: University of Notre Dame Press, 2001), 203; Beth Tompkins Bates, "A New Crowd Challenges the Agenda of the Old Guard in the NAACP, 1933–1941," *American Historical Review* 102, no. 2 (April 1997): 357; I. A. Newby, *Black Carolinians: A History of Blacks in South Carolina from 1895 to 1968* (Columbia: University of South Carolina Press, 1973), 296.

NAACP saw itself as the nation's lynching watchdog. Because it maintained local chapters throughout the South and enjoyed close ties to Black newspapers, the group quickly learned about vigilante murders, wherever they occurred. It collected this local information and disseminated it nationally.[409] The NAACP also dispatched representatives[410] to investigate lynchings, since, in Executive Secretary Walter White's words, "little confidence could be placed in the reports" of local officials.[411] A powerful symbol of the group's urgent fight against racist vigilantism was a large flag that hung with disturbing regularity outside the windows of its New York offices. It read: "A Man was Lynched Yesterday."[412]

The NAACP may have been particularly interested in Tessie Earle's case because it involved Article VI. Executive Secretary White liked civil-damage statutes and considered South Carolina's to be the gold standard.[413] In the 1930s, the NAACP included a county-liability provision in a proposed federal antilynching bill. When asked whether this measure would be constitutional, NAACP lawyers noted that state courts had consistently upheld similar provisions. The first example that they cited was Article VI.[414] Representing Tessie in a county-liability case would enable NAACP lawyers to wield a respected legal weapon.

The group also appreciated the public relations potential of the Earle case. When choosing among possible test cases, the NAACP routinely considered whether a prospective client was likely to evoke public sympathy.[415] Tessie Earle passed that test. Early in 1948, half a year after Earle's Manhattan trip, NAACP attorney Franklin H. Williams reflected on her case's potential public impact. "I do not think that this case is so old" as to have

---

409. W. Fitzhugh Brundage, interviewed by Olivia Daniels, University of North Carolina, Chapel Hill, April 2, 2018. Janken, interviewed by Olivia Daniels.

410. William F. Pinar, "The N.A.A.C.P. and the Struggle for Antilynching Federal Legislation, 1917–1950," *Counterpoints* 163 (2001): 721. A Langston Hughes poem noted that White's Caucasian appearance was an asset in his battle against southern lynchings. Langston Hughes, "The Ballad of Walter White," in Kenneth R. Janken, *White: The Biography of Walter White, Mr. NAACP* (New York: New Press, 2003).

411. Janken, *White*, 187, 216.

412. "A Man was Lynched Yesterday," Library of Congress, accessed Sept. 27. 2022, https://www.loc.gov/pictures/item/2015647092/.

413. Quoted in Roger Didier, "Lynching Exposed," *Washington Tribune*, March 29, 1934, 4.

414. "N.A.A.C.P. News," *Wyandotte (Kansas City, KS) Echo*, Nov. 19, 1937, 1.

415. Brundage, interviewed by Olivia Daniels.

lost its "terrific news value," Williams wrote privately to Thurgood Marshall. "Here we have a case packing a terrific emotional appeal."[416] In other words, both parties stood to benefit. Tessie Earle would get A-list legal representation. In return, the NAACP would get a case that would generate positive publicity and might even rally support for a federal antilynching law.[417]

Although the case was straightforward, lawyers did have a few decisions to make. One was how much money to seek. To rousing Midtown cheers, the National Negro Day Committee had dramatically announced plans to sue for $500,000. Perhaps aware that any award would have to be approved by an all-white jury, and that extravagant requests in the past had failed, NAACP lawyers aimed comparatively low: $5,000.[418]

Another question was whom to sue. The National Negro Day Committee had proposed suing Willie Earle's lynchers directly. The NAACP chose not to do this. Such litigation would present the same obstacles that doomed the criminal trial: speak-no-evil witnesses and see-no-evil jurors. Still, it might have been worth trying. A victory would have made an important statement about justice. A loss, from the NAACP's perspective, could have been better still. Even a weak echo of the indignation that followed the criminal acquittals following the Earle lynching could have boosted support for a federal antilynching law. But the NAACP chose not to devote its scarce legal resources to this labor-intensive struggle. Perhaps it concluded that no amount of indignation would be enough to drive a federal antilynching bill through congressional quicksand.

The National Negro Day Committee also planned to sue the city of Greenville. This made no sense. Article VI applied to counties, not cities. But which county should the NAACP sue? After all, the Willie Earle lynching began in the Pickens County jail and ended over the Greenville County line. The 1895 Constitutional Convention left this issue unresolved. "Suppose they take him [a hypothetical lynching victim] to another county to lynch him; which county is responsible?" a delegate asked during the Arti-

416. Williams continued: "Naturally, we will have to refresh the public's mind through proper build-up, which of course, this Association can do." Memorandum from Franklin H. Williams to Thurgood Marshall, Feb. 10, 1948, NAACP Papers, correspondence, copy in author's possession and available upon request.

417. Harold R. Boulware to Franklin H. Williams, April 10, 1948. NAACP Papers, correspondence.

418. Earle v. Greenville County, 540; Gravely, *They Stole Him Out of Jail*, 304.

cle VI debate in 1895. Nobody answered.[419] Early investigations into the Willie Earle lynching raised some geographical uncertainty. "There was question just which county was the scene of the slaying," the Raleigh *News and Observer* reported. "Earle's body was found . . . at the edge of a scrub-pine thicket two-tenths of a mile inside Greenville County. A trail of blood spots leading to the body indicated he may have been killed elsewhere and hauled to the spot."[420]

NAACP lawyers prudently sued both counties.[421] Greenville was more liable, they thought, since it apparently was the scene of the actual murder. But as attorney Boulware explained to his colleagues, "suing both counties" would get them "to place the blame on one another." "Pickens County will certainly prove that the death occurred in Greenville in court, and Greenville will then have no room to contest this as a fact."[422] Just as Boulware expected, both counties demurred and claimed that the essential elements of the lynching had occurred elsewhere.[423] And as Boulware predicted, the trial court sided with Pickens County, since the most fundamental element of a lynching, the actual killing, had occurred in Greenville County. The trial judge therefore released Pickens County from liability but left the case against Greenville County intact.[424]

Greenville County appealed to the State Supreme Court, arguing that the greater share of blame belonged to the county where the lynching began, not the one where it ended.[425] Greenville should not have to pay for the Pickens County jailer's negligence. Greenville lawyers also cited South Carolina precedent to argue that death was not a necessary part of lynching,[426] and that the primary object of Article VI was to deter future lynchings, not to compensate victims' families for past lynchings. Finding

419. "Considering Corporations," *The State*, Nov. 12, 1895, 2.

420. "Negro in South Carolina Taken from Jail," 1.

421. S.C. Supr. Ct., transcript of Record of Earle v. Greenville County, et al., vol. 351, 4–5 (1959).

422. Harold R. Boulware to Franklin H. Williams, Jan. 5, 1949, NAACP Papers, correspondence.

423. Transcript of Record of Earle v. Greenville County, 6–8.

424. Ibid., 13–14; "S.C. Judge Says He'll Hold County for Earle's Death," *Atlanta Daily World*, April 2, 1949, 1.

425. Earle v. Greenville County, "Argument of Appellant," vol. 351, 10.

426. Ibid., 7, 11; Transcript of Record of Earle v. Greenville County, 13. In support of this argument, Greenville County cited Kirkland v. Allendale County, 128 S.C. 541 (1924).

Pickens County liable, Greenville argued, would have the most powerful deterrent effect.[427]

On the other side of the appeal were two respondents: Pickens County and Tessie Earle. Both wanted the Supreme Court to uphold the trial court's ruling. Pickens County argued that "forcible seizure" of a prisoner did not a lynching make.[428] What if the mob had seized Earle from jail, only to return him unharmed? Surely that would not constitute a lynching, the county argued.[429] The shotgun blasts that took Earle's life were fired in Greenville County. Greenville was liable, having had the "last clear chance" to prevent the lynching. Punishing this failure would inspire county residents to work harder to prevent future lynchings, the NAACP argued.[430]

Late in 1949, the South Carolina Supreme Court ruled in favor of Tessie Earle and Pickens County, on grounds that liability fell to "the county where . . . lynching takes place." Although some elements of the lynching had taken place in Pickens, the decisive ones had occurred in Greenville County. There the liability lay.[431]

The Black press cheered. Tessie Earle "got the green-light . . . from the State Supreme Court to go ahead with her suit for damages," the *Baltimore Afro-American* approvingly reported. "The court held that Earle was lynched in Greenville County by a mob that took him forcibly from the Pickens jail," and that it would be "quibbling to say that the complaint fails to allege a lynching in Greenville County" simply because "all of the stated elements" of a lynching were not present.[432]

The Supreme Court ruling paved the way for a jury trial back in Greenville County. Before this could occur, however, the two parties settled out of court. Greenville County agreed to pay Tessie Earle $2000.[433] NAACP lawyers guessed that no Greenville County jury would award more than that.[434]

427. Earle v. Greenville County, "Argument of Appellant," vol. 351, 12–14; citing Kirkland v. Allendale County.

428. Earle v. Greenville County, "Argument of Respondent," 2.

429. Ibid., 2.

430. Ibid., 4–6; Earle v. Greenville County, "Memorandum on Behalf of Respondent, Tessie Earle," 8–10.

431. Earle v. Greenville County.

432. "Lynch Victim's Mother Permitted to Sue County," *Baltimore Afro-American*, Nov. 26, 1949, 2.

433. "$2000 Paid in Lynch Case," *New York Times*, March 17, 1950, 7.

434. Gravely, *They Stole Him Out of Jail*, 307.

By settling, Greenville County capped its financial exposure, limited legal expenses, and avoided additional bad press. Tessie Earle guaranteed herself some money while avoiding the stress of another trial. The NAACP freed legal resources to devote to areas that had recently become top priorities: voting rights, employment discrimination, and school segregation.[435] Although some NAACP officials had been keen on the public-relations aspects of Tessie Earle's suit, others may have worried that a high-profile trial victory in a southern state court would make federal action on lynching appear less necessary. Moreover, Tessie Earle's suit was not a test case. Victory would not change the law. Settlement was acceptable to all.

One final obstacle remained. Emma Brown, widow of Thomas Brown, the murdered cab driver, filed a civil suit against the Estate of Willie Earle for $10,000. Brown's suit cited the "excruciating physical and mental pain" inflicted on the Brown family by "the brutal assault of the said Willie Earle."[436] As long as Emma Brown's suit lasted, Tessie Earle would not be allowed to cash her settlement check. Finally, late in 1956, the courts ruled that Article VI payments belonged to Tessie Earle, not her son's estate. Therefore, Emma Brown, who wanted Willie Earle to be found posthumously liable for the death of her cab-driving husband, had no claim to that money. In early 1958, over a decade after her son's death by lynching, Tessie Earle received her Article VI settlement award. With interest, it totaled $3,000.[437]

Conclusion

Every murder has multiple victims. The surviving relatives of Willie Earle, like those of Thomas Brown, sustained deep emotional wounds. Tessie Earle's never healed. "Grandma Tessie . . . never got over" Willie's lynching, her granddaughter later recalled. "It caused distress for the whole family, but particularly for her."[438]

435. See August Meier, "The NAACP as a Reform Movement, 1909–1965: To Reach the Conscience of America," *Journal of Southern History* 59 (Feb. 1993): 24–25; Frederickson, "The Slowest State," 166; Gravely, *They Stole Him Out of Jail*, 303.

436. "News in Tabloid," *Baltimore Afro-American*, Feb. 26, 1949, 5.

437. Gravely, *The Stole Him Out of Jail*, 220; Tessie Earle (Robinson) v. Emma D. Brown, S.C. Ct. Comm. Pleas, (Nov. 26, 1956). Our thanks to Will Gravely for providing us with a photocopy of this ruling.

438. Eloise Earle, quoted in Vince Jackson, "Clemson Family Remembers State's Last

Black distress radiated far beyond South Carolina. Following the mass acquittals of Willie Earle's murderers, one national Black leader wailed, "How long, O God, will a man be treated worse than a beast just because his skin is black!"[439]

Indignation spurred action. The acquittals caused Black Greenvillians to organize, causing one local civil rights pioneer to conclude that "Willie Earle's death was not in vain."[440] Black residents boycotted the taxicab companies whose drivers had lynched Willie Earle. They petitioned Greenville to license Black cabbies. Doing so, they hoped, would open jobs to Black drivers while also reducing conflicts between Black passengers and white cabbies. The time had come to "Jim Crow the taxicabs, like they Jim Crow[ed] . . . everything else," reasoned one Black man.[441] Black South Carolinians also demanded representation on juries. State courts served "both races," and therefore "ought to have juries on which both races . . . are represented," they argued.[442] Fairer juries would produce more justice—and fewer lynchings. "Lynchers would be less inclined to lynch were they assured beforehand that their penalty would be partially fixed by the people they wronged."[443]

The Earle lynching also stirred white Greenvillians. Some sought personal atonement. Late one night, following the acquittals, a local Black minister heard a knock at his door. There stood a lyncher, sobbing. "Reverend, I am a marked man," the cabbie wept, for the lynchers' names were "on every tongue," and people, "white and black, show[ed] them visible contempt." The Black minister kneeled with the white lyncher and "prayed for his soul."[444]

Lynching Victim," *Independent Mail* (Anderson, SC), Feb. 17, 2011, http://archive.independentmail.com/news/local/clemson-family-remembers-states-last-lynching-victim-ep-413434413-349365891.html/

439. Benjamin E. Mays, "South Does it Again," *Pittsburgh Courier*, Jun. 14, 1947, 7. Mays, a South Carolina native, was president of Morehouse College.

440. Oral history interview of A. J. Whittenburg by Will Gravely, Greenville, SC, December 13, 1982, University of South Carolina Digital Collections, https://digital.tcl.sc.edu/digital/collection/gravely/id/32/.

441. Bird, "Lynching Town Glad Pressure of Trial Is Off," 3.

442. "Lynching, An Incorporation," *Atlanta Daily World*, June 4, 1947, 6, originally from the *Lighthouse Informer*, a Black paper published in South Carolina.

443. Ibid.

444. McCray, "The Need for Changing," 5. According to this article, the minister related this story to McCray personally the previous week. McCray was a Black South Carolina journalist. Herb Frazier, "McCray, John Henry," *South Carolina Encyclopedia*.

Other whites sought atonement on a broader scale. White Greenville, according to the Black press, did "some serious stock-taking," with the "express purpose of improving the lot of its colored citizens."[445] The city vowed to improve Black conditions in health, sanitation, law enforcement, transportation, recreation, and employment. "I covered the trial of Willie Earle's alleged lynchers from the vantage point of a seat in the [segregated] balcony of the Greenville County Court," a Black journalist wrote three years later.

> I was exposed to the virus of racial prejudice in its worst form. And I saw the accused white men freed of all charges in spite of the overwhelming evidence against them. . . . But . . . Greenville is taking some steps on its own in trying to dim the bitter memory of the Willie Earle lynching stigma. And if the Greenville experiment is as successful as its sponsors hope for, and becomes a pattern for the entire South, then the community, paradoxically enough, will have the lynching . . . to thank.[446]

The reform spirit spread beyond Greenville. Shortly after the acquittals, in July of 1947, US District Court Judge J. Waites Waring, of Charleston, struck down the South Carolina Democratic Party's all-white primary. "It is time for South Carolina to rejoin the union," declared Waring, who was white. "I cannot see where the skies will fall" if Black South Carolinians vote, he added.[447] The lawyers who convinced Judge Waring to strike down the white primary included Thurgood Marshall and Harold Boulware, both of whom also represented Tessie Earle.[448] Black litigation, a product of Reconstruction, survived Jim Crow and ultimately helped to weaken it.

The Willie Earle episode contributed to a national change of heart. The mass acquittals sparked northern protests[449] and fueled a national campaign for a federal antilynching law.[450] According to a Gallup poll taken in

---

445. Albert L. Hinton, "Behind the Headlines: Willie Earle May Not Have Lost His Life in Vain After All," *Norfolk Journal and Guide*, June 10, 1950, 14.

446. Ibid. See also, Archie Vernon Huff Jr., *Greenville: The History of the City and County in the South Carolina Piedmont* (Columbia: University of South Carolina Press, 1995), 401.

447. Elmore v. Rice, 72 F. Supp. 516, 527 (1947); "U.S. Judge Outlaws 'Private Club' Rule," *Baltimore Afro-American*, July 19, 1947, 1.

448. "U.S. Judge Outlaws 'Private Club' Rule," *Baltimore Afro-American*, July 19, 1947, 1.

449. "Quick Federal Action against Lynchers Demanded," *People's Voice*, June 7, 1947, 3.

450. "Anti-Lynching Day Urged," *New York Times*, June 7, 1947, 30.

the summer of 1947, shortly after the mass acquittals, 69 percent of American respondents, including 56 percent of southerners, now favored such a law.[451] Ten years previously, national support for a federal antilynching law stood at just 44 percent.[452] In the autumn of 1947, *To Secure These Rights*, a report prepared by President Truman's Committee on Civil Rights, discussed the Earle case, lamented the "almost complete immunity from punishment enjoyed by lynchers," and perceptively described lynching as "the ultimate threat" that reinforced "all the other disabilities placed upon" Black people.[453] Within a year, Truman desegregated the federal workforce, including the military, denounced lynching as a crime "against which [he could not] speak too strongly," and sent Congress a ten-point civil rights program that included an antilynching proposal.[454]

Not everyone moved Left, however. Following their respective antilynching episodes, Ben Tillman and Strom Thurmond both moved Right. The two leaders' paths differed, however, and that difference reveals a gradual weakening of white supremacy over the twentieth century's first half.

For most of his time as South Carolina governor, Ben Tillman both favored white supremacy and opposed lynching. After moving to the US Senate and achieving more of a national profile, however, he adjusted. He retained white supremacist goals, becoming arguably the nation's "leading exponent" of "white rule"[455] but abandoned antilynching means. While governor, he had sought to discourage federal intervention by restraining the lynching mindset in the South. Now, as Senator, he sought to discourage federal intervention by inflaming the lynching mindset in the North. During the century's opening decade, seemingly whenever the Senate was not in session, Tillman, like a Gettysburg-bound Robert E. Lee, charged north and preemptively attacked white northerners who might otherwise have

451. "Gallup Poll Reveals 69% Want Federal Lynch Law: Acquittal of 28 S.C. Lynchers Causes Change of Heart; 56% of Southerners Favorable," *Baltimore Afro-American*, July 12, 1947, 15.

452. Gallup Organization, Gallup Poll # 1937-0106, China and Japan/Automobiles/Finances, Question 13, USGALLUP.37-106.Q11, Gallup Organization, Roper Center for Public Opinion Research, Cornell University, Ithaca, NY,, 1937.

453. United States President's Committee on Civil Rights, *To Secure These Rights: The Report of the President's Committee on Civil Rights* (New York: Simon and Schuster, 1947), 24.

454. Harry Truman, "The Text of President Truman's Message on Civil Rights," *New York Times*, Feb. 3, 1948, 22; "Anti-Lynching Law, Civil Liberties Unit Sought by Truman," *New York Times*, Feb. 3, 1948, 1.

455. "Tillman Says the Whites Must Rule," *New York Herald*, Nov. 14, 1898, 4.

been tempted to defend Black rights. He spoke in cities and towns, from New England to the Pacific Northwest. His go-to topic was "The Race Problem." He attacked relentlessly, racist artillery booming: "All men are not created equal and the 'niggers' are not fit to vote";[456] "the negro race is inferior to the white race";[457] "God made the white man out of better clay";[458] the Black man was "only one shade better than a baboon."[459] He challenged white listeners to imagine how they would respond if they lived, as he did, in a majority-Black state. "Who wants to be governed by negroes?" he asked his northern listeners. "Answer me, you in the audience. Nobody?"[460]

A frequent target of Tillman's wrath was the Fifteenth Amendment. Citing no evidence, Tillman asserted that "nine-tenths of the people in the Northern states now believe[d] that the country made a grave mistake in passing the constitutional amendments which give the negro the right to vote."[461] The remedy was simple: Repeal! "To hell with such a law that puts black feet on white necks," Tillman thundered one night in Cleveland. "What do you say?"

"You're right," answered half a dozen Ohioans.[462]

No lecture was complete without a discussion of lynching. Although Tillman had strongly opposed lynching during most of his governorship, and at the 1895 convention, he packed only prolynching arguments in his northbound satchel. His "eloquent"[463] justifications stressed the need to defend white women against Black men. When the unthinkable occurred—that crime too awful to name—lynching was not just excusable. It was praiseworthy, he said. Lynchings saved white women the trauma of testifying in court, gave Black fiends exactly what they deserved, and brutally discouraged future attacks.[464] Northern whites would do no less, Tillman believed. If not, he told a Rhode Island crowd in 1899, he would blush to

456. "Whites Must Rule in South: Senator Tillman Speaks to a Wisconsin Audience," *San Antonio Express*, Aug. 5, 1901, 2.

457. "The Race Problem as Viewed in the South," *Worcester Daily Spy*, March 19, 1902, 1.

458. "Tillman is Unbridled," *Charlotte Observer*, Nov. 27, 1906, 8.

459. Ibid.

460. "Tillman Speaks to Quiet Crowd," *Plaindealer*, Dec. 8, 1906,

461. "Disfranchisement Is Tillman's Solution," *Bellingham (WA) Herald*, Sept. 26, 1907, 4.

462. "Tillman Speaks to Quiet Crowd," 1.

463. "Whites Must Rule in South," *San Antonio Express*, Aug. 5, 1901, 2.

464. "The Race Problem as Viewed in the South," 1.

know them.[465] "When niggers assault our women[,] we lynch them," he told an Ohio audience. "You have some lynchings of your own up here . . . showing that you have some red blood left."[466]

Some Black northerners protested.[467] Some white northerners objected.[468] Some elite white southerners lamented his "coarse speech and plantation manners."[469] But overall, Tillman's white supremacist message landed.[470] His prolynching, northern lectures were "frequently applauded."[471] "The people of the North are becoming more and more informed on the subject of the negro," Tillman happily remarked in 1905. "They are respecting our actions."[472] A Black South Carolinian despondently agreed: "Senator Tillman not only has a large number of sympathizers through the South, but I believe he has a larger number in the North."[473] Had Robert E. Lee experienced equal success in his northern campaign, the Confederate States of America might yet exist.

Decades later, another gifted South Carolina politician followed Ben Tillman's path from Edgefield County to the national stage. J. Strom Thurmond learned his politics from "Pitchfork" Ben.[474] Both men served four years as South Carolina governor, during which they took conspicuous antilynching stances. Both men subsequently served long careers in the US Senate. But whereas Tillman's turn-of-the-century defense of Jim Crow included full-throated endorsements of both white supremacy and lynching, Thurmond's midcentury segregationism did not. Though widely considered to be "one of white supremacy's leading spokesmen,"[475] Strom Thurmond thought it prudent both to distance himself from white supremacist

465. "He Lectures New England," *Boston Journal*, Sept. 5, 1899, 2; "The Race Problem as Viewed in the South," 1.

466. "Tillman Speaks to Quiet Crowd,"

467. "Troubles of Senator Tillman," *New York Age*, Nov. 29, 1906, 4.

468. "Tillman Roasted!," *Cleveland Gazette*, Aug. 17, 1901, 1. See also "Tillman Is Excoriated," *Duluth (MN) News Tribune*, Aug. 12, 1901, 5.

469. "Tillman's Lynching Speech," *Charlotte Observer*, Aug. 7, 1901, 4, quoting *The State*.

470. New York City Democrats made Tillman the guest of honor at their "annual blowout" in 1906. "Tillman to Be Honored," *Portland (OR) New Age*, Feb. 3, 1906, 4.

471. "Tillman Speaks to Quiet Crowd," 1; "The Race Problem as Viewed in the South," 1.

472. "Ben Tillman Is an Advocate of Lynch Law," 1.

473. "Mr. Tillman and the Negro," *Springfield Republican*, June 27, 1903, 13.

474. "Last-Ditch Southerner," *New York Times*, Aug. 30, 1957, 20.

475. "Senator Strom Thurmond Says," *Pittsburgh Courier*, Dec. 21, 1957, 10. See also *New York Age*, Aug. 19, 1950, 11.

extremes and consistently to oppose lynching. The virulence of the Jim Crow virus was abating.

As we have seen, the Willie Earle lynching of 1947 pushed the federal government to the left on civil rights. According to Newton's First Law of Southern Politics, that moved South Carolina Governor Strom Thurmond and other Jim Crow defenders to the right. During the presidential election of 1948, a group of white southerners calling itself the States' Rights Democrats, or Dixiecrats, broke away from the national party.[476] "We stand for the segregation of the races and the racial integrity of each race," their platform declared.[477] For president, the Dixiecrats chose Strom Thurmond. The South Carolinian's acceptance speech crackled with Tillmanesque passion. Thurmond "brought howls of rage" when he asked delegates to picture what it would mean if "white folks were compelled to admit Negroes into [their] swimming pools and theaters."[478] But that would never happen, Thurmond vowed. "There are not enough laws on the books of the nation, nor can there be enough, to break down segregation in the South."[479] One Black commentator described Thurmond's presidential campaign as but "a revamped Tillmanism."[480] Thurmond lost in 1948. Thereafter, he repeatedly won, serving forty-seven years in the US Senate. Among his claims to fame was history's longest senate filibuster—twenty-four hours and eighteen minutes—wielded in opposition to a voting rights bill.[481]

And yet, although Thurmond resembled Tillman in some ways, he differed in others. Unlike Tillman, who proudly waved the banner of "white supremacy," Thurmond claimed to be "perturbed" by the label.[482] Thurmond reportedly "cracked down on his 'white supremacy' followers" dur-

---

476. Harlan Trott, "Bolting Democrats in South Form States' Rights Party," *Christian Science Monitor*, July 19, 1948, 1.

477. American Presidency Project, "Platform of the States Rights Democratic Party," UC Santa Barbara, item number 4, accessed Sept. 4, 2022, https://www.presidency.ucsb.edu/documents/platform-the-states-rights-democratic-party.

478. Trott, "Bolting Democrats in South Form States' Rights Party," 1.

479. Strom Thurmond, quoted in "Southern Revolters Inflamed: Name Presidential Candidates on Anti Civil Rights Plank," *Norfolk Journal and Guide*, July 24, 1948, 1.

480. Dean Gordon B. Hancock, "Between the Lines," *Plaindealer*, Sept. 17, 1948, 7.

481. Walt Hickey, "The Longest Filibuster in History Lasted More than a Day—Here's How It Went Down," *Business Insider*, March 6, 2013, https://www.businessinsider.com/longest-filibuster-in-history-strom-thurmond-rand-paul-2013-3.

482. John Popham, "Thurmond, Candidate of Rebels, Decries White Supremacy Idea," *New York Times*, July 20, 1948, 1.

ing his 1948 presidential run, telling reporters that his campaign was about states' rights, not white supremacy.[483] A decade later, while claiming to oppose a civil rights bill on the grounds of federalism only, Thurmond insisted: "I am not interested one whit in the question of white supremacy."[484]

One of Thurmond's go-to moves when seeking to counter charges of racism was to position himself as a "bitter foe of lynching"[485] and to remind listeners of his strong antilynching stance during the Willie Earle affair.[486] Thurmond feared that southern inaction on lynching might prompt Congress to pass a federal antilynching law that could, in turn, beget additional federal action. Thurmond knew that lynching was deeply unpopular and did not want civil rights proponents to capitalize on the issue.[487] "We are all opposed to lynching," he told a Maryland audience in 1948. "It is nothing but murder—the worst form of murder."[488] (He then reminded listeners that murder was a state crime, not a federal crime.[489]) And unlike Ben Tillman decades earlier, Thurmond carved out no exception for alleged cases of rape. Lynching was "the worst form of murder," no matter the circumstances.[490] The distance separating Ben Tillman from his protégé suggests how much the politics of lynching evolved, even among staunch segregationists, during the twentieth century's first half.[491]

One of Strom Thurmond's arguments against a federal antilynching law during his 1948 presidential run was that it was unnecessary, since the South "ha[d] almost wiped out lynching" on its own.[492] That was an exaggeration. But it was not outlandish. In South Carolina, lynching peaked at the end of the nineteenth century, then declined steadily: sixty-four South Carolina lynchings in the 1890s, forty-three in the 1900s, twenty-nine in the 1910s, eleven in the 1920s, eight in the 1930s. Willie Earle's lynching, in

483. Ibid.

484. "Last-Ditch Southerner," *New York Times*, Aug. 30, 1957, 20.

485. "Thurmond Calls Lynching Murder," *New York Times*, July 18, 1948, 3.

486. Popham, "Thurmond, ," 1.

487. "'Rebel' Democrat's Platform: Lynching Case Recalled," *Manchester Guardian*, July 21, 1948, 6; Popham, "Thurmond," 1.

488. "Thurmond Attacks Civil Rights Points," *New York Times*, Oct. 3, 1948, 40.

489. Ibid.

490. "Thurmond Brands Civil Rights as Red Inspired," *Atlanta Daily World*, Sept. 1, 1948, 2; "Thurmond Calls Lynching Murder," *New York Times*, July 18, 1948, 3.

491. "Progress of Justice," *New York Times*, Jan. 3, 1948, 12.

492. "Thurmond Warns of Rights Strife," *New York Times*, Aug. 1, 1948, 44.

1947, was the state's fourth that decade, and the only one in the nation that year. To date, South Carolina has recorded no other lynching.[493]

Problems, of course, persisted. As lynching declined, capital punishment rose, peaking nationally in the 1930s. The inverse relationship between the two forms of killing was more than coincidental. Lynching opponents consistently urged mobs to let the law take its course. Too frequently, the law's course entailed a rushed conviction and a hasty death sentence. Capital punishment, like lynching, was disproportionately southern and disproportionately Black.[494] Police brutality was another racialized law-enforcement concern that some activists saw rising as lynching fell. "Who knows this any better than Negroes?" a Black pundit rhetorically asked in 1948. "We must fight just as vigorously to end police brutality as we are fighting to put an end to . . . lynching."[495] Work remained.

As for Article VI, racial progressives have long misunderstood it. When Tessie Earle won her settlement in the 1950s, some observers wrongly assumed that her victory was unprecedented. "For the first time in recorded history in the U.S.," a Black newspaper reported, "the family of a lynch victim was compensated by the authorities."[496] In fact, as described above, a long line of Black litigants had previously won Article VI compensation. More recently, the Equal Justice Initiative (EJI), which has worked hard to raise awareness of lynching history, wrongly assumed that Tessie Earle lost her case.[497] In fact, she won and received $3,000. And the definitive study of Ben Tillman and white supremacy, far from untangling the origins of Article VI, fails to mention it.[498]

Existing accounts misunderstand two important things. They overlook the extent to which Article VI, from its inception forward, was supported by white elites, most of whom were devoted white supremacists. Admit-

493. Tolnay and Beck, "Public Vic List."

494. Robert M. Bohm, *DeathQuest: An Introduction to the Theory and Practice of Capital Punishment in the United States*, 4th ed. (Waltham, MA: Anderson Publishing, 2011), 10–12; "Executions in the U.S., 1608–2002: The Espy File," Death Penalty Information Center, accessed June 18, 2020, https://deathpenaltyinfo.org/executions/executions-overview/executions-in-the-u-s-1608-2002-the-espy-file.

495. "Yes One Lynching, But," *Atlanta Daily World*, Jan. 6, 1948, 6.

496. "State Pays Family of Lynching Victim," *New York Amsterdam News*, Jan. 6, 1951, 2.

497. "White Mob Lynches Willie Earle Near Greenville, South Carolina," Equal Justice Initiative, accessed Sept. 4, 2022, https://calendar.eji.org/racial-injustice/feb/17.

498. Kantrowitz, *Benjamin Tillman.*

tedly, occasional white demagogues promoted lynching as a virtuous response to perceived Black threats.[499] But these leaders were the exception.[500] Most elite southern whites—clergy, press, bench, bar, political leaders—regarded lynching as, to quote a group of South Carolina ministers in 1911, a stain on the state's "honor and dignity."[501] Antilynching white supremacy was no oxymoron. Indeed, it was the dominant political force in South Carolina for most of the Jim Crow era. Its adherents favored disfranchisement and segregation but opposed lynching. They believed that their opposition to lynching would strengthen Jim Crow. In the short run, though not the long run, they may have been right. Throughout, the most important lynching debates in South Carolina did not pit white people against Black people, as misleadingly suggested by the acquittal photograph at the beginning of this chapter. They pitted upper-class white people against lower-class white people.

Another underappreciated feature of Article VI history is how frequently—and how successfully—Black litigants invoked the measure in court. The law's architects relied on financial disincentives to change behavior. Raise the cost of lynching, they reasoned, and demand would fall. But the measure was not self-enacting. In order for its market mechanisms to work, the relatives of lynching victims had to sue. And they had to win. Considering the context—Jim Crow-era South Carolina—neither was guaranteed.

Most surviving family members of lynch victims, like most people, most of the time, did not go to court. Some may have been unaware of Article VI. Others probably were unsure how to sue. Others may have been scared—and with good reason. Every step of the legal process brought risks.[502] Filing any civil suit against white people could be dangerous, for it challenged local traditions of deference. The risks multiplied in postlynching suits, for attackers had already demonstrated a willingness to use violence.[503] Once litigation began, plaintiffs had to present evidence, lifting the

499. "Laws Unjust to Lynchers?" *The State*, Aug. 11, 1911, 4.

500. "Indignation in South Carolina," *Dallas Morning News*, Nov. 14, 1911, 1; "The People's Own Progressive," *Macon Telegraph*, July 21, 1912, 4.

501. "Ministers Speak in Law's Behalf," *The State*, Oct. 19, 1911, 6.

502. [No Title], *Savannah Tribune*, Nov. 25, 1916, 4.

503. Myisha Eatmon to John Wertheimer, personal communication, May 28, 2020. When asked about the sorts of risks that Black litigants might face if they sued under Article VI, Section 6, Ben Tillman biographer Stephen Kantrowitz speculated: "It would have been an

veil of feigned ignorance behind which local whites preferred to mask lynchings. And if a surviving family member won, taxes might rise—never a popular result.

Given these many risks, the number of surviving family members willing to file Article VI cases was impressively high. At the very least, twelve different lynchings resulted in Article VI litigation—about 10 percent of the state's post-1895 lynching total.[504] This is surely an undercount. For instance, our lowball figure does not include the case of Ada Thompson, widow of 1933 lynch victim Bennie Thompson. According to press reports, Ada Thompson "engaged lawyers . . . to file suit against [Greenwood] county for $2000."[505] We chose not to count her planned case because we cannot prove that she ever filed it, although she probably did. Similarly, although the first case in our count was Isaac Brown's 1898 suit against Orangeburg County, a newspaper report published the *previous* year referred to "cases"—plural—that had already arisen under Article VI.[506] We did not count these early cases because we could not document them. But we have good reason to believe that they exist.[507]

In addition to our numerator—twelve Article VI cases—likely being too low, our denominator—one hundred and twenty South Carolina lynchings after 1895—is probably too high. The data set upon which we rely lists seventeen of those one hundred and twenty lynchings as either "probable" or "possible." "Only" 103 post-1895 lynchings in South Carolina are confirmed.[508]

But even our conservative count finds that, at the very least, 10 percent

---

extremely foolhardy . . . thing to do to actually bring a case in the early twentieth century on the basis of such a claim." Stephen Kantrowitz, in Madison, Wisconsin, interviewed via Skype by Frank Carroll, in Davidson, North Carolina, April 18, 2018. My thanks to both Myisha and Steve for generously sharing their knowledge.

504. According to Tolnay and Beck, one hundred and twenty lynchings occurred in South Carolina after 1895, when Article VI was enacted. Tolnay and Beck, "Public Vic List."

505. "South Carolina Widows to Sue for Lynching of Mates," *Washington Tribune*, Nov. 30, 1933, 8.

506. [No Title], *Cleveland Gazette*, May 29, 1897, 2.

507. Similarly, although our count includes just two Article VI cases as of 1904, a South Carolina newspaper in that year reported that Article VI cases had already been filed "in *several* counties of the State [emphasis added]," further evidence that we are under-counting. "Lawlessness in South Carolina: Its Causes and Remedies," *The State*, Dec. 25, 1904, 5.

508. Tolnay and Beck, "Public Vic List."

of South Carolina's post-1895 lynchings resulted in Article VI suits. Black people were missing from the courtroom photograph with which this chapter began but were hardly missing from South Carolina courts in the Jim Crow era. Nor were they ineffective as litigators. In Article VI cases, Black litigants usually won.

Did Article VI work? It is hard to say. The measure certainly failed to live up to the more extravagant claims made on its behalf.[509] Far too many lynchings occurred in South Carolina following the law's enactment for anyone to claim clear victory. Admittedly, South Carolina lynchings did decline steadily following the measure's adoption. But lynching declined everywhere. South Carolina's post-1895 drop was steeper than those of some states but gentler than those of other states. South Carolina and North Carolina, the two southern states with county-liability laws, had two of the lowest lynching levels in the region. Civil-liability laws may have dampened enthusiasm for lynching in these two states. Then again, the existence of comparatively mild lynching cultures in the Carolinas might have facilitated the passage of those laws in the first place. And this experiment is not perfectly controlled. South Carolina's Article VI received a lot of nationwide attention. Its deterrent effects may have crossed state lines.

The difficulty of assessing the measure's effectiveness did not deter legal scholar James Chadbourn. In the 1930s, Chadbourn analyzed all eleven postlynching civil liability laws then in existence nationally. He examined South Carolina's law especially closely, since it had been used more than any other.[510] Chadbourn concluded that Article VI worked. As of his publication date, postlynching fines had been imposed upon six South Carolina counties. Prior to being fined, those counties had all experienced lynching levels that matched or exceeded the state average. After the fines, lynching levels in those counties dropped—to zero. Statewide lynching levels dropped too.[511] If Chadbourn is right, Article VI worked well. To the list of Black antilynching activities—journalism, migration, armed self-defense, political action—perhaps we should add litigation.

Tessie Earle was not passive following her son's lynching. Like many

509. See "Taxation of Lynching," *Cleveland Gazette*, March 16, 1907, 2; and "Anti-Lynch Law," *Columbus Ledger*, Feb. 25, 1916, 4.

510. Chadbourn, *Lynching and the Law*, 50.

511. Ibid., 48-51.

Black predecessors, in a state where courthouse seating was separate and unequal, she sued and won civil damages. Her legal victory did not balance the scales of justice. It did not bring back her son. But it forced an official acknowledgment that lynching was not just a wrong but a public wrong. Her successful legal campaign begs the question: What is justice?[512]

One month after the all-white "acquittal photograph" was snapped, Black journalist John McCray wrote about the ghost of Willie Earle,[513] a specter that rose from Earle's "decaying remains" to haunt the living by decrying the injustice of lynching. Earle's ghost "flits from breast to breast, from race to race, from mind to mind," McCray wrote, reminding them of Earle's unjust death and touching "the hearts of men and women" who are "blind to color" and who believe "in the rights of men."[514]

The Ghost of Willie Earle hovers still.

---

512. One Black commentator darkly considered this question in light of Tessie Earle's lawsuit: "Nobody bothered to ask" Willie Earle "whether or not he valued his life at $2,000 or more. Even if they had been able to communicate with his spirit, the answer would have been anything but satisfactory. Even a ghost would find it . . . difficult to talk with half his head shot away!" Hinton, "Behind the Headlines," D12.

513. For more on the ghost of Willie Earle, see Nancy Roberts, *South Carolina Ghosts: From the Coast to the Mountains* (Columbia: University of South Carolina Press, 1983), 81–92; Terrance Zepke, *Best Ghost Tales of South Carolina: Haunted Houses, Plantations, Inns, and Other Historic Sites* (Sarasota, FL: Pineapple Press, 2004), 21–22; and Jason Profit, *Haunted Greenville, South Carolina* (Charleston, SC: Haunted America, 2011).

514. McCray, "The Need for Changing," 5.

Conclusion

In South Carolina, from the 1840s through the 1940s, race and the law intertwined. On the one hand, advocates of white supremacy established racial categories in the law, sorted people among them, and allocated rights and restrictions accordingly. The resulting distinctions inevitably disadvantaged people of color. On the other hand, the legal system provided a forum within which racial distinctions could be contested.

The ability of Black South Carolinians to challenge racial subordination varied substantially with time. Prior to 1865, South Carolina law provided a sturdy framework for a thoroughly racialized slave society. One's legally designated race, more than any other factor, channeled one's life prospects. By law, white South Carolinians could not be enslaved, but Black South Carolinians were assumed to be so. Even the state's tiny "free-Black" population was, in the words of a prominent legal scholar of the day, "a degraded caste, of inferior rank."[1] White South Carolinians used legal tools to limit the growth of the free-Black community. Their goal was to tighten the legal correlation between race and freedom status. On the eve of the Civil War, some white South Carolinians called for all free Black people in the state to be enslaved or deported.[2]

During this era, Black South Carolinians had almost no ability to mount public claims. No Black South Carolinians, free or enslaved, could vote[3] or serve as legislators.[4] There were no Black judges. There were no Black law-

1. This statement applied nationally, including in South Carolina. James Kent, *Commentaries on American Law*, vol 2 (New York: O. Halsted, 1832), 258.

2. Michael P. Johnson and James L. Roark, eds., *No Chariot Let Down: Charleston's Free People of Color on the Eve of the Civil War* (Chapel Hill: University of North Carolina Press, 1985).

3. South Carolina Constitution of 1790, art. I, § 4.

4. Ibid., art. I, § 6, § 8.

yers. There were no Black jurors. Black witnesses could not testify in superior court—or against white people in any court.[5] Black people could not carry guns.[6] State law even formally barred Black people, enslaved or not, from assembling privately "in a confined . . . place of meeting." If they attempted to do so—such as, say, to share grievances or plan protests—officers of the law were "authorized to enter and if necessary, to break open doors" to disperse the gathering. The law also authorized those officers to impose "corporal punishment" on the "slaves, free negroes, mulattos, or mestizos" so assembled.[7]

Enslaved South Carolinians, who accounted for over 98 percent of the state's Black population and a majority of the state's total population, faced all of these race-based constraints, and more. Unlike "free" Black people, the enslaved were not allowed to file lawsuits or receive an education.[8] Even if they had been inclined to "work within the system" to ameliorate their oppression, there was no system within which they could work.[9] Some enslaved people responded to the absence of legal options by acting illegally. They often unhappily learned that the law treated enslaved people most fully as people, not property, when they committed crimes. Admittedly, enslaved people occasionally benefited from court rulings. For exam-

5. John Belton O'Neall, *The Negro Law of South Carolina* (Columbia, SC: J. G. Bowman, 1848), 13.

6. Ibid., 16.

7. Ibid., 23–24.

8. Note that litigation did offer some Black southerners some access to legal remedies. See Kimberly M. Welch, *Black Litigants in the Antebellum South* (Chapel Hill: University of North Carolina Press, 2017); Dylan Penningroth, *The Claims of Kinfolk: African American Property and Community in the Nineteenth-Century South* (Chapel Hill: University of North Carolina Press, 2003); Anne Twitty, *Before Dred Scott: Slavery and Legal Culture in the American Confluence, 1787–1857* (New York: Cambridge University Press, 2018); Kelly M. Kennington, *In the Shadow of Dred Scott: St. Louis Freedom Suits and the Legal Culture of Slavery in Antebellum America* (Athens: University of Georgia Press, 2017); Martha S. Jones, *Birthright Citizens: A History of Race and Rights in Antebellum America* (Cambridge: Cambridge University Press, 2018); Laura Edwards, *The People and their Peace: Legal Culture and the Transformation of Inequality in the Post-Revolutionary South* (Chapel Hill: University of North Carolina Press, 2009); and Loren Schweninger, *Appealing for Liberty: Freedom Suits in the South* (New York: Oxford University Press, 2018).

9. Ethan Kytle and Blaine Roberts made this point in a Skype interview with the students of Davidson College's HIS 454, April 5, 2019: Julia Bainum, Patrick Casey, Laura Collins, Caroline Macaulay, Tommy May, Meghan Rankins, Seth Rinkevich, Jack Sheehy, Marcus Whipple.

ple, the South Carolina courts ultimately allowed Amy, the formerly enslaved sexual partner of Elijah Willis, to inherit his estate following his death and her out-of-state manumission. But that ruling reflected the courts' regard for Elijah's rights, not Amy's.

During the post–Civil War Reconstruction period, approximately 1865 to 1877, Black access to the public sphere swelled, and Black South Carolinians experienced something approaching full citizenship. They could receive an education, assemble freely, discuss openly, file lawsuits, and testify in court. Additionally, Black men voted, practiced law, served in public office, and sat proportionally on juries.

The Republicans who orchestrated South Carolina's Reconstruction revolution did some of their most important legal work with erasers, not pens. In addition to expunging remnants of slave law,[10] they systematically deleted racial categories from state law. Their magnum opus, the South Carolina Constitution of 1868, contained no racial designations whatsoever. Its guiding ethos was color-blindness. The word "negro" did not appear in it. Neither did "black," "white," "mulatto," or "Indian." The document did mention the words "race" and "color," but only to assert their legal irrelevance. The right to vote, the new constitution declared, shall be determined "without distinction of race, color or former condition."[11] Public schools shall be free and open to all "without regard to race or color."[12] Lest the underlying principle be missed, the constitution declared that, henceforth, "Distinction on account of race or color, in any case whatever, shall be prohibited."[13] In practice, plenty of customary segregation persisted throughout the Reconstruction period.[14] But in theory, the Constitution of 1868 declared that "all classes of citizens"—all—"shall enjoy equally all common, public, and legal and political privileges."[15]

It would not last. By century's end, self-proclaimed "white supremacists" had retaken power by means that included fraud, violence, and rac-

10. S.C. Const., art. I, § 2 (1868).

11. Ibid., art. 8, § 2.

12. Ibid., art. 10, § 10.

13. Ibid., art. 1, § 39.

14. Joel Williamson, *After Slavery: The Negro in South Carolina During Reconstruction, 1861–1877* (Chapel Hill: University of North Carolina Press, 1965); Howard N. Rabinowitz, "From Exclusion to Segregation: Southern Race Relations, 1865–1890," *Journal of American History* 63, no. 2 (Sept. 1976): 325–50.

15. S.C. Const., art I, § 2 (1868). See also art. 1, § 1.

ism. There was nothing surreptitious about their racial politics. "White supremacist" was not an insult hurled by politically correct elites against fringe activists. It was a banner that dominant white political leaders wrestled to control[16] and then proudly waved from the balconies of power. "There are only two flags. The white and the black. Under which will you enlist?" asked John Gary Evans in 1895, while rallying support for Black disfranchisement. Evans was no crackpot extremist. He was the state's governor. In his 1895 "White Supremacy" proclamation, he challenged white South Carolinians to choose. Would it be the "white . . . flag of Anglo-Saxon civilization and progress" or "the black flag of the debased and ignorant African, with the white traitors who are seeking to marshal the negroes in order to gain political power?"[17] Revealingly, among the villains in Governor Evans's proclamation were judges, whom he denounced for occasionally impeding disfranchisement through their legal rulings.[18] He vowed not to let their legal snares obstruct white supremacy: "law or no law, court or no court, the intelligent white men of South Carolina intend to govern. . . . We are ready to lead the fight under the white man's flag."[19]

The region-wide political tide with which Evans swam was overwhelming. In a vicious cycle, Black voting rights shriveled, Black legislative representation dwindled, and around it went. Each rotation left Black South Carolinians more vulnerable. By century's end, a huge swath of the region's working and poorer classes had been disfranchised, with important consequences for national as well as state politics.

South Carolina's ascendant white supremacists reinserted racial categories into state law. Once again, legalized racial classifications—"negro," "white," "mulatto," "colored"—constricted life prospects. White families persuaded white officials to expel insufficiently white students from all-

---

16. In 1894, white supremacist leader Ben Tillman unseated US Senator Matthew Butler. In that 1894 campaign, Butler criticized Tillman, but he did not criticize white supremacy. "'White supremacy' is a very precious thing . . . and I would lament the day when it is lost," Butler proclaimed. He added that he had done "more in one day to establish 'white supremacy' in South Carolina" than Tillman and his corrupt ring had done in their entire lives. "White Supremacy: Gen. Butler Tells the Croakers a Thing or Two," *The State* (Columbia, SC), Sept. 9, 1894, 8.

17. "White Supremacy: Gov. Evans, of South Carolina, Issues a Sensational Proclamation," *Jackson Daily Citizen* (Michigan), May 15, 1895, 3.

18. Ibid.

19. Ibid.

white public schools. White registrars scribbled the letter "C" next to the names of "colored" people on lists of prospective jurors—and then studiously skipped over most of those names when assembling juries.

But although Jim Crow-era white supremacists effectively doused the flames of Reconstruction-era racial democracy, they could not extinguish the embers. Most obviously, the ban on slavery survived. During Reconstruction, Black State Supreme Court Justice Jonathan Jasper Wright had attempted to replace slavery with an egalitarian system of labor law based on the free-labor contract. Wright's dreams died at the end of Reconstruction. Hierarchical master-servant relations would dominate post-Reconstruction labor law in South Carolina. Through it all, however, slavery remained dead, and not even the most rabid white supremacist credibly threatened to resuscitate it. Emancipation was one Reconstruction-era reform that stuck.

Education was another. Jim Crow schools were, by definition, racially segregated. But education for nonwhite children remained legal. Indeed, it remained constitutionally mandated. The same 1895 Constitution that effectively disfranchised most Black voters ordered the General Assembly to continue providing free public schools for "all children."[20] The constitution also mandated state support for Black higher education, where faculty "representation" was to be given to "men and women of the negro race."[21] This explains why South Carolina State University, still "the state's sole public college for black youth," traces its origins to 1896, the year after the disfranchising constitution went into effect.[22] Black literacy, negligible under slavery, climbed steadily through the Jim Crow years.

The right of Black South Carolinians to assemble, also negligible under slavery, likewise endured through the Jim Crow years. Even after the "Retreat from Reconstruction,"[23] Black people retained the newly won freedom to gather for political protest, religious worship, or any other lawful reason. Black political meetings, such as the "immense" antilynch-

20. S.C. Const., art XI, § 5 and § 7 (1895).

21. Ibid., art. XI, § 8.

22. "History of SC State University," South Carolina State University, accessed consulted August 7, 2021,https://www.scsu.edu/aboutscstate/historyofscstateuniversity.aspx. See also William C. Hine, *South Carolina State University: A Black Land-Grant College in Jim Crow America* (Columbia: University of South Carolina Press, 2018).

23. William Gillette, *Retreat from Reconstruction, 1869–1879* (Baton Rouge: Louisiana State University Press, 1982).

ing protest that occurred in Columbia in 1892, remained possible.[24] Black churches,[25] schools,[26] private colleges,[27] and fraternal organizations[28] proliferated and helped Black people to fight injustice in ways impossible under slavery.

Black lawyers were another Reconstruction-era novelty that endured.[29] They selectively challenged Jim Crow abuses, often winning. Even when they lost, their efforts publicized the incompatibility of explicit racism with the rule of law. Indeed, courts were likely the best white-dominated venues in the South within which racism could be openly challenged.[30]

Black freedom, education, association, and legal activism: these legacies of Reconstruction, along with favorable national and international contexts following World War II, contributed to Jim Crow's grudging relaxation. Thereafter, new challenges awaited. As with slavery and its overthrow in the mid-nineteenth century, Jim Crow and its decay in the mid-twentieth left behind complex legacies, including both deep, structural problems and an enhanced ability to challenge them.

---

24. "Let up on the Lynchings. An Earnest Appeal by Negroes in Mass Meeting. Resolutions Adopted," *The State* (Columbia), June 1, 1892, 8.

25. William E. Montgomery, *Under their Own Vine and Fig Tree: The African-American Church in the South, 1865–1900* (Baton Rouge: Louisiana State University Press, 1993).

26. Howard Rabinowitz, "Half a Loaf: The Shift from White to Black Teachers in the Negro Schools of the Urban South, 1865–1890," *Journal of Southern History* 40, no. 4 (Nov. 1974): 565–94.

27. "Historically Black Colleges in South Carolina," Sciway, accessed August 7, 2021, https://www.sciway.net/edu/colleges/black.html.

28. Theda Skocpol and Jennifer Lynn Oser, "Organization Despite Adversity: The Origins and Development of African American Fraternal Associations," *Social Science History* 28, no. 3 (Fall 2004): 367–437.

29. Lewis Burke, *All for Civil Rights: African American Lawyers in South Carolina, 1868–1968* (Athens: University of Georgia Press, 2017).

30. See, for example, Burke, *All for Civil Rights*; and R. Volney Riser, *Defying Disfranchisement: Black Voting Rights Activism in the Jim Crow South* (Baton Rouge: Louisiana State University Press, 2010).

Index

www.ingramcontent.com/pod-product-compliance
Lightning Source LLC
LaVergne TN
LVHW050023250826
846302LV00009B/68
* 9 7 8 1 9 4 3 2 0 8 3 2 6 *